Business Law

For business and marketing students

Third edition

Richard Lawson
Douglas Smith

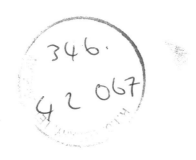

Butterworth-Heinemann
Linacre House, Jordan Hill, Oxford OX2 8DP
A division of Reed Educational and Professional Publishing Ltd

A member of the Reed Elsevier plc group

OXFORD BOSTON JOHANNESBURG
MELBOURNE NEW DELHI SINGAPORE

First published 1989
Reprinted 1990
Second edition 1992
Reprinted 1992
Third edition 1997

British Library Cataloguing in Publication Data
Lawson, R. G. (Richard Grenville), 1943–
    Business law. – 3rd ed.
    1.   Business law – England
    I.   Title   II.   Smith, Douglas
    346.4'2'067

ISBN 0 7506 2570 8

Printed and bound by Scotprint, Great Britain

Preface

This book is primarily aimed at students taking business law units on undergraduate degree programmes. There is already a plethora of law texts on the subject but this offering is designed to make the subject both accessible and readily understandable. Each sub-topic is broken down into relevant common law principles or statutory provisions and these are clearly explained together with illustrative case examples. Where appropriate, further comments are made in the margin so as to leave an uncluttered main text.

Business law is a large field with a considerable body of case and statute law. At first sight this may be rather intimidating but, if the student carefully reads through the text, tackles the review questions that are periodically set and attempts the questions given at the end of each chapter, then the authors confidently expect that students will be well prepared for any assignment or examination that they may have to take.

Douglas Smith would like to a colleague, Lesley Lomax for her help on the product liability and professional negligence chapters.

Richard Lawson
Douglas Smith

Contents

Introductory comments

This book as a learning aid

Both common and statute law are developing sources of law. Largely driven by the leviathan growth of European law, British domestic statute law continues to increase. This means that there is a considerable amount of law and this is particularly true of business law which is already highly developed. Students taking business law on either a degree programme or professional course should not feel intimidated by the volume or complexity of law they will be expected to cover. A student of average ability who is prepared to *work reasonably diligently*, by adopting a systematic approach to study, ought to be capable of achieving a very good standard in assignment and examination work.

To facilitate learning, the format of this book is that each topic is given a short introduction, designed to place what is going to be dealt with in a contextual background, followed by a list of key concepts which indicate the crucial aspects of the topic. Relevant common law principles or statutory provisions are fully explained, with illustrative case law liberally used to show how the law has been applied to actual business problem situations. Incorporated into the text are periodic review questions, and students should attempt these as they appear before starting the next sub-topic. To consolidate learning, at the end of each topic is a summary of what has been discussed, and a student who is not confident that they have fully understood the material ought to re-read the appropriate part of the text before proceeding to tackle the questions set at the end. Where a fuller understanding is required, such as for assignment work, recommendations for further reading are given.

Assignment and examination technique

Examiners can only award marks for what is correctly provided, not for what is wrongly stated or omitted. Unfortunately, all too often, failure in an examination or assignment is the result of poor response technique. The following comments are intended to assist candidates to improve in this important area. If the advice is adhered to it should result in a more successful outcome, which is particularly satisfying to a student who has worked hard at the subject.

Before you start writing

Read the instructions on the examination paper or assignment carefully, and make sure that you follow them. It is also essential, in an examination, to allocate appropriate time for each question to be answered and to discipline yourself to keep to this plan. For example, in a three-hour paper where four questions are required to be answered, you should leave 10 minutes for reading the paper and 10 minutes for revision and correction at the end. Consequently, you will have 40 minutes per question. Despite the temptation to write at length on one or more questions, you are urged not to exceed the 40-minute time allowance per question, otherwise you may later run out of time. Therefore, give time management the importance it deserves!

Read the questions carefully and decide exactly what they call for, and which of them you will attempt to answer. Make full use of your recommended reading time to select the set of questions best fitted to your own level of knowledge. Avoid any question whose meaning you are uncertain of, and do not tackle a multiple-part question because you feel confident in some parts, but not in others. Once you have chosen which questions to answer, then answer those specific questions and not others which you wish had been set.

Be aware of the types of questions you will encounter. They will be of two types:

- the essay
- the problem format.

The essay type   These will attempt to test your knowledge and recall in a certain area of law, e.g. 'Explain the *Nemo dat habet* rule and discuss exceptions to it.' The expected style is: an introduction followed by a discussion or argument followed by a conclusion. Students who have completed a good revision programme may prefer this type of question, which is intended to test factual knowledge as well as critical and analytical abilities in relation to a general area of law.

Pay special attention to the key word given in the essay you are asked to do.

1 *Examine*   You need to explain the relevant legal principles or provisions. Where the examination relates to a broad concept, such as 'Examine the role of consideration in contract law', then in an examination there will be time to provide little more than an outline of the sub-principles involved.

   If the subject matter of the question is narrower, such as 'Examine to what extent a prior contractual obligation can be a valid consideration', then more detailed treatment, derived from an investigation into appropriate case law, will be required.
2 *Critically examine*   You need to be more judgemental and much less descriptive in the explanation given. What is required is a detailed exposition of the principle(s) being examined, which incorporates a discussion of respective strengths and weaknesses.
3 *Evaluate*   You need to provide an informative commentary on the law. The approach to follow is to use selective judicial statements to construct a sound argument for or against whatever proposition is being questioned.
4 *Discuss*   You need to provide a detailed critical statement of law with illustrations of its application. An exhaustive, but solely descriptive, account is insufficient.

The problem format   These will consist of a situation within which one or more legal principles will operate. Students will be required to analyse the situation and say whether or not liability will apply. At degree level, problems are likely to consist of subtly altered facts, taken from decided cases, which are intended to get students to examine a range of possible outcomes. Not only is knowledge and recall needed, but these must be applied to the problem situation. Always try to be systematic in the treatment of such problems. You are advised to adopt this approach:

1 State the legal principle(s), or rule(s) of law (common law or statutory), which you believe apply.
2 Provide legal authority to support what you have stated.
3 Relate 1 and 2 to the problem situation, referring to any exceptions or defences which may operate, together with legal authority for them.
4 Provide a reasoned conclusion in which you say whether or not someone is liable.

Generally, the essay question is a closed one while the problem question will frequently be open in that more than one outcome can be identified. There will always be a most appropriate outcome, but candidates putting forward reasonable alternatives, justified by legal authority, may well be able to obtain a reasonable or better mark.

On beginning to write

Follow the 'ABC Rule':

- *Accuracy*   Make sure that what you say is correct and as precise as the level of your knowledge will permit.
- *Brevity*   Do not use unnecessary words, still less unnecessary sentences or paragraphs. However, avoid the opposite extreme, such as saying 'X is liable' without saying why. Always provide a full but concise exploration.
- *Clarity*   Use short sentences and, wherever possible, simple words. Keep your language simple and write legibly. Consider what you want to say before commencing to write. If you do this then vague statements ought to be avoided.

Also remember to be:

- *Orderly*   Plan the structure of your answer. Make an essay plan before you start each question.
- *Relevant*   Do not include material which has no valid bearing on the question. Avoid the temptation to display your knowledge by wandering from the question set.
- *Thorough*   Do not omit essential points. Space should be left at the end of each examination response for any later correction or addition.

Things to avoid

Writing in the first person. Even though the question requires you to offer advice to X, it is always expected that advice will be tendered in the third, not the first person.

Use of semi-slang expressions, jargon or unclear abbreviations, and any attempt to be flippant. A law assignment or examination is not, admittedly, an English test, but remember that you are most probably sitting an examination at a university or for a professional body, and a good standard of English is expected.

Lengthy introductions. Introductions should be kept short; long ones are wasteful of time and gain no extra marks. It is sensible to have an introduction in the form of a definition. If answering a question on misrepresentation, for example, then say, 'Misrepresentation is a materially untrue statement which induces someone to enter into a contract. In the question it appears that…'. You may then proceed to give your substantive answer comments. Regrettably, many students prefer to begin by writing at length on what does not directly apply, e.g. 'First of all, before dealing with misrepresentation, it is important to say that a contract consists of…'. There then follows up to two sides or more of material which, while correct, is meaningless to the answer and earns no marks.

Providing facts to cases. You should always attempt to support legal principle by citing legal authority. This should consist of referring to cases by name only, e.g. *Carlill* v *Carbolic Smoke Ball Co.*, to support the principle that it is possible, though exceptional, for an advertisement to be an offer and not an invitation to treat. If unable to recall the names of the parties, then write the minimum necessary to show which case you refer to, e.g. 'in the case of the broken crankshaft which had to be sent to a manufacturer' (*Hadley* v *Baxendale*). It may be reassuring to fill up paper with a recitation of case facts but be warned – this is a sign of a weak student desperate to fill up paper rather than getting to grips with the legal principles themselves.

Where reasonable reference to case facts is justified is where it is used to distinguish between an apparent similarity with the facts of a decided case and facts given in the problem to be solved. This use of case facts should show that while at first sight the citation is attractive, it may, because of a crucial minor dissimilarity, not be followed. In respect to extensive references (or quotations) to judgments, these should only be made if a point of law is contentious. When used it ought to be pointed out that the judgment (opinion) referred to is not regarded by all as being a definitive statement of the law.

Volunteering information. Unless directly required, other comments or observations should not be provided. Similarly, do not cite legal principles or refer to cases and statute aimlessly. First, you are wasting time; second, if what you volunteer is wrong then it will detract from what you have already correctly said.

Table of cases

Van den Berghs & Jurgens Ltd v Burleigh [1987] 337, 181

Vawdrey v Simpson [1896] 1 Ch 166, 20

Verelst's Administratrix v Motor Union Ins Co [1925] 2 KB 137; 133 LT 364; 41 TLR 343; 69 SJ 412, 311

Veritas Shipping v Anglo Canadian Cement Ltd [1966} 1 Lloyd's Rep 76, 347

The Wagon Mound [1961] (Overseas Tankship (UK) Ltd v Morts Dock and Engineering Co Ltd) AC 388, 24, 210

Wagstaffe, John, Ltd v Police [1965] NZLR 973, 176

Waithman v Wakefield [1897] 1 Camp 120, 120

Walford v Miles [1992] 2 AC 128, 43

Wallis Sons & Webb v Pratt & Haynes [1910] 2 KB 1003, 79

Walters v Morgan [1792] 2 Cox Eq Cas 369; 30 ER 169, LC, 337

Walton v British Leyland (UK) Ltd [1978] QBI, 212, 218

Warrington v Early (1853) 23 LJQB 47, 262

Watteau v Fenwick [1893] 1 QB 346, 115, 117

Weld-Blundell v Stephens [1920] AC 956, 285

Weller and Co v Foot and Mouth Disease Institute [1966] 1 QB 569; [1965 3 WLR 1082; [1965] 560, 228, 229

Westminster Bank Ltd v Zang (1966) AC 182, 268

Westminster City Council v Pierglow Ltd (1994), 186–7

White v Jones [1993] 3 ALL ER 481, 234, 240

Willesford v Watson [1873] 8 Ch App 473; 42 LJ Ch 447; 28 LT 428; 37 JP 548; 21 WR 350, 346

Williams and Glyn's Bank Ltd v Barnes [1981] Comm LR 205, 280

Williams v Fawcett [1986] QB 604, 24

Williams v Roffey Bros [1990] 1 QB 1, 54

Williams v Summerfield [1972] 2 QB 512, 283

Williamson v Rider [1963] 1 QB 89, 251

Willis v Wood [1984] CCLR 7, 141

Wilson v Best Travel Ltd [1993] 1 All ER 353, 93

Wings Ltd v Ellis [1985] AC 272, 183

Winspear v Accident Insurance Association [1880] 6 QBD 42; 43 LT 459; 45 JP 110; 29 WR 116, 306

Witty v World Services Ltd [1935] Ch 303, 177

Woods v Martins Bank Ltd [1958] 3 ALL ER 166, 277

Woolcott v Sun Alliance and London Alliance Co [1978] 1 WLR 493; [1978] 12 ALL ER 1253; [1978] 1 Lloyd's Rep 629, 300

Woollatt v Stanley (1923) 138 Lt 620, 262

Worcester Works Finance Ltd v Cooden Engineering Co Ltd [1972] 1 QB 210, 87

Yeoman Credit Ltd v Gregory [1963] 1 WLR 343, 259

Yianni v Edwin Evans and Sons [1982] QB 438; [1981] 3 WLR 843; 125 SJ 694, 241–243

Yonge v Toynbee [1910] 1 KB 215, 129, 281

Young v Bristol Aeroplane Co Ltd [1944] KB 718, 24, 25

Zambia Steel and Building Supplies Ltd v James Clark and Eaten Ltd [1986] 2 Lloyd's Rep 225, 338

1 The English legal system

Introduction

The term 'legal system' has no specific definition. It is, however, generally understood as referring to the ways in which laws are made in a jurisdiction, the types of law which are made, the court structure, and the role and function of various personnel. This is the approach which is adopted in this chapter.

Although there are many areas where the position described is the same throughout the United Kingdom, this chapter is specifically devoted to the position in England and Wales.

Objectives

The first objective will be to make clear the role of Parliament in making laws, and the extent to which Parliament is sovereign.

Account will also be given of other sources of law, notably that branch of the law normally referred to as the 'common law'. It will also be explained that, whatever its source, the law can be subdivided into various categories.

Given the position of the United Kingdom as a member of the European Union, a further objective will be to explain how European Union law is made, and its relationship to law having its origin solely within the United Kingdom.

Account will also be given of the court structure, the importance attached to previous court decisions within the English legal system (the so-called 'doctrine of precedent') of various legal personnel and of the legal profession.

Key concepts

- Law as derived from legislation and judge-made law
- Differing categories of legislation – Acts of Parliament and subordinate legislation
- How Acts are made
- Powers of House of Lords
- Differing categories of Act
- Equity as distinct from common law
- Distinction between civil and criminal law

- Categories of civil law
- Criminal and civil courts
- The doctrine of precedent
- Solicitors and barristers
- Law Officers
- The relationship between domestic law and European Union (EU) law
- Supremacy of EU law.

Legislation

By 'legislation' is meant law which is made by, or under the authority of, Parliament. Legislation is subdivided into Acts of Parliament, which is law made by Parliament directly; and subordinate legislation, which is law made under the authority of Parliament, usually expressed in an Act of Parliament.

Acts of Parliament

When going through the parliamentary process, the measure which will eventually become an Act is known as a 'bill'. Most such bills come from government departments and will have been drafted by officials known as parliamentary draftsmen. Bills can also be introduced by individual Members of Parliament. A ballot is held among the MPs for the right to introduce private members' bills. Quite often, such bills do become Acts, though generally they need government support.

Parliament is 'sovereign'

Parliament is not restricted in its powers to create, alter or repeal law. An Act of Parliament cannot be questioned in or by the courts but must always be applied by them. This is what is meant by saying that Parliament is 'sovereign'.

'Money' bills must start life in the Commons

Parliament consists of the House of Commons and the House of Lords, and a bill can be introduced into either House with the exception of 'money' bills. A bill is a money bill if it is so certified by the Speaker of the House of Commons. The annual budget, eventually enshrined in that year's Finance Act, is the prime example of a money bill.

Limited power of Lords to block legislation

For a bill to become an Act of Parliament, it must satisfy the procedure of both Houses, which means essentially that it must pass through three readings in each House. The main work is done during the second reading. The first reading is the presentation of the bill in principle; the third reading is also usually a matter of form when the particular House approves the changes which have been made to the original proposal during the second reading.

Delaying powers of House of Lords

The powers of the House of Lords to delay the further progress of measures approved by the House of Commons was considerably restricted by the Parliament Acts of 1911 and 1940. The position can be summarized as follows:

- A money bill (see above) which has passed all its stages in the Commons, is to receive the royal assent without the approval of the House of Lords, unless it has been passed by the Lords within one month of it being sent to that House, provided that it was in fact sent to the Lords at least one month before the end of the Parliamentary session.
- The power of the Lords to reject any bill seeking to extend the maximum life of Parliament beyond five years remains unaffected.

- If any other category of public bill (see below) passed by the Commons but rejected in the Lords is passed again by the Commons in the next session of Parliament and is not passed by the Lords unamended (except for amendments approved by the Commons), the Commons may forward the bill for royal assent. The Parliament Acts further provide that this procedure can apply only when at least one year elapsed between the second reading of the bill in the Commons in the first session and the third reading in the Commons in the second session.
- The power of the Lords to block private bills (see below) is unaffected by the Parliament Acts.

A bill which has been through all its parliamentary stages receives the royal assent, whereupon it becomes an Act of Parliament. It is very rare for the monarch personally to give the assent. As a rule, the assent is notified to each House by the Speaker of the Commons and the Lord Chancellor (the Speaker's equivalent in the House of Lords) under the powers provided in the Royal Assent Act 1967.

Categories of Act

Acts are 'public' Acts if of general application, such as the Sale of Goods Act 1979. An Act is a 'private' Act if it deals purely with personal matters or matters specific to one area of the country. An example is The Letchworth Garden City Heritage Foundation Act 1995. There are some differences in parliamentary procedure in the case of a private bill than in that of a public bill.

A final category of Act is the 'hybrid' Act, being an Act introduced as having general application, but which affects the private interests of particular bodies or individuals. An example is the Channel Tunnel Act 1987. Part of the parliamentary procedure applicable to such bills is that of the private bill.

Subordinate legislation

It is extremely common for Acts of Parliament to give a government minister, a local authority or a public corporation the power to make regulations and to state the penalties for breach of such regulations. There is a vast amount of such 'subordinate' legislation, usually in the form of statutory instruments, of which there are often more than 2000 a year, compared with the 150 or so Acts of Parliament.

Most legislation is subordinate legislation

Control over statutory instruments

The Act of Parliament under which a statutory instrument is made will often require the draft instrument to be laid before Parliament to be the subject of a vote in favour ('affirmative resolution') before it comes into effect. An example is the statutory instrument made under the Fair Trading Act 1973, following examination of a course of conduct by the Consumer Protection Advisory Committee. If affirmative resolution is not provided for in the Act, the 'negative resolution' procedure has effect, which means that the instrument will come into force unless there is a vote against it within 40 sitting days in either House (Statutory Instruments Act 1946 and the Laying of Documents before Parliament (Interpretation) Act 1948).

Parliament has established a joint select committee on statutory instruments which consists of members of both Houses and which reports to Parliament. Its terms of reference include consideration of every statutory instrument laid or laid in draft before Parliament, with a view to seeing whether the special attention of Parliament should be drawn to the instrument on one of a number of grounds, e.g. that it is obscurely worded, appears to impose charges on the subject or the public

Committee scrutiny of instruments

Instruments
must be made
as required by
enabling Act

revenue, or purports to have retrospective effect unauthorized by the Act under which it was made.

If a statutory instrument is not made in accordance with the provisions of the Act under which it was made, it can be challenged in the courts and struck down.

Case example
R v Secretary of State for Health (1992)

Acting under powers contained in the Consumer Protection Act 1987, the Secretary of State made the Oral Snuff (Safety) Regulations 1989. The Act requires the Secretary of State, before making regulations, to consult such organizations as appear to him representative of interests substantially affected by the proposals. The applicants in this case were the only persons affected by the ban contained in the regulations and this, the court said, required the Secretary of State to 'show a high degree of fairness and candour' towards these applicants. Since he had concealed from the applicants scientific advice given to him which led directly to the ban contained in the regulations, an order would be made quashing the regulations.

Bylaws

Another type of subordinate legislation is the bylaw. These may be made by local authorities, public corporations, and certain other bodies authorized by Act of Parliament. Bylaws are restricted to the locality or undertaking to which they apply. Bylaws are not made by statutory instrument.

The Local Government Act 1972 states that bylaws must be made in accordance with 'standard procedure' except where the enabling statute provides otherwise. The procedure is that the bylaws are to be made under seal and submitted to the Secretary of State for the Environment unless some other party is specified. The 'confirming authority' then decides whether or not to confirm the bylaws which take effect one month after confirmation unless some other date is specified.

Bylaws can be challenged on the grounds that they are outside the powers conferred by the relevant Act under which they were made, that they are contrary to law or for any other reason.

Case example
Nash v Finlay (1901)

A bylaw stated that: 'No person shall wilfully annoy passengers in the streets.' This was held void for uncertainty.

Repeals

Acts may be
repealed by
statutory
instrument

It was formerly the case that Acts of Parliament could only be repealed by Act of Parliament. However, the Deregulation and Contracting Out Act 1994 provides that any 'enactment', which will include an Act or statutory instrument passed before the end of the 1993–1994 session of Parliament, which imposes a burden on business may be repealed by statutory instrument. Such instruments are subject to the affirmative resolution procedure (see above).

Review questions

1 Explain the procedure by which an Act of Parliament is made.
2 What limitations exist over the powers of the House of Lords?
3 Explain what is meant by 'subordinate' legislation.
4 Give an account of what is meant by 'negative' and 'affirmative' resolution and indicate the way in which statutory instruments are subject to review.

The common law

In addition to the law to be found in Acts of Parliament and subordinate legislation, there is also the 'common law' – which may be regarded as those legal principles developed over the centuries by the courts without the help of Parliament. The law of contract and the law of tort, for example, derive in great part from the common law. Because Parliament is sovereign (see above), any conflict between the common law and legislation (including subordinate legislation) has to be resolved in favour of the legislation.

Judges also 'make' law

Common law and equity

The term 'common law', as describing the law made by judges, also, confusingly, means those rules developed by the 'common law' courts (such as the early King's (or Queen's) Bench, the Court of Common Pleas and the Court of Exchequer), as well as those developed by the (often rival) 'courts of equity' (such as the Court of Chancery). As the name implies, these latter developed their own legal principles based on principles of fairness or 'equity'. Much of the law of trusts, for example, was developed by these courts. The common law and equity courts were fused by the Judicature Acts 1873–1875, and all courts can now administer both the rules of equity and common law. In the event of a conflict, the rules of equity prevail (Judicature Act 1873, s. 25(11)).

'Equity' as distinct from 'common law'

Categories of law

It is customary to regard the law as falling into one of two separate categories: the civil law and the criminal law. Each is a mixture of common law and legislation, though it is probably true to say that legislation is the greater part of the criminal law.

Where there is a breach of the criminal law, the action is called a prosecution and is brought against a 'defendant' in the name of the Crown or public official who is empowered to bring prosecutions, such as the Director of Public Prosecutions, or a local trading standards authority. Prosecutions can also be brought by the Crown Prosecution Service which, following the Prosecution of Offences Act 1985, largely took over the powers of prosecution hitherto held by the police.

Distinction between criminal and civil law

It is also possible, though very rare, for the person directly affected by the commission of a crime to bring the proceedings themselves in a private prosecution.

If the prosecution is successful, the defendant can be fined or imprisoned, or both, depending on the penalties set out for the offence which they have committed. The courts also have the power to grant an absolute or conditional discharge. Fines, including fines paid in the event of a private prosecution, go to the state. However, in criminal cases, the courts do have the power to order compensation to be paid to affected parties under the Powers of Criminal Courts Act 1973.

Civil law

The civil law essentially regulates the rights of private citizens against each other. For that reason, the state plays no active role, and actions are brought by private individuals, known as 'plaintiffs', against other such individuals, known (as in criminal law) as 'defendants'. In this context, 'individuals' means not just human beings ('natural persons'), but also any 'legal person', such as a company. If a money award (usually in the form of 'damages') is made by the court following a successful action, this goes directly to the plaintiff.

Although the criminal law is usually regarded as a whole (though there are of course specialist areas such as consumer protection, road traffic, crimes against the person), the civil law is regarded as being composed of separate categories.

Subdivisions of civil law

The two best-known categories of civil law are the law of contract and the law of tort. The latter, which takes its name from the Norman-French for 'wrong', covers such matters as negligence, trespass to land, defamation. Other branches of the civil law are: company law; partnership law; the law relating to negotiable instruments (e.g. cheques); family law and property law. It would be wrong to suppose, however, that these categories are entirely independent. Family law and property law could well overlap, and many aspects of, say, company law are also within the ambit of the law of contract.

Overlap of criminal and civil law

It is perfectly possible for the same set of facts to involve both categories of law. The supply of falsely described goods can cause an infringement of the Trade Descriptions Act 1968 (criminal law) and of the Sale of Goods Act 1979 (civil law). Each cause of action is, however, separate, and has to be fought in different courts (see below). Under the terms of the Civil Evidence Act 1968, a criminal conviction is evidence in subsequent civil proceedings that the defendant committed the offence; so a conviction under the Trade Descriptions Act is evidence under the Sale of Goods Act that the goods were falsely described. The Act does say, however, that the conviction is evidence, not proof.

Review questions

1 Explain what is meant by the 'common law' and the 'rules of equity'.
2 What is the essential difference between the criminal and the civil law?
3 Describe some of the subdivisions of the civil law.
4 What is the effect of the Civil Evidence Act 1968?

The court structure – the criminal courts

Magistrates' courts

Each county is divided into petty sessional divisions, and these may be regarded as the magistrates' courts' districts. Each such court is composed of one or more magistrates or justices of the peace (the terms are interchangeable). Magistrates are appointed by the Lord Chancellor. There are 411 magistrates' courts in England and Wales.

The vast majority of the 30 000 or so magistrates are 'lay' magistrates: that is to say they are people with no legal qualifications who are unpaid, but who receive allowances and expenses. They are chosen from what is sometimes called 'the list of the great and good'. Each bench of lay magistrates is assisted by a salaried clerk who assists the magistrates on questions of procedure and law and who is responsible for the administration of the court. Clerks will have had a five-year magistrates' court qualification.

Magistrates generally without legal qualification

A small number of magistrates (those in inner London and some of the major cities) will be stipendiary magistrates who are salaried and who will be persons with a seven-year general qualification.

But some magistrates are qualified

If an offence is stated to be a 'summary' offence, then it can only be tried in a magistrates' court. Certain offences under the Consumer Credit Act 1974, for example, can only be tried summarily. If an offence is one triable 'either way', proceedings can be brought in the magistrates' court or in the Crown Court (see below). Offences under the Trade Descriptions Act 1968 are triable either way. If the prosecution thinks that the offence calls for penalties beyond the powers of the magistrates' court, it will institute proceedings in the Crown Court. It is reckoned that around 96 per cent of criminal cases are in fact tried summarily.

Exclusive right to try summary offences

Sentencing powers

The maximum fine that a magistrate can impose will be contained in the legislation under which the charge is brought. In no case will it exceed the 'statutory maximum' as set out in the Criminal Justice Act 1991, which is currently £5000. The maximum period of imprisonment which may be imposed is six months, though magistrates can impose consecutive sentences for a total of 12 months if the accused has been convicted of at least two offences triable 'either way' (Magistrates' Courts Act 1980 s. 133).

Magistrates also act as examining magistrates prior to a case being heard on indictment in the Crown Court. They have to decide if there is enough evidence on which a jury, properly directed, could convict (Magistrates' Courts Act 1980 s. 6).

Magistrates can fine and imprison

A person convicted by a magistrates' court may appeal to the Crown Court (see below) against conviction, sentence, or both, though they can only appeal against sentence if they pleaded guilty (Magistrates' Courts Act 1980 s. 108). Appeals will be made to the Divisional Court of the Queen's Bench Division (see below) by defence or prosecution on the grounds that the magistrates were wrong in law or acted in excess of their jurisdiction (s. 111 of the 1980 Act).

Crown Courts

The Crown Courts are divided into circuits covering a large number of towns and are themselves ranked as first-, second- or third-tier courts. First- and second-tier courts are served by High Court judges, circuit judges and recorders (these are persons who have at least a 10-year Crown Court or county court qualification). Third-tier courts are served only by recorders, with the result that

Crown Courts are ranked in tiers

some of the very serious offences, such as murder, cannot be tried at third-tier courts.

The powers of the Crown Court are set out in the Supreme Court Act 1981. It has exclusive jurisdiction over all offences tried by jury on indictment. It also has the power to deal with persons committed for sentence by magistrates' courts because their sentencing powers are inadequate, and to hear appeals from magistrates' courts against conviction or sentence. An appeal against conviction takes the form of a full re-hearing of the case.

Magistrates have limited powers in Crown Courts

Lay magistrates cannot act as judges of the Crown Court by themselves, only with a High Court judge, a circuit judge or a recorder. They must, however, be part of the Crown Court when it hears appeals from magistrates' courts and also when it is sentencing persons who have been committed for sentence by the magistrates' court, although the Lord Chancellor can dispense with this requirement. The number of magistrates so sitting must be not fewer than two nor more than four. Rulings on questions of law are for the judges, but decisions on other questions, such as sentences, are made by all members of the court, which means that, on such matters, the judge can be outvoted (*R* v *Orpin* (1974)).

Appeals against Crown Court rulings

Where the Crown Court has given its decision on an appeal from a magistrates' court against conviction or sentence, the prosecution or defendant, if of the view that the decision was wrong in law or in excess of jurisdiction, can appeal to a divisional court of the Queen's Bench Division (see below).

Case example
R v *Crown Court at St Albans, ex parte Cinnamond* (1981)
A discretionary sentence may be wrong in law or in excess of jurisdiction if it is harsh and oppressive or so far outside the normal sentence imposed for the offence as to enable the divisional court to hold that the sentence involves an error of law.

Where the judgment appealed from relates to a trial on indictment then the appeal will be to the Court of Appeal (Criminal Division) (see below).

Queen's Bench Division (divisional court)

A divisional court of the Queen's Bench Division of the High Court (see below) hears appeals from the magistrates' courts and appeals from the Crown Court which have been heard by that court on appeal. The court consists of two or more judges (though usually two), one of whom will be the Lord Chief Justice or a Lord Justice of Appeal (see below). An appeal by case stated must be on the ground that the determination or decision was wrong in law or in excess of jurisdiction. The case is not re-heard, being confined to legal argument.

Court of Appeal (Criminal Division)

Rights of appeal

The Court of Appeal (Criminal Division) was established by the Criminal Appeal Act 1968 as most recently amended by the Criminal Appeal Act 1995.

A person convicted on indictment may appeal to the court: (a) against their conviction on any ground of appeal which involves a question of law alone; and (b) with the leave of the court or upon the certificate of the judge who tried them that it is a fit case for appeal against their conviction; (c) with the leave of the court against any sentence (not being a sentence fixed by law) passed on him for the offence of which he was convicted, whether passed on their conviction or in subsequent proceedings. In specified circumstances, a person convicted of an offence by a magistrates' court and committed to the Crown Court for sentence or to be dealt with may, with the leave of the criminal division, so appeal.

In the case of an appeal against conviction, the court, acting under the Criminal Appeal Act 1995, shall allow an appeal if it thinks that the conviction was, under all the circumstances, 'unsafe'. The court shall dismiss an appeal against conviction in any other case.

Decisions on appeal

Case example
R v Clinton (1993)

The appellant had been charged with kidnapping and indecent assault. The case against him depended almost entirely on matters of identification. There were, however, many discrepancies in the description of him. His defence counsel asked him if he wished to give evidence and, when he stated that he did not, no further discussion on the matter took place. The appellant was not called on to give evidence, nor was he advised to do so, and no evidence was called on his behalf to rebut the prosecution's evidence. The result was that these discrepancies were not put to the jury, and the judge was unable to give a full direction as to the discrepancies or to answer properly questions asked by the jury.

The Court of Appeal (Criminal Division) held that the circumstances in which a court was entitled to overturn a jury when the grounds of appeal consisted wholly or mainly of criticism of the conduct of defence counsel would be very rare. Where defence counsel made decisions as to the conduct of the trial, particularly whether or not to call the defendant, in good faith, after proper consideration of the competing arguments and, where appropriate, after due discussion with his client, his decisions could not render a guilty verdict unsafe or unsatisfactory, nor could allegations of incompetence on counsel's part amount to a material irregularity. Conversely, and exceptionally, where it was shown that defence counsel's decision whether or not to call the defendant was taken either in defiance of or without proper instructions, or when all the promptings of reason and good sense pointed the other way, it was open to the court to set aside the verdict of the jury if counsel's conduct of the trial rendered the verdict unsafe or unsatisfactory. On the facts of this case, the appellant had a strong positive case which had not been presented to the jury as a result of the conduct of his counsel and those advising him before the trial and of the prosecution, and that conduct rendered his conviction unsafe and unsatisfactory.

The above case was heard before enactment of the 1995 Act. It remains good authority, however, in relation to convictions judged 'unsafe'.

Under the provisions of the Criminal Justice Act 1968, the Attorney-General may refer a sentence imposed by the Crown Court to the Court of Appeal if the sentence appears to be unduly lenient. On such a reference, a more severe sentence may be imposed.

Lenient sentences may be reconsidered

Case example
Attorney-General's Reference (No 22 of 1992)

Following a plea of guilty to a charge of wounding with intent to do grievous bodily harm, the Crown Court deferred passing sentence for six months following a social inquiry report which recommended such deferral. The Court of Appeal substituted a sentence of 30 months

---

The prosecution has no right of appeal against acquittal on indictment. However, under the provisions of the Criminal Justice Act 1972, the Attorney-General may refer to the Court of Appeal, and ultimately to the House of Lords (see below), a point of law arising at a trial on indictment where the accused was acquitted. The opinion of the court on the reference does not affect the actual acquittal but does provide authority on the relevant point of law.

Constitution of
court

The criminal division normally sits in two courts: one composed of the Lord Chief Justice and two judges of the Queen's Bench Division, and the other a Lord Justice of Appeal and two Queen's Bench judges. In exceptional cases, a court will consist of five judges. By way of exception to the general requirement that criminal appeals must be heard by three judges, the Supreme Court Act 1988 provides that two judges may hear an appeal against sentence. A single judge may deal with applications for leave to appeal.

Who makes up
the Court of
Appeal

The Court of Appeal consists of the Master of the Rolls, the President of the Family Division (see below), the Vice-Chancellor and Lord Justices of Appeal. A Lord Justice (and this title is also applied to females) must, under the provisions of the Supreme Court Act 1981, be someone who has a 10-year High Court qualification, or who is a judge of the High Court. In addition, the Act states that any High Court judge (see below) may be required to sit in the Court of Appeal if this is necessary.

References on
acquittal

Criminal Cases Review Commission

Establishment of
review body

The Criminal Appeal Act 1995 established a Criminal Cases Review Commission, the purpose of which is to investigate and, where appropriate, refer to the courts, cases of possible wrongful conviction or sentence. The Commission may refer to the Court of Appeal any conviction or sentence which has been tried on indictment. The Commission may also refer to the Crown Court any conviction or sentence in any case which has been tried summarily. Before the Commission may refer a case, new issues must be raised by way of argument or evidence. The Commission may not, unless there are exceptional circumstances, make a reference unless the convicted party has already appealed, or leave to appeal has been refused.

The House of Lords

The House of
Lords exercises
judicial
functions

The function of the House of Lords when sitting as a court is discharged by its Appellate Committee. The Appellate Jurisdiction Act 1876 provides that, at the hearing of an appeal, at least three of the following must be present: the Lord Chancellor; the Lords of Appeal in ordinary; and such peers who hold or have held high judicial office, such as former Lord Chancellors.

A Lord of Appeal must have a Supreme Court qualification, and certain rights of appointment are given to qualified personnel from Scotland and Northern Ireland. Normally five Law Lords hear an appeal.

Under the provisions of the Criminal Appeals Act 1968, the House of Lords may hear appeals by either party either from a decision of the Court of Appeal (Criminal Division) or a divisional court. However, the court below must have certified that a point of law of general public importance is involved; that court, or the House of Lords itself, must be satisfied that the point of law is one which should be considered by the House; and either the lower court or the House of Lords must have granted leave to appeal.

Review questions

1 Give an account of the nature and function of magistrates' courts and state what their sentencing powers are.
2 What is meant by 'offences triable either way' and what is the significance of the term?
3 What cases are heard by the Crown Court and by whom are its powers exercised?
4 To what extent may magistrates sit in the Crown Court and what are their powers?
5 In what circumstances can an appeal be made from the magistrates' courts and the Crown Courts to the divisional court?
6 Under what circumstances may an appeal be made to the Court of Appeal (Criminal Division)?
7 When the Court of Appeal (Criminal Division) hears appeals against conviction, under what circumstances must it (a) uphold and (b) dismiss the appeal?
8 Under what circumstances can the length of a sentence be increased?
9 Although there can be no appeal against an acquittal on indictment, the Attorney-General does have certain relevant powers. What are they?
10 What is the function of the Criminal Cases Review Commission?
11 Under what circumstances can an appeal be made to the House of Lords?
12 Give an account of the composition of: the divisional court; the Court of Appeal Criminal Division; and the House of Lords.

The court structure – the civil courts

Magistrates' courts

The magistrates' courts (for their general composition, see above) also have a limited civil jurisdiction. Under the provisions of the Magistrates' Courts Act 1980, this jurisdiction can extend to the recovery of certain civil debts, such as electricity, gas, council tax and income tax; to the grant and renewal of licences; and to family proceedings.

Magistrates also have powers under various enactments (such as the Matrimonial Causes Act 1973, the Children Act 1989 and the Maintenance Enforcement Act 1991). When hearing family proceedings, the court must be composed of not more than three magistrates, including, where practicable, a man and a woman. Unless the court directs otherwise, only the officers of the court, the parties and their legal representatives, witnesses and reporters may be present. There are strict limitations on what may be published.

Important functions as to family proceedings

Appeals generally lie to the Crown Court (see above) with a further, or alternative, appeal on a point of law to the Queen's Bench or, in family proceedings, to the Family Division (see below). In this last case, there is no alternative of an appeal to the Crown Court.

Crown Court

The Crown Court (for details of its composition, see above) has a limited civil role, this being principally to hear appeals concerned with betting, gaming and liquor licensing (see, for example, the Betting, Gaming and Lotteries Act 1963 and the Licensing Act 1964).

Limited civil function for Crown Court

County courts

The county court has civil jurisdiction only. Under the provisions of the County Courts Act 1984, England and Wales are divided into county court districts, each with its own courthouse, office and staff, grouped into a number of circuits. Each circuit has assigned to it one or more circuit judges who must have a 10-year Crown Court or 10-year county court qualification or have held a full-time appointment for at least three years as one of a number of listed officers; or be a recorder (see above).

Jurisdiction exclusively civil The jurisdiction of the county court, as laid down in the 1984 Act, is unlimited in general list cases. The Act itself lists a number of matters as coming within the jurisdiction of the county court. These include:

- general jurisdiction in actions in contract and tort. There is a presumption that cases with a value of £50 000 or more will be tried in the High Court (see below);
- money recoverable by statute;
- actions for recovery of land and actions where title in question;
- certain jurisdiction in equity, where the sum involved is not greater than £30 000, such as proceedings for the administration of the estate of a deceased person. The £30 000 limit can be exceeded in certain cases;
- admiralty proceedings;
- probate proceedings.

The county court has other jurisdiction allocated by other enactments covering such matters as: divorce, judicial separation; guardianship and adoption; bankruptcy, winding-up of companies; matters under legislation dealing with rent, landlord and tenants; housing and consumer credit.

Financial limits and importance determine allocation of cases

Cases are allocated for trial according to the substance, importance and complexity of the issues involved. As a rule, cases involving amounts below £25 000 will be tried in the county court; those involving amounts between £25 000 and £50 000 will be tried in the High Court (see below) or the county court; while those involving amounts above £50 000 will be tried in the High Court. The decision as to allocation will be made according to the above criteria and the availability of judges. All personal injury cases where the amount involved is less than £50 000 will start in the county court.

District judges have jurisdiction to try cases in the county court where the amount involved does not exceed £5000. The district judge must have a seven-year general qualification. Appeals are to the Court of Appeal (Civil Division) (see below), except in bankruptcy proceedings where appeal is to a single judge of the High Court.

Small claims

There is no specific small claims' court. However, under s. 65 of the County Courts Act, provision can be, and has been, made for the reference of cases to arbitration, popularly called 'small claims'. A defended action in the county court must be referred to arbitration if the sum does not exceed £3000. Disputes involving more than this sum can be so referred if both parties agree. If a party

The small claims procedure allows for informal hearings

does object, the court can decide if the matter is to go to arbitration. Hearings before an arbitrator take place in private and without the formalities normally associated with court proceedings. The arbitrator will normally be the district judge, but either party may apply to the judge for the appointment of a more suitable person.

Rescission of reference to arbitration

The county court rules specify that a reference to arbitration may be rescinded, and the matter tried instead in court, if the district judge is satisfied that:

- a difficult question of law or a question of fact of exceptional complexity is involved; or
- fraud is alleged against a party; or
- the parties are agreed that the dispute should be tried in court; or
- it would be unreasonable for the claim to proceed to arbitration having regard to its subject matter, the size of any counterclaim, the circumstances of the parties or the interests of any other person likely to be affected by the award.

Case Example
Afzal v *Ford Motor Co. Ltd* (1994)

A number of actions were brought by employees in respect of minor personal injuries. The district judge granted their applications that the actions be tried in court on the ground that it would be unreasonable for the claim to proceed to arbitration having regard to its subject matter, the circumstances of the parties and, in particular, the fact that the employees could not be expected to frame their own claims in industrial accident cases (where breaches of statutory duty, medical evidence and discovery of documents might play a large part) without legal representation. The Court of Appeal said that a court should not rescind an automatic reference to arbitration merely because a question of law was involved or the facts were complex, since the county court rules made it clear that a question of law had to be difficult and a question of fact exceptionally complex if a claim were to be tried in court. Furthermore, these were not matters which could be reintroduced in relation to cases where reference to arbitration was unreasonable, since 'subject matter' meant something sufficient to one or more of the parties to justify trial in court, such as: a claim for damages for trespass which might have far-reaching consequences for the rights of the parties; a claim involving owner-ship of a family heirloom; or test cases in which the rights of others were likely to be affected by the award.

The Court of Appeal went on to say that the law applicable in employer liability cases was often straightforward and, while the facts could be complex, in most instances the question was whether the employer had taken reasonable care or exposed the employee to an unnecessary risk of injury, and the medical issues were unlikely to be complex when the sum claimed was under £1000 (this being the small claims limit at the time). Furthermore, the hardship of an employee representing himself against legally represented employers was one faced in all cases where the resources of the parties were unequal, and was a matter for the arbitrator to take into account in the procedure to be adopted for arbitration, rather than being a decisive factor against proceeding to arbitration in the first place. The appeal was allowed and the cases were sent back for individual consideration by the district judge.

Inflating claims to avoid arbitration

Plaintiffs might deliberately inflate their claims to a level above the limit to avoid automatic reference to arbitration.

Case example
See the *Afzal* case above

Some of the employees had sought to pre-empt automatic reference to arbitration by claiming damages limited to £3000 (the small claims limit then being £1000) even though there was no reasonable prospect of recovering more than a few hundred pounds. In each case, the trial judge had held that the claims should have been dealt with by arbitration and awarded only those costs appropriate to an automatic reference to arbitration.

The Court of Appeal held that the intentional overstatement of the amount involved in a claim to avoid a procedure which had been laid down by Parliament and incorporated in rules of court was a clear abuse of process. The test for determining whether a claim had been unjustifiably inflated to avoid automatic reference was whether the plaintiff could reasonably expect to be awarded more than £1000 and, if not, it would be an abuse to claim damages of more than £1000. Parties should also bear in mind, the court said, that the overstatement of the amount of damages, or the raising of a speculative and insupportable defence, might be regarded as unreasonable conduct and hence allowing an award of costs against that party.

An award made under the small claims procedure is entered as a judgement in court proceedings and is enforceable as such.

Injunctions

A district judge has the power in arbitrations to grant both interlocutory and final injunctions (with some limited exceptions) and to order specific performance (*Joyce* v *Liverpool City Council* (1995)).

Costs in arbitration

Normally, no costs are allowed in arbitration other than fixed costs on the summons. It is, however, clear that an attempt to manipulate the arbitration procedure to gain a costs advantage will amount to unreasonable conduct justifying an award of costs (*Newland* v *Boardwell*; *MacDonald* v *Platt* (1983) and see the *Afzal* case above).

Appeals from arbitration

There is no right of appeal against a decision resulting from arbitration. The judge does have power, though, on application to set an award aside.

The High Court of Justice

High Court subdivided into three divisions

Under the Supreme Court Act 1981, the High Court of Justice, along with the Crown Court and the Court of Appeal, make up the Supreme Court. The Act provides for three divisions of the High Court as detailed below. High Court judges must have a 10-year High Court qualification or have been a circuit judge who has held office for at least two years. To reduce delays, the Lord Chancellor can appoint deputy High Court judges on a temporary basis.

Chancery Division

A number of matters are assigned to the 'original' jurisdiction of the Chancery Division (that is matters which commence in the Chancery Division). These include:

- the administration of the estates of deceased persons;
- the redemption and foreclosure of mortgages;
- the execution of trusts;
- the rectification and cancellation of deeds;
- partnership actions;
- bankruptcy;
- the sale, exchange or partition of land, or the raising of charges on land;
- all causes and matters under legislation relating to companies.

The appellate jurisdiction of this Division is much more limited. It hears income tax appeals from the commissioners of the Inland Revenue and a divisional court hears appeals from the county court on bankruptcy matters.

The Division consists of the Lord Chancellor as its head, though he never sits, a Vice-Chancellor and a set number of judges. It sits in London and a number of major towns.

Wide original jurisdiction, but limited hearing of appeals

Family Division

The original functions of the Family Division deal with all aspects of family law, such as proceedings for divorce, annulment of marriage and judicial separation, proceedings for the determination of title to property in disputes between spouses, proceedings concerning the occupation of the matrimonial home and wardship of court, guardianship and adoption proceedings.

The appellate function of this Division is concerned in the main with appeals from decisions of the magistrates' courts in family and care proceedings. Some of these appeals are heard by a divisional court.

This Divisions consists of a president and a set number of judges. It sits in London and at first-tier crown courts.

Family Division too has extensive original, but limited appellate, functions

Queen's Bench Division

The principal aspects of the Division's work lie in contract and tort. Financial limits apart (see above), there is an overlap between the functions of this Division and the county court. Admiralty matters, such as salvage claims, are heard in this Division by specialist judges who may sit with lay assessors in the Admiralty Court.

It has already been seen that the Queen's Bench Division has appellate criminal jurisdiction (see above). In terms of its appellate civil jurisdiction, a single judge or, where the decision of the High Court is final, a divisional court, has jurisdiction to hear appeals from certain tribunals and certain other appeals. A single judge, or, where the court so directs a divisional court, hears appeals by way of cases stated on various civil matters from magistrates' courts (excluding family and care proceedings which are dealt with in the Family Division), the Crown Court and certain other bodies.

The Queen's Bench Division fulfils some important supervisory roles. It can issue writs of habeas corpus to secure the release of individuals who might be detained, and, on application for judicial review, it has the power to make 'prerogative orders' against magistrates' courts, county courts and, except to matters relating to trial on indictment, the Crown Courts, tribunals and other decision-making bodies of a public nature, such as local authorities, the Take-over Panel and the

Queen's Bench Division has wide original and appellate functions

Court can direct orders to various bodies

Advertising Standards Authority (see *R* v *Panel on Take-overs and Mergers* (1987) and *R* v *Advertising Standards Authority* (1990)).

The prerogative orders are the orders of mandamus, prohibition and *certiorari*. An order of mandamus compels the body to whom it is directed to carry out a definite duty imposed on it by law. An order of prohibition is used to prevent a body which is under a duty to 'act judicially' or to 'act fairly' from acting in excess of its jurisdiction or from otherwise acting unfairly. An order of *certiorari* covers much the same area but is used after the particular body has done something and it is desired to review what has been done and, if necessary, quash what was done on the ground of excess of jurisdiction, denial of natural justice or error of law on the face of the record.

Case example
R v *Paddington (South) Rent Tribunal* (1955)
An order of mandamus was granted against a rent tribunal which had wrongly held that it had no jurisdiction to hear and determine an application properly made to it.

Case example
R v *Kent Police Authorities* (1971)
An order of prohibition was granted to prohibit a police authority from appointing a particular doctor to determine certain matters as part of the compulsory early retirement procedures being brought into operation in respect of the applicant for the order. The doctor was barred as a matter of natural justice from acting in this judicial capacity because of a previous examination and assessment of the applicant.

Case example
R v *Liverpool Corpn* (1972)
Certiorari was granted to quash a decision of a local authority to grant 50 new hackney carriage licences, the decision to grant the increase being taken in breach of the authority's duty to act fairly.

Applications for judicial review are heard by a single judge unless the court directs a hearing by a divisional court. Applications for habeas corpus are heard by a divisional court.

The Commercial Court

This is a branch of the Queen's Bench Division which sits in London, Liverpool and Manchester to which specialist judges are appointed. The Rules of the Supreme Court say that the Commercial Court can deal with commercial actions including 'any cause arising out of ordinary transactions of merchants and traders and, without prejudice to the generality of the foregoing words, any cause relating to the construction of a mercantile document, the export or import of merchandise, affreightment, insurance, banking, mercantile agency and mercantile usage.'

The basic features of the operation of this court are speed, and simplicity and flexibility in terms of procedure. The strict rules of evidence may be relaxed, and judges are available at short notice at any stage of the action at the initiative of either party.

The head of the Queen's Bench Division is the Lord Chief Justice and a set number of judges are assigned to it. It sits in London and at first-tier Crown Courts.

Appeals from its original jurisdiction lie to the Court of Appeal (Civil Division) as do appeals

Commercial Court ensures speedy hearings for commercial matters

from the appellate jurisdiction of any division. However, a special procedure introduced by the Administration of Justice Act 1969 provides that appeals in most civil cases go straight to the House of Lords. This procedure may only be used where:

- the parties so agree;
- the High Court grants a certificate to sanction it (which it may do only if satisfied that a point of law is involved which is of general public importance and which relates either to the construction of an Act or statutory instrument, or else is one in respect of which it considers itself bound by a decision of the Court of Appeal or House of Lords;
- the House of Lords grants leave to appeal.

'Leap-frog' procedure allows direct appeals to House of Lords

Court of Appeal (Civil Division)

The membership of the Court of Appeal has been described above. This division hears appeals from:

- decisions in civil matters from the High Court. Under the provisions of the Supreme Court Act 1981, appeals from the determination of an appeal by a divisional court require the leave of that court or of the division itself;
- decisions of the county court, except in bankruptcy where appeal is to the Chancery Division. In certain cases, the leave of the judge or of the division is required;
- decisions of the Employment Appeals Tribunal, Restrictive Practices Court, lands tribunal and certain other tribunals.

Except in the case of certain appeals from tribunals and from the Restrictive Practices Court, appeals are by way of re-hearing, which means that the court reviews the whole case by way of consideration of the notes of the trial and in the light of argument. Witnesses are not recalled and fresh evidence is not normally admitted.

Most appeals are by way of re-hearing

An appeal is usually heard by three members of the division, but, in certain circumstances, as in the case of appeals from the county court, an appeal may be heard by two members. A single judge may determine an application for leave to appeal and other incidental matters.

House of Lords

The membership of the House of Lords has been discussed above. It hears civil appeals from the Court of Appeal (Civil Division) if the House or that court has granted leave. It also hears appeals from the High Court under the 'leap-frog' procedure (see above).

Certain special courts and tribunals

Judicial Committee of the Privy Council

In a (diminishing) number of cases, the Privy Council is the final court of appeal from the courts of some Commonwealth countries. It sits in London and is normally composed of five Law Lords, but judges from Commonwealth countries also occasionally sit. It can also hear appeals from decisions of the disciplinary committees of the medical, dental and related professions.

Privy Council as Commonwealth court

Restrictive Practices Court

The Restrictive Practices Court operates under the provisions of the Restrictive Practices Act 1976. The Act is designed to prevent businesses from entering into agreements which restrict competition or fix prices. Goods and services are covered. The court investigates such agreements to determine if they are contrary to the public interest. It also deals with issues of resale price maintenance under the Resale Prices Act 1976, again to determine if an agreement is contrary to the public interest.

Employment Appeals Tribunal

The Tribunal operates under the provisions of the Industrial Tribunals Act 1996. Its jurisdiction is entirely appellate. It can hear appeals on points of law from industrial tribunals on matters relating to: unfair dismissal, redundancy payments, equal pay, sex discrimination, contracts of employment, trade unions and employment protection.

Lands Tribunal

This was established under the Lands Tribunal Act 1949. It hears appeals from: local valuation courts; cases for the assessment of compensation for the compulsory acquisition of land; applications for the variation, modification or discharge of restrictive covenants under the Law of Property Act 1985.

Other tribunals

A wide range of other matters come before various tribunals. Disputes about entitlement to various social welfare benefits come before social security appeals tribunals and the Social Security Commissioners. Disputes as to assessments in numerous categories of tax, duties and levies comes, *inter alia*, before the General and Special Commissioners for Income Tax, VAT tribunals, and betting levy appeals tribunals. Immigration and deportation disputes are heard by the Immigration Adjudication and Immigration Appeals Tribunal. Questions as to the continued detention of individuals under mental health legislation are decided by mental health review tribunals. Complaints about the conduct of medical and other practitioners are heard by family practitioner committees. Decisions about the licensing of public service vehicles and their drivers, routes and charges are taken by the Traffic Commissioners, the Licensing Authority for Goods Vehicles, and the Transport Tribunal. Appeals against refusals of credit licences are heard by the Consumer Credit Appeals Tribunal.

Supervision of tribunals

The decision of a tribunal may be challenged by applying to the Queen's Bench Division for judicial review (see above). Tribunals are also subject to the Council on Tribunals established by the Tribunals and Enquiries Act 1971. Under s. 1 of the Act, the Council must:

- keep under review the constitution and working of specified tribunals and, from time to time, report on their constitution and working;
- consider and report on such matters as are referred to the Council under the Act with respect to tribunals other than the ordinary courts of law;
- consider and report on such matters as may be referred as above, or as the Council may determine to be of special importance, with respect to administrative procedures involving, or which may involve, the holding by or on behalf of a minister of a statutory inquiry.

Restrictive Practices Court examines anti-competitive agreements

Tribunal hears appeals on many work-related issues

A very wide range of matters is covered by tribunals

Role of tribunals subject to supervision

Coroners' courts

Coroners' courts are regulated by the Coroners Act 1988. A coroner must be a barrister, solicitor or registered medical practitioner who has a five-year general qualification. Although the coroner has jurisdiction over such matters as treasure trove and, in London, the outbreak of fires, his jurisdiction is principally concerned with inquests into the death of persons whose bodies are 'lying within this district', where there is reasonable cause for suspecting that the person has died a violent or unnatural death, or a sudden death the cause of which is unknown, or has died in prison or that the death occurred while the deceased was in police custody, or resulted from an injury caused by a police officer in the purported execution of his duty. In such circumstances, an inquest must be held.

Review questions

1 What civil jurisdiction is enjoyed by the magistrates' courts and Crown Courts and to whom do appeals from their decisions lie?
2 Give an account of the small claims procedure, and indicate what attitude the courts take when a claim is framed so as to avoid the appropriate limit.
3 What is the jurisdiction of the county court and what basis is used to decide the allocation of cases between it and the High Court?
4 Explain the functions of the separate divisions of the High Court.
5 Give an account of the supervisory role of the High Court, and explain what is meant by the 'prerogative orders'.
6 What function is performed by the Commercial Court?
7 What is the appellate jurisdiction of the Court of Appeal (Civil Division)?
8 Under what circumstances can appeal be made to the House of Lords? Explain what is meant by the 'leap-frog' procedure.
9 What function is performed by the Judicial Committee of the Privy Council?
10 There are a number of other specialized courts. Which are they and what are their particular areas of concern?
11 To what extent is the work of tribunals subject to scrutiny?

Arbitration

A dispute may be referred to arbitration in any one of three ways. The governing legislation is found in the Arbitration Act 1996.

Reference by agreement out of court

An arbitration contract can take one of two forms:

- a contract might provide that all disputes between the parties are to be referred to arbitration;
- an agreement concluded after the dispute has arisen, seeking to submit that dispute to arbitration.

Many contracts provide for future disputes to be taken to arbitration, as do various trade association codes of practice. If a party to an arbitration agreement brings court proceedings instead of going to arbitration, the other party may apply for the proceedings to be stayed.

Case example
Home and Overseas Insurance Co. Ltd v Mentor Insurance Co. (UK) Ltd (1989)

The Court of Appeal held that in cases where there is an arbitration clause, especially when the dispute turns on the construction or implication of terms or trade practice, the court should not, on an application made prior to the arbitration, permit full-scale argument on the terms of the agreement between the parties, since the parties have agreed on the chosen tribunal, and the defendant is fully entitled prima facie to have the dispute decided by that tribunal in the first instance, to be free of court intervention until the dispute has been determined. He is also entitled to be free of such intervention thereafter, if the dispute has been determined in his favour, unless the plaintiff obtains leave to appeal and successfully appeals.

Courts can stay court proceedings in favour of arbitration agreements

The courts have usually shown a willingness to stay proceedings, and it is for the party opposing the stay to show why it should not be granted (*Vawdrey* v *Simpson* (1896)). If the arbitration agreement is not a domestic one, the court must stay proceedings, unless satisfied that the agreement is null and void, inoperative or incapable of being performed, or that there is in fact no dispute between the parties with regard to the matter agreed on to be referred.

'Autonomy' of arbitration clauses

It is a general principle that an arbitration clause is a separate agreement and survives any failure of the main contract itself.

Case example
Harbour Assurance Co. (UK) Ltd v Kansas General International Assurance Co. Ltd (1993)

Certain contracts of reinsurance contained an arbitration clause providing for the arbitration of 'all disputes or differences arising out of' the agreement. A question had arisen as to whether or not the reinsurance contracts were legal. The High Court had refused to stay proceedings on the ground that the principle of autonomy could not be applied so as to enable an arbitrator to determine whether or not the contract in which the arbitration clause was illegal.

The Court of Appeal held that the principle of autonomy could give jurisdiction to an arbitrator to determine a dispute over the initial validity of the contract itself provided that the arbitration clause was not itself directly impeached. The court also held that an issue as to the initial illegality of the contract was also capable of being referred to arbitration, provided that any initial illegality did not directly impeach that clause. In every case, the logical question was not whether the issue of illegality went to the validity of the contract, but whether it went to the validity of the arbitration clause. Accordingly, the illegality pleaded in this case did not affect the validity of the clause, which, on its proper construction, was wide enough to cover a dispute as to the initial illegality of the contract. The appeal was therefore allowed and the proceedings stayed.

Scott v *Avery* clauses

These are clauses where the agreement is that there is no right to refer a dispute to court until after an arbitration award has been made. Since no right of action in the courts accrues until the arbitration takes place, failure to observe the provisions of such a clause provides a complete defence to court action (*Scott* v *Avery* (1856)).

Arbitrators are themselves given the right to dismiss claims for want of prosecution, but this is a discretion which is to be exercised only in exceptional circumstances (*Lazenby & Co.* v *McNicholas Construction Co. Ltd* (1995)).

Appointment of arbitrators

It is normal to have one arbitrator, though the parties may choose more. If they do so, the possibility of an even split is avoided by the fact that the arbitrators are empowered at any time to choose an umpire, and must do so at once if they cannot agree. A majority decision is binding unless the arbitration agreement indicates otherwise.

Where, for whatever reason, the parties are unable or unwilling to appoint an arbitrator as specified in the agreement, the High Court may make an appointment and the person appointed may, in some circumstances, be a judge of the Commercial Court (see above).

The award and its enforcement

The Acts do not provide for any particular form for the award, but it must be expressed in final, unambiguous and internally consistent terms (see for example *Tomlin* v *Fordwick Corporation* (1836)). The High Court, unless the parties have excluded this, may request an arbitrator to give reasons for his award.

The award may order a money payment, or specific performance of a contract (except where it relates to land), and it may also direct the payment of costs, though these may be dealt with in the original arbitration agreement.

If the unsuccessful party does not honour the award, the award may, with the leave of the High Court, be enforced as a judgement of the court. In addition, such conduct by the unsuccessful party is a breach of contract and the award may be enforced in an action upon that breach (see *Agromet Motoimport Ltd* v *Maulden Engineering Ltd* (1985)).

Applying to the courts

Resort to the courts in relation to the substance of the arbitration (as opposed to procedural or ancillary matters) is possible only where there is an appeal against the award or where there is an application for the determination of a preliminary point of law.

Limited right to approach courts

An appeal lies against an arbitration award on any question of law, but not of fact, but, unless all parties agree, leave of the court is required.

Guidelines laid down for considering the granting of leave recognize a distinction between an arbitration on the terms of a standard form contract and one that arises from a one-off contract (see *The Nema* (1981) and *The Antaios* (1984)). In the latter case, leave should be granted only if the judge is satisfied on 'a mere perusal' of the reasoned award that the arbitrator was 'obviously wrong'. If, however, the judge feels by such perusal that the argument might convince him of the correctness of the decision, leave should not be given.

Guidance as to when leave to appeal to High Court allowed

In the case of standard form contracts the guidelines are less stringent, but leave should still only be granted if a 'strong prima facie' case has been made out that the arbitrator was wrong.

> ### Case example
> ### *Ipswich Borough Council* v *Fisons plc* (1990)
> A disagreement had arisen in relation to a lease granted by the Council to the company. The High Court held that the above guidelines were inapplicable outside shipping and commercial contracts, but the Court of Appeal ruled that this was a 'profound error'.

Further appeals

Beyond the High Court, appeal may be made to the Court of Appeal if the High Court certifies that there is a point of law at stake which is of general public importance, or is one which for some other reason should be considered by the Court of Appeal, and if either court gives leave. A further appeal to the House of Lords is permissible only if either court gives leave.

Preliminary point of law

Except where the parties have given their consent, the court cannot determine a point of law which has arisen in the course of arbitration unless the arbitrator has consented and the court is satisfied that its determination might substantially reduce the parties' costs, and that the question of law involved could substantially affect the rights of one or more parties to the agreement.

Exclusion agreements

Jurisdiction of court may be ousted

The High Court may not grant leave to appeal with respect to a question of law arising out of an award, nor accept a reference for the determination of a preliminary point of law, without the consent of the parties if the parties have agreed in writing to exclude such references to the High Court. However, in the case of a domestic arbitration agreement, such an exclusion agreement is valid only if entered into after the relevant arbitration has begun.

Reference by statute

Arbitration may be required by statute. For instance, s. 33 of the Trade Descriptions Act 1968 provides that compensation in relation to goods seized by an enforcement officer is to be determined by arbitration. Like provisions are found in s. 34 of the Consumer Protection Act 1987.

The provisions of the Arbitration Acts will apply unless the relevant statute provides otherwise. It is to be noted that, in the case of a reference by statute, the parties cannot make use of exclusion agreements (see above) to oust the jurisdiction of the courts.

Reference to arbitration by the court

Under the provisions of the Supreme Court Act 1981 the High Court may refer any case within its jurisdiction, or any particular issue in such a case, to be tried by an official referee (a circuit judge assigned for such business), a senior officer of the court, or, where the issue is of a technical nature requiring special knowledge, to a special referee. Such references can be made against the wishes of the parties. The award of the arbitrator is entered as a judgement in court proceedings. In certain circumstances, an appeal will lie to the Court of Appeal. The High Court may also use these officers to conduct an enquiry and make a report. If adopted, wholly or partially, the report is as binding as a judgement.

The powers of the county court to refer matters to arbitration under the County Courts Act 1984 have been considered above.

Consumer arbitration agreements

The Consumer Arbitration Agreements Act 1988 provides that, where a consumer has made an agreement for the resolution of future disputes by arbitration, such agreement is unenforceable unless:

- written consent was given after the particular dispute arose;
- the consumer has submitted to arbitration in pursuance of the agreement, regardless of which dispute might have been involved;
- the court so orders. There is no such power, however, if the proceedings fall within the small claims limit (see above).

The Act further provides that a consumer will generally have to abide by an arbitration agreement if the proceedings would not have been within the jurisdiction of the county court (see above).

Review questions

1 There are essentially three ways in which disputes can be referred to arbitration. Give a brief account of each.
2 What principles apply when one party to an arbitration agreement seeks to take the matter to court?
3 What is meant by the 'autonomy' of arbitration clauses?
4 What procedures govern the appointment of arbitrators, and how are their awards enforced?
5 What is meant by a '*Scott* v *Avery* clause'?
6 What guidelines have been laid down by the courts as to when appeals can be made from determinations at arbitration?
7 To what extent is it possible for the parties to an arbitration agreement to agree to oust the jurisdiction of the courts?
8 In what circumstances may a court refer matters to arbitration?
9 Explain the effect of the Consumer Arbitration Agreements Act 1988.

The doctrine of precedent

It is fundamental to the operation of the English legal system that previous judgements are treated as binding future courts. There is no statute laying down the operation of the doctrine, and the rules have therefore been laid down entirely by the courts themselves.

Rules of precedent developed by the courts

House of Lords

Until 1968, the House of Lords was bound by its own decision. In that year, the Lord Chancellor (see below) announced as follows: 'too rigid adherence to precedent may lead to injustice in a particular case and also unduly restrict the proper development of the law. [Their lordships] proposed therefore to modify their present practice and, while treating former decisions of this House as normally binding, to depart from a previous decision when it appears right to do so.'

House of Lords not bound by previous decisions

The House of Lords has said that it will not review one of its previous decisions unless it feels free to depart from both the reasoning and the decision, and unless it is satisfied that so to do would be relevant to the resolution of the dispute in the case before them, notwithstanding that the previous decision had given rise to concern (*Food Corp. of India* v *Antclizo Shipping Corp.* (1988)).

The House of Lords is free to depart from an earlier decision if an argument had not been placed before the previous court and which argument would, if placed, have led the House to rule differently (*Moodie* v *IRC* (1993)).

Court of Appeal (Civil Division)

This court is bound by decisions of the House of Lords and by its own previous decisions. Any departure from previous decisions of its own has been said to be 'in principle undesirable' and to be considered only if the previous decision is 'manifestly wrong'. Even then, it will be necessary to take account of whether the decision purports to be one of general application and whether there is any other way of correcting the error, by, for example, appeal to the House of Lords (*Langley* v *NW Water Authority* (1991)).

Guidance has been given as to the exceptional circumstances where the court can ignore its own previous decisions (see *Young* v *Bristol Aeroplane Co. Ltd* (1944); *Davis* v *Johnson* (1978)). These are:

- where two previous decisions conflict: the decision not followed will then be deemed to be overruled;
- a decision which is inconsistent with a ruling of the House of Lords, even though not actually overruled by the House of Lords;
- decisions given in error, which, for example, overlooked a relevant statute or binding decision.

The court cannot, however, claim not to follow a decision of the House of Lords which it believed to be in error (*Cassell & Co. Ltd* v *Broome* (1972)).

The Court of Appeal can also depart from a previous case if there is more than one of its decisions which is 'manifestly wrong', and there is no 'realistic possibility' of an appeal to the House of Lords to correct the position (*Williams* v *Fawcett* (1986)).

It is also the case that the court can ignore a previous decision if that decision has subsequently been disapproved by the Privy Council, even though this is not strictly a court which is part of the English legal system (see above).

> ### Case example
> ### Doughty v Turner (1964)
> In *Re Polemis* (1921), the Court of Appeal had ruled that the test for liability in tort depended on whether the loss followed the tort as a direct consequence, but in *The Wagon Mound* (1961), the Privy Council disapproved of that decision. The Court of Appeal felt free in these circumstances not to follow *Re Polemis*.

Court of Appeal to follow House of Lords and, save for exceptional cases, its own previous decisions

If a Court of Appeal decision goes to the House of Lords, and the House decides the appeal on grounds not argued in the Court of Appeal, being of the view that the issue decided in the Court of Appeal did not arise, the Court of Appeal's decision is not binding on a subsequent Court of Appeal (*R* v *Secretary of State for the Home Department* (1989)).

The authority of a two-judge court should be regarded as the same as a three-judge court, since, under present practice, the allocation of work between such courts is not determined by whether there will be no need for other than brief argument or the point is of minimal importance other than to the parties (*Langley* v *NW Water Authority* (1991)).

Court of Appeal (Criminal Division)

The position is generally as described in relation to the Civil Division (see above). However, an ordinary court of three judges may deviate more easily from previous decisions because the liberty of the individual may be at stake (*R* v *Gould* (1968)). A full court, which consists of five judges, can overrule previous decisions of the Criminal Division.

More flexibility in departing from own previous decisions

Divisional courts

In relation to civil cases, the divisional courts of the Family, Chancery or Queens Bench Divisions are bound by rulings of the Court of Appeal (Civil Division) and of the House of Lords. These courts are not, however, bound by their own decisions, but will follow them unless convinced that the earlier decision was wrong (*R* v *Greater Manchester Coroner, ex parte Tal* (1985)). They can also depart from their previous decisions if the principles in *Young* v *Bristol Aeroplane Co. Ltd* apply (see above) (*Huddersfield Police Authority* v *Watson* (1947)).

High Court

A High Court judge is bound by decisions of the Court of Appeal, the House of Lords and of divisional courts (*Huddersfield Police Authority* v *Watson* (1947)). They are not bound by other High Court decisions but will follow them unless convinced that the earlier decision is clearly wrong, and then only with a clear statement of their reasons for not following the earlier decision (Re *Hillas-Drake* (1944)).

Where a High Court judge is faced with conflicting High Court decisions, they must take the later decision as correct, unless convinced that the later decision was wrong because, for example, a binding or persuasive precedent had been overlooked (*Colchester Estates (Cardiff)* v *Carlton Industries plc* (1984)).

High Court generally follows its own decision

Crown Court

The Crown Court is bound by decisions of higher courts, but, it would seem, not by decisions of the divisional court (*R* v *Colyer* (1974)). Crown Court rulings cannot themselves give rise to binding precedents, mainly because there is no proper system for the reporting of Crown Court judgements (see below).

County courts and others

County courts, magistrates' courts and other inferior tribunals are bound by the decisions of higher courts. Their rulings cannot give rise to binding precedents, again mainly because of the absence of law reports (see below).

Lower courts bound by higher courts but cannot produce their own binding precedents

Law Reports

The system of precedent relies heavily on a proper system for the reporting of judgements. Although law reporting has been in existence since the time of Bracton in the thirteenth century, it was not until 1865 that law reporting became formalized. Then, the Incorporated Society of Law Reporting was founded. It is a joint committee of the Inns of Court, the Law Society and the Bar

Council (for the functions of these bodies, see below). The Council is responsible for the *Law Reports* and, since 1953, for the *Weekly Law Reports*.

There are in addition a considerable number of commercial law reports, such as the *All England Law Reports*, the *Road Traffic Reports*, the *Justice of the Peace Reports* and many other reports covering specialized areas, such as *Lloyd's Law Reports*. The Incorporated Council also publishes the *Industrial Cases Reports*. Recent developments have included the establishment of various on-line and fax systems for the reporting of judgements. In addition, some newspapers carry law reports edited by qualified barristers, the best known, perhaps, being the reports published in *The Times*.

There are both official and commercial law reports

The House of Lords has held that transcripts of unreported judgements of the Court of Appeal (Civil Division) may not be cited on appeals to the House except with its leave, and that will only be given if counsel gives an assurance that the transcript contains a statement of a relevant principle of law whose substance is not found in any reported judgement (*Roberts Petroleum Ltd* v *Bernard Kenny Ltd* (1983)). The Court of Appeal, however, has not taken this attitude to the citation of its judgements (*Lee* v *Walker* (1985)).

Review questions

1 Give an account of the doctrine of precedent and state which courts are bound by which other courts.
2 In what circumstances may the House of Lords ignore its own previous decisions?
3 What principles have been laid down as to the circumstances in which either Division of the Court of Appeal may depart from its own previous rulings?
4 To what extent do decisions of a three-judge Court of Appeal have a greater authority than a two-judge court?
5 What account must a High Court or divisional court take, respectively, of other decisions of the High Court and divisional court?
6 To what extent are binding precedents created by decisions of the Crown Court, county court and magistrates' court?
7 Give a brief account of the system of reporting court judgements.

Profession divided into various 'practitioners'

Legal profession

Barristers

Barristers do not form partnerships, but work together in what are called 'chambers', sharing rent and expenses. Their work consists of drafting legal documents and in giving 'opinions' on points of law, as well as appearing as advocates (for the rights of barristers to appear in court and conduct litigation, see below). For the most part, clients can only contact barristers through a solicitor (see below).

Barristers are members of one of the four Inns of Court. Those wishing to become barristers must apply to become a student of one of the Inns (Middle Temple, Inner Temple, Lincoln's Inn and Gray's Inn) and pass appropriate examinations. Successful candidates will then become the 'pupil' of a senior barrister or attend an approved practical training course. The Bar as a profession is represented by the General Council of the Bar.

Solicitors

Unlike barristers, solicitors are usually in partnerships, although a solicitor can be a sole practitioner. They act as advisers on commercial, family and personal matters, convey land, draft wills, and prepare cases involving litigation.

To become a solicitor, a person must be articled to a solicitor already in practice, pass the examinations conducted by the Law Society, and be admitted by the Master of the Rolls.

The Law Society is responsible for the profession, its Council being the ultimate authority. (For their rights to appear in court and conduct litigation, see below.)

Legal executives

Legal executives are qualified legal assistants who work in solicitors' offices. Their professional body is the Institute of Legal Executives. (For their rights to appear in court and to conduct litigation, see below.)

Conveyancing services

The Solicitors Act 1974 limited the categories of person who could provide conveyancing services. The Courts and Legal Services Act 1990, however, provides that this limitation is not to apply to 'authorized practitioners'. This is essentially a matter of being authorized by the Authorized Conveyancers Board set up by the Act.

In addition, the Administration of Justice Act 1985 established the Council for Licensed Conveyancers to grant licences and to regulate practitioners in the provision of conveyancing services.

Conveyancing not a monopoly of solicitors

Rights of audience

The position as to rights of audience is regulated by the Courts and Legal Services Act 1990. The expression is defined to mean 'the right to exercise any of the functions of appearing before and addressing a court including the calling and examining of witnesses.'

The right to an audience before a court arises where the particular person has such a right granted by the appropriate authorized body. This is a reference to the General Council of the Bar; the Law Society and any professional or other body designated as an authorized body by Order in Council. The Institute of Legal Executives has made a successful application to become such a body.

Rights of audience depend on membership of an 'authorized body'

The Act preserves the rights of barristers and solicitors to those rights of audience which they had as at 7 December 1989. The Courts and Legal Services Act also empowers the Lord Chancellor (see below) to give solicitors the right to appear in such Crown Courts as he directs.

Right to conduct litigation

This too is governed by the Courts and Legal Services Act. The 'right to conduct litigation' means the right to: (a) exercise all or any of the functions of issuing a writ or otherwise commence proceedings before any court; and (b) to perform any ancillary functions in relation to proceedings, such as entering appearances to actions. The position parallels that above in that the relevant person must be a member of an 'authorized body', defined here to mean the Law Society and any other body authorized by Order in Council. Solicitors are deemed to have been granted by the Law Society the rights to conduct litigation which were exercisable by the profession before 7 December 1989.

Review questions

1 Explain the differences between solicitors, barristers and legal executives.
2 What is meant by 'rights of audience' and 'right to conduct litigation' and who has such rights?
3 Who may provide conveyancing services?

The law officers

The Lord Chancellor

The Lord Chancellor occupies the highest judicial office

The Lord Chancellor is the Speaker of the House of Lords and head of the judiciary. He controls the administration of the courts. He advises the Crown on the appointment of judges, is responsible for the appointment of justices of the peace, and advises on the appointment of recorders and stipendiary magistrates. Unlike the Speaker in the House of Commons, he may take part in debates and may vote in divisions, but he has no casting vote. The office is political and the holder sits in the Cabinet.

The Attorney-General

The Attorney-General is usually a member of the House of Commons and a member of the governing party. He is head of the English Bar and prosecutes in important criminal cases and represents the Crown in civil matters. He also advises the government departments on legal matters, and the courts on matters of parliamentary privilege.

The Attorney-General also has the power to institute litigation on behalf of the public, for example to stop a public nuisance or the commission of a crime. Generally, individuals do not have a sufficient interest in law to institute action in such cases. Where a person does not have sufficient interest, they can ask the Attorney-General to take proceedings in what is known as a 'relator action'. The relator is the individual who asks the Attorney-General to act, and the relator is responsible for the court costs. If the Attorney-General declines to act, he cannot be compelled to do so (see *Gouriet v Union of Post Office Workers* (1977)). The Attorney-General is barred from private practice.

The Solicitor-General

Both the Attorney-General and Solicitor-General are usually MPs

Like the Attorney-General, the Solicitor-General is almost always a member of the governing party in the House of Commons. His duties are similar to those of the Attorney-General and he is in many ways his deputy. The Law Officers Act 1944 provides that any functions undertaken by the Attorney-General may be discharged by the Solicitor-General if the office is vacant, if he is unable to act through illness or absence, or where the Attorney-General authorized him to act. The Solicitor-General is barred from private practice.

The Director of Public Prosecutions

The Prosecution of Offences Act 1985 states that the Director of Public Prosecutions is to be appointed by the Attorney-General (see above) and must be a person who has a general qualification.

The Act lists his functions as follows:

- to take over the conduct of all criminal proceedings, except in relation to proceedings specified by the Attorney-General, which are instituted on behalf of a police force;
- to institute and have the conduct of any criminal proceedings in any case where it appears to him that the importance of the case makes it appropriate that proceedings should be instituted by him; or where it is otherwise appropriate for proceedings to be instituted by him;
- to take over the conduct of all binding over proceedings instituted by a police force;
- take over the conduct of all proceedings begun by summons issued under those provisions of the Obscene Publications Act 1969 relating to the forfeiture of obscene articles;
- to give, to such extent as is considered appropriate, advice to the police on all matters relating to criminal offences;
- to appear for the prosecution, when so directed by the court, in relation to various appeals;
- to discharge such other functions as from time to time may be assigned to him by the Attorney-General.

Wide ranging functions of DPP

Crown Prosecution Service

The Crown Prosecution Service was established by the Prosecution of Offences Act 1985. It consists of the Director of Public Prosecutions (see above); the Chief Crown Prosecutors (see below) and such other staff as are appointed by the DPP. Crown prosecutors are designated by the DPP from members of the service who have a general legal qualification. England and Wales are divided into areas, and for each area the DPP appoints a Chief Crown Prosecutor. Under the provisions of the Courts and Legal Services Act, Crown prosecutors have the rights of audience which they had prior to the Act, which were broadly those of solicitors, but the Act allows for such rights to be altered in the future.

Independent prosecution service for England and Wales

The Legal Services Ombudsman

The Courts and Legal Services Act established the position of Legal Services Ombudsman appointed by the Lord Chancellor. He has two main functions: to investigate the way in which complaints have been handled by the relevant professional bodies; and he has the power to investigate the original complaint as to the provision of legal services. Following his investigations, the Ombudsman may make recommendations which can include the payment of compensation. These are not binding, but any person failing to comply with a recommendation is to publicize that failure and the reasons for it, in such form as the Ombudsman may require.

Decisions of Ombudsman not binding

Review questions

1 What are the roles of the Lord Chancellor, the Attorney-General and the Solicitor-General, and what qualifications are required for appointment?
2 What are the powers of the Attorney-General with regard to instituting litigation, and what is meant by a 'relator action'?
3 Explain the functions of the Director of Public Prosecutions.
4 Give an account of the constitution of the Crown Prosecution Service.
5 What is the remit of the Legal Services Ombudsman and what is the extent of his powers following an investigation?

The United Kingdom as a Member of the European Union

The United Kingdom entered what was then called the Common Market in 1973 by virtue of the enactment in the United Kingdom Parliament of the European Communities Act 1972. Including the United Kingdom, there are now 15 member states in the Union. The 'constitution' of the Union is to be found in the Treaty of Rome 1957. The Treaty on European Union, signed in Maastricht in 1992, created a European Union moving towards economic and monetary union with intergovernmental co-operation in certain areas. This was implemented in the United Kingdom by the European Communities (Amendment) Act 1993.

European Union 'enlarged' by agreement with EFTA states

The European Union has joined with the member states of the European Free Trade Area (Iceland, Liechtenstein, Norway and Switzerland) to form the European Economic Area. There is free movement of goods, persons, services and capital within the area, as well as uniform rules on competition and state aid. The EFTA states generally adopt Union legislation.

The institutions of the European Union

European Commission

The European Commission is responsible for initiating and drafting legislation, implementing the decisions of the Council of Ministers of the European Union (see below), administering the various EU funds (such as the European Social Fund, the Cohesion Fund). The Commission has autonomous powers under which it may act without reference to the Council in areas such as the Common Agricultural Policy and customs union.

The Commission is essentially the executive arm of the EU

The Commission consists of 20 Commissioners: Austria, Belgium, Denmark, Finland, Greece, Ireland, Luxembourg, Netherlands, Portugal and Sweden each have one. France, Germany, Italy, Spain and the United Kingdom each have two. The European Parliament (see below) is consulted before the member states appoint the President of the Commission, and Parliament must approve the full Commission. Commissioners serve for five years. Commissioners are required to act in the best interests of the Union as a whole, and are not under the authority of their national government.

Council of Ministers of the European Union

Legislation is initiated by the Commission (see above) but its final adoption generally depends on the Council.

Council is law-making body

Each member state has the following votes in the Council: Austria 4; Belgium 5; Denmark 3; Finland 3; France 10; Germany 10; Greece 5; Ireland 3; Italy 10; Luxembourg 2; Netherlands 5; Portugal 5; Spain 8; Sweden 4; United Kingdom 10. Some measures, notably on taxation, have to be adopted unanimously, and there are also occasions (see below) when the law-making procedure requires unanimity. Unanimity is also generally required for action in relation to a common foreign and security policy, or in relation to co-operation in home affairs. For the most part, however, the Council can adopt measures by a simple majority or by a qualified majority. This latter requires 62 votes of the possible 87 votes which may be cast.

Council can act by majority, though unanimity sometime required

The Council consists of representatives from each member state at ministerial level, authorized to commit the government of that member state. Meetings are attended by different ministers. For example, agriculture ministers will discuss farm prices; employment ministers labour and social affairs. Major Union issues will be matters for the foreign ministers.

European Parliament

This is directly elected by the citizens of the Union. Its role is to adopt the Union's budget, give its opinion on proposed legislation and propose amendments (see further below), and to investigate complaints of maladministration in the other institutions of the Union. Under the amendments adopted at Maastricht, the Parliament has been given the power of 'negative assent' which means that it can veto legislation in certain areas (such as education and culture) by an absolute majority. The Parliament also has the 'right of initiative', which enables it to request the European Commission to draft legislation in areas where it feels EU action is required.

Directly elected Parliament has number of powers

Parliament's consent is also required for the accession of new members.

Committee of the Regions

This was established by Maastricht. It drafts legislation on policy areas such as health, culture and certain funds, and where the Council or Commission considers it appropriate. It consists of 222 representatives from local and regional authorities in the member states.

Union business assisted by number of committees

Economic and Social Committee

This is an advisory body also consisting of 222 representatives from the various economic and social sectors in the member states. It is divided into three groups – employers, workers and various interests (such as agriculture, small and medium-sized businesses and transport). The Committee draws up opinions on all draft legislation referred to it by the Commission.

Conciliation Committee

This is made up of members or representatives of the Council and Parliament in equal numbers. It is convened when the Council and Parliament disagree on a legislative proposal (see more on the law-making process below) and it seeks to draw up and approve a text satisfying both bodies.

COREPER

This is an acronym for the Committee of Permanent Representatives of the member states. It is composed of civil servants and is where the initial discussion of proposals takes place between the member states.

Court of Auditors

Auditors act as
financial
watchdog

The Court consists of 15 members appointed by the unanimous decision of the Council after consultation with the Parliament. Its main task is to check that all Union revenue has been collected, that all expenditure has been validly incurred, and that financial management is sound. It issues an annual report.

The European Court of Justice and the Court of First Instance

The Court of Justice consists of 15 judges assisted by nine Advocate-Generals. The members of the Court are appointed for six years by agreement between the governments of the member states. Their independence is guaranteed.

The Court's role is to ensure that the European treaties are interpreted and applied in accordance with the law. The Court can find that a member state has failed to fulfil its obligations. A member state not complying with a judgement of the Court may be fined. The Court also reviews the legality of measures taken by any of the Union's institutions and it has the power to judge when they are in breach of the Treaties by failing to act.

The Court also gives preliminary rulings, on an application by a national court, on the interpretation or validity of points of EU law. If a legal action produces a disputed point of law of such a kind, a national court may seek a ruling from the Court: it must do so if there is no higher court of appeal in the member state, in which case the judgement of the Court is binding.

Case example
H. P. Bulmer Ltd v *Bollinger SA* (1974)

It was decided by the Court of Appeal that the High Court and Court of Appeal have the jurisdiction to interpret Community law and that they are not obliged to grant a right of appeal to the European Court of Justice. However, if the case goes to the House of Lords on appeal, the House must refer the matter to the Court if either party so desires.

The obligation to refer to the Court does not arise if the question raised is not relevant to the outcome of the proceedings, if it has already been answered in a previous ruling of the Court, or if the correct interpretation is so obvious as to be beyond reasonable doubt (*CILFIT* v *Ministry of Health* (1982); *Magnavision NV SA* v *General Optical Council (No 2)* (1987)).

The Court of First Instance deals with disputes concerning the EU institutions and their staff and with EU competition rules. The CFI also has jurisdiction in all direct actions by citizens and firms against EU institutions except in anti-dumping matters. It consists of 12 judges. Appeals on points of law are only dealt with by the Court of Justice.

European Court
as interpreter of
EU law

The legislative instruments

Regulations

Direct
applicability of
regulations

Under the Treaty of Rome, the Union may adopt regulations. These apply the same law throughout the Union and apply in full in all member states. In addition, regulations are 'directly applicable', which means that they do not specifically have to be adopted by the member states. Instead they confer rights or impose duties in exactly the same way as domestic laws.

Directives

The purpose of a directive is to ensure uniformity in the law throughout the Union but to make allowance for national traditions and structures. A directive is binding on member states as to the objective to be achieved, but leaves the precise attainment of that purpose to whatever method is chosen by the individual member state.

Member states have options as to how Directives implemented

Although, unlike regulations, directives do not have direct effect, the European Court of Justice has held that, where a member state has not implemented a directive, nationals of that state can rely on the directive before the national court to secure such rights as are provided by the directive, and can even claim compensation where loss is sustained because of the failure to implement the directive (Cases of *Frankovich* and *Boniface* (1991)).

Case example
Faccini Dori v *Recreb Srl* (1995)

A contract had been made in Italy which was within the terms of Council Directive 85/577 on contracts made by consumers away from business premises. The contract was made at a time when Italy was in breach of the time limit for the implementation of that directive. The European Court of Justice ruled that, in the absence of measures implementing a directive, consumers could not make use of the right of cancellation provided for in the directive nor enforce such rights in the national court since directives were addressed to member states and hence could not impose obligations on individuals. However, the Court said that national courts, when applying national law, had to interpret it as close as possible to the principles contained in the directive so as to achieve the intended result. Moreover, if the result required by the directive could not be obtained by such interpretation, the member state would have to make good the damage caused to individuals by the failure to implement the directive if (a) the purpose of the directive was to grant rights to individuals; (b) it was possible to identify the contents of those rights from the provisions of the directive; and (c) there was a link between the breach of the member state's obligations and the damage suffered.

Reliance may be placed even on directive not formally implemented

---

Decisions

A decision of the Commission or Council may be addressed to member states, individuals or corporations and is binding on those addressed. An example of an individual decision would be a Commission ruling that a firm had acted in breach of the competition rules contained in the Treaty of Rome. Such decisions can include the imposition of a fine. An example of a decision addressed to a member state would be a Community instruction requiring a member state to abolish or amend measures of state aid to national undertakings.

Recommendations and opinions

Recommendations and opinions delivered by an institution of the Union have no legal effect Recommendations will urge those addressed to adopt a particular form of behaviour; opinions are used when the particular institution is called on to state a view on a current situation or particular event in the Union or a member state. A recommendation was, for example, adopted in 1992 on codes of practice for the protection of consumers in respect of contracts negotiated at a distance.

Recommendations and opinions have no binding effect

Resolutions

Unlike the various instrument discussed above, the Treaty of Rome does not provide for resolutions. However, both the Council, the Parliament and the Commission do occasionally adopt resolutions which do, not, of course have legal effect. In 1992, for example, the Council adopted a resolution on future priorities for the development of consumer policy.

The legislative process

The proposal procedure

As was seen above, it is the Council which in most cases is responsible for the adoption of a legislative proposal. However, before it actually reaches a decision, there are various stages to be completed.

The Commission will draft a measure which it can adopt by a simple majority, and this is then forwarded to the Council. The Council will then check to determine if it is required by Union law to refer the matter to other Union institutions, such as the European Parliament or the Economic and Social Committee. If they are to be consulted, they communicate their opinion back to the Council.

Once these consultations have taken place, the Commission proposal is once more placed before the Council, possibly amended to take account of the opinions expressed during the consultation process. Adoption by the Council is the final stage of the legislative process.

This form of procedure operates where neither the co-operation or co-decision procedures are stated to apply (see below).

So-called 'proposal procedure' just one form of adopting proposals

The co-operation procedure

The co-operation procedure involves a bigger role for the Parliament. It is applicable primarily in matters relating to the internal market, social policy, economic and social cohesion, and research and development. The procedure is essentially as follows:

Enhanced role for Parliament in co-operation procedure

1 The Commission proposal is sent not just to the Council but also to the Parliament. This gives the proposal a first reading, and it then notifies the Council of its opinion.
2 The Council then adopts a 'common position' which is sent to the Parliament for a second reading. Parliament then has three months to choose one of the following:
   (i)   to accept the common position, in which case the Council can adopt the proposal;
   (ii) it may do nothing, in which case it is to be taken to have accepted the common position and the Council can adopt it;
   (iii) it may reject the common position, in which case the proposal can only be adopted by the Council acting unanimously;
   (iv) it may propose changes to the common position. The question is then whether the Commission is prepared to accept these amendments. If it does, the Council may adopt the proposal by a qualified majority (see above) or, if it is departing from the Commission's proposal, unanimously. If the Commission does not accept the amendments, adoption by the Council must be unanimous.

It is always open to the Council effectively to block a measure by not taking any decisions at all on amendments proposed by Parliament or on the amended Commission proposals.

The co-decision procedure

The following is the essence of the co-decision procedure. It encompasses measures relating to: the free movement of workers; freedom of establishment (including special rules for foreign nationals and recognition of diplomas); freedom to provide services; the harmonization of legislation for the establishment and operation of the single market; educational and vocational training; youth, culture and health; consumer protection; research and development; and certain environmental programmes.

1 The Commission makes a proposal which is sent to the Council and the Parliament. There is a first reading by the Parliament and its opinion goes to the Council.
2 The Council can then accept the proposal by a qualified majority (see above) or, if it is departing from the proposal, unanimously. Either way, a common position is adopted, and the matter is then referred to the Parliament for a second reading. Parliament is now in the co-decision stage and it has three months in which to do one of the following:
    (i)   it may adopt the common position, or do nothing, in which case the Council may adopt the proposal;
    (ii)   if it wishes, it may make amendments to the common position. The procedure is then to set up a conciliation committee consisting of representatives from the Council and the Parliament in equal proportion to negotiate a compromise. If a compromise is agreed on, the proposal is adopted by a joint decision of the Council and Parliament.
    (iii) it may reject the common position outright, in which case the Council may convene the conciliation committee, and the procedure is then as in (ii).
3 Where the conciliation committee fails to negotiate a compromise, the Council may, within six weeks, confirm its common position, amended as desired by Parliament, by a qualified majority. Parliament may, however, reject this position by an absolute majority of its members at third reading. In this case, the proposal is defeated, thus giving the Parliament a right of veto.

Co-decision procedure puts Council and Parliament on equal footing

Infringement proceedings

The European Commission or another member state (in practice almost always the Commission) may bring a member state before the European Court of Justice if it believes that that member state has failed to fulfil an obligation imposed by EU law. If the Court finds against the particular member state, that state is required to take the measures needed to conform.

Case example
R v Secretary of State for Employment (1996)

It was held by the European Court of Justice that the United Kingdom, in allowing women to claim free prescriptions from the age of 60, but compelling men to wait until 65, was in breach of EU law on the equal treatment of men and women in matters relating to social security. The Department of Health then immediately issued a press release entitled 'Exemption from prescription charges to be equalized for men and women from tomorrow' which provided for men and women to receive free prescriptions from age 60.

Case example
Barber v Guardian Royal Exchange Assurance Group (1990)

The European Court of Justice ruled that the provisions as to equal treatment were infringed by an occupational pension scheme which applied differing age qualifications between men and women. Although this did not apply to state pensions, the United Kingdom took the view that it would be impossible in practical terms to maintain differing ages for men and women in this context and made provision in the Pensions Act 1995 for the state retirement age to be 65 for both sexes.

Penalties can be imposed for failure to observe court rulings

If a member state fails to comply with a judgement it can be ordered to pay a lump-sum fine or a penalty payment.

Preliminary rulings

National courts may seek guidance on EU law

This refers to the procedure by which a national court can seek guidance on EU law from the Court. Where a national court is required to apply provisions of EU law in the case before it, it may stay the proceedings and ask the Court for questions regarding the validity of the EU legislation at issue and/or the interpretation of any legislation. The Court answers in a judgement, not in an advisory capacity.

Case example
Secretary of State for Social Security v Thomas (1993)

Social security legislation applied different age qualifications between men and women in relation to certain disablement allowances. Female applicants were refused allowances by adjudication offers, but their appeal succeeded before the Social Security Commissioners, whose decision was upheld by the Court of Appeal, on the grounds that the legislation infringed EU law. The Secretary of State for Social Security appealed to the House of Lords who referred the matter to the European Court of Justice for its ruling.

Primacy of EU law

EU law prevails over conflicting national law

There is nothing in the Treaty of Rome which expressly gives EU law superiority over national law in the event of a conflict between the two. The principle of the primacy of EU law has, however, been established by the European Court of Justice. It has established that, first, the member states have transferred sovereign rights to a community created by them. They cannot reverse the process by means of subsequent unilateral measures inconsistent with the concept of that community. Second, it is a principle of the Treaty of Rome that no member state can call into question the status of EU law as a system uniformly and generally applicable throughout the EU (*Costa* v *ENEL* (1964)).

The notion that EU law is paramount can mean that United Kingdom courts have the authority to suspend the operation of what is otherwise a valid enactment.

Case example
Factortame Ltd and Others v Secretary of State for Transport (No 2) (1991)

Acting under the provisions of the Merchant Shipping Act 1988, the Secretary of State made certain regulations dealing with a register of British shipping vessels. Certain English companies did not qualify under the regulations because most of their directors and shareholders were Spanish. They challenged the legislation on the grounds that it deprived them of certain rights granted by the EU. The divisional court requested a preliminary ruling from the European Court of Justice on the substantive provisions of EU law and granted the applicants interim relief to the effect that the relevant United Kingdom legislation was to be disapplied and the Secretary of State restrained from enforcing it. The Court of Appeal allowed an appeal and set aside the order for interim relief. The applicants appealed to the House of Lords, which held that the common law did not provide the power to set aside otherwise valid legislation pending a reference to the European Court. The House of Lords, however, referred this matter to the European Court, which ruled that a national court was required to set aside a rule of national law which it considered was the sole obstacle preventing it from granting interim relief in a case before that court concerning Community law if to do otherwise would impair the full effectiveness of the subsequent judgement to be given on the substantive issue of the existence of the rights being claimed under Community law.

Following this ruling from the European Court, the House of Lords held that a court should exercise its discretion according to the balance of convenience and should, in so doing, take account in particular of the importance of upholding the law of the land in the public interest, bearing in mind the need for stability in society and the duty placed on certain authorities to enforce the law in the public interest. However, the court should not restrain an apparently authentic law unless satisfied that, having regard to all the circumstances, the challenge to its validity was prima facie so firmly based as to justify the taking of such an exceptional course. Applying those principles to the present case, the applicants had a strong case to present to the European Court that the evidence presented by the Secretary of State was not sufficient to outweigh the obvious and immediate damage which would continue to be caused to them if they were not to be granted the interim relief, and therefore the balance of convenience favoured the granting of interim relief to the applicants whose appeal against the decision of the Court of Appeal was therefore allowed.

In exceptional cases, the courts can set aside national law if in conflict with EU law

Review questions

1 Give an account of the make-up of the European Commission and of the Council of Ministers of the European Union.
2 What is the basic role of the European Parliament?
3 There are two courts interpreting EU law: the European Court of Justice and the European Court of First Instance. What is their composition and what is their role?
4 Apart from the above, there are a number of other EU institutions. State what they are and give an account of their functions.

5 Give an account of the process by which the EU makes law, paying particular attention to the co-decision and co-operation procedure.
6 Explain the differences between regulations and directives, and state the extent to which directives can be relied on by individuals even if not incorporated into national law.
7 In the context of the European Court of Justice, what is meant by infringement proceedings and preliminary rulings? What powers does the Court have to enforce its rulings?
8 To what extent is EU law supreme? Set out what you consider to be the implications of the Factortame case.

Chapter summary

- The English legal system is a common law system. The source of law within this system is that of statute law, which includes Acts of Parliament and statutory instruments, and the law made by the judges (which is sometimes also called 'the common law').
- The English legal system is also broadly divided into the civil and the criminal law. To reflect this distinction, a separate hierarchy of civil and criminal courts has been established.
- The above hierarchy works on the doctrine of precedent, so that, although there are certain exceptions, a lower court will always be bound by the decision of a higher court. This in turn has given rise to an extensive system of law reports, both official and commercial.
- To help overcome the delays and expense that going to court can often involve, parties can choose instead to have their disputes resolved by arbitration. This takes place within a statutory regime. A small claims court has also been established with quicker, cheaper procedures for litigants who wish to pursue small claims without incurring heavy costs.
- The court system is also supplemented by a number of specialist courts, such as the Restrictive Practices Court and the Employment Appeals Tribunal. Many of these specialist courts are subject to review by the Council on Tribunals.
- Practising lawyers are barristers or solicitors, each with their own separate roles. There are also legal executives and licensed conveyancers. The rights of audience and the right to conduct litigation are subject to the provisions of the Courts and Legal Services Act 1990. There are in addition a number of law officers, such as the Director of Public Prosecutions, the Attorney-General and the Solicitor-General. Generally, prosecution for criminal offences is in the hands of the Crown Prosecution Services established by the Prosecution of Offences Act 1985.
- The chapter also sets out the legal consequences of the United Kingdom's membership of the European Union. It describes the precise nature and function of various Union bodies and institutions, and gives an account given of how EU law is made, the role of the European Court of Justice, and of the supremacy of EU law over national law.

Discussion questions

1 To what extent is it true to say that, for the most part, substantive law is now to be found in texts which are not themselves Acts of Parliament? If this is the case, to what extent do you think that this is a situation over which Parliament exerts adequate control?
2 'The doctrine of precedent ensures that the courts apply a consistent view of the law.' To what extent is this true?
3 It has been said that, following the enactment of the Courts and Legal Services Act 1990, the difference between the various branches of the legal profession have become of less importance. Is this a proposition with which you agree?
4 The formal court structure is inadequately equipped to meet the requirements of specialized branches of the law, or the needs of individual litigants. Discuss the validity of this statement and the measures which have been taken to overcome the problem.
5 'The English legal system does not recognize the separation of powers.' Discuss the accuracy of this statement vis-à-vis the various law officers.
6 What is meant by 'parliamentary sovereignty' and to what extent is it true to say that, given the United Kingdom's membership of the European Union, Parliament is no longer supreme?

Recommended reading

English Law, Smith and Keenan (1986), Pitman.
Principles of Law Government Law (2nd edn), Cross (1997), Sweet & Maxwell.
Law and Institutions of the European Communities (6th edn), Lasok and Bridge (1994), Butterworths.

2 Contract

Objectives

The purpose of this chapter is to explain how a binding contract is made. It will analyse the key issues of offer and acceptance and the doctrine of consideration. Particular attention will also be paid to how the contents of a contract are categorized; the circumstances in which a contract can be brought to an end; and the rights and liabilities which arise in the event of a breach of contract.

Key concepts

- The categories of contract
- The consensual nature of contract expressed through offer and acceptance
- The relative importance of contract terms
- The capacity of parties to enter into contracts
- The element of consideration
- The doctrine of privity of contract
- The incorporation of contract terms
- The classification of contract terms
- The control of exclusion clauses
- The effect of mistake and misrepresentation
- The remedies available to the victim of a breach of contract.

Categories of contract

Essentially, contracts are divided into two categories. Specialty contracts are contracts which are binding simply because they have been signed, sealed and delivered. However, the effect of the Law of Property (Miscellaneous Provisions) Act 1989 has effectively put an end to the requirement for sealing. Such contracts are generally of little relevance and hence are not covered in this chapter. Far more important is the simple contract, the requirements of which are discussed below. It should be noted that these requirements are based on common-law principles and are not to be found in any Act of Parliament.

Relationships with compulsory suppliers

If a party is under a statutory duty to supply goods or services, then the arrangements into which that party enters with its customers are not contracts. Examples are the NHS, the compulsory acquisition of property, and the gas and electricity companies: *Pfizer Corporation* v *Ministry of*

Health (1965); *Sovmots Investments Ltd* v *Secretary of State for the Environment* (1977); *Norweb plc* v *Dixon* (1995).

Legal capacity

If a party to a contract is suffering from some mental disability, or is drunk, and this state of affairs is known to the other party to the contract, the first party is entitled to avoid the contract. However, the Sale of Goods Act 1979 does say that a reasonable price must be paid for the relevant goods.

If a party has not yet reached majority, which was established at 18 by the Family Law Reform Act 1969, they are obliged to pay only for necessaries. These are defined by the Sale of Goods Act as 'goods suitable to the condition in life' of the minor and 'to his actual requirements at the time of the sale and delivery'.

Case example
Nash v *Inman* (1908)

A Cambridge undergraduate from a comfortable background ordered 11 fancy waistcoats from a Savile Row tailor. The court did not accept that these were necessaries and the tailor was, therefore, not entitled to payment.

If the contract entered into by the minor is one which gives them an interest in some matter of a permanent nature, such as a lease, they are bound by it unless they repudiate it during infancy or within a reasonable time of reaching their majority. A minor cannot take a legal estate in land because of the provisions of the Law of Property Act 1925 and the Settled Land Act 1925, but a lease can convey something called an 'equitable' title, which is short of a full legal title. In other cases, a contract made by a minor is ineffective unless they confirm it after reaching the age of 18.

The Minors' Contracts Act 1987 provides that where a contract cannot be enforced against a minor, or they repudiate a contract made when a minor, this does not affect the validity of any guarantee given in respect of that contract. The Act also states that where a minor has acquired property under an unenforceable contract, they may be required by the court, where this is 'just and equitable', to return the property or property representing that which they have acquired.

Companies

The operation of the *ultra vires* doctrine, which once had the effect of putting in doubt contracts made by a company outside its stated powers, has been effectively abrogated by the Companies Act 1989. The position now is that a third party dealing with a company is no longer under any obligation to check that company's capacity and there is no question of a contract made by a company being invalid because it is outside the purpose of the company as defined in the company's memorandum.

Review questions

1 In what circumstance is a minor, or someone suffering from mental incapacity, obliged to pay for the goods they have obtained?
2 How would you define 'necessaries'?
3 When can a company be held to contracts made by it outside the terms of its memorandum of association?

Offer and acceptance

It is an established principle that, before parties can be said to have made a binding contract, one party must have made a clear, unequivocal offer, and the other side must have provided a no less clear and unequivocal acceptance of that offer. It should also be realized that the courts have also defined an 'invitation to treat', which is a statement or declaration inviting the other to come up with an offer. It is not itself an offer and so does not lend itself to immediate acceptance. This was established in *Pharmaceutical Society of Great Britain* v *Boots* (1953) and reaffirmed in *Fisher* v *Bell* (1961). This is why shoppers can never demand to be sold goods which have been inadvertently underpriced. The display of the goods at that price is not an offer to sell, but an invitation to treat. The shopper then makes the offer which the shop owner can accept or reject at their discretion.

There can be no acceptance of an invitation to treat

Case example
Harvey v *Facey* (1893)

A potential buyer sent a telegram asking for the lowest cash price. The reply which stated the lowest price was held to be an invitation to treat only, and not as an offer to sell at that price.

No acceptance by silence

A person may not arbitrarily impose on another to the effect that that other's silence will be deemed an acceptance of an offer.

Case example
Felthouse v *Bindley* (1862)

One party wrote to another offering to buy a horse, adding that if a reply was not received, the horse would be deemed to have been sold to him. No reply was made. The court held that this silence had not amounted to acceptance of the offer.

However, where the party to whom an offer is made himself indicates that the offer is to be taken as accepted if he does not indicate to the contrary within a reasonable time, that can constitute acceptance: *Gebr Van Weelde Scheepvaartkantor BV* v *Cia Naviera Sea Orient SA* (1985); Re *Selectmove Ltd* (1995).

Agreements to agree

An agreement to make a contract, as well as an agreement to negotiate, is unenforceable because each lacks the element of certainty (*Walford* v *Miles* (1992)).

Acceptance and counter-offers

Acceptance of an offer must be absolute and unqualified. If it is not, then the original offer is rejected and can only be reinstated if made afresh.

Case example
Hyde v *Wrench* (1840)

A farm was offered for sale at £1000. A counter offer was made at £950, but was increased two days later to the original offer price. It was held that no binding contract had come into existence since the counter offer of £950 had destroyed the original offer which had not been repeated. A mere inquiry for further information, however, is not the same as a counter-offer.

Case example
Stevenson v *McLean* (1880)

A company offered to sell iron at £2 a tonne. The company to whom this offer was made asked if the sellers would accept £2 for delivery over two months or, if not, the longest limit available. No reply was received and a telegram was sent accepting the original offer. It was held that a binding contract had been created. The buyers had not made a counter offer, but had only inquired as to possible terms of business. The original offer had not been rejected and was still available for acceptance.

Case example
Norfolk County Council v *Dencora Properties* (1996)

The parties were landlord and tenants. Under the terms of the lease, Dencora, as landlords, gave the Council a right to terminate the lease in writing after a certain period had passed. Any such notice would then take effect within two years.

This meant that the notice had to be given before 25 March 1993. The November before, the parties had got together to discuss a possible change to that March date. Following that meeting, the Council wrote to the landlord asking if the giving of notice could not wait until not later than March 1995 and suggesting that the notice thus given would take effect after one year and not the two stated in the contract. The reply which came back referred to the rent and said that, if agreement could be reached on a couple of points, there was a good chance that the tenants could stay. A letter then followed on 7 December from the landlords which said that, in order to assist, 'we are prepared to postpone the notice period to break the lease to 1995 or 1996, but not both. The two-year notice must still remain.' This letter was acknowledged by the Council, which said that it was considering other options and would get back to Dencora early in 1993.

The Council resumed the correspondence on 18 February that year, noting that it was unclear as to what exactly their needs would be with regard to the relevant premises. To vacate by March 1997 would cut things too fine; to vacate by March 1998, it was said, could be too long. Agreement was given to the two-year notice period, but the Council asked if this could be given at any time, but not earlier than March 1995. The Council said it could then gauge with some accuracy as to when they could vacate Dencora's premises. That was rejected by Dencora on 22 February. The Council wrote back on 5 March saying that they were prepared to accept the offer to be able to break the lease in 1998 by serving notice in 1996.

The Court of Appeal ruled that the letter of 7 December was an offer not an invitation to treat. If, furthermore, it was an offer which survived until 5 March, then the letter of that date from the Council accepted it. They had used in that letter the words 'we are prepared to accept', and it appears that Dencora had argued that this formulation stopped short of a clear acceptance. The court, however, ruled that nothing turned on these words, which could just as well have been left out.

This left everything to turn on the letters of 18 and 22 February. In the first of these, the Council had asked if the two-year notice period could be given at any time, so long as it was not given before March 1995. They argued that this was no more than a mere enquiry. The court held, however, that the true construction of this letter was that, 'for understandable reasons', the Council was making a counterproposal. It was felt that the Council was here making a clear rejection of the 7 December offer and coming up with proposals of its own. To say: 'I ... ask if this (two-years' notice) could be given at any time' was felt to be the language of counter-offer. Its effect was 'to sweep the offer of 7 December off the negotiating table so that it was no longer there to accept'.

This left for determination one last question: was this counter-offer itself accepted? The letter of 22 February had stated the landlord's 'regret' that the terms of the letter of 18 February were 'not acceptable'. This was a 'clear rejection' of the counter-offer. The court also said that, even if the offer of 7 December had survived to 22 February (which it had not), then the terms of the later letter suggesting that the tenants could put the property on the market when they were ready to vacate had clearly revoked it. By the time 5 March came round, there was nothing left to accept. The court therefore ruled that there had been no binding contract made to alter the terms of the lease.

In the course of reaching its judgement, the court said: 'If this court were devising a code of offer and acceptance for the law of contract, there would be something to be said for treating an offer as surviving ordinary efforts to renegotiate it, whether by exploratory enquiry or by counter-offer, until such time as the offer, if not accepted, was withdrawn either explicitly or by the effluxion of a stipulated or plainly excessive period of time. But, for over a century, people have arranged their affairs and been advised by their lawyers that they can safely do so on the basis of two propositions: that an offer, to be capable of binding acceptance, has to be explicit and exact; and that such an offer, if met by a counter-offer, lapses and cannot be revived by subsequent acceptance.'

Where each party to the contract responds to the other side with their own terms and conditions, and the other side purports to accept, but subject to their own terms and conditions, this gives rise to a series of offers and counter-offers in what is often referred to as the 'battle of the forms'.

Case example
Butler Machine Tools Co. Ltd v *Ex-Cell-O Corporation* (1979)

Sellers quoted for the price of machinery. That offer was stated to be subject to their own terms and conditions which were to 'prevail over any terms and conditions in the buyer's order'. The buyers placed an order on their own terms. At the bottom of the buyer's order form was a tear-off slip which stated: 'We accept your order on the terms and conditions stated thereon.' The sellers returned this slip. The Court of Appeal held that the buyer's order was a counter-offer which had the effect of destroying the original offer. The sellers, by completing and returning that tear-off slip, had accepted the counter-offer. If the sellers had not returned the slip, then the probable result would have been that there would have been no contract until the goods had been delivered and accepted by the buyer. Lord Denning suggested that there may be occasions when the correct solution to the 'battle of the forms', where the parties are under the impression that they have reached an agreement, is to construct an agreement out of both sets of terms.

Case example
Hitchins (Hatfield) Ltd v *H. Butterfield* (1995)

'We are left in this court with an artificial exercise of a kind that lawyers sometimes have to undertake.' The defendants were builders' merchants. When they came together to do business – and this was the first time they had dealt with each other – they did so in relation to four lots of bricks: a sample; Redland standard stock bricks; special bricks; and arch bricks. It was in relation to this last that the dispute ultimately arose.

The essence of the dispute was whether Hitchins could recover damages for late delivery of the arch bricks. And that in turn depended on whether their terms governed the contract; whether the other side's did; or indeed, whether there were no terms at all other than those which would be implied by the Sale of Goods Act 1979.

As just noted, there were, apart from the Arch contract, two other contracts for bricks negotiated between the parties. The Court of Appeal regarded an understanding of these contracts as essential to an understanding of the crucial arch contract.

It went back to November 1987 when Hitchins wrote to Butterfield asking for a quotation for arch bricks. The reply dealt with arch bricks, but also referred to Redland and special bricks. A week or so before that, Butterfield had responded to a different enquiry when they sent a quotation for special bricks on the back of which were to be found their conditions of sale. That document also referred to delivery dates. Those conditions of sale included this: 'We accept no responsibility for delay or non-delivery due directly or indirectly to strike, fire, act of state, *force majeure* or other circumstances beyond our control.' The next stage was for a reply to come from Hitchins to the reply to that November letter. This letter answered the query about special bricks, and referred to the arch bricks, and stated that an official confirmation would be sent. This was indeed sent, but this referred to the Redland bricks. Crucially, it had at its foot and as part of the form a portion headed: 'This portion to be detached at perforation and returned by supplier on date of receipt to [name and address of Hitchins].' That slip also referred to Butterfield, followed by the words: 'We acknowledge receipt of your order and confirm that delivery will be effected in accordance with the instructions and conditions given thereon.'

Just a few days later, on a 'precisely similar form', Hitchins sent off a confirmation order in relation to the special bricks. The confirmation orders sent out by Hitchins in relation to both the Redland and the special bricks contained their own terms and conditions, paragraph 10 of which read: 'Time is of the essence of the contract.'

A telex followed in sharp order from Butterfield confirming that the bricks had been ordered. The next document was an acceptance of order from Butterfield headed with the order number for the Redland bricks, stating: 'Your order is accepted on the standard terms of our conditions of sale and where any points are at variance with those on the order, then our conditions will apply.' That related to Redland bricks. The court accepted that a similar document had been sent in relation to the contract for the sample bricks.

Following the order from Butterfield for the Redland bricks, there were a number of messages between the parties relating to the contract for the special bricks and for the arch bricks. In particular, there was a letter to Butterfield which contained a delivery schedule relating to the Redland and special bricks. This stated that: 'All outstanding confirmation orders … will be forwarded to yourselves in the near future for acknowledgement, as agreed.' It was, the court said, 'at some date after that', when Butterfield received from Hitchins the last in the series of confirmation orders. This order referred, by way of addendum, to the specials and Redland contracts, and it also contained a description of the arch bricks.

The court noted that the 'parties … could quite easily have discussed the terms of the contract. [Butterfield] could have declared, for example, that they would not do business with [Hitchins] except on their own terms. Then the difficulty which has given rise to this litigation would have been avoided. Instead, each side made desultory efforts to make its own conditions prevail.'

In the present case, both parties accepted that the contracts were to be governed by one set or other of standard terms. Butterfield, it was noted, had put in their standard terms right at the outset as soon as the sample bricks had won approval. Although, the court continued, the conditions were attached to the quotation for the special bricks, it was nonetheless arguable that 'when thereafter the order was placed orally for Redland bricks, it was impliedly subject to [Butterfield's] conditions if only because standard terms were intended to apply and at that stage [Hitchins'] conditions had not been proffered.' The court stressed that, on each occasion when Hitchins sent off their confirmation order with the tear-off slip seeking to impose their terms and conditions, that slip was never returned. Those confirmations, the court said, had no material effect on the contracts to which they related. On each occasion on which they had been sent, the order had already been accepted. At best, the court felt, the confirmation of order and its slip was 'an invitation to render [Hitchins'] terms applicable, but since in no case was the invitation accepted by the return of the slip', the attempt failed.

In the case of the Redland bricks the attempt which failed was an attempt to introduce Hitchins' terms *ex post facto*. When Butterfield's formal acceptance of the order was sent, there was no consideration of any variation to introduce their conditions, but when these were received by Hitchins 'without demur', the court 'may well have been entitled' to assume that Hitchins had accepted the intention that Butterfield's standard conditions of sale should govern their contractual relationship.

The court also regarded it as unarguable that the order for the special bricks was subject to Butterfield's terms because they were included in the quotation of November 1987 of which Hitchins' buyer was aware. While other bricks might have been added, that was a variation, it said, which did not affect the terms of the earlier offer. As for the arch bricks, when their specification had been established, and the order placed by phone, it was, as the latest in a series of contracts between the same parties, 'impliedly subject to the same terms and conditions as its predecessor'.

The essential position, the court said, was this: when Hitchins 'rested content' with Butterfield's formal acceptance of the order of November 1987, which incorporated the latter's conditions, they were 'resigning themselves' to contracting on Butterfield's terms, even if strictly speaking these were not part of the Redland contract. That the term 'addendum' had been used in relation to the contracts for special and arch bricks indicated, it said, that the parties intended them to be a series of contracts made on the same terms.

As an alternative route, it was also suggested that the starting point was the finding 'on the clearest evidence' that the parties intended their relationship to be governed by one or other of the rival terms and conditions, and that the contracts were to be in documentary form. Given these findings, 'the absurdity' of imagining that different parcels of bricks were to be sold on different terms, the fact that the negotiations for the various categories of brick were being conducted concurrently, and sometimes in the same letter, given too that the later orders were described as 'addenda' to the Redland order, it was felt that the critical question as to whose terms were to rule was to be answered by reference to the Redland contract. This was because they had 'conspicuously declined' to return the tear-off slip; and because, by their own letter sent in December 1987, they expressly accepted Hitchins' order but upon their own terms and conditions. Hitchins had argued that the Redland contract had been concluded orally before the letter from Butterfield. It was suggested that this argument should be rejected because it ignored the finding in the lower court that the parties had intended to reduce their agreement to written form, at least to the extent of determining which set of terms was incorporated. The law, it was said, allows retrospective contracts, so it must be the case that it allows the 'retrospective imposition of conditions in a case such as this where both parties clearly envisaged such a result.'

There was also rejection of the argument that the last shot in the contract for arch bricks consisted in Hitchins' confirmation bearing their own contract terms. This was because it was 'wholly artificial and impermissible' to regard each separate contract as requiring individual consideration. Once the main course of trading had begun on Butterfield's own terms, 'it would have needed altogether clearer evidence than any existing here to alter that established here.'

Case example
In the matter of an arbitration between *Jayar Impex Ltd* and *Toaken Group Ltd* (1996)

Acceptances must be unqualified acceptances of the offer and not introduce any fresh terms. Note that where parties 'accept' an offer, but on their own terms, the 'battle of the forms' provides, in effect, that the last party to present its terms will be the winner

The relevant contract related to the sale and purchase of Nigerian gum arabic. Although there were many differences in the evidence tendered by sellers and buyers, the court concluded that there had been an oral contract made for the purchase of 40 tons, orally amended two days later to 47 tons. It was also prepared to accept that the sellers referred to the eventual despatch of a written contract form.

It was the case that such a form was drawn up some four days following the alteration in the contract tonnage. This purported to describe the sellers as buyers' agents when, said the judge, they were no such thing. There was a reference to the 'Spot terms and conditions of the International General Produce Association Ltd'. There was, though, no reference to certain matters which had been discussed and agreed upon. The form also stated: 'Important – Please sign, date and return this document.' In fact, the buyers neither signed nor returned it, but simply filed it away.

The buyers were not themselves members of the IGPA and the party acting for the buyers in this case had not previously contracted with the sellers on their terms. There had, some 30 months previously, been a contract between the sellers and buyers in which IGPA terms had been mentioned, but the buyers had negotiated through a party not involved in the current negotiations.

A few days after the written contract had been sent and filed, execution of the contract started. The buyers subsequently alleged that the goods were defective, but further deliveries were collected by the buyers. In response to complaints from the latter, the sellers said that, if prompt payment were not forthcoming, they would seek arbitration under the terms of the written contract. The question thus arose as to whether the sellers' contract form was binding on the buyers.

Three arguments were advanced by the sellers in favour of their contention. First, it was said that the oral agreement was binding, but that this agreement already contained the written agreement because reference had been made in the conversation to the written contract.

Rix J regarded this argument as only acceptable if this contract was known in advance to be identical to the oral contract; or if there were an established course of dealing between the parties. The latter alternative was not relied on by counsel; and it would, the judge found, be 'most unbusinesslike' to infer that the buyers would accept the written contract no matter what it should turn out to contain.

The sellers also argued that there was never in fact a contract at all until the buyers had accepted the contract form, since the parties oral conversation had itself contemplated a written agreement.

This too was dismissed. The argument assumed no agreement save by reference to the written contract, in which case the parties' agreement was subject to a written contract never executed by the buyers. Furthermore, the sellers were actually prepared to accept certain terms as part of the contract when they were not mentioned in the document. There was also the point that the sellers' written submissions to one of the arbitrators stated that the agreement was reached by telephone.

The main argument related to the sellers' further contention that the telephone agreements were binding, but later varied by consent through the buyers' acceptance of the sellers' contract form. In favour of this view, attention was drawn to the absence of any objection to the contract form when received, to the collection of the goods without any objection to that form, and to a reference to a contract number in a fax sent some time after the buyers had started collection of the goods. The sellers maintained that this was not to rely on acceptance by silence, because the circumstances of this case would create a belief that a positive objection would be forthcoming, especially since the parties had looked to the expression of their oral agreement in written form.

The judge rejected this alternative approach, stressing the following factors:

(i)   The incorporation of the IGPA terms was 'undoubtedly' a proposed amendment to the existing contract by way of addition.
(ii) The spot terms contained therein were particularly stringent and would cut back on what would otherwise be the buyers' statutory rights and remedies. Any such variation was not to be 'lightly inferred'.
(iii) The written contract did not contain a number of terms which were admitted to be part of the agreement between the parties.
(iv) The written contract would have changed the role of the sellers to buyers' agent, something which would have fundamentally changed the nature of the contract and which, again, could be achieved only 'on the plainest evidence of assent' by the buyers.
(v)   The written contract itself contemplated that it would take effect only on signature and return, something which was never done.
(vi) The collection of the goods by the buyers was as referable to the existing oral agreement as it was to the written contract. In principle, said the judge, it was for these sellers to query the matter with the buyers expressly rather than relying on the latters' silence.
(vii) The reference contained in the fax was in any event to the sellers' invoices not to the contract form. The judge rejected the argument that the reference to any contract number was an acceptance of there being some governing document. If a reference is included in an invoice, and the recipient responds by quoting that reference, 'that signifies nothing concerning a written contract'.

In the circumstances, therefore, the court ruled that the contract between the parties was not to be found in the sellers' contract form, but was based instead on the oral agreement.

Communication of acceptance

An acceptance of an offer must reach the other side if the parties are in face-to-face negotiations. It is enough to post an acceptance, however, if the parties were negotiating instead through the post

If the parties are in face-to-face communication (or its equivalent, such as communication by telephone, fax, e-mail or telex), then the rule is that the acceptance must actually reach the other side.

> ### Case example
> ### *Entores Ltd* v *Miles Far Eastern Corp.* (1955)
> A London company sent a telex to an Amsterdam company with an offer to buy certain goods. The latter accepted by telex received in London. The contract was held to be made in London because that was where the acceptance was received. See too *Brinkibon* v *Stahag Stahl und Stahlwarenhandelgesellschaft* (1983).

If the parties are negotiating in circumstances which are not the equivalent of face-to-face negotiations, then the acceptance does not have to be received by the other side.

> ### Case example
> ### *Adams* v *Lindsell* (1818)
> A letter offering to sell goods was posted on 2 September. On 5 September, the buyer posted his acceptance. It reached the seller on 9 September who had in fact sold the goods to a third party the day before. A binding contract had been made with the first buyer since his letter of acceptance had been posted prior to the sale to the third party and this created a binding contract as at the moment of posting, regardless of when the letter arrived.

However, if the circumstances of the negotiations make it clear that an acceptance must reach the other side, then this is what must happen (*Holwell Securities Ltd* v *Hughes* (1974)).

Lapse of time and revocation

If an offer is not accepted within a reasonable time, it lapses automatically. What amounts to a reasonable time is a question of fact to be decided on all the circumstances of the case.

> ### Case example
> ### *Ramsgate Victoria Hotel* v *Ramsgate* (1866)
> A person offers to buy shares in June, the offer being accepted in November. It was held that this was after the lapse of a reasonable time, so that the offer had lapsed and could not be accepted.

> ### Case example
> ### *Chemco Leasing* v *Rediffusion* (1987)
> An offer was made in January to assume certain liabilities. The offer was accepted in November. The court held that, since about four months was a reasonable time for the offer to remain open, a reasonable time had passed and the offer could not be accepted.

Offers can be revoked at any time, except where there is a binding commitment to keep them open. Offers may also lapse

If a party says that they will keep an offer open for a certain time, that promise is only binding on them if the other side provides some consideration (see below) in return for that promise. Where the party making an offer is not bound to hold it open for a specified period, they can revoke it at any time. However, the revocation must reach the other side, although there is no requirement that it must be communicated directly.

Case example
Dickinson v *Dodds* (1876)

An offer to sell property was stated to be open until Friday. The day before, the buyer learned through a third party that the property had been sold to a third party. He was held unable then to accept the offer because he knew of its revocation. See too *Cartwright* v *Hoogstoel* (1911).

Review questions

1 What is the difference between an invitation to treat, an offer and an acceptance?
2 In what circumstances must an acceptance of an offer actually reach the party making the offer?
3 How long does a person have to decide whether or not to accept an offer?

Intention to create a legal relationship

A binding contract will only come about if the parties intend there to be a binding relationship between themselves. This is normally presumed in commercial cases, but is presumed to the contrary in purely social relationships. For that reason, a failure to turn up after acceptance of an invitation to dinner could not lend itself to an action for breach of contract.

Case example
Balfour v *Balfour* (1919)

The defendant was a civil servant in Ceylon. He promised to pay his wife a weekly sum while they lived apart. He failed to do so and she sued for breach of the agreement. The court held that no legal relationship had been contemplated and that her action must fail. See too *Pettitt* v *Pettitt* (1969); *Jones* v *Paddavatton* (1969).

If acts are done in performance of an agreement which was not of itself intended to be binding, those acts will have legal consequences if done in relation to the acquisition, improvement or addition to real or personal property (see *Pettitt* v *Pettitt* above).

It should also be appreciated that if the parties to a domestic or similar arrangement intend it to be binding, then the courts will implement their wishes.

Domestic arrangements are presumed not to be binding, whereas business arrangements are. Such presumptions can, in both cases, be displaced

> ## Case example
> ### *Simpkins* v *Pays* (1955)
> Three members of a household, the owner, her granddaughter and a paying guest, took part in a weekly newspaper competition. Entries were in the name of the owner. She refused to share the winnings saying that there was no intention to create a legal relationship, this being nothing more than a friendly adventure. The court, while accepting the general principle, felt that this was a case where there was a 'mutuality in the arrangements between the parties' which gave rise to a binding agreement. The presumption that arrangements between businesses are binding can also be displaced by the circumstances.

> ## Case example
> ### *Rose, Frank & Co.* v *Crompton Bros* (1923)
> The relevant document stated: 'This arrangement is not entered into … as a formal or legal agreement and shall not be subject to legal jurisdiction in the Law Courts … but is only a definite expression and record of the purpose and intention of the parties…'. It was held that this displaced the ordinary presumption that business arrangements were binding.

Review questions

1   When is it possible for a purely domestic agreement to become a legally binding contract?
2   When is it possible for a commercial agreement not to be a legally binding contract?

Consideration

Specialty contracts (see above) are binding in the absence of consideration, but, in other cases, this is an essential element. In essence, the doctrine of consideration is that each party must give something, or do something, to the other. There is no requirement that the respective elements of consideration must be anything like commensurate in value. If an offer to buy a new car for £1 is accepted, this gives rise to a binding contract, provided the parties intended to create a legal relationship (see above).

The benefits provided by one party to another need not be anything like equal in value

> ## Case example
> ### *Thomas* v *Thomas* (1842)
> A widow had been promised by her husband that she should have the house in which they lived. The executors promised to convey the house provided she paid £1 in rent and kept the house in good repair. The executors broke this agreement. The court, which declined to be influenced by the husband's wishes, because motive was 'not the same thing with consideration', held that the £1 a year in rent was good consideration. It was said that consideration 'means something which is of value in the eyes of the law, moving from the plaintiff: it may be some detriment to the plaintiff or some benefit to the defendant.' See too *Bunn* v *Guy* (1803); *Currie* v *Misa* (1875).

Categories of consideration

Consideration is normally divided into these categories:

- executory
- executed
- past.

The first of these arises when a promise is made in return for a promise, as when one party promises to deliver goods in return for payment. Everything here is in the future, hence the consideration is 'executory'. Consideration is 'executed' when it is promised in return for an act, such as a reward promised for the return of lost property. Consideration is 'past' when it is made subsequent to the completion of a particular transaction. Executed or executory consideration are valid forms of consideration, but past consideration is not.

Case example
Re *McArdle* (1951)
Children, by their father's will, were entitled to a house following their mother's death. During her life, the mother made a number of improvements to the house, following which they signed a document agreeing to pay her for these improvements. It was held that, as all the work on the house had been completed before the document was signed, this was a case of past consideration and the document could not therefore be supported as a binding contract.

Agreement to perform existing duties

If a party offers to perform duties or obligations which they are already bound to do, then their further offer to perform those duties is not consideration.

Case example
***Stilk* v *Myrick* (1809)**
A ship's captain promised certain members of his crew that, if they worked the ship home, they would be paid the wages of those who deserted. It was held that, since the seaman were already contractually obliged to work the ship home, their further promise to do so was no consideration. See too *Collins* v *Godefroy* (1831) and *Atlas Express Ltd* v *Kafco Ltd* (1989).

If, however, a party agrees to perform more than they are obliged to do, that extra performance will provide good consideration.

Case example
***Glasbrook Bros Ltd* v *Glamorgan CC* (1925)**
Mine owners who feared violence asked for police protection greater than the police authorities thought necessary. This extra level of policing was held to be sufficient consideration.

Past
consideration is
not valid
consideration.
Nor is an
agreement to
perform an
existing
obligation

Case example
Williams v Roffey Bros (1990)

The defendants made an agreement to refurbish a block of flats and subcontracted part of the work to the plaintiffs. It was a term of the contract that the plaintiffs would receive interim payments based on the work completed. After completing some of the contract and undertaking preliminary work on the remainder, the plaintiffs found they were in financial difficulties.

The defendants were liable under a penalty clause of the main contract if the work were not completed on time and were aware of the plaintiffs' financial problems. They therefore agreed to an extra payment. They later claimed that this offer of extra payment was not supported by any consideration provided by the plaintiffs.

It was held that where, in the absence of economic duress or fraud, one party to a contract agrees to make a payment over and above the contract price in order to secure completion of the contract on time, and thus obtains a benefit, such as avoiding payment of a penalty, the obtaining of that benefit could amount to consideration for payment of the extra sum. The defendants also obtained a benefit in avoiding the need of having to find a replacement contractor.

It is also the case that payment of a smaller sum than that owed is not consideration, unless there is some consideration for the smaller sum, such as an agreement to pay the smaller amount sooner than the full amount would have been due.

Case example
D and C Builders Ltd v Rees (1966)

Builders carried out work for the defendants who delayed payment knowing that the builders were close to bankruptcy. They then offered £300 in satisfaction of the debt of £482. The builders were held entitled to the balance since there had been no consideration for acceptance of the smaller sum.

Case example
Re Selectmove Ltd (1995)

However, there are limits to the application of the doctrine that, in some cases, a promise to perform an existing obligation can amount to good consideration. It has been held that the principle that a promise to perform an existing obligation can amount to good consideration where there were practical benefits to the party receiving the performance is confined to cases where the obligation involved a supply of goods or services. The principle cannot be extended to an obligation to make a payment, such as a tax payment

Promissory estoppel

The doctrine of promissory estoppel is used as a way of avoiding some of the harsher aspects of the doctrine of consideration.

Case example
***Central London Property Trust Ltd v High Trees House Ltd
(1947)***
The plaintiffs had leased a block of flats to the defendants. The following January, because of
the outbreak of war, the rent was reduced. Early in 1945, the plaintiffs claimed that they were
entitled to the full rent agreed in 1939. It was agreed by the court that the rent could be raised
for the future, but the back rent could not be recovered even though there was no consideration for the reduction. It was stated, as a principle of the doctrine of promissory estoppel, that if
A makes a promise to B intending that promise to have legal consequences, and B acts upon that
promise, then A cannot go back on his promise and enforce his rights with retrospective effect.

*Promissory
estoppel allows
a party to rely
on promises
where there is
no
consideration*

The doctrine can, however, only act as a defence and not as a cause of action.

Case example
Combe v Combe (1951)
As part of a divorce settlement, a husband promised his wife a certain payment as maintenance. She did not apply to the court for maintenance, but this was not following any request
from the husband. The court dismissed the wife's action, stating that the case discussed above
did not create new causes of action where none had previously existed: 'It only prevents a
party from insisting upon his strict legal rights, when it would have been unjust to allow him
to enforce them, having regard to the dealings which have taken place between the parties.'

Furthermore, the doctrine will not apply where the alleged promise was made by someone who
had no authority to make the promise, nor where it would be inequitable to allow reliance on a
promise (Re *Selectmove* (1995)).

Review questions

1 What is the difference between, and the significance of, executory, executed and past
   consideration?
2 To what extent can the promise to perform an existing obligation amount to consideration?
3 How does the doctrine of promissory estoppel operate?

Privity of contract

The doctrine of privity of contract means that only the parties to a contract have any rights or
duties under it.

Case example
Beswick v Beswick (1968)
A coal merchant contracted to sell his business to his nephew, one of the terms being that he
would pay his aunt £5 a week. It was held that she had no personal right to sue on the contract
because she was not one of the contracting parties. It should perhaps be added that she was
entitled to enforce the agreement, but only in her capacity as administratrix of her husband's
estate. See too *Tweddle v Atkinson* (1861).

*Third parties
have no rights
or duties under
a contract*

The terms of a contract – incorporation of contract terms

Terms are incorporated into a contract only if made available or presented to the other side before the contract is made.

Case example
Olley v Marlborough Court Ltd (1948)

A couple arrived at a hotel and made their booking at reception. In their room, there was a notice which contained certain purported contract terms. It was held that this notice was presented to the parties only after the contract had been made, at the reception desk, and hence could not form part of the contract.

Case example
Thornton v Shoe Lane Parking Ltd (1977)

A driver obtained a ticket from an automatic machine before entering a car park. The court said that the driver had accepted an offer of a parking space when he placed his money in the slot. The terms of the contract were therefore presented to him after the contract was made and hence did not bind the driver.

It has yet to be decided whether a party is bound by contract terms, presented to them before the contract is made, but when in practical terms they are incapable of not proceeding with the contract. A person at the front of a line of cars has no real choice but to proceed into the car park, even if they do not wish to park on the basis of the terms presented to them. The question was not specifically answered in the Thornton case, but the court did seem of the opinion that, in such circumstances, the contract terms would not be binding.

If a person has signed a document containing the terms of a contract, presented before the contract was made, the signatory is bound by the terms even if they were not read by him (see *L'Estrange* v *Graucob* (1934)).

Terms to be in contractual documents

Terms cannot be regarded as incorporated into a contract if they are not contained in what may be fairly described as a contractual document.

Case example
Chapleton v Barry UDC (1940)

The plaintiff hired deckchairs from a pile stacked near a notice. A person hiring the deckchairs was given tickets which he retained for inspection. It was held that the terms printed on the ticket had not been incorporated into the contract since no reasonable person would have considered the ticket to be anything other than a receipt for the money paid.

> **Case example**
> ## *Grogan v Robin Meredith Plant Hire* (1996)
> A telephone agreement had been made between Triact, a civil engineering contractor, and Meredith Plant Hire for the supply to the former of a driver and machine. Neither of the parties referred to any particular terms to govern the contract; in particular, no reference was made to the standard terms of the Contractors Plant Association commonly used in contracts of this particular category. However, at the end of the first and second weeks, a time sheet was presented by the driver to Triact's site working agent, someone who had authority to hire machinery on behalf of his employers. At the bottom of this sheet, and just above the place for signature, were the words: 'All hire undertaken under CPA conditions. Copies available on request'.
>
> The status of the time sheet, and this declaration, arose when an accident occurred causing personal injury to the plaintiff. Judgement was entered by agreement in the form of a sum of £82 798.17 and the question arose whether Meredith were entitled to an indemnity under the terms of the CPA terms and conditions.
>
> The court said that the central question was whether the time sheet fell within the class of document which the recipient knew, or would reasonably expect, to contain relevant contractual provisions. The test was whether a particular document purported to be a contract or to have contractual effect. The evidence showed that Meredith regarded the time sheet as essentially an administrative document designed to indicate the hours worked in the performance of an existing contract. It was further said that the central question in this appeal was whether the time sheet could be considered as a document having administrative effect or as an administrative document enabling the parties to agree on the sums owing, and the court accepted that it should be read only as the latter. The court rejected the argument that a document did not have to be a contractual document if it were signed; that it was necessary to look at a signed document only to see what it said. That was an argument dismissed by the Court of Appeal as 'too mechanistic' and 'contrary to a long line of authority'. It was therefore held that the particular CPA terms had not been incorporated into the contract.

Contract terms are valid only if presented to the other side before a binding contract is concluded

Incorporation by course of dealing

It may be the case that the parties have generally dealt on the basis of certain terms and conditions. If, in one particular case, those terms are not specifically produced, they may still be held to have been incorporated into the contract by virtue of their course of dealing.

> **Case example**
> ## *Henry Kendall & Sons v William Lillico & Sons* (1969)
> A verbal contract was followed the day after with a note containing the terms of the contract. The parties had been dealing with each other for over three years and there had been around 100 such notes. The recipient had known of the written conditions on the note and had never queried or even read them. It was held that the terms on the note had been incorporated through the parties' established course of dealing.

It will be a question for all the circumstances of the case as to whether a sufficient course of dealing has been established.

> ## Case example
> ### Hollier v Rambler Motors Ltd (1972)
> The plaintiff telephoned the defendant garage owners with instructions for the undertaking of certain repair work. During the previous five years, the plaintiff had been to the defendants on three or four occasions for repair work. On the two previous occasions, but not on this particular occasion, the plaintiff had signed a contract note. It was held that there was no sufficient course of dealing to incorporate this contract note into the latest of the contracts.

The understanding of the parties

Closely following the above principle is the idea that terms can be incorporated into a contract through the understanding of the parties.

> ## Case example
> ### British Crane Hire Corp. v Ipswich Plant Hire (1974)
> The defendants urgently needed a piece of equipment. This was despatched. Nothing was said as to the conditions of hire; these were later sent for signature, but were in fact never signed. The parties had contracted twice over the preceding year, and these contracts had been on the basis of the written terms. The court doubted if this established a course of dealing. Even so, the court held that the terms had been incorporated into the contract because of the common understanding of the parties that the hiring was to be on the plaintiffs' usual terms of contract. See too *Keeton Sons & Co. Ltd v Carl Prior Ltd* (1986).

Onerous terms

If a contract term is particularly onerous, a matter to be decided upon in all the circumstances of the individual case, it must be given especial prominence before it can be held to be part of the contract.

> ## Case example
> ### Interfoto Picture Library Ltd v Stiletto Visual Programmes Ltd (1971)
> Following a telephone conversation, certain pictures were delivered by hand in a bag. The contract was made when the arrival of the bag was acknowledged over the phone. The bag also contained a delivery note containing the terms and conditions of the contract. One of these terms, relating to the amount to be paid if the photographs were not returned by a specific time, was accepted by the court to be particularly onerous. It was held that, though the delivery note was incorporated into the contract, this particular term had no effect because it had not been drawn specifically to the attention of the other party.

Case example
AEG (UK) Ltd v *Logic Resource Ltd* (1995)

The buyers had ordered from the sellers 49 cathode ray tubes for use in radar equipment. The price was £14 800. The buyers were intending to export the goods to customers in Iran.

The goods, when delivered to Iran, were found to be defective. The tubes would not fit into the particular equipment since the pins were too long. It was therefore necessary for the tubes to be air-freighted back to the sellers for modification. This cost £4000. When the buyers received the sellers' invoice, they promptly deducted this particular outlay.

The order from the Iranians had been received by the buyers in 1988. They had then got in touch with the sellers who had taken over production from the previous manufacturers, MOV, and sent off an order. In response, the sellers sent off confirmation. This set out the details of the equipment and added, at the bottom, and in small capital letters, these words: 'ORDERS ARE SUBJECT TO OUR CONDITIONS OF SALE – FOR EXTRACT SEE REVERSE'. Five conditions were set out on the reverse headed: 'Extracts from our Conditions of Sale'. Those five conditions were then set out and then there was what the Court of Appeal called 'an important statement'. This ran: 'A copy of the full Conditions of Sale is available on request'. In fact, no copy was ever requested by the buyers. The relevant term stated that: 'The purchaser shall return the defective parts at his own expense to the supplier immediately on request of the latter.' If this term was allowed its maximum influence, the buyers would of course not be entitled to deduct the cost of the air freight from the amount outstanding. This particular clause was not on its own. It was, in fact, a subclause in a set of terms which were gathered together under the heading of 'warranty'.

The first subclause in this warranty contained a guarantee from the sellers that the goods were free from defects caused by faulty materials and bad workmanship. It added that, if the goods were not in fact manufactured by the sellers, then the supplier was prepared to warrant the goods only to the extent of any warranty provided by the manufacturer to the supplier. A further term provided that the buyers would have to notify the suppliers of any defect within seven days of its discovery and also tender proof of purchase and guarantee. Once the goods were back with the suppliers, the buyers were required to allow them 'the time and opportunity requested as estimated' by the sellers. The contract also stated that the buyers were to pay the costs of any tests run on the goods where the sellers denied liability. Even if the sellers were liable, the extent of any liability was not to be anything more than making good the defects or issuing a credit note. The 'warranty' also sought to dispense with the buyers' rights under the Sale of Goods Act 1979 (to goods of 'merchantable quality and which were reasonably fit for their purpose' by virtue of a subclause reading: 'All other warranties or conditions are hereby expressly excluded'. Another clause stated that the sellers were not to 'be liable in any event for any consequential loss'.

It was noted by the court that the disputed clause was drafted in a way one has seen in other standard terms: 'what it gives with one hand it takes away with the other ... [it] gives warranty cover. It is very restricted warranty cover, for bad workmanship. The only way it can be taken advantage of is to send the goods back'. The clause in the present case was, the Court of Appeal said, to be considered in its context and, once this was done, it could only be stigmatized as 'extremely onerous'. Since nothing had been done by way of bringing the term to the attention of the buyers, the clause was struck down.

Review questions

1 What is the crucial point of time for determining whether terms have been successfully incorporated into a contract?
2 What is the position if a party has in effect no choice but to proceed with a contract, even though they may not wish to contract on the basis of the terms presented to them?
3 In what circumstances may terms be incorporated by the previous course of dealing between the parties?
4 What provisions apply to the incorporation of particularly onerous terms?

Express and implied terms

The terms on which the parties specifically agree are generally known as the 'express' terms of the contract. These are contrasted with the 'implied' terms of the contract, these being incorporated into the contract even though the parties have not specifically agreed to their inclusion or even considered them.

Most obviously, terms can be implied through the operation of an Act of Parliament, such as under the Sale of Goods Act 1979 (see Chapter 3). Terms can also be implied if they are customary in the trade (see *Harley & Co.* v *Nagata* (1917); *Peter Darlington Partners Ltd* v *Gosho Co. Ltd* (1964)).

Terms can also be implied if they are necessary to give the contract 'business efficacy'.

> ## Case example
> ## *The Moorcock* (1889)
> A contract permitted the plaintiff to unload his ship at the defendant's jetty. Both parties knew that the ship would ground at low tide. A term was implied on the grounds of business efficacy to the effect that, so far as reasonable care could provide, the river bed would not be in such a condition as to damage the boat.

Contract terms will be express – specifically agreed to by the parties – or implied

Under the heading of 'business efficacy', the courts have also implied into a contract between a driving school and a customer that the car would be covered by insurance (*BSM* v *Simms* (1971)); and that a footballer will be given a reasonable opportunity to score the requisite number of goals when his transfer contract provided that an extra sum would be paid should he score 20 goals (*Bournemouth and Boscombe Athletic Football Club* v *Manchester United Football Club Ltd* (1980)).

Review question

What is meant by 'express' and 'implied' terms, and when may a term be implied on the basis of business efficacy?

Classification of contract terms

It is traditional to divide contract terms, whether they be express or implied, into two categories: the major terms of a contract are called 'conditions'; the minor terms of a contract are called 'warranties'. (For the relevance of the distinction, see Remedies.) The precise name given to a term is not necessarily relevant, since a term can be a warranty, even though the contract might call it a 'condition' (*Schuler AG* v *Wickman Machine Tool Sales Ltd* (1974)).

Contract terms are usually divided into conditions and warranties – the difference depending on their relative importance

In determining into which category a contract term falls, it is first necessary to see if the matter has been decided by Act of Parliament. For instance, the Sale of Goods Act 1979 and the Supply of Goods and Services Act 1982 (see Chapter 3) specifically classify certain contract terms as conditions or warranties.

If there is no relevant statute, but the classification of the particular term has earlier been decided by binding authority, then the decision reached in that case will be followed (*The Mihail Angelos* (1971)).

If there should be no statute nor binding precedent, then the question as to whether the term is a condition or warranty will be examined with particular reference to the intention of the parties. The courts have also said that, if there is no precise statutory or judicial classification of a contract term, then it will be classified as an intermediate or innominate term, with the remedies for breach depending on the gravity of the breach (*Hong Kong Fir Shipping Co. Ltd* v *Kawasaki Kishen Kaisha* (1962)).

Review question

How are contract terms categorized and how do the courts determine into which category a term falls?

Exclusion clauses and unfair terms

It is often the case that the terms of a contract will seek to exclude or limit a person's liability in the event of a breach of contract by them. The courts have never liked such clauses and have always stressed that they must be construed strictly, and that any ambiguity will be interpreted in favour of the victim of the breach.

Exclusion clauses are interpreted very much in favour of the innocent party

> ## Case example
> ### *White* v *John Warwick & Co. Ltd* (1953)
> The plaintiff hired a cycle on terms which stated that 'nothing in this agreement shall render the owners liable for any personal injuries to the riders of the machine hired.' It was held that the drafting of this clause was apt to exclude liability for any breach of contract, but not for the tort of negligence.

Case example
Hollier v *Rambler Motors Ltd* (1972)

The exclusion clause ran: 'The company is not responsible for damage caused by fire to customers' cars on the premises.' Although the only possible source of liability would be in negligence, and even though it could therefore be argued that the clause must inevitably extend to negligence, the court ruled that the clause could in fact be read as simply a warning that the defendants would not be responsible for a fire caused without negligence.

It was said in *Smith* v *South Wales Switchgear Ltd* (1978) that, in order to exclude liability for negligence, the relevant clause must refer specifically to 'negligence' or to some acceptable synonym.

Legislative control

While the foregoing cases remain valid precedents regarding the construction and interpretation of exclusion clauses, the work of controlling such clauses has been in greater part taken over by legislation, namely the Unfair Contract Terms Act 1977 and the Unfair Terms in Consumer Contracts Regulations 1994. These enactments are separate, and a disputed clause has to be assessed under each before it can be said to be valid. It should also be realized that there are a number of categories of contract which are excluded from the respective scope of the enactments, and reference should be made to them for further information.

The Unfair Contract Terms Act

The 1977 Act imposes strict controls on the extent to which a party can exclude his liability in negligence

The Act provides that no clause can exclude or limit liability for any act of negligence which results in death or personal injury: s. 2(1). If an act of negligence results in any other category of loss, such as damage to property, then the clause will be valid only if it is reasonable (see below): s. 2(2). A consumer (that is to say someone not acting in the course of a business) cannot be made to indemnify another for that other's negligence except where the indemnity clause is reasonable: s. 4. Section 5 provides that, where consumer goods are defective because of the negligence of a manufacturer or distributor, nothing in any guarantee can exclude or restrict liability for loss or damage caused by negligence.

Section 3 of the Act imposes a series of controls in relation to contracts on 'written standard terms'. There is no definition provided of 'written standard terms', but case law has determined that a contract will still be on written standard terms even though some of its clauses might have been individually negotiated, so long as the exclusion clause was not one of these: *McCrone* v *Boots Farms Sales* (1981); *The Salvage Association* v *CAP Financial Services Ltd* (1992); *St Albans City and District Council* v *International Computers Ltd* (1994).

If a contract is on written standard terms, and it contains any or all of the following categories of clause, such a clause will be valid only if reasonable (see below):

- a clause seeking to exclude or restrict liability for breach;
- a clause seeking to allow a substantially different performance from that which was reasonably expected;
- a clause which seeks to allow no performance at all.

Sections 6 and 7 of the Act control clauses which seek to exclude or restrict the terms implied by the Sale of Goods Act 1979 and the Supply of Goods and Services Act 1982. These provisions are dealt with in the next chapter.

Where a clause is valid only if it is reasonable, s. 11 of the Act says that it is unreasonable unless and until the contrary is proved. The person relying on the clause is required to show that, in all the circumstances of the case, the clause was a reasonable one to incorporate, having regard to those matters which were, or ought reasonably to have been, in the contemplation of the parties when the contract was made. If what is relied on is a term contained in a notice which is not part of a contract, the test is whether it is fair and reasonable to allow reliance on the notice having regard to all the circumstances when the particular liability arose.

Certain clauses contained in contracts on written standard terms are subject to the reasonableness test

---

Case example
Smith v Bush; Harris v Wye (1989)

A surveyor's contract contained a term disclaiming any kind of assurance as to the accuracy or validity of the report. The survey was in fact carried out negligently and the purchase was duly made. It was held that, in considering whether the disclaimer could be relied on, the general pattern of house purchases and the extent of the work and liability accepted by the surveyor had to be kept in mind. Having regard to the high cost of houses and high rates charged to borrowers, it was neither fair nor reasonable for mortgagees or surveyors to impose on purchasers the risk of loss arising from incompetence or carelessness on the part of surveyors. In the circumstances, the disclaimers did not pass the reasonableness test.

Case example
Lease Management Services Ltd v Parnell Secretarial Services (1994)

An agreement was made for the lease of a photocopying machine. It was expressly stated to have a certain capacity. The agreement excluded all liability 'in respect of any conditions, warranties or representations relating to the condition of the equipment or to its merchantability or suitability or fitness for the particular purpose for which it may be required whether such conditions warranties or representations are express or implied and whether arising under the agreement or under any prior agreement or in oral or written statements made by or on behalf of the lessor or its agents in the course of negotiations in which the lessee or its representatives may have been concerned prior to the agreement.' The court ruled that this clause was unreasonable since: 'Self-evidently, it cannot be reasonable to exclude liability for breach of warranty or condition which has been expressly given.'

Review questions

1 What is the general judicial attitude to exclusion clauses and to clauses seeking to exclude liability for negligence in particular.
2 How does the Unfair Contract Terms Act 1977 control clauses seeking to exclude liability for negligence?
3 Outside issues affecting negligence liability, what other clauses are subjected by the Act to the reasonableness test?

The unfair terms in consumer contracts regulations

These regulations implement EU law. They apply to contracts with a consumer (that is those not acting in the course of a business), including oral contracts, where the contract has not been individually negotiated. It is stated that an agreement is always regarded as not individually negotiated if it has been drawn up in advance.

The regulations state that any written contract term which is not in 'plain, intelligible language', and where there is a doubt as to that term's meaning, will be interpreted against the party who is seeking to rely on it. This in fact is only to put in specific form the general rules of interpretation discussed above in relation to the interpretation of clauses generally.

The regulations control 'unfair' terms where these are contained in contracts within its scope as defined above. A term is stated to be unfair if 'contrary to the requirements of good faith [it] causes a significant imbalance in the parties' rights to the detriment of the consumer'. In deciding on this, account must be taken of the nature of the contract goods and services and, as at the time the contract was made, of the circumstances 'attending the conclusion of the contract and ... all the other terms of the contract or of another contract on which it is dependent'. A schedule to the regulations indicates matters to which particular regard must be paid when determining issues of unfairness, such as the strength of the bargaining position of the parties. A further schedule provides an 'indicative' list of terms which may be regarded as unfair, although in any individual case a term so listed might turn out in all the circumstances not in fact to be unfair. If a term is shown to be unfair, the burden of so showing lying on the consumer, then it has no legal effect. The rest of the contract will continue in force if it is capable of continuing without the unfair term.

> If a term in a consumer contract is unfair, then it will not be binding

The regulations state that what are called 'core provisions' shall not be subject to the fairness test. A core provision is one which defines the main subject matter of the contract, or which concerns the adequacy of the price or remuneration. Matters such as the description of the goods and the comparison of what was paid with the value of what was received would be core provisions. Although core provisions cannot themselves be subject to the regulations, such provisions can be taken into account when considering the fairness of other terms in the contract.

> The Director General of Fair Trading may prevent the use of unfair terms

The regulations require the Director General of Fair Trading to consider any complaint that a contract term drawn up for general use is unfair. When acting on a complaint, he may seek an injunction against anyone using or recommending the use of such a term in consumer contracts. As an alternative, he may accept undertakings. The Director General is also empowered to arrange for the dissemination of information and advice on the operation of the regulations.

Review questions

1 To what contracts do the regulations apply?
2 By what criteria are contract terms judged to be 'unfair' and what is the consequence of a term being judged unfair?
3 What enforcement measures may be taken to control the use of unfair terms?

The effect of mistake on a contract

The traditional way of dealing with the effect of mistake on a contract is to ask whether the mistake is one which is common, in the sense that all the parties to the contract have made the same mistake; is mutual, where the parties are at cross purposes; or whether the mistake is unilateral, meaning that only one side is mistaken, and this is known to the other contracting party.

Common mistake

As a general rule, a common mistake does not affect the validity of the contract.

> **Case example**
> ### Grist v Bailey (1967)
> Parties agreed on the sale and purchase of a house subject to an existing tenancy. The sale price was lower than it would otherwise have been because both parties wrongly thought that the tenancy was protected. The contract was held to be valid.

However, if the mistake goes to the existence of the very subject matter of the contract, then the contract will be declared null and void.

> **Case example**
> ### Galloway v Galloway (1914)
> Parties executed a deed of separation in the mistaken belief that they were married. The separation deed was declared to be a nullity. See too *Cooper* v *Phibbs* (1867).

If there has been a common mistake, and whether or not it is one which has the effect of putting an end to the contract, the courts may exercise their discretion to eliminate a perceived injustice. In *Grist* v *Bailey* (see above), where the court held the contract to be valid, the plaintiff's action for specific performance was dismissed on terms which required the defendant to enter a fresh contract at the appropriate price.

Common mistake does not usually put an end to a contract unless it removes the very basis of the contract

Mutual mistake

In the event of a mutual mistake, that is to say where the parties are at cross-purposes, the courts consider the position from the point of view of a third party.

> **Case example**
> ### Scriven Bros & Co. v Hindley & Co. (1913)
> An auction was to sell both hemp and tow. One lot was for hemp, the other for tow, the same shipping marks being entered against each. The successful bidder believed both were hemp. Witnesses said that tow and hemp had never previously been landed from the same ship with the same mark. The court held that, such was the confusion, no contract came into being. A notional third party would have been unable to say just what the contract was for. See too *Wood* v *Scarth* (1858).

Where the parties have made a mutual mistake, how things seem to a third party will be crucial

Unilateral mistake

If the unilateral mistake was fundamental to the agreement, then no contract will come into existence.

Case example
Webster v Cecil (1861)

The defendant, who had already refused an offer of £2000 for his land, then offered to sell it for £1250. The mistake was known to the other side, and it was held that no contract had come about.

Many of the cases of unilateral mistake involve cases where a person has claimed to be someone he is not.

Case example
Lewis v Averay (1971)

A person claimed to be a well-known actor and sought to buy a car which he had seen advertised. The advertiser accepted his cheque after being shown a film studio pass. The court held that a valid contract had been made, though one that could be rendered void by the innocent party. Although the victim of fraud, the innocent party had intended to deal with the person in front of him. See too *King's Norton Metal Co.* v *Eldridge* (1897); *Phillips* v *Brooks Ltd* (1919).

Case example
Ingram v Little (1961)

The plaintiffs sold their car to a person claiming to be a Mr Hutchinson with an address in Surrey. One of the plaintiffs checked the phone book and found that such a person did live at the stated address. The sale went through. It was held that no contract had been made since, on the facts, the plaintiffs had only meant to deal with Mr Hutchinson and not the fraudster. See too *Cundy* v *Lindsay* (1878).

A contract may be void for unilateral mistake if a contracting party claims to be someone they are not

It is not easy to see the distinction between these two sets of cases, and it may be doubted whether *Ingram* v *Little* is still good law, though so far it has not been overruled. Where a contract has been induced by fraud, but a valid contract sill exists (as in *Lewis* v *Averay*), the innocent party can render the contract void, so long as an innocent third party has not become involved. This is what had happened in that case.

Review questions

1 What is meant by 'common', 'mutual' and 'unilateral' mistake?
2 What is the effect on a contract of these categories of mistake?
3 How can the rights of an innocent victim of a unilateral mistake be affected by a third party?

Misrepresentation

If a person wishes to contest the validity of a contract on the basis that they were the victim of a misrepresentation made by the other party, they must show that the misrepresentation involved a misrepresentation of fact.

Case example
Bisset v Wilkinson (1927)

A statement was made as to the capacity of a particular piece of land. This was said to be a mere statement of opinion which could not give rise to an action for misrepresentation.

It is also the case that a misrepresentation will be actionable only if the other party relied on it as one of the reasons for entering the contract.

Case example
Horsfall v Thomas (1862)

The plaintiff was asked to make a gun to a particular specification. The gun was delivered, but with a concealed defect. The defendant had never inspected it and so the misrepresentation as to soundness had not affected him.

Case example
Smith v Chadwick (1884)

A prospectus contained false information. The plaintiff admitted, however, that he had not been influenced by this information. He had, therefore, no relevant claim.

To be actionable, a misrepresentation must be a statement of fact and be relied on by the other side

Silence can amount to misrepresentation if it distorts a representation already made.

Case example
With v O'Flanagan (1936)

A doctor wished to sell his practice, stating what its income was. Following that statement, the income fell substantially, but this was not disclosed. It was held that this silence amounted to a misrepresentation.

The effects of misrepresentation

The remedies available to the victim of a misrepresentation will depend on the category into which the misrepresentation falls.

Innocent misrepresentation

A misrepresentation is 'innocent' if it was made in the genuine belief that it was correct and with reasonable grounds for that belief.

At common law, the victim has a right to rescind the contract (but see Loss of right to rescind below). The only compensation he may claim is a recovery of any expenses directly imposed by the contract (*Whittington v Seale-Hayne* (1900)). However, under s. 2(2) of the Misrepresentation Act 1967, the court can order the contract to remain in force and award damages instead.

Negligent misrepresentation

A misrepresentation is 'negligent' when it was made by a person who believed it to be true, but who had no good grounds for this belief. At common law, the victim of such a misrepresentation is entitled to rescind the contract (but see Loss of right to rescind below) and to claim damages (*Hedley Byrne & Co. Ltd* v *Heller & Partners Ltd* (1964)). The right to damages is also provided by s. 2(1) of the 1967 Act. In fact, it is more prudent to sue under the Act, since an allegation of negligence will be deemed true unless the contrary is proved: in an action brought at common law, the person alleging negligence will be required to prove their case. Under s. 2(2) of the Act, a court can order a contract to remain binding and for compensation to be paid in place of rescission. If the victim is already entitled to damages, these damages must reflect any further damages he is paid as compensation for loss of the right to rescind (s. 2(3)).

Fraudulent misrepresentation

The innocent party's rights will depend on the type of misrepresentation. Generally, there is a right to claim damages

A misrepresentation is 'fraudulent' if it is made 'knowingly, or without belief in its truth, or recklessly, careless whether it be true or false' (*Derry* v *Peek* (1889)). The victim is entitled to rescind the contract (but see Loss of right to rescind below) and to claim damages. The damages will compensate for the actual loss flowing from the fraudulent misrepresentation (*Clark* v *Urquhart* (1930); *Smith New Court Securities Ltd* v *Scrimegour Vickers Ltd* (1994)). There is nothing in the Misrepresentation Act relevant to fraudulent misrepresentation.

It will be seen that there is a close correspondence between negligent and fraudulent misrepresentation as far as the remedies are concerned. Since fraud is difficult to prove, actions tend to be for negligent misrepresentation.

Loss of right to rescind

The victim of a misrepresentation will lose their right to rescind if they affirm the contract with full knowledge of the misrepresentation.

> ### Case example
> ### *Long* v *Lloyd* (1958)
> A lorry was misrepresented as being 'in exceptional condition'. Two days after purchase, defects appeared and the buyer accepted an offer that the seller pay half the cost of repair. This amounted to affirmation of the contract and so the buyer lost his right to rescind.

The right to rescind is also lost if the parties cannot be restored to the position they occupied before the contract was made.

> ### Case example
> ### *Laguanas Nitrate Co.* v *Laguanas Syndicate* (1899)
> A syndicate sold a nitrate mine to a company under a contract which contained misrepresentations. It was held that the right to rescind had been lost because the mine had been worked and the parties could not be restored to their original position.

The right to rescind will be lost if an innocent third party has obtained an interest in the subject matter of the contract.

Case example
White v Garden (1851)

Plaintiffs contracted with A for the purchase of 40 tonnes of iron which A had obtained by fraud from the defendants. The latter delivered it to the plaintiffs on A's instructions. The plaintiffs paid on receipt, but the defendants seized the iron when they discovered the fraud. It was held that the seizure was wrongful. The contract with A could not be rescinded since the goods had come into the hands of the plaintiffs, who were innocent third parties.

In _Phillips_ v _Brooks Ltd_ and _Lewis_ v _Averay_ (see above) innocent third parties had become involved and hence the contract with the fraudulent party could not be rescinded.

Finally, an innocent party loses the right to rescind if more than a reasonable time has passed before the election to rescind is made.

Case example
Leaf v International Galleries (1950)

A painting believed by both parties to be a Constable was found five years later not to be such. Too long a period had elapsed to allow rescission. It must be remembered that the loss of the right to rescind does not affect any right to damages.

There are various ways in which a party can lose the right to rescind

Review questions

1 What are the categories into which a misrepresentation can fall and what are the remedies available in each of these categories?
2 In what circumstances is the right to rescind for misrepresentation lost?

Excluding liability for misrepresentation

Section 3 of the Misrepresentation Act 1967 states that a contract term which seeks to exclude or restrict liability is valid only if it satisfies the reasonableness test laid down in the Unfair Contract Terms Act 1977 (see above). In addition, such clauses will also be subject to the provisions of the Unfair Terms in Consumer Contracts Regulations 1994 (see above).

Case example
South Western General Property Co. v Marten (1983)

Particulars of sale at an auction misrepresented the position as to planning permission. The successful bidder later sought rescission of the contract on the grounds of misrepresentation. It was held that the sellers could not rely on an exclusion clause since the buyer had had no chance to check for himself on the accuracy of the particulars. In these circumstances, the clause was not a reasonable one.

Clauses excluding liability for misrepresentation are subject to statutory control

Frustration

The basic rule is that contracts are 'absolute'. This means that once a party has accepted contractual obligations, they cannot later argue that subsequent events made it impossible for them to perform.

> ### Case example
> ### *Hills* v *Sughrue* (1846)
> A shipowner agreed to load his ship with certain goods at a place in West Africa. He was held liable in damages even though those goods were unobtainable.

To mitigate the severity of this rule, the courts have developed the doctrine of frustration. Although there is some argument as to the precise rationale underlying the doctrine, it is probably best summed up in the following words: 'frustration occurs whenever the law recognises that without default of either party a contractual obligation has become incapable of being performed because the circumstances in which performance is called for would render it a thing radically different from that which was undertaken by the contract' (*Davis Contractors Ltd* v *Fareham UDC* (1956)).

Although contractual obligations are generally 'absolute', supervening events may invoke the doctrine of frustration

> ### Case example
> ### *Taylor* v *Caldwell* (1863)
> A music hall was hired out but destroyed before it could be put to use. It was held that the contract had been frustrated.

> ### Case example
> ### *Robinson* v *Davison* (1871)
> A pianist agreed to play at a concert. He fell ill and could not play. It was held that the illness frustrated the contract. See too *Krell* v *Henry* (1903).

> ### Case example
> ### *Gamerco* v *Missouri Storm Inc.* (1995)
> A pop concert was arranged. The promoters were obliged by the contract to obtain a permit for the use of a particular stadium. The permit was issued but then revoked. It was held that this revocation amounted to frustration. If, however, the essence of the contract remains, the doctrine of frustration will not apply.

> ### Case example
> ### *Herne Bay Steam Boat Co. Ltd* v *Hutton* (1903)
> To coincide with the coronation, a boat was chartered to see the royal naval review at Spithead and to cruise around the fleet. The coronation was cancelled.
>
> It was held that the contract had not been frustrated since, although there could be no review, it remained possible to cruise around the fleet.

The effect of frustration

When a contract has been judged to be frustrated, all obligations under it are discharged. In addition, the Law Reform (Frustrated Contracts) Act 1943 further provides:

1 All sums paid under the contract before discharge may be recovered.
2 If the person who received payment under the contract has incurred expenses in its execution, they may retain or recover from the payer all or part of their expenditure if the court considers it just so to do.
3 All sums payable under the contract cease to be payable.
4 Any valuable benefits obtained from the other party's actions under the contract must be paid for if the court thinks this just.

In the Gamerco case (see above), where the pop group had received an advance payment and claimed to be entitled to set off expenses against that advance, the court held that, in the circumstances, no deduction was appropriate.

The Act can be excluded by the express terms of the agreement. In addition, it does not cover: charter parties; contracts for the carriage of goods by sea; agreements for the sale of goods which perish before the risk has passed to the buyer; and insurance contracts. In all such cases, the common law applies and this provides:

1 Both parties are discharged from obligations which have not yet accrued.
2 If the price, or any part of the price, has been paid, it can be recovered if there has been a total failure of consideration.
3 If there is a total failure of consideration, no part of the price can be retained for expenses incurred.
4 Payments made cannot be recovered if there has been only a partial failure of consideration.
5 It is not possible to compel one party to pay for a benefit received where the contract was to perform one indivisible service and nothing had been received.

Case example
Fibrosa Spolka Akcyjna v Fairbairn Lawson Combe Barbour Ltd (1942)

An agreement was made in 1939 to sell and deliver to a company in Poland. Part of the price was paid in advance. The contract was frustrated by the outbreak of war. The Polish company requested the return of part of the advance payment. This was refused on the grounds, that considerable work had already been performed on the goods. It was held that the advance payment could be recovered because there had been a total failure of consideration.

The principle of this case only operates where there has been a total failure of consideration. It does not allow for the recovery of an advance payment if there has been only a partial failure of consideration. Again, the recipient of the payment will be obliged to return it, but without any set-off for expenses incurred.

The effects of frustration will vary according to whether the contract is within the 1943 Act or not

Review questions

1 What contracts are excluded from the operation of the Law Reform (Frustrated Contracts) Act 1943?
2 If a contract is within the 1943 Act what effect will frustration have on that contract; and what effect will frustration have in the case of the excluded contracts?

Remedies for breach of contract

Reference was made above to the distinction made between those terms of a contract which are conditions, and those which are warranties (see above).

In the case of a condition, or an intermediate term which is treated as a condition (see the discussion of the Hong Kong case above), the innocent party is entitled to claim damages and to rescind the contract. The circumstances in which they lose the right to rescind are the same as those set out in relation to misrepresentation (see above).

In the event of a breach of warranty, or of a term to be treated as a warranty, the innocent party is only entitled to damages. The contract remains in force.

The rules for determining damages

Recoverable damages are limited to those in the contemplation of the party in breach

A party in breach of contract is liable only to make good that loss which they contemplated as a probable result of the breach of contract. This is known as the Rule in *Hadley* v *Baxendale* (1854).

> ## Case example
> ## *Victoria Laundry (Windsor) Ltd* v *Newman Industries Ltd* (1949)
> A laundry business ordered a new boiler. It was delivered damaged and late. The business was held entitled to recover for loss of normal business profits, but not for the loss of certain exceptional government contracts since these had not been known to the other side and had not therefore been contemplated as a probable loss.

In limited circumstances, the innocent party is also entitled to claim damages for their disappointment, but such cases are limited to contracts whose essence was to provide pleasure, such as a holiday contract (*Jarvis* v *Swans Tours Ltd* (1973); *Jackson* v *Horizon Holidays Ltd* (1975)) or to build a swimming pool (*Ruxley Electronics and Construction Ltd* v *Forsyth* (1995)). Companies, however, cannot claim damages for disappointment (*Firesteel Cold Rolled Products Ltd* v *Anaco Precision Pressings Ltd* (1994)).

Penalty and liquidated damages clauses

Penalty clauses cannot be enforced

To remove the need for a court to determine the amount of damages in the event of breach, contracts sometimes contain a term specifying the amount to be paid should there be a breach. The validity of such clauses depends on whether they are genuine attempts at estimating the likely loss (when they are known as 'liquidated damages' clauses): or whether they are simply intended to punish a party for his breach of contract (when they are known as 'penalty' clauses). Only the former are enforceable.

> **Case example**
> ## Dunlop Pneumatic Tyre Co. Ltd v New Garage and Motor Co. Ltd (1915)
> Manufacturers supplied tyres to dealers under terms which prevented them from selling below list price or to certain named parties. Five pounds was to be paid for each breach. It was held that this was a genuine pre-estimate of loss and so could be enforced.

Note that such agreements are now caught by restrictive trading law. This does not, however, affect the validity of this case as regards damages clauses.

> **Case example**
> ## Ford Motor Co. (England) v Armstrong (1915)
> A dealer agreed not to sell cars or parts below list price, nor to resell to dealers or to exhibit cars bought under the agreement. In the event of breach, £250 was to be paid. It was held that this amounted to a penalty since it could not be regarded as a genuine pre-estimate of loss.

Note the remarks made above as to the impact of restrictive practices legislation. See too *Irish Telephone Rentals* v *Irish Civil Service Building Society* (1994).

The courts have also held that there is no distinction in law between a penalty for non-payment of sums due under a contract and a penalty imposed for the breach of some other obligation; nor between a penalty requiring the payment of money and one which requires the transfer of property. Any such clause would be unenforceable: *Jobson* v *Jobson* (1989).

Duty to mitigate

The victim of a breach of contract is not allowed to do nothing and let the damages mount up against the other side. They are instead obliged to undertake all reasonable measures to mitigate the loss being suffered. It will be a question of fact in the circumstances of the case as to whether the victim of the breach has taken all reasonable steps.

The innocent party must mitigate their loss if this is reasonable

> **Case example**
> ## Payzu Ltd v Saunders (1919)
> Under a contract to deliver goods by instalments, the buyers failed to pay punctually for the first instalment. The seller treated this as repudiation of the contract, but offered to continue with the deliveries if cash was paid with each order. This offer was rejected and the buyer sued for breach. The seller was liable to damages since the circumstances did not warrant his repudiation. On the other hand, it was also held that the buyers should have mitigated their loss by accepting the seller's offer.

> **Case example**
> ## Pilkington v Wood (1953)
> A solicitor was negligent in handling the conveyance of particular property. It was argued that he should have mitigated his loss by taking proceedings against the vendor to correct the defect in the title he had obtained. It was held that it was not reasonable to expect the purchaser to do this since an action against the vendor would have involved argument on a difficult point of law as to which the outcome was not clear.

It is well-established that the victim of a breach is not normally expected 'to act outside the normal course of business or incur unusual expenditure in an attempt to mitigate his loss, particularly where there is an element of speculation about whether it will pay dividends' (*Barclays Mercantile Highland Financing Ltd* v *Dunning* (1994)).

Review questions

1   What is the rule for working out what damages a person in breach of contract is liable to pay?
2   To what extent is it possible for the victim of a breach of contract to claim compensation for disappointment? What is the position with regard to companies?
3   What is meant by the duty to mitigate?

Specific performance

Instead of seeking damages, the victim of a breach of contract may instead prefer the contract to be performed. This will require the grant by a court of an order for specific performance, which is, however, rarely granted. Specific performance is a discretionary remedy and a plaintiff will generally have to show that: damages will not be an effective remedy; enforcement of the order will not require constant court supervision; the contract is enforceable by both parties; and that the plaintiff has acted fairly and honourably. The 'dominant principle has always been that equity will only grant specific performance if, under all the circumstances, it is just and equitable to do so' (*Stickney* v *Keeble* (1915)).

In limited circumstances, contracts may be enforced by decree of specific performance or an injunction

The courts also have the discretionary power to issue injunctions. A 'prohibitory' injunction enforces a negative promise (such as a promise not to sell a particular item). A 'mandatory' injunction orders a person to undo something he has done in breach of contract. An injunction will not be granted if its practical effect would be to compel the performance of a contract which is not capable of specific enforcement.

Case example
Lumley v *Wagner* (1852)
The defendant agreed to sing at the plaintiff's theatre twice a week for three months and not to work elsewhere. It was held that she could be restrained by injunction from breaking this promise.

If, however, the effect of the injunction is such that it would compel the defendant to work for the plaintiff (which could not be achieved by specific performance) then the injunction would not be granted.

Case example
Page One Records Ltd v *Britton* (1968)
A pop group promised not to make recordings for anyone except the plaintiff, who they appointed as their manager for five years. An injunction to restrain the group from breaking this promise was refused as it would 'as a practical matter' force them to continue working for the plaintiff.

Review question

In what circumstances can the victim of a breach of contract seek to compel performance or stop non-performance?

Assignment

All rights under a contract can be assigned by s. 136 of the Law of Property Act 1925. To be effective, the assignment must be in writing, signed by the person making the assignment (the 'assignor'); and be absolute and not solely by way of charge. Express notice must be given to any party against whom the assignor was entitled to claim.

If these formalities are not complied with, the assignment is 'equitable' only. This means that a subsequent assignment to a person (the 'assignee') who has no notice of the previous assignment will be effective unless that assignee had notice of the earlier assignment.

A person entitled to the benefit of a contract may transfer that benefit to another person

There can be no assignment of a contract for personal services, such as a contract to write a book.

Assignment must be distinguished from a novation. A novation occurs where a new contract is substituted for an existing contract.

Review question

Explain the difference between a statutory and an equitable novation.

Chapter summary

- Generally a contract is binding whether or not it is in written form.
- Consideration is the key element in the formulation of a binding contract. It is irrelevant that the consideration given by the parties is not of equivalent value.
- The terms of a contract differ in importance and the remedies for breach of a particular term will depend on its importance.
- Where an apparently binding contract has been formulated on the basis of a misapprehension caused by one party to the contract, the other may, in certain circumstances, be able to terminate that contract. There are also times when supervening events can put an end to a contract.
- The fine print of a contract will not always restrict the rights and remedies of a party. Much will depend on the reasonableness and fairness of the particular term.
- The victim of a breach of contract is entitled to damages, usually based on the contemplated loss.

United Kingdom application

The foregoing account of the law applies in the main solely to England, Wales and Northern Ireland. Scottish contract law differs materially in certain respects, and students are advised to consult specialist Scottish texts such as Gloag on the Law of Obligations.

Case study exercise

Adlaw Services, a one-man firm specializing in marketing law advice, bought a computer system from a local company, Southern Island Hardware. This was the third such system the firm had bought from SIH, the previous two being purchased within the previous six years.

No contract had ever been tendered to Adlaw Services in advance of either of the two previous contracts. Instead, the invoice, when it arrived a few days after installation, contained a lengthy set of terms and conditions. This pattern was followed on the occasion of the third purchase.

Unlike the previous two purchases, this third was not successful. There were many problems with the hardware, and Adlaw Services was unable to function properly while the hardware was being repaired.

Eventually it was, but Adlaw Services reckoned to have lost some £2000 worth of business while the hardware was being repaired. The firm eventually put in a claim for this lost business. In response, SIH pointed to this term in the terms and conditions: 'We accept no liability for any kind or amount of loss or damage whatsoever, whether such loss is direct or consequential, and whether that loss is caused by any act or negligence or default on our part.'

Student task

You are asked to consider whether the above clause has any effect on the principle of the claim, and whether the claim itself, in the absence of such clause, is sustainable.

Discussion questions

1 What effect does a misrepresentation as to the identity of a contracting party have on the contract?
2 If one party is compelled by law to enter into an arrangement with another, this does not give rise to what the law calls a contract. Discuss the validity of this statement.
3 Distinguish between the following:
    (a) conditions
    (b) warranties
    (c) intermediate terms.
4 'The victim of a breach of contract is not entitled simply to sit back and let damages mount up at the expense of the party in breach.' Is this a true statement of the law?

Recommended reading

The Law of Contract (13th edn), Furmston, Cheshire and Fifoot (1996), Butterworths.
Contract Cases and Materials (3rd edn), Beale, Bishop and Furmston (1995), Butterworths.
An Outline of the Law of Contract (5th edn), Treitel (1995), Butterworths.
Exclusion Clauses and Unfair Contract Terms (4th edn), Lawson (1995), FT Law & Tax.

3 Sale of goods and supply of services

Introduction

The sale and purchase of goods is one of the most important areas of commerce and also of the law of contract. It is, however, one of the few areas where the law of contract has been codified into an Act of Parliament. The questions of whether a contract has been entered into will be subject to the usual contractual principles discussed in the preceding chapter. This chapter will concentrate on the statutory provisions which have been enacted to regulate this particular contractual relationship.

For the most part, concentration will be on the Sale of Goods Act 1979. There are, however, other enactments which, though smaller in range, have codified the law relating to contracts which resemble contracts of sale, but which are technically in some other category. It will be seen that these codifications have established a regime which is essentially identical for all contracts under which the ownership or possession of goods passes.

This chapter also examines the duties imposed on those who provide services.

Objectives

The purpose of this chapter is to examine the legal framework of a particular category of contract: namely those dealing with contracts for the sale of goods and contracts for the supply of services.

Key concepts

- Statutory control
- Terms implied by the Supply of Goods (Implied Terms) Act 1973, the Sale of Goods Act 1979 and Supply of Goods and Services Act 1982
- Terms subdivided into conditions and warranties
- Nature of seller's liability
- Contracts of conditional sale and hire purchase
- Property and risk
- Exclusion clauses
- Remedies for breach.

Sale of Goods Act 1979

So that the Sale of Goods Act 1979 and its subsequent amendments can be properly understood, it is necessary to say a few words in advance as to its history. The common law on the sale of goods (meaning the law that had been developed over the years by the courts) was consolidated for the first time in the Sale of Goods Act 1893. This Act was amended in the following years and it was repealed and its various amendments were all consolidated in the Sale of Goods Act 1979 which has itself been subsequently amended in some important aspects. Because the current legislation therefore dates, in effect, from 1893 and before, many of the cases cited are earlier than the current legislation.

Scope of the Sale of Goods Act

The Act only covers contracts of sale, these being defined in s. 2(1) as contracts where ownership passes in exchange for money (which is not limited to cash, but covers all forms of payment). Any contract which differs from this model, even though goods and money may change hands, cannot be a contract of sale. Contracts of barter, where goods are exchanged for goods, are not contracts of sale. Nor are contracts where services are supplied with goods. For example, a plumber who puts in a new tap does not do so as part of a contract of sale. That is because he both supplied the tap and the service of installing it.

A contract for sale is where the parties exchange goods for money

Contracts of conditional sale and hire purchase

It is necessary to distinguish these two categories of contract because, although they closely re-semble each other, and their effect is the same, it is only contracts of conditional sale which are within the Sale of Goods Act.

In a contract of hire purchase the essence of the contract is that the customer only commits themselves to hiring the goods for a specific period. At the end of that period, they have an option to buy the goods which they need not exercise, though in practice they always will because the money they will have paid will cover the cost of purchase. The price to pay the option is nominal and is often paid as part of the regular instalments. In a conditional sale, however, the customer commits themselves at the outset to making the purchase, and pays off the price in instalments. It is because, in this latter case, the customer is bound to the purchase, and does not have an option on whether to buy, that only conditional sales are within the 1979 Act. Instead, hire purchase contracts are governed by the Supply of Goods (Implied Terms) Act 1973.

Hire purchase contracts are outside the Sale of Goods Act

Review questions

1 To what contracts does the Sale of Goods Act 1979 apply?
2 What is the difference between a contract of conditional sale and a contract of hire purchase?

Implied terms

The Sale of Goods Act identifies in contracts of sale certain implied terms. The Act specifically subdivides these into 'conditions' and 'warranties'. There is no definition of 'condition' in the Act, but it has been judicially defined to mean a term which goes 'directly to the substance of the contract, or, in other words [is] so essential to its nature that [its] non-performance may fairly be considered by the other party as a substantial failure to perform the contract at all … usage has consecrated the term "condition" to describe an obligation of [this] class' (*Wallis Sons & Webb* v *Pratt & Haynes* (1910)).

The Act defines a 'warranty' (s. 61(1)) as 'an agreement with reference to goods which are the subject of a contract of sale, but collateral to the main purpose of such contract …'. In the case just mentioned, the court said that, while warranties must be performed, they are 'not so vital that a failure to perform them goes to the substance of the contract'. In short, a 'condition' is a major term of the contract; a 'warranty' is a minor term. It will be explained below that the remedies available to a buyer depend on whether the breach is of a condition or a warranty.

> Conditions are major terms of a contract; warranties are minor ones

Review question

What is the difference between a condition and a warranty?

Conformity with description

Section 13(1) of the Act says that if a sale is by description, then the goods must conform to that description. This covers oral and written descriptions, or a combination of both, and also self-applied descriptions, such as the packaging of goods. This provision is stated to be a 'condition'.

> Goods must be as described

Case example
Pinnock v *Lewis* (1923)
A contract described the product as copra cake, which was to be used as a cattle feed. The goods delivered combined copra cake with castor beans. The court held that the quantity of beans so changed the nature of the product that it no longer fitted the description 'copra cake'.

Case example
Raynham Farm v *Symbol Motor Corporation* (1987)
A car sold as 'new' had, some months previously, been damaged by fire in the Netherlands after being exported from the United Kingdom. It was returned to this country where a great deal of repair work was done. The court accepted that a certain amount of very minor damage could be sustained by a car which could still properly be described as 'new'. The damage suffered in this case, however good the quality of the repairs, prevented such a description being made, not least because there would always be a lurking doubt that the fire had caused additional damage which had not been detected.

There will, however, be cases where, although there might be some admixture or alteration in the substance or the character of the product, it retains enough of its identity for it not to have been misdescribed.

> It is a question of fact – sometimes difficult to determine – as to when goods are not as described

Case example
Ashington Piggeries Ltd v *Christopher Hill* (1971)
Herring meal was contaminated with a substance which made it unsuitable for feeding to mink, the purpose for which it had been bought. It was ruled that the product had been correctly described as 'herring meal' even though not suitable for its intended purpose.

The requirement that goods must conform to their description is stated by the Act to apply only when goods are sold by description.

> **Case example**
> ### *Harlingdon & Leinster* v *Christopher Hull Fine Art Ltd (1990)*
> A firm of art dealers was asked to sell certain paintings described in a catalogue as being the work of a certain German painter. They themselves only specialized in British paintings and took them to an auction house which expressed an interest. They also contacted the plaintiffs who specialized in German paintings, telling them that they did not know much about the German school. An employee of the plaintiffs examined the paintings and agreed to buy the paintings without seeking further details. The paintings were forgeries.
>
> The court held that the goods had not been sold by description. For that to happen, the buyer had to rely on the description, and the facts showed that this had not been the case. The plaintiffs had not relied on the description and so, although the goods might have been misdescribed, there was no breach of s. 13.

The buyer must rely on the description

Section 13(3) provides that, just because goods are selected by the buyer from goods exposed for sale, this does not prevent the sale from being a sale by description. This provision ensures that when, for example, goods are selected from a supermarket shelf, those goods can still be sold by description even though no words are ever exchanged.

Review questions

1 In what circumstances will goods no longer conform to their contract description?
2 In what circumstances will a contract be one by description?

Excluding the implied term
The validity of exclusion clauses to exclude the implied term is dealt with below.

Satisfactory quality

Section 14(1) of the Sale of Goods Act 1979, as introduced by the Sale and Supply of Goods Act 1994, provides that where goods are sold in the course of a business, those goods must be of 'satisfactory quality'. Purely private transactions are excluded. This provision is a 'condition'. The Act states that goods are of a satisfactory quality if they meet the standard 'that a reasonable person would regard as satisfactory, taking account of any description of the goods, the price (if relevant) and all the other relevant circumstances.' It goes on to say that 'quality' includes state or condition and that the following matters, among others, are in appropriate cases aspects of the quality of goods:

- fitness for all the purposes for which goods of the kind in question are commonly supplied
- appearance and finish
- safety
- durability.

Under the law prior to the 1994 amendment, the 1979 Act required goods to be of 'merchantable quality', and it was this requirement that was removed by the 1994 amendment. Although there is considerable overlap between 'merchantable quality' and 'satisfactory quality', many of the cases dealing with the former requirement cannot be safely accepted as precedents for the new law. It is likely, however, that the following cases would be decided the same way now.

Goods sold in business transactions must be of satisfactory quality

> ## Case example
> ### *Bernstein v Pamson Motors (Golders Green) Ltd* (1987)
> A new car broke down when the buyer had had it for just three weeks and when he had driven only some 220 km. It was held that the car was not of merchantable quality. This was because, while the car had been repaired to 'good as new', there would always be doubt as to the area of potential damage caused by the seizing up of the engine; second, the fact that the engine had seized while being driven on a motorway meant that the car had been unsafe. It is certain that this car would also have been held not to have been of satisfactory quality.

> ## Case example
> ### *Rogers v Parish (Scarborough) Ltd* (1987)
> A new Range Rover was purchased for about £16 000. It proved unsatisfactory and it was replaced by another which turned out no better. Although drivable, it had faulty oil seals and defects in the engine, gearbox and bodywork. Despite several attempts at repair, problems persisted with the engine and gearbox. The court ruled that the car was not of merchantable quality, since consideration had to be given not merely to drivability, but also to comfort, ease of handling and pride in the vehicle's outward appearance. There can be no doubt that this finding would be the same under the new law.

In the *Harlingdon & Leinster* case, the court ruled that the painting was still of merchantable quality, even though not by the painter ascribed to it. The point was that it could still be resold, albeit at a lower price, and was still capable of aesthetic appreciation. Again, it is likely that the painting would now be judged to be of satisfactory quality.

Review question

What is meant by the duty to provide goods of satisfactory quality?

Excluding the implied term

The implied condition as to satisfactory quality can, in certain circumstances, be avoided by the use of an exclusion clause. This is dealt with below. Apart from such clauses, the Act itself states that the implied condition is inapplicable when the matter making the quality of the goods unsatisfactory is:

In some circumstances a buyer loses his right to satisfactory goods

- specifically drawn to the buyer's attention before the contract is made; or
- something which examination of the goods made by the buyer before the contract was made ought to have revealed.

81

There has been no case law on the first example, but it is not thought that it is necessary for a seller specifically to refer to 'defects'. It would be enough that he pointed out facts which were defects.

In the second example, the buyer must actually have examined the goods. It is not enough that they were offered the chance to examine the goods and declined it. It is, furthermore, only the examination which was actually made which is relevant, not some different or more rigorous examination which could have been made, but which was not.

Review questions

1 What is meant by the duty to provide goods which are of 'satisfactory quality'?
2 Other than by the use of an exclusion clause, in what circumstances may a buyer lose their right to goods of satisfactory quality?

Fitness for purpose

Goods to be
reasonably fit

It is an implied condition that goods supplied in the course of a business must be reasonably fit for the buyer's purpose where this purpose is made known, expressly or by implication. Purely private transactions are excluded. Where the goods have only one normal purpose, a seller will be taken to know the purpose for which the goods are wanted.

Case example
Priest v *Last* (1903)

A hot water bottle was held to be bought for a particular purpose although it had only the one purpose.

If the goods have a special purpose, this must be disclosed to the seller.

Case example
Griffiths v *Peter Conway Ltd* (1939)

A buyer of a coat contracted dermatitis. This was, however, because of an abnormally sensitive skin. It was held that the buyer should have advised the seller of the special use in advance. Since this had not been done, and although the coat was not fit for this buyer's purpose, there was no breach of the statutory requirement.

This case was approved by the House of Lords in *Slater* v *Finning Ltd* (1996).

Excluding the implied term

The terms as to reasonable fitness can in certain circumstances be excluded by an exclusion clause. The Act itself further provides that a seller is under no obligation to provide goods which are reasonably fit for their purpose if the buyer did not rely on the seller's skill and judgement; or did rely but were unreasonable in so doing. It has been said that, in the usual case of goods being purchased from a retailer, 'reliance will be in general inferred from the fact that a buyer goes to the shop in the confidence that the tradesman has selected his stock with skill and judgement' (*Grant* v *Australian Knitting Mills* (1936)). If the buyer is aware that the seller can only supply them with one particular brand of the goods in question, (as in a public house which is tied), then there will be evidence that the buyer has not relied on the seller's skill and judgement (*Wren* v *Holt* (1903)).

Case example
Baker v *Suzuki* (1993)
The buyer of a motor cycle was injured in an accident involving the motor cycle. The court ruled that the machine was, in fact, reasonably fit for its purpose but added that the term was inapplicable since the buyer had not relied on the seller's skill and judgement. The buyer 'knew what he wanted when he came in, and chose one of the two vehicles the seller had of that description for… reasons that he arrived at on his own.'

Like satisfactory quality, the duty as to reasonable fitness can also be excluded

Review questions

1 Under what circumstances is a seller under a duty to supply goods which are reasonably fit for their purpose?
2 When, other than in the case of an exclusion clause, does a buyer not have a right to goods which are reasonably fit for their purpose?

Strict liability

Where a seller fails in their duty to provide goods which conform to their description, are of satisfactory quality or are reasonably fit for their purpose, they are in breach of contract even if they were in no way to blame for the failure.

Case example
Frost v *Aylesbury Dairy Co. Ltd* (1905)
A bottle of milk was contaminated by the presence of a bacillus. The seller was held to be in breach of the Act even though the presence of the bacillus was not then discoverable by the use of any care or diligence.

Duty to pass title

Section 12 of the Act states that the seller must have the right to sell the goods. This is expressly stated to be a condition. This provision applies to private transactions as well as to those made in the course of a business. If the goods have to be returned to the true owner because of a breach by the seller, the buyer is entitled to recover all the purchase price without giving any allowance for any use that might have been made of the goods.

Case example
Rowland v *Divall* (1923)
The buyer bought a car and resold it to a third party. It was then discovered that the seller had no right to sell, and the car was repossessed from the third party. The buyer was held entitled to recover the full price and was not required to make any allowance for the use enjoyed by the third party. See too *Butterworth* v *Kingsway Motors Ltd* (1954).

There are also two implied warranties which require a seller to provide goods which are free from any undisclosed charge or encumbrance not known to the buyer prior to the contract; and to guarantee that the buyer will enjoy quiet possession of the goods except in relation to charges or encumbrances known to the buyer before the contract was made.

Case example
Mason Burningham (1949)
A typewriter was sold by a party who had no right to sell. It was repossessed from the buyer who obtained damages because of the breach of his right to quiet possession.

Case example
Microbeads AC v Vinhurst Road Markings Ltd (1975)
The seller sold equipment used for marking roads. A third party obtained a patent over the equipment after the contract had been made. Patent law enabled the third party to take possession of the equipment. It was held that the seller had failed to give the buyer quiet possession. See too *Healing (Sales) Pty Ltd v Inglis Electrix Pty Ltd* (1968); *Lloyds & Scottish Finance Ltd v Modern Cars and Caravans (Kingston) Ltd* (1966).

Where the goods have to be returned, a buyer is entitled to recover from the true owner compensation for anything they might have done which has enhanced their value.

Case example
Greenwood v Bennett (1973)
The seller sold a car which he had stolen. The buyer spent over £200 on repairs. When it was discovered, the police commenced proceedings to determine the rightful owner. In these proceedings, the car was ordered to be returned to its true owner, but compensation was to be paid to the buyer for the cost of repairs.

The principle of this case was subsequently consolidated in s. 6 of the Torts (Interference with Goods) Act 1977.

Review questions

1 What obligations are imposed on a seller with regard to title?
2 To what extent may a buyer recover the purchase price when the goods have to be returned to their rightful owner?
3 Is the buyer who returns the goods entitled to any compensation for what they may have spent on those goods?

Excluding the implied term

The buyer must get a sound title

The position with regard to exclusion clauses is dealt with below. Quite apart from any exclusion clause, however, the Act itself provides for a seller to pass only a limited title. If it appears from the circumstances that the seller intends only to pass such title as they or a third party might have, they are subject only to the two following warranties (see above):

1 that all charges and encumbrances known to the seller have been disclosed;
2 that none of the following will disturb the buyer's quiet possession:
   (a) the seller;
   (b) a third party (but only where the aim is to transfer that third party's title); and
   (c) anyone who claims under the seller or third party, except in relation to a disclosed charge or encumbrance.

A seller may pass only a limited title

Where the true owner loses their title

Although the basic rule is that the true owner of goods may recover them when they have been sold by a party who had no right to sell them, there are a number of cases where this is not so. It can be stated here that the instance of sales in market overt was repealed by the Sale of Goods (Amendment) Act 1994.

The owner is not always entitled to get their goods back when they have been sold without their consent

Agency

According to ordinary legal principles, a seller can pass a valid title if they are acting as the owner's agent and acting within their actual, ostensible or usual authority.

> ## Case example
> ## *Tingey & Co. Ltd v Chambers & Co. Ltd* (1967)
> The owners of an engine sent it to a firm for sale. No clear-cut terms for sale were stipulated, and the firm eventually sold the engine under its own name. The court held that the owner of the engine had 'so acted in relation to this engine as to clothe its agent with apparent authority to sell as principal and is thus precluded, as against the buyer, who was induced bona fide to act on the faith of that apparent authority, from denying that it had given such an authority.'

Estoppel

An owner may be precluded from setting up their title by their conduct. This is known as the principle of estoppel.

An owner can be 'estopped' from setting up their title

> ## Case example
> ## *Eastern Distributors v Goldring* (1957)
> A, as part of a plan to deceive a hire purchase company, signed and delivered forms to B which enabled the latter to represent that he had A's authority to sell a car which belonged to him. A was thereby estopped from setting up his title against the party who had bought the car from B.

> ## Case example
> ### *Central Newbury Car Auctions Ltd* v *Unity Finance Ltd* (1957)
> A person offered to buy a car on hire purchase terms. He gave a car in part-exchange, but this was itself subject to a hire purchase contract, and he drove away in the new car. His proposal to buy this car on hire purchase was, however, rejected by the finance company. The new car was later found in the possession of a party who had bought it in good faith. The case for estoppel was based on the fact that the owner had allowed the new car to be driven away complete with its registration book. This argument was, however, rejected because the registration book was not a document of title and even contained a warning that the person in whose name the car is registered may not be the owner.

The provisions relating to estoppel will not apply if the person making the sale actually does sell, in the sense of immediately giving title to the buyer. It will not apply if the person making the sale does so under an agreement where the passing of the title is deferred until some later date (*Shaw* v *Commisison of Police of the Metropolis* (1987)).

Sale under a voidable title

A voidable title may suffice

Section 23 of the Act provides that, where a seller has a voidable title to goods, and sells those goods before this title has been rendered void, the buyer acquires a good title if they buy in good faith and without notice of the defect in the seller's title.

> ## Case example
> ### *Lewis* v *Avery* (1971)
> An owner advertised his car for sale, selling it to a person who falsely claimed to be a named actor. The buyer thereby acquired a voidable title, but the car had been resold before the true owner rendered the title void. See this case further discussed in Chapter 2.

> ## Case example
> ### *Newtons of Wembley Ltd* v *Williams* (1964)
> The owner of a vehicle obtained from him by false pretences had taken all possible steps to trace the offender and had issued a stop notice to the Hire Purchase Information Bureau. Since this had been done before resale, it was held that the voidable title had been rendered void. See too *Car and Universal Finance Co. Ltd* v *Caldwell* (1965).

Seller in possession

Seller may resell if they remain in possession

Section 24 of the Act (and in almost identical terms, s. 8 of the Factors Act 1889) provides that, where a seller retains possession of the goods after sale, but then makes a further pledge, sale or 'other disposition' to a second buyer, who takes in good faith, passes a good title to the second buyer.

Case example
Pacific Motor Auctions Pty Ltd v *Motor Credits (Hire Finance) Ltd* (1965)

Dealers in vehicles sold a number to another party under a 'display agreement' whereby the dealers remained in possession for display. The dealers were paid 90 per cent of the price and were authorized to sell the vehicles as agents for that other party. The dealers fell into financial difficulties and their authority to sell was revoked. However, the dealers still sold a number of the vehicles to purchasers who took in good faith. It was held that these purchasers obtained a valid title from a seller in possession. See too *Worcester Works Finance Ltd* v *Cooden Engineering Co. Ltd* (1972).

However, if the seller resumes possession after having released the goods to the buyer, as where they borrow them back, their possession will not be as a seller in possession and therefore the above provisions will not apply (*Mitchell* v *Jones* (1905)).

It should be noted that the second buyer must take actual or constructive possession of the goods if they are to obtain a good title. Thus, if a person sells goods to A, retaining possession, and then sells to B, and still retains possession, A has a better claim to the goods (see *Forsythe International (UK) Ltd* v *Silver Shipping Co. Ltd* (1994) discussed below under Buyers in possession). The transfer of possession must also be voluntary (see again the *Forsythe* case below).

Buyer who obtains possession may pass good title

Buyer in possession

Section 9 of the Factors Act, and s. 25(1) of the Sale of Goods Act, provide that where a person has bought or agreed to buy goods, obtained possession of goods, or the documents of title to goods, with the seller's consent, any delivery of transfer by the buyer to a third party taking in good faith and without notice of any rights of the original seller 'shall have the same effect as if the person making the delivery or transfer were a mercantile agent in possession of the goods or documents of title with the consent of the owner.' A 'mercantile agent' is defined by the Factors Act as 'a person who, in the ordinary course of business, has authority to sell or buy goods, or to raise money on the security of goods.' A typical mercantile agent is a car dealer; another is an auctioneer.

Case example
Lee v *Butler* (1893)

Goods were bought under the terms of a conditional sale agreement. The goods were sold before title had passed. The person who undertook this sale was in good faith and so title passed to him. See also, *Forthright Finance Ltd* v *Carlyle Finance Ltd* (1997).

It must be remembered that a conditional sale agreement is different from a hire purchase agreement (see above). Under the latter, a person is not committed to making the purchase. For that reason, the rules as to a buyer in possession have no application to hire purchase contracts (see *Helby* v *Mathews* (1895)). The position is further complicated by the fact that the Consumer Credit Act 1974 provides that, where the amount of credit extended to a person buying under a conditional sale agreement does not exceed £15 000, and the buyer is an individual or a partnership or any other unincorporated body of persons not consisting entirely of bodies corporate, then the agreement is to be treated as a hire purchase agreement. Students should be aware that the £15 000 figure can be altered at any time, and they should always check for the latest figure.

One particular problem which had arisen in the interpretation of the provisions relating to the buyer in possession is this. Suppose a thief steals goods from the owner, and then sells them to a third person. The thief is not a buyer in possession, so that third person could not acquire a good title under these provisions. But suppose that the third party then sells to a fourth party. It could be argued that the third party is a buyer in possession, and that they can therefore pass a good title to the fourth party.

Case example
National Employers Mutual General Insurance Association Ltd v Jones (1990)

The court ruled that, because the thief never had title to the goods, he could not be said to have 'sold' the goods to the third party who was therefore not a buyer in possession. The absence of a genuine contract of sale on the part of the thief would mean, the court said, that however many further sales of the stolen goods there might be, none of the buyers could be classified as buyers in possession.

It will be recalled that the provisions relating to the buyer in possession are to apply as if the buyer in possession were a mercantile agent in possession with the consent of the owner. There are provisions relating to mercantile agency (see below) which prescribe that an unauthorized sale by a mercantile agent only has effect if they are selling in the ordinary course of his business. The problem in relation to the buyer in possession provisions is that, if the buyer in possession is not a mercantile agent, they cannot be said to be acting in the ordinary course of business. The problem has not been resolved, but the better approach would be to treat the relevant words as meaning that the sale by the buyer in possession has effect as if they were a mercantile agent acting in the ordinary course of their business, and not as meaning that they must be judged as though they were such an agent and whether they were or were not acting in the ordinary course of their business (*Jeffcott* v *Andrew Motors Ltd* (1960); *Lambert* v *G&C Finance Corporation Ltd* (1963); *Newtons of Wembley Ltd* v *Williams* (1965); *Forsythe International (UK) Ltd* v *Silver Shipping Co. Ltd* (1994)).

As with the position regarding the seller in possession, the provisions as to the buyer in possession only apply when the third party obtains actual or constructive possession. Furthermore, the transfer of possession must be voluntary.

Case example
Forsythe International (UK) Ltd v Silver Shipping Co. Ltd (1994)

Unauthorized sales by mercantile agents can oust the true owner's title

A party contracted with charterers to supply bunker oils to a vessel which was on a time charter from the owners. The vessel was withdrawn from charter by the owners ahead of time because of non-payment of hire. At that time, the vessel was carrying bunker oil supplied by that party but not paid for. The owners contended that title had passed to them because the charterers were buyers in possession, and they had obtained possession. The court held that the delivery to the owners had to be voluntary. In this case, the transfer was involuntary since it had come about by virtue of the owners' termination of non-payment of hire and not because of any act of the charterers.

Mercantile agency

The Factors Act 1889 states that where a mercantile agent is in possession of goods with the consent of the owner, they can, when acting in the ordinary course of business, pass a good title to someone taking in good faith even when not authorized to make the sale. A party is a 'mercantile agent' or 'factor' if, in the ordinary course of business, they are authorized to sell or buy goods, or to raise money on the security of goods. This includes such businesses as that of car dealer and auctioneer.

Case example
Folkes v *King* (1923)

A car owner delivered his car to a dealer for sale at not less than £575. The dealer sold at £340 to a buyer who took in good faith. It was held that, as the dealer was a mercantile agent in possession of goods with the consent of the owner, the buyer obtained a good title.

Even though the mercantile agent's consent might have been obtained by deception, this nonetheless amounts to consent for the purposes of the Factors Act.

Case example
Pearson v *Rose & Young* (1951)

A car owner left his car with a dealer to see what offers would be made. The dealer was, however, not authorized to sell. The dealer had intended from the outset to sell, but his possession, even though obtained by deception, was still held to be with the owner's consent, thus allowing him to pass a title to a buyer in good faith. See too *Du Jardin* v *Beadman* (1952).

It should be noted that, under the 1889 Act, consent is assumed unless the contrary is proven.

It is also necessary that the mercantile agent obtained possession in his capacity as such an agent. The owner 'must consent to the agent having [the goods] for a purpose which is in some way or other connected with his business as a mercantile agent. It may not actually be for sale. It may be for display, or to get offers, or merely to put in his showroom; but there must be consent to something of that kind before the owner can be deprived of his goods' (*Pearson* v *Rose & Young* (1951)). See too *Cole* v *North Western Bank* (1975). If, therefore, the owner is unaware that the party to whom they give the goods is a mercantile agent, the latter does not obtain possession under the provisions of the Act (*Henderson* v *Prosser* (1982)).

Case example
Astley Industrial Trust v *Miller* (1968)

A car was provided to a self-drive car hire business. As an ancillary activity to this business, they also sold second-hand cars. They resold this car before title had passed. It was held that the Factors Act did not apply as they had obtained possession as operators of a car hire business and not as mercantile agents.

It will be recalled that the Factors Act will apply only when the mercantile agent is selling in the ordinary course of their business. This means 'acting in such a way as a mercantile agent in the ordinary course of business would act, that is to say, within business hours, at a proper place of business, and in other respects in the ordinary way in which a mercantile agent would act, so that there is nothing to lead the [other party] to suppose that anything is done wrong, or to give notice that the disposition is one which the mercantile agent has no authority to make' (*Oppenheimer* v *Attenborough* (1908)). Thus, a transaction whereby payment is made not to the mercantile agent but to one of their creditors may well be outside the ordinary course of business (see the *Oppenheimer* case). Whether a transaction has taken place in the ordinary course of business is a question of fact which depends on the circumstances of the particular case.

Sale under special powers

Sales may be made under special powers

Section 21(2) of the Sale of Goods Act expressly allows for the title of the true owner to be ousted by a sale made under any special common law or statutory powers of sale, or under the order of a court.

There are a large number of statutory powers, such as the power of a sheriff to sell goods seized under a writ of execution (Bankruptcy and Deeds of Arrangement Act 1913; the powers of an innkeeper to sell goods over which they have a lien under the Innkeepers Act 1878; the powers conferred by the Torts (Interference with Goods) Act 1977; and the powers relating to pawns under the Consumer Credit Act 1974).

An example of a common-law power of sale is that of a pledgee, but this right may in certain cases have to be executed under the provisions of the Consumer Credit Act 1974.

The Hire Purchase Act 1964

Special provision for motor vehicles

The Hire Purchase Act 1964 covers those cases where a motor vehicle is being bought under either hire purchase or conditional sale terms. Where a motor vehicle being obtained in such circumstances is sold to a private consumer (i.e. someone not buying the course of a trade or business) and they take in good faith and without notice of the seller's defect in title, they obtain a good title in that motor vehicle.

> ### Case example
> ### *Dodds* v *Yorkshire Finance* (1992)
> The purchaser of a car had stipulated that the receipt for her payment was to contain a declaration that the car was not the subject of an existing hire-purchase agreement. The Court of Appeal said that good faith was to be equated with honesty. The purchaser's evidence was that, when this declaration had been given, 'I was not suspicious any more.' It was held that she had been a purchaser in good faith.

Review questions

1 What is the normal position when goods are sold without the consent of the owner?
2 Outline those circumstances in which the owner of goods loses their right to reclaim them.
3 When will the owner be 'estopped' from setting up their title against a third party?
4 What is the position when goods are (a) sold by a buyer in possession and (b) by a seller in possession?

5 What rules apply to unauthorized sales by a mercantile agent?

6 What special rules apply to the sale of a motor vehicle?

Hire purchase contracts

The Supply of Goods (Implied Terms) Act 1973 applies only to contracts of hire purchase (see above). It implies into such contracts implied terms as to description, satisfactory quality and reasonable fitness for purpose which are identical in all respects to those applying in contracts of sale (see above).

The 1973 Act deals only with the implied terms and does not, therefore, set out the position with regard to the effect of sales without title. However, the provisions of the Sale of Goods Act, as representing the common law, and the relevant provisions of the Factors Act 1889 may be taken as applicable. The provisions as to buyers in possession will not of course apply since a person taking on hire purchase is not a person who has bought or agreed to buy goods. Reference should be made in particular to the provisions of the Hire Purchase Act 1964 also discussed above.

Identical terms implied into contracts of hire purchase as in contracts of sale

Exclusion clauses

The position is the same as with contracts for the Sale of Goods Act 1979 (above) and reference should also be made to the consideration of exclusion clauses and the Unfair Contract Terms Act below.

Review question

What terms are implied into contracts of hire purchase and under what enactment?

Other contracts for the transfer of goods

There are various other contracts under which possession or ownership of goods passes but which are not subject to the Supply of Goods (Implied Terms) Act 1973 or the Sale of Goods Act 1979.

Trading Stamps Act 1964

When a customer exchanges the trading stamps they have obtained on a purchase of goods (Green Shield stamps are the classic example), they have the benefit of certain implied 'warranties' (for the definition of a 'warranty', see above). These are:

- that the promoter of the trading stamp scheme has the right to give the goods in exchange for the stamps;
- that the goods are free from any charge or encumbrance not disclosed or known to the customer before obtaining the particular goods;
- that the customer will obtain quiet possession of the goods except so far as that quiet

possession may be disturbed by the owner or other person entitled to the benefit of any charge or encumbrance so disclosed or known;
- that the goods are of satisfactory quality.

It is to be noted that, unlike the corresponding provisions of the Sale of Goods Act, these terms are not conditions. Furthermore, there is no requirement that the goods shall conform to their description or be reasonably fit for their purpose. It is more than likely, however, that such terms will be implied at common law.

Review question

What duties are imposed on a party who exchanges trading stamps for goods?

Exclusion clauses

Warranties implied on redemption of trading stamps

The Act states that the implied warranties apply notwithstanding any term in the contract to the contrary.

The Supply of Goods and Services Act 1982

This Act applies to contracts for the transfer of ownership in goods except contracts governed by the Sale of Goods Act 1979, the Supply of Goods (Implied Terms Act) 1973, and the Trading Stamps Act 1964 (see above). It is also expressly stated that it does not apply to transfers to be made by deed where there is no consideration; nor to a contract which is intended to operate by way of mortgage, pledge, charge or other security. The Act also applies to contracts for the lease or hire of goods.

Various conditions and warranties implied into contracts for transfer of possession and ownership

In all cases within the 1982 Act, terms are implied which are identical to those implied under those provisions of the Sale of Goods Act dealing with description, satisfactory quality, fitness for purpose and title (see above) but with two exceptions: in the case of contracts of lease or hire, though, there is no implied term as to freedom from encumbrances or charges, though this may well be implied at common law; and in no case is there any right to pass or offer only a limited title, though this too may well be implied at common law.

Review questions

1 To which contracts relating to goods does the Supply and Services of Goods Act 1982 apply?
2 What duties are imposed on those who supply goods under contracts within the Act?

Supply of services

Certain terms implied into contracts of services

The 1982 Act, which consolidated the common law, also implies certain terms into contracts of the provision of services. Where a service is provided in the course of a business, there are implied terms that: the service will be provided within a reasonable time, unless a specific time has been expressly agreed; and that the service will be effected with reasonable care and skill, though the Act does allow a party to promise that they will use more than reasonable care and skill (see *Greaves & Co. (Contractors) Ltd* v *Baynham Meikle & Partners* (1975)). Whether the contract is made in the course of a business or not, the Act also implies a term that, unless the amount of the charge has been agreed in advance, only a charge which is reasonable will be made.

Case example
Wilson v *Best Travel Ltd* (1993)

A holidaymaker at a Greek hotel, booked in England through English tour operators, sustained injuries after falling through glass doors at the hotel. The doors complied with Greek safety regulations, but not those which would have applied in England. It was held that, since the hotel had been inspected by the tour operators, since the doors complied with local regulations, and since the holidaymaker would not have refused the hotel because of the state of the doors, the tour operators had acted with reasonable care and skill.

It is to be noted that these are 'terms' and are not divided up into either 'conditions' or 'warranties' (see above). The effect will presumably be, therefore, that a serious breach will be treated as a breach of a condition, whereas a relatively minor breach will be treated as a breach of a warranty (see above).

Review question

What obligations are imposed on those who supply services and into what category do these obligations fall?

Exclusion clauses

See below.

Exclusion clauses

The Unfair Contract Terms Act 1977 makes a distinction between contracts made between businesses and those made with a consumer. Section 12(3) of the Act states that a person is assumed to be a consumer until the contrary is proved. Subject to this, s. 12(1) states that a person is a consumer if: they neither make the contract in the course of a business nor hold themselves out as so doing; the other party does make the contract in the course of a business; and where the contract is one of sale, hire purchase or for the transfer of ownership or possession (see above).

Controls are imposed on the use of exclusion and limitation clauses

---

Case example
R&B Customs Brokers Co. Ltd v *UDT Ltd* (1988)

A company purchased a car from a finance company. This was the second or third which they had acquired on credit terms in their business as freight forwarding agents. This particular car was for both company and personal use. It was held that the purchase was only incidental to the purchaser's business and that, in such a case, a degree of regularity was required before the transaction could be said to be an integral part of their business. The company was therefore dealing as a consumer. See too *Rasbora* v *JCL Marine Ltd* (1977).

If a contract is made with a consumer, then no term is effective to exclude or limit liability for breach of any of the implied terms as to title, description, satisfactory quality or reasonable fitness for purpose. It is furthermore a criminal offence, under the provisions of the Consumer Transactions (Restrictions on Statements) Order 1976 (SI 1976 No 1813), to include in a contract with a consumer any such term.

Where the contract is made between businesses, the implied terms as to title cannot be excluded or limited, but the other terms can be excluded or limited if the relevant exclusion or limitation clause is reasonable. Section 11(5) states that a term is unreasonable until the contrary is proved. The court is required to consider whether the disputed term was one which it was reasonable to include in all the circumstances of the case, and to have regard to various matters listed in a schedule to the Act (such as the relative bargaining strength of the parties). In some cases, regard is to be had to the availability of insurance to the party seeking to impose the particular term.

Case example
The Salvage Association v *CAP Financial Services Ltd* (1992)

A contract for the supply of computer software imposed a maximum liability of £25 000 in the event of breach. The parties were of equal bargaining power, the contract was freely negotiable, and there were competing sources of supply. Advice had also been sought from solicitors, accountants and insurance brokers. At the same time, the figure of £25 000 was arbitrary and unrelated to company turnover, the level of insurance cover, the value of the contract, or the degree of financial risk. It was also the case that it had been agreed that the liability limit should be generally increased to £1 million, and it was not explained why this had not been done in this particular case.

Other factors were also considered by the court. First, that the task was not particularly demanding and well within the relevant party's range of skills There had never been any suggestion that the party seeking to rely on the clause would fail to perform the contractual task. It was also the case that the other party was not able to obtain insurance cover against non-performance at anything like reasonable cost, if it all. Weighing all these various factors, the court concluded that the clause in question was unreasonable. See too: *Photo Production Ltd* v *Securicor Transport Ltd* (1980); *BTE Auto Repairs* v *H&H Factors Ltd* (1990); *Edmund Murray* v *BSP International Foundations Ltd* (1992); *W Photoprint Ltd* v *Forward Trust Group Ltd* (1993); *St Albans City and District Council* v *International Computers Ltd* (1994); *Lease Management Services Ltd* v *Purnell Secretarial Services Ltd* (1994); *Fillite (Runcorn) Ltd* v *APV Pasilac Ltd* (1995).

Contracts within the Supply of Goods and Services Act

Controls on exclusion clauses differ under Supply of Goods and Services Act

A different regime applies in relation to those contracts within the Supply of Goods and Services Act 1982 (see above). The Act itself provides that the provisions as to title cannot be excluded or limited, except in relation to contracts for the hire or lease of goods, where the provisions as to title can be excluded or limited by a clause which passes the reasonableness test (see above).

In relation to the terms relating to description, satisfactory quality and fitness for purpose, a distinction is again drawn between business and consumer contracts. In the former case, reasonable exclusion clauses are effective; in the latter case, any exclusion clause is automatically invalid. In this case, however, no criminal offence is committed by the inclusion of such a void term in a consumer contract (contrast the position under the Consumer Transactions (Restrictions on Statements) Order explained above).

The unfair terms in consumer contracts regulations

These were fully discussed in Chapter 2. They do not in any way affect the position described above.

Review questions

1   What exclusion clauses are automatically void and which are subject to the reasonableness test?
2   In what circumstances can the presence of an exclusion clause in a contract give rise to a criminal offence?
3   What does a court have to consider when applying the test of reasonableness?
4   What use can be made of exclusion clauses in the case of contracts, whether for services or goods, falling within the Supply of Goods and Services Act 1982?

Passing of property

'Property' is defined in s. 61(1) of the Sale of Goods Act 1979 as the 'general property' in goods. To all intents and purposes, 'property' means the full rights of ownership. Section 17(1) provides that 'property' passes at the moment specified in the contract. However, to cater for those contracts where the parties have said nothing as to when property is to pass, s. 18 lays down five rules for determining when property is to pass. These rules refer to 'specific goods', which are defined in s. 61(1) as goods agreed on and identified at the time the contract is made; i.e. the very goods with which the buyer will be supplied.

Ownership passes when contract says so or in accordance with statutory rules

Rule 1

Where there is an unconditional contract for the sale of specific goods in a deliverable state, the property passes to the buyer when the contract is made. Section 61(1) says that goods are in a 'deliverable state' when they are in such a condition that, under the contract, the buyer would be bound to take delivery.

The five rules for when property is to pass

Case example
Dennant v Skinner & Collom (1948)

Goods were knocked down at auction to the highest bidder. Payment was made by cheque and the goods taken away. The cheque was not honoured. It was ruled that property had passed when the bid was accepted, so that a term in a document signed subsequently to the effect that property only passed when the cheque was met had no effect.

Rule 2

Where there is a contract for the sale of specific goods, and the seller is bound to do something to put them into a 'deliverable state' (see this term defined in Rule 1), property passes when that thing is done and the buyer has been notified.

Case example
Underwood Ltd v Burgh Castle Brick and Cement Syndicate (1922)

An engine was sold when bolted to a factory floor. It was held that property had not passed when the contract had been made.

Rule 3

Where there is a contract for the sale of specific goods in a deliverable state (see Rule 1) and something remains to be done, such as weighing, before the price is determined, property passes when it is done and the buyer notified.

Case example
Nanka Bruce v Commonwealth Trust Ltd (1926)

Cocoa was sold to a buyer who resold to a third party. This party was to weigh it to determine how much the buyer owed the seller. It was held that the Rule did not apply because it was not the seller who did the weighing.

Rule 4

Where specific goods are supplied on the basis of sale or return, property passes when the buyer adopts the transaction, or when they keep them after the date for return, or (if no date is fixed for return), they retain them for longer than a reasonable time.

Case example
Poole v Smith's Car Sales (Balham) Ltd (1962)

A car was left with dealers, but no time limit given. It was unsold for three months. During this period, the owner made several requests for the car's return. It was held that property had passed in these circumstances and that the dealers were liable for the price.

Rule 5

This Rule deals with 'unascertained' or 'future' goods. 'Future' goods are defined in s. 61(1) as goods to be manufactured or acquired by the seller after the contract was made. There is no definition of 'unascertained' which can be taken as a reference to goods of the contract description of which only a part is needed to fulfil the contract, but which part has yet to be decided.

Section 16 of the Act states that where there is a contract for the sale of unascertained goods, property cannot pass until those goods are ascertained.

Case example
Re Stapylton Fletcher Ltd (1995)

Wine merchants held stock in common for customers. When a customer purchased wine, it was removed from the trading stock and placed in reserve. In the case of one of the wine merchants, a master card recorded the names of the customers and the number of cases allo-

---

cated to each customer. The individual cases of wine, however, were not marked with a particular customer's name. As wine was delivered to each customer and new wine acquired, the master index was updated. The other merchant made no attempt to allocate the wines either to specific customers or as between the company and its customers generally.

It was held that, if there was no delivery, but merely a segregation in the hands of the seller for retention by him, it was the segregation of the stock from the company's trading assets, whether done physically or by giving instructions to a bonded warehouse keeper, which caused the goods to be ascertained for the purposes of s. 16. The goods then became identified as those to be handed over for storage in performance of the contract of sale and the purchaser then became a 'tenant in common' of the entire stock in the proportion that his goods bore to the total in store for the time being. A 'tenancy in common' exists where two or more people own all of a particular item or stock. On the facts of the present case, where a number of cases or bottles of identical wines were held, apart from the trading stock, in store for a group of customers, those cases or bottles were ascertained and property passed by common intention, and not by virtue of Rule 5. By contrast, wines which had been stored in a warehouse without having been allocated to customer orders (either by marks on the cases or by an inventory) or even as between the seller and its customers generally were not ascertained at the time receivers were appointed and so the customers' only remedy lay in damages.

Once goods have become ascertained, Rule 5 states that property passes if the goods are in a deliverable state and have been unconditionally appropriated to the contract by one party with the assent of the other. Assent may be expressed or implied and given before or after the appropriation. Rule 5 gives as an instance of unconditional appropriation the delivery of goods by the seller to the buyer, or to a carrier for transmission to the buyer, where the seller has not reserved the right to dispose of the goods.

Case example
Pignatoro v Gilroy (1919)
One hundred and forty bags of rice were sold, the bags being unascertained. The buyer paid by cheque and asked for a delivery order which was sent for 125 bags. The seller said that the balance was awaiting delivery at his place of business. These were stolen. It was held that property had passed since the seller had appropriated the balance to the contract and the buyer had agreed to this by his conduct.

Case example
Wardar's Import & Export Co. Ltd v W Norwood & Sons Ltd (1968)
The seller sold 600 boxes of frozen kidneys from a consignment of 1500. The buyer's carrier took delivery the next day of the 600 boxes when the delivery note was handed over. It was held that property had passed since there had been an unconditional appropriation.

It must be remembered that the rules only apply where the parties have not themselves indicated when property is to pass. In Re *Stapylton Fletcher Ltd* (discussed above), where a number of cases of bottles of identical wines were held, segregated from trading stock, or in store for a group of customers, the cases or bottles would be sufficiently appropriated, even though not immediately appropriated to each individual customer. Property accordingly was held to pass by the common intention of the parties and not under the provisions of Rule 5. The result was that each customer became a tenant in common in the proportion that their goods bore to the entire stock. By contrast, wines which had been stored in a warehouse without having been allocated to customers' orders, either by marks on the cases or by an inventory, or even as between the sellers and its customers generally, were not ascertained at the time receivers were appointed and the relevant buyers' remedies lay in damages.

Goods forming part of a bulk

New rules for sales from bulk

The passing of property in goods forming part of a bulk has been affected by the Sale of Goods (Amendment) Act 1995 and the preceding discussion must be read in the light of this Act. Under the new provision, a buyer who has paid for some or all of goods which form part of an identified bulk becomes an 'owner in common' of the bulk, and each buyer's share in the bulk is that which the quantity bought and paid for by that buyer bears to the quantity in the bulk. Where the aggregate of the undivided shares of buyers exceeds the whole of the bulk, each buyer's share is proportionately reduced. 'Bulk' is defined as meaning a mass or collection of goods of the same kind contained (a) in a defined space or area, and (b) such that any goods in the bulk are interchangeable with any other goods in the bulk of the same number or quantity. Where a buyer had paid the price for only some of the goods due to them from the bulk, any delivery to them from the bulk is to be ascribed in the first place to the goods in respect of which payment was made. Payment of part of the price for any goods is to be treated as payment for a corresponding part of the goods. Each owner in common is deemed to have consented to a delivery from the bulk to any other owner in common of goods due to them under their contract and to any dealing with or removal, delivery or disposal of goods in the bulk by any such person, and no cause of action lies against such a person in respect of any such actions.

The effect of this change in the law is to make it clear that, in cases in which the parties have bargained in terms of a given quantity from a larger bulk, the subject matter of the contract is not the unidentified quantity, but the bulk itself. So, a contract to sell 100 bottles from an identified stock of 1000 is treated as a contract to sell a 10 per cent interest in the entire stock. The parties are always free to bargain for co-ownership by stipulating for the sale and purchase of a given percentage or fraction of the bulk, and the new law would have no effect.

Review questions

1 What is the basic rule as to when property is to pass?
2 What is meant by 'specific', 'future' and 'unascertained' goods?
3 What are the rules which govern the passing of property in specific goods?
4 What rules govern the passing of property in unascertained goods?
5 What rules are now applicable regarding sales from bulk?

Retention of title clauses

Once property in goods has passed to the buyer, the seller can no longer use those goods as security should the buyer fail to pay. It therefore became common, starting with the decision in *Aluminium Industrie BV* v *Romalpa Aluminium Ltd* (1976) for sellers to insert 'retention of title' clauses into the agreement. Under such a clause, which can take one of several forms, a seller stipulates that property remains theirs until all sums outstanding under the contract have been paid. In the so-called 'all monies' clause, the seller goes a stage further and retains title in particular goods until all sums are paid both under the particular contract and all other contracts between them. Such clauses were upheld in *Thyssen* v *Armour Edelstahlwerke AG* (1991). There have been many cases on aspects of retention of title (see for example Re *Bond Worth* (1980); *Clough Mill* v *Martin* (1985); *Compaq Computer Ltd* v *Abercorn Group Ltd* (1991); *Modelboard Ltd* v *Outer Box Ltd* (1992)).

Sellers may retain property pending payment

> ## Case example
> ## *Chaigley Farms Ltd* v *Crawford, Kaye & Grayshire* (1996)
> Cattle had been supplied to an abattoir under the terms of a retention of title clause which provided for the supplier to 'retain ownership until all the goods invoiced have been paid for in full'. The document containing this clause noted that it was only on the basis of such a clause that the supplier would be able to trade with the abattoir in the purchase of 'livestock'. The supplier contended that 'this was effective to protect not only the live animals delivered but also the dead meat after slaughter.' The court held that there was an effective retention of title clause so long as the animals were alive. It was also held that the slaughter of the cattle extinguished the supplier's retention of title. There was an 'inescapable difference' between a live animal and a dead one. It was pointed out that animals were 'goods' for the purposes of the Sale of Goods Act 1979, and the fact that the parties may have intended or contemplated that the retention clause should extend to the carcasses could not support an extended meaning of 'goods', nor could the clause be given such a wider interpretation on grounds of business efficacy.

These cases are highly technical and raise many difficult points of law. Readers are strongly advised to refer to specialist texts.

Review question

Under what circumstances is a seller likely to want to use a retention of title clause?

Risk passes with property

Section 20 of the Act provides that the party who has property in the goods takes the risk of any damage or deterioration in them. If, therefore, property has passed to the buyer under the contract, or by virtue of the operation of any of the above rules, then they must take the risk of anything happening to them, even if it happens before they take possession.

> ### Case example
> ### *Mitchinson* v *Otaihape Farmers' Meat and Produce Co. Ltd (1920)*
> The buyer selected 280 sheep from a flock of 1100. These were put into a separate pen. Property thereby passed to the buyer. Later that day, the sheep were destroyed by fire. It was held that the buyer had to pay the price since the risk had passed to him with the property (see too the *Wardar's* case discussed above under Rule 5).

The Act goes on to say that the parties can provide in the contract that risk and property need not go together. It is therefore always possible for the contract, expressly or by implication, to provide that the buyer takes the risk, even though the property is still with the seller. Conversely, it can also state that the risk remains with the seller, even though property has passed to the buyer.

The buyer's remedies

On breach, buyer can claim damages and reject goods

Where a seller is in breach of the implied conditions as to title, conformity with description, satisfactory quality and fitness for purpose (see above), this entitles the buyer to reject the goods and to claim damages. On rejection, and unless otherwise agreed, the Sale of Goods Act says that it is not the responsibility of the buyer to return the goods, meaning that the seller must at their own expense arrange for their collection or return.

The right to reject can be lost by acceptance

The buyer can, however, lose the right to reject (but not the right to claim damages) if they have 'accepted' the goods. This is governed by s. 35 of the Sale of Goods Act 1979 which provides that goods are accepted, and the right to reject is lost, in the following cases:

1 Where the buyer 'intimates' acceptance; or takes delivery of the goods and does an act which is inconsistent with the ownership of the seller. In both these cases, however, the Sale of Goods Act, as amended by the Sale and Supply of Goods Act 1994, states that the buyer is not taken to have accepted the goods under either of these heads if they have not had the chance of examining the goods to check up that they conform to the requirements of the contract. Furthermore, if the buyer is a 'consumer' (see above) they cannot lose this right of examination by agreement, waiver or otherwise. These provisions mean that simply signing receipts, delivery or acceptance notes does not of itself amount to acceptance if there has been no opportunity for prior inspection.

2 Where the buyer retains the goods for more than a reasonable time without rejecting them. A 'reasonable time' is stated in s. 61(1) to be a question of fact which depends on all the circumstances of the case. However, by an amendment introduced by the 1994 Act, consideration must be given in determining whether a reasonable time has elapsed to whether the buyer had a prior opportunity of examining the goods to see if they were as required by the contract.

Although there are no equivalent provisions in the Supply of Goods (Implied Terms) Act 1973 (see above) nor in the Supply of Goods and Services Act 1982 (see above), these provisions probably represent the common law applying to contracts governed by these two Acts.

Acts not constituting acceptance

The Sale and Supply of Goods Act also specifically changed the law, but only in relation to contracts within the 1979 Act (see above), by stating that a buyer is not deemed to have accepted goods under any of the above headings just because:

1 They ask for, or agree to, their repair by or under an arrangement with the seller.
2 The goods are delivered to another under a sub-sale or other disposition.

Prior to this particular amendment, a buyer who resold goods would be taken to have done an act which was inconsistent with the seller's ownership, and hence to have accepted the goods.

Commercial units

The 1994 Act further provides, again only in relation to contracts within the 1979 Act (see above), that where the contract of sale relates to one or more 'commercial units', a buyer who accepts any of the goods in the unit is to be taken as accepting all the units. A 'commercial unit' is a unit, division of which would materially impair the value of the goods or the character of the unit. For instance, a buyer who accepted one volume from an encyclopaedia sold as a set would be taken to have accepted the whole set. Similarly, the buyer who had accepted one shoe would be taken to have accepted the pair.

These provisions will not apply if there is a term to such effect, express or implied, in the contract.

Right of partial rejection

An amendment to the law brought about by the 1994 Act provides for a right of partial rejection, but only in relation to contracts within the 1979 Act (see above). This will arise if the buyer has the right to reject because there has been a breach affecting some or all of the goods, and the buyer accepts some of the goods, including, where there are goods not affected by the breach, those which are so unaffected. The Act provides that such acceptance does not prevent the buyer from rejecting the rest of the goods. This provision gives rise to the following possibilities. The buyer may:

• accept all the conforming goods and reject all the non-conforming goods;
• accept all the conforming goods and some of those not conforming, and reject the rest;
• reject all the goods;
• keep all the goods;
• keep most of the goods, rejecting the most defective.

For instance, if a buyer purchased 100 tiles, and found that 40 were defective, they will be able to retain the 60 and reject the 40; or retain the 60 and some of the 40 and reject the rest. They will also be entitled to reject all 100.

These provisions apply unless there is a contrary intention contained, expressly or by implication, in the contract.

Where rejection is unreasonable

The 1994 Act also took away the right to reject in certain cases where the exercise of the right to reject would be unreasonable.

Insignificant breaches may prevent rejection

The position now, except in cases where the buyer is a consumer (see above), is that where there is a right to reject because of breach of the provisions as to description, quality and fitness for purpose (see above), and the breach is so slight that it would be unreasonable to reject, the buyer is limited to a claim in damages and may not reject the goods. These provisions will not apply if a contrary intention, expressly or by implication, appears in the contract. The Act also puts on the seller the burden of showing that it would be unreasonable to allow rejection.

The foregoing amendments apply not just to contracts of sale, but also to contracts governed by the Supply of Goods (Implied Terms) Act 1973 (see above) and contracts relating to the transfer of property or of hire within the Supply of Goods and Services Act 1982 (see above).

Shortfalls and excesses

Parallel provisions apply when more goods, or fewer goods, than were ordered are delivered. Under the Sale of Goods Act, the buyer has the right, where the seller delivers less than the contract quantity, to reject them. The amendment, which applies only to non-consumer sales (see above) states that this right to reject is lost if the shortfall is so slight that rejection would be unreasonable.

The Sale of Goods Act also states that if the seller delivers more than they should, then the buyer may accept the contract quantity, or they may reject all that have been delivered.

Under the amendment, applying again only to non-consumer sales (see above), the buyer is not able to reject the whole if the excess is so slight that rejection would be unreasonable. They will still be able to reject the excess, however, even though this may be slight. It is for the seller to show that the shortfall or excess is slight.

These provisions as to shortfalls and excesses apply only to contracts within the 1979 Act (see above).

Measure of damages

Buyer entitled to loss contemplated as a result of breach

It is laid down in the Sale of Goods and at common law (see *Hadley* v *Baxendale* (1854)) that a buyer is entitled to compensation for such loss arising from the breach of contract as was contemplated by the seller as the probable result of the breach. Since this is also laid down at common law, this principle will also apply to contracts within the Supply of Goods (Implied Terms) Act 1973 (see above) and contracts within the Supply of Goods and Services Act 1982 (see above).

> ## Case example
> ### *Parsons (Livestock) Ltd* v *Uttley, Ingham & Co. Ltd* (1978)
> The sellers sold a pig hopper. When installing it, they left the ventilator closed with the result that the pig feed became mouldy. The animals became ill, triggering off a serious illness. The value of the affected animals was in the region of £10 000. It was held that, although the extent of the loss could not have been contemplated, the seller could still have reasonably expected that illness would occur, so he was liable for the full extent of the loss.

Case example
Re *Hall and Pim's Arbitration* (1928)
Sellers sold corn which was then sold and resold down a line of buyers and sellers. Since it was known that the corn would be resold, the sellers who failed to deliver were liable for loss of resale profits.

The buyer is, however, under a duty to take all reasonable steps to mitigate their loss. They cannot just do nothing and allow the damages to multiply at the seller's expense.

Case example
***Payzu Ltd v Saunders* (1919)**
Under a contract to deliver goods by instalments, the buyers failed to make punctual payment for the first instalment. The seller regarded this as repudiation of the contract, but offered further deliveries at the contract price for cash. This offer was rejected. The price of the goods rose and the buyers sued for breach.

It was held that the seller was liable in damages because the buyer's late payment did not permit him to treat the contract as repudiated. On the other hand, it was also held that the buyer should have mitigated his loss by accepting the seller's offer of delivery in return for cash. This meant that the buyer's damages were not the difference between the contract and the market prices, but the loss which he would have incurred had the seller's offer been accepted.

Specific performance

A buyer does not have a right to an order from the court compelling the seller to perform the contract. The court has an absolute discretion and will not generally grant an order where damages will be an adequate remedy.

The buyer can ask the court to order performance of the contract

---

Case example
***Societe des Industries Metallurgiques SA v Bronx Engineering Co. Ltd* (1975)**
The court refused to order a seller to delivery of a machine, although it was over 220 tonnes in weight, cost some £270 000, and could only be bought in the market with a 9 to 12 months' delivery date.

Case example
***Sky Petroleum Ltd v VIP Petroleum Ltd* (1974)**
A buyer sought specific performance of a contract under which the seller had agreed to supply all its requirements for 10 years. Because of the unusual state of the oil market at the time the order was sought, damages would not be adequate compensation for failure to deliver and specific performance was awarded.

Review questions

1 On breach of condition, what are a buyer's basic remedies?
2 Under what circumstances may a buyer lose the right to reject?
3 What acts have been specified by the Sale and Supply of Goods Act 1994 as not of themselves amounting to acceptance?
4 In what circumstances will the fact that a breach is slight deprive the buyer of rights of rejection?
5 In what circumstances will a court order the seller to perform the contract?

The seller's remedies

Seller has rights to sue for price or claim damages

If the property in the goods has passed (see above), this means that they belong to the buyer. The seller in such circumstances is given the right under s. 49(1) of the Sale of Goods Act to sue for the price, but not to the return of the goods. This reflects the common law and so also applies to other contracts outside the Sale of Goods Act where property has passed (see above). Section 49(2), which would also reflect the common law, also gives the seller a right to sue for the price, regardless of whether property has passed, if a day has been set for payment and that day has passed. Because property has not passed, though, the seller is alternatively allowed to sue for return of the goods or damages for non-acceptance (see below).

Measure of damages

Section 50 of the Sale of Goods Act provides that the seller can sue for the loss naturally arising from the breach, which will normally be the loss suffered if the goods have to be sold in the market for less than the buyer would have paid. This reflects the common law, so the position will be the same for those contracts not governed by the Sale of Goods Act.

Unpaid seller has certain rights over goods

Rights over the goods

Lien

Under s. 41 of the Sale of Goods Act 1979, the seller has the right to keep possession of the contract goods if unpaid. When payment is made, they must release the goods. The seller loses the right to this lien if they deliver the goods to a carrier for transmission to the buyer without reserving a right of disposal; if the buyer or their agent lawfully obtains possession of the goods; or if the seller themselves waive their lien. The exercise of a lien does not of itself terminate the contract.

Stoppage in transit

The 1979 Act gives the seller the right to stop the goods in transit, but this is only so where the buyer has ceased to pay their debts in the ordinary course of business, or is unable to pay their debts as they fall due. The seller may exercise their right to stop the goods by taking possession or by giving notice to the carrier. On being given notice, the carrier must redeliver according to the seller's directions, but at the seller's expense. The exercise of the right to stop the goods does not of itself put an end to the contract. The right to stop the goods comes to an end when the transit itself comes to an end. Under the Act, this will occur when: the buyer or their agent takes possession from the carrier; the buyer or their agent takes possession before the transit has ended; if, after arrival of the goods at their due destination, the carrier or their agent wrongly refuses to deliver to the buyer or their agent; if the carrier acknowledges that they hold on behalf of the buyer but retain the goods after they have reached their destination; or if the goods, in certain circumstances, are delivered to the master of a ship chartered to the buyer. If the goods are rejected by the buyer and the carrier retains possession, the transit is not at an end even if the seller has declined to take the goods back. The Act also provides that, if part of the goods has been delivered to the buyer, the right to stop in transit remains in relation to the balance, unless the circumstances show an agreement to give up possession of all of the goods.

Resale

The Sale of Goods Act gives the seller the right to resell the contract goods in these cases: where such a right was expressly given in the contract; where the goods are perishable; and where the seller gives the buyer notice of their intention to resell and the buyer does not tender the price within a reasonable time.

Case example
***Ward* v *Bignall* (1967)**

The buyer purchased two cars. He put down a deposit but subsequently refused to pay the balance. He was told that, if the full price were not paid by a certain date, the cars would be resold. Only one of them was resold. The seller claimed the balance of the purchase price after giving an allowance for the deposit and the one resale. This was refused since it was held that the resale of the one car had rescinded the entire contract. The seller was instead entitled to damages based on the total contract price minus the deposit and the amount realized on the one resale, less also an agreed value for the car which had not been resold.

These provisions as to lien, stoppage and resale are based on the common law and will apply to contracts within the Supply of Goods (Implied Terms) Act 1973 and the Supply of Goods and Services Act 1982 (see above).

Review questions

1 Under what circumstances may a seller sue for the contract price?
2 Give an account of the rights which the seller has over the contract goods.
3 On what basis will a seller's damages for breach of contract be estimated?

Chapter summary

- The law relating to the sale and supply of goods is a branch of the law of contract, but much of it has been codified in legislation.
- Contracts involving the sale or supply of goods are, depending on the precise nature of the contract, dealt with by different enactments, though the legal requirements are essentially the same in each case.
- Obligations are imposed by legislation on sellers as to title, description, quality and fitness.
- Obligations are also imposed on those who provide services.
- Controls are imposed over the exclusion of these obligations, principally by use of the reasonableness test.
- A number of rules are laid down as to when the ownership in goods passes to the buyer.
- Risk normally passes with ownership.
- Retention of title clauses are often used to give the seller greater security.
- A seller who sells goods without authority may nonetheless be able in specified circumstances to pass a good title to a buyer.
- On a breach by a seller, the buyer has rights to damages and, in some cases, to rejection, though this latter can be lost through acceptance of the goods.
- A buyer may also lose the right to reject where the breach is a trivial one.
- The seller may, in certain circumstances, sue for the price, or claim damages. The seller also has a number of rights in relation to the goods.

United Kingdom application

The provisions of this chapter generally apply throughout the United Kingdom, though it should be noted that, in a fairly restricted area, the law in Scotland can differ.

Case study exercise

A, a car dealer, sells a second-hand car to B, who is a private buyer buying for personal and domestic use. B cannot take delivery straightaway, and the car is left with A overnight. Before B comes in the morning, the car is slightly damaged by an intruder. B does not notice this and takes the car away. Almost straight away, B realizes that the car is not exactly as he was expecting. The steering wheel squeaks, the glove box will not stay shut, the radio works intermittently, and the hub caps keep falling off. He asks A to attend to these problems, as well as to the damage which he has now noticed, which A does. However, the problems persist and B drives back to A's garage and announces that he has had enough and wants a return of the purchase price and damages.

A points to the written contract between them, stressing that B signed it, and that one clause reads as follows: 'The buyer hereby agrees that this car is subject to no terms express or implied by or under any legislation.'

Student task

Consider the above sequence events, bearing in mind in particular the legislative provisions as to the quality of goods, the passing of risk, exclusion clauses and a buyer's rights on breach.

Discussion questions

1 To what extent is it true to say that, although the treatment of various types of contracts relating to goods are dealt with in different Acts of Parliament, the treatment of such contracts is broadly the same?
2 The general rule is that a seller can only give such title as they themselves possess or as they are authorized to pass. To what extent is it true to say that the number of exceptions virtually does away with this rule?
3 To what extent has the notion of freedom of contract been undermined by the Unfair Contract Terms Act 1977 and the Unfair Terms in Consumer Contracts Regulations 1994?
4 Given that the enactments considered in this chapter distinguish in some important areas between contracts with consumers and those with businesses, has the time come for a separate Consumer Sales Act?

Further reading

The Sale of Goods (9th edn), Atiyah (1995), Pitman Publishing.
This is probably the leading textbook on the Sale of Goods Act and is generally recommended reading.
The Supply of Goods and Services Act 1982, Lawson (1982), FT Law and Tax.
Deals only with the 1982 Act.
Exclusion Clauses and Unfair Contract Terms (4th edn), Lawson (1995), FT Law and Tax.
See generally Chapters 8 to 10.

4 Agency

Introduction

The appointment of an agent is one of the most common forms of commercial arrangement entered into between business enterprises. You may appoint others to work on your behalf because you may be unable to perform the task required because you lack the necessary level of expertise; alternatively you may find the practice of appointing others more effective in terms of time and cost than personally performing them.

However, the circumstances which give rise to the arrangement and the precise nature of the relationship created are many and varied. A considerable body of case law concerning the relationship of principal and agent has been developed by the English courts over many years. At the heart of the relationship is *trust*. The principal must trust that the agent will work in their (the principal's) best interest. If the agent abuses that trust then the principal could suffer loss of money, opportunity and reputation. Also the agent must trust that the principal will pay them for their efforts.

In addition to the common law, commercial agents are now subject to the Directive on Commercial Agents and also are liable under domestic and European Union (EU) competition law.

Agency law is based on contractual principles. If contract law has been mastered to a good level of understanding then large amounts of agency law will tend to fall into place. In contract law the normal position is that one party will make a contract directly with another, e.g.

direct contractual relationship

With agency there is a tripartite arrangement whereby an intermediary (the agent) is used to put their employer (the principal) into a contractual relationship with another (the third party), e.g.

indirect contractual relationship

As far as contractual capacity is concerned, clearly both the principal and third party must have contractual capacity when the contract is created. However, as the agent is not a contractual party it is not necessary that he or she has contractual capacity. Therefore, while commercially dangerous it is legally possible to have a minor acting as an agent!

Objectives

The purpose of this chapter is to provide a framework on which agency principles may be placed. These principles have been developed largely to protect the principal against agents who abuse their position for their own advantage. While agency law has been almost exclusively common law in origin, now, under the Commercial Agents Regulations 1993, a major European dimension aspect has been introduced.

Key concepts

- The concept of agency
- The methods which create an agency relationship
- The duties and obligations of the principal and agent
- The concept of the undisclosed principal
- The termination of the agency appointment
- The effect on agency of the Commercial Agents Regulations 1993.

Definition of *an agent or agency*

Various writers have provided definitions of agents or agency. One authoritative writer said that:

The principle–agent relationship is a contractual one

> Agency is the relationship that exists between two persons where one, called the agent, is considered in law to represent the other, called the principal, in such a way as to be able to affect the principal's legal position in respect of strangers to the relationship by the making of contracts or the disposition of property.
>
> Fridman, *The Law of Agency*, 1990

A judicial definition is:

> [an agent is] a person invested with a legal power to alter his principal's legal relations with third parties
>
> *Towle* v *White* [1873]

Therefore, an agent is invested with a legal power to alter their principal's legal relations with a third party. A wider definition is now provided by the Directive on Commercial Agents. Under this a *commercial* agent (not a *professional* agent) is a person:

> who has continuing authority to *negotiate* the sale or the purchase of goods on behalf of another person called the principal.

Under English agency law the determining characteristic of an agent was that they had to have the authority to alter their principal's legal relations, whereas the Directive says that anyone with the authority to negotiate, without necessarily establishing a legal relationship, will be an agent.

The reason why it is useful to have a definition of agent and agency is that it establishes the liability of the parties to each other. Where both deal with each other as principals then each will be directly liable to the other for any breaches that occur. But if one acts as an agent then normally they will, once the contract has been concluded, 'drop out' and bear no personal liability on the contract they have helped to create. The injured party will then have to seek out the principal for compensation.

Although the term is commonly used commercially not all who call themselves agents are in fact agents in law. In law the term agent has a precise meaning which, from the discussion above, is a person who acts with their principal's authority to bring about a contract between the principal and the third party. A motor distributor proclaiming themselves agents for the Ford Motor Company are not agents in law as they merely buy in goods from a supplier for the purpose of resale. The distributor does not create a contract between the customer and the Ford Motor Company but contracts in their own right. Similarly with estate agents. While there are always possible exceptions, such as where an estate agent is employed to manage property so that they are authorized, on the landlord's behalf, to engage workers to maintain the property, the normal position is that an estate agent does not actually contract for their client but merely carries out instructions to locate a buyer (*Lamb & Sons* v *Goring Building Company* (1932)).

The term agent is frequently used in a commercial not legal sense

Review questions

Without rereading the definition section of this chapter:

1 How would you define the agency relationship?
2 Is a travel agent a true agent in law?
3 If yes, then whose agent is the travel agent, the holiday company or the customer?

Main types of agent

1 *Auctioneers* A person who is engaged to sell property and conduct sales or auctions. They are agents for the vendor before and after a sale, but may also in certain circumstances be the agent for the purchaser after the sale.
2 *Banker* The bank is an agent of the customer in relation to paying out and receiving proceeds on cheques.
3 *Broker* An intermediary between contracting parties who has no possession of a principal's goods and only dealing in debit and credit notes between the vendor and purchaser. The term broker is a portmanteau one in that there are a number of different brokers, e.g. commodity broker, credit-broker, insurance-broker, stockbroker, etc. Increasingly, brokers have been subject to statutory regulation, e.g. Consumer Credit Act 1974; Insurance Brokers Act 1977 and the Financial Services Act 1987.
4 *Cohabiting woman* An implied agent of a male cohabiting partner unless he advertises otherwise. There is no need for a legally married relationship to exist, only that the parties appear to be living together as husband and wife.
5 *Company director* They are agents of the company when acting as part of a board of directors but may also, in certain circumstances, bind the company when acting alone.
6 *Del-credere* One who undertakes that clients (third parties) introduced by them will pay

Such an agent effectively acts as a guarantor for the third party for the goods sold. If they do not pay then the principal may enforce the promise against the *del-credere* agent. As they incur a higher risk they correspondingly charge a higher commission. It must be appreciated that only liability for non-payment by the third party is accepted. The practice of using this type of agent arose in the export trade where frequently manufacturers were uncertain of the creditworthiness of foreign buyers.

7 *Factor (mercantile)* Unlike brokers they have possession or control of goods and may in the customary course of their business buy, sell, pledge or insure them. They are governed by the Factors Act 1890.

8 *Partners* Each partner is an implied agent of the partnership as a whole as well as their other fellow partners in respect to normal activities of the firm (s. 5, Partnership Act 1890).

There are two commonly termed agents who are not in fact legal agents. These are:

The court will ignore the 'label' the parties have afixed

1 *Canvassing agent (Marketing agent)* Their authority does not extend to creating a binding contract on behalf of their principal but is limited to introducing customers. Their authority may, however, allow them to make representations about goods or services offered by their 'principal' and in this respect the 'principal' will be bound.

2 *Commission agent* Here the principal will appoint a person (termed agent) to deal on their behalf but on the understanding that when dealing with third parties they deal in their own name and not that of the principal. Therefore, third parties have no direct right of action against the principal. The contract between the principal and agent is analogous to an agency one, but as the agent does not bring their principal into a contractual relationship with the third party they are not a true agent but a quasi one.

Classes of agent

These may be divided into five categories:

General agents are the commonest class

1 *General* Those having authority to carry out all business of a certain kind for their principal. A partner is a general agent of their firm.

2 *Special* Those having limited authority for a particular purpose. A bank is a special agent for the clearing of customer cheques.

3 *Universal* Those who carry on all the affairs of their principal. Any transaction the principal can enter into the universal agent will also be able to enter into on their behalf. This class of agent is rare as principals are naturally reluctant to give an agent such sweeping authority.

4 *Commercial* The EU Directive on Commercial Agents 1986 defines a commercial agent as:

> a self employed intermediary who has continuing authority to negotiate the sale or purchase of goods on behalf of another person or to negotiate and conclude the sale or purchase of goods on behalf of and in the name of the principal.

5 *Professional* This class is composed of those who do not come under the Directive as being commercial agents. They do not deal in goods but provide services such as insurance, books, solicitors, travel agents, etc.

Creation of the agent's authority

The acts of an agent can only bind the principal if the agent has the authority to act. The authority which is possessed by an agent may arise in the ways outlined below.

Express authority

The general rule is that no particular formalities are required. The appointment may be created orally or in writing. Exceptions are where the appointment must be in writing. An example of the need for a written appointment is where the agent is required to create or dispose of an interest in land, then under s. 53(1) and s. 54 Law of Property Act 1925 the agents own appointment must be in writing. Should the agent be required to execute a deed then they must have been themselves appointed by deed (*Berkeley* v *Hardy* (1826)) unless the principal was present and consented to the agent entering into the deed (*Ball* v *Dunstonville* (1791)).

Increasingly, where the elderly appoint an agent to look after their affairs they do so by giving a 'power of attorney' to the agent so that he or she can act for them. The power of attorney formerly had to be given under seal (s.1 Powers of Attorney Act 1971), but now a signed and witnessed document will do (s.1 Schedule 1, Law of Property (Miscellaneous) Act 1989); should the donor want the power of attorney to continue after loss of mental capacity then the procedure given in ss 1 and 2 the Enduring Powers of Attorney Act 1985 must be followed.

Any ambiguity in the appointment may be read against the principal

Where the express appointment is not clear as to the extent of the agent's authority a court may be prepared to give the benefit of the doubt to the agent.

> ## Case example
> ### *Ireland* v *Livingston* (1872)
> L wrote to I asking that he ship 500 tons of sugar. The letter said that to get the best price plus or minus 50 tons would be suitable. I sent 400 tons in one consignment intending to send the rest later. L refused to accept the 400 tons and cancelled the later delivery. The House of Lords said that where the written appointment was ambiguous, provided the agent acts in good faith and follows a reasonable interpretation of the document of appointment then he will be regarded as acting within his actual authority.

However, the courts are increasingly less willing to say that an agent is able to interpret the agency contract because, with modern methods of communication, the reasonable course of action is for the agent to contact the principal for clarification (see *European Asian Bank AG* v *Punjab and Sind Bank (NZ)* (1983)).

Implied authority

Here the court will look at the perceived intentions of the parties. This commonly may be based upon their conduct.

The courts will use an objective approach

Case example
Hely-Hutchinson v *Bray Head Ltd* (1967)

The chairman of a limited company, although never officially appointed, acted as managing director and made a number of contracts on behalf of the company. The board of directors never protested these contracts. One contract made by the chairman was to guarantee a debt for a third party.

The Court of Appeal held that the board of directors, by allowing the chairman to act as managing director, had impliedly authorized him to enter into the contract. The company was therefore bound by the guarantee given.

Implied authority arises from the circumstances. For convenience it may be divided into:

Customary authority

This is derived from market practice or business usage.

Case example
Scott & Horton v *Godfrey* (1901)

In this case the custom of the stock exchange allowed stockbrokers to act as agents simultaneously for a number of principals when buying shares on their behalf from one seller.

Traditionally, the courts have always been reluctant to be too willing to recognize trade customs in order that customary authority of an agent may be established. To do so the evidence must be particularly strong.

The guidelines of Ungoed-Thomas LJ in *Cuncliffe-Owen* v *Teather & Greenwood* (1967) need be followed. These were that the usage:

- must be certain in that it is clearly established;
- must be notorious in that it is so well known in the market that it allegedly exists that those who conduct business in that market contract with the usage as an 'implied term';
- must be reasonable.

Case example
Robinson v *Mollett* (1874)

It was alleged that there was a trade custom in the London area to allow a market which enabled agents in that market to buy in bulk in their 'own name' in order to satisfy their principals orders. This purported custom was said to be unreasonable as it went against the very basis of the agent–principal relationship in that the 'agent' was not an intermediary to put the principal into a contractual relationship with a third party but was merely selling goods directly himself.

Usual authority

All persons within a certain class will be deemed to be an agent

This may be based on the status or position a person occupies. As, overwhelmingly, people with such status or in such a position are usually agents, the law will say that everyone with that status or position is to be treated, when acting in the normal scope of their duties, as being an agent. Examples are a company secretary while buying office equipment, a solicitor acting for a client, and a shop manager making a refund to a customer.

> ## Case example
> ### *Panorama Development Ltd* v *Fidelis Furnishing Fabrics Ltd* (1971)
> A company secretary hired Rolls-Royce limousines in his company's name but for his own personal use. On discovery the company refused to pay for the hire cars. The Court of Appeal held that a person occupying the position of a company secretary could be expected to have the authority to hire luxury cars then usual authority would apply and the company would in consequence be liable.

Whether or not it is reasonable for a third party to rely on the usual authority of an agent is dependent on:

- the kind of business carried on by the principal;
- the kind of status or position occupied by the agent;
- whether or not there are established business practices which will map out what an office-holder can be expected to do.

In *British Bank of the Middle East* v *Sun Life Assurance Company of Canada (UK) Ltd* (1983), the House of Lords found that a branch manager of an insurance company with branches throughout the UK did not have usual authority to make certain contracts because there was no established business practice of what contracts such a manager could make.

But what if the authority of the agent is limited?

Even though a principal may expressly prohibit their agent from carrying out certain tasks, the principal may still be liable to the third party where the agent breaks the prohibition.

The law is anxious to protect innocent third parties

> ## Case example
> ### *Watteau* v *Fenwick* (1893)
> Humble owned a public house which he sold to Fenwick. After the sale Humble remained at the public house as a manager but Fenwick expressly told him never to order cigars. Fenwick broke the prohibition and ordered cigars on credit from Watteau. On Fenwick's refusal to pay, Watteau successfully sued him for the value of the cigars. It was said to be reasonable for an innocent third party to rely on the authority usually held by a person with the status of a public house manager to order bar supplies.

The *Watteau* v *Fenwick* case has a problem attached to it. This problem will be discussed at the end of Apparent authority.

For liability to attach to the principal, even though they have tried by a prohibition to limit their agent's authority, it is necessary that:

- the prohibited act is reasonably incidental to the duties the agent is employed to carry out
- that the third party was unaware that the agent had been prohibited from doing that act.

Apparent or ostensible authority (or agency by estoppel)

A principal holds out an 'agent' at own risk

This method of creating an agency relationship is based on promissory estoppel. It is where the principal holds out to the third party that the agent has the necessary authority to act for them. Because of the principal's words, conduct or omission it appears to the third party that the agent holds such authority and the third party relies on it. The conditions required were set out in *Rama Corporation Ltd* v *Proved Tin and General Investments Ltd* (1952) by Slade J:

- a representation is made by the principal to the third party
- the third party relies on this representation, and
- the third party as a consequence of his reliance alters his position.

Where the above conditions apply then the principal will be estopped (that is prevented) from alleging that the 'agent' had the necessary authority.

Apparent authority may apply even though there is no formal principal–agent relationship in existence. More commonly it applies where the principal has restricted the agent, such as by limiting them only to making contracts up to, say, £50 000, but they have failed to inform the third party of the limitation, therefore if the agent contracts in excess of £50 000 the third party may claim that apparently to them the agent had the necessary authority to make a contract for that amount. All that is required is that the principal held out (that is made a representation) to the third party that the 'agent' did have authority to act for them and that the third party had relied on this holding out. Holding out can be by word or conduct e.g. the representation can be express or implied.

> ### Case example
> ### *Summers* v *Salomon* (1857)
> Salomon owned a jewellery shop and employed a manager to run it. The established practice was that the manager would order goods for the shop on credit which Salomon later paid for. Summers was a regular supplier of these goods. Subsequently the manager was given notice and without telling Summers that he had given up his agency appointment ordered goods from him in Salomon's name and then absconded with them. It was held that a representation could be implied from previous dealings that the manager continued to appear to be Salomon's agent so that Salomon was liable to Summers for the value of the goods.

The most influential case on apparent authority is *Freeman and Lockyer* v *Bucklehurst Park Properties (Mangal) Ltd* (1964). In the Court of Appeal, Diplock LJ gave what has become the definitive explanation of apparent authority. (NB: the word 'contractor' is used as an alternative to third party.)

An 'apparent' or 'ostensible' authority, on the other hand, is a legal relationship between the principal and the contractor or created by the representation, made by the principal to the contractor, intended to be and in fact acted on by the contractor, that the agent has authority to enter on behalf of the principal into a contract of a kind within the scope of the 'apparent' authority, so as to render the principal liable to perform any obligations imposed on him by such contract. To the relationship so created the agent is a stranger. He need not be (although he generally is) aware of the existence of the representation. The representation, when acted on by the contractor by entering into a contract with the agent, operates as an estoppel, preventing the principal, from asserting that he is not bound by the contract. It is irrelevant whether the agent had actual authority to enter into the contract.

Lord Keith in *Armagas Ltd* v *Mundogas SA, The Ocean Frost* (1986), restated Diplock's general principle as:

Ostensible authority comes about where the principle, by words or conduct, has represented that the agent has the requisite actual authority, and the party dealing with him in reliance on that representation. The principal in these circumstances is estopped from denying that actual authority existed.

Apparent authority can never arise where the third party knows that the agent's authority is limited to such an extent that the agent does not in fact have the necessary authority. Here the third party will be unable to say that when entering into a transaction he relied upon the principal's representation.

Apparent authority and usual authority

The distinction between these two principles is that the apparent authority is based on the conduct of the principal and its effect on the third party, whereas with usual authority the agency arises from an examination of the contract of agency in relation to business practice so that the agent obtains implied powers derived from his status or position. The similarities between these two principles are:

- in both a principal may be liable for the acts of an agent even though the agent never had the principal's real authority;
- in both the principal makes a representation to the third party which is relied upon. In apparent authority it is a representation by words or conduct, whereas in usual authority the representation takes the form of appointing an agent with a certain status or position so that the third party may reasonably assume that the agent holds the principal's authority.

These similarities have led to difficulties. On occasions judges have used language to describe usual authority which closely resembles apparent authority. Ideally it would be convenient to delete usual authority and have apparent authority covering all agency by representation. The problem with this approach is *Watteau* v *Fenwick* (1893), the case invariably used to illustrate usual authority. In it the principal, Fenwick, had not been disclosed by the agent, Humble, to the third party, Watteau. For apparent authority to apply the principal *must* be disclosed. For this reason it seems that not all representational circumstances can be fitted into apparent authority and that another category, usual authority, is required. *Watteau* v *Fenwick* is unsatisfactory in that it states that the appointment of a person with a certain status or position that carries with it usual powers will bind the principal to contracts made within these usual powers even though the third party did not know of the agency aspect. Because agency is essentially a tripartite arrangement, *Watteau* v *Fenwick* is said to be incorrectly decided as *de facto* the third party contracted only with the 'agent'. While the case has not been expressly overruled, Bingham LJ in *Rhodian River Shipping Co.* v *Halla Maritime Corporation* (1984) said that it is a 'case which a court should be wary of applying'.

Inconsistency of judicial language has caused problems

Review question

Explain the difference, if any, between usual and apparent authority of an agent.

Agency by operation of law

Agency by imposition of law may arise in three ways: co-habitation; necessity; and statue. The parties intentions are irrelevant.

Co-habitation

Co-habitation is now largely a historical relic

Agency by co-habitation is now dated and should be interred. However, at common law where a couple are living together in a household as husband and wife, the wife is presumed to be her husband's agent in relation to pledging his credit to obtain necessaries in order to support their lifestyle. It must be established that the creditor gave credit to the wife as her husband's agent and did not give it to her personally. If personally given then agency by co-habitation does not apply.

The rule that a deserted wife could make her husband responsible for contracts of necessaries was abolished by s. 41 Matrimonial Proceedings and Property Act 1970.

The husband may rebut the presumption that his wife is his agent by proving one of the following:

- that he had expressly told her not to pledge his credit;
- that he had made his wife a satisfactory allowance so that she did not need to pledge his credit;
- that the goods obtained were not necessaries but luxury items;
- that he had expressly told the supplier not to give his wife any credit.

> ## Case example
> ### *Miss Gray Ltd* v *Earl Cathcast* (1922)
> A 'wife' obtained clothes to the value of £215 by pledging her 'husband's' credit. The husband refused to pay and proved that he gave an annual allowance of £960.
> The husband had rebutted the presumption of agency by co-habitation.

Necessity

Agency by necessity operates within narrow limits

The law is reluctant to allow a stranger to deal with the property of another but circumstances may arise where it is deemed necessary to allow a person charged with the task of looking after another person's goods (known as a bailee) to make contracts on behalf of a principal although the bailee had no actual authority whatsoever.

Historically, agency of necessity occurred where a vessel suffered storm damage and put into a foreign port for emergency repairs. The captain, on behalf of the owner, would authorize the repairs and the third party (the repairer) would later claim from the shipowner.

For agency of necessity to apply four conditions must be satisfied:

1 It was impossible for the agent (bailee) to communicate with the principal. If the intending agent can obtain instructions from the principal then they must attempt to do so. A failure to try to contact the principal will mean that agency of necessity cannot arise.

Case example
Spinger v Great Western Railway (1921)

S contracted with the GWR for a cargo of tomatoes to be transported from Jersey to Weymouth by ship and then onto London by rail. On arrival at Weymouth the vessel was delayed in unloading due to a dock strike. When finally unloaded, the GWR, fearing that the tomatoes would soon perish, sold the cargo locally making no attempt to contact S for instructions.

Held: The GWR had to compensate S for the difference in price between the Weymouth and higher Metropolitan price.

This condition was reaffirmed as still being required by the Court of Appeal in the *Choko Star* (1990).

As a result of better communications agency of necessity now seldom occurs.

2   There must be a commercial necessity. A necessity may be equated to an emergency.

Case example
Sachs v Miklos (1948)

M had generously agreed to store some of S's furniture. Much later he himself needed the storage space but was unable to contact S to tell him to remove the furniture. M then sold the furniture claiming to do so as the agent of S.

The Court of Appeal said that no commercial emergency was present.

---

3   The 'agent' must have acted in the interests of his or her principal.

Case example
Prager v Blatspiel (1924)

B bought skins in Romania as the agent of P but because of World War I was unable to send them to P. Being unable to contact P, B, claiming to be an agent of necessity, sold the skins before the war ended.

B had not acted in P's interest for he could have stored the skins and delivered them when the war had ended.

---

4   The actions taken by the agent must in all the circumstances have been reasonable.

Case example
Great Northern Railway v Swaffield (1874)

S sent a horse by the GNR. On arrival at the delivery station there was no one there to collect the horse. The GNR sent it to a local livery stable but S later refused to pay the charges.

GNR's conduct had been reasonable – they could not let the horse starve.

Statute

The finance company is deemed to be the principal

1 *S. 56(2) Consumer Credit Act 1974*   During negotiations leading to a consumer credit agreement a negotiator is deemed to be the creditor's agent. An example is a car dealer who arranges, as a credit broker, the hire purchase agreement between a consumer and the finance company; the car dealer is deemed to be the agent of the finance company so that the finance company as principal will be liable for any misstatements the dealer makes.

   Similarly, covered by s. 56(2) is a supplier who negotiates with a consumer for goods which the consumer will pay for by credit tokens, e.g. Visa or Mastercard. Again the supplier is deemed to be the agent of the creditor – credit token company.

2 *S. 5 Partnership Act 1890*   All general partners are agents of both the firm and of one another in relation to the normal business of the firm. Therefore, a partner who acts within their normal duties will bind the firm.

Ratification (or subsequent authority)

A principal may adopt an agent's unauthorized act

If an agent contracts with a third party as an agent of a principal but without the principal's authority, the principal can subsequently adopt the transaction as their own, i.e. they can ratify it. However, the principal must have:

- full knowledge of the circumstances or an intention to ratify whatever the facts are;
- a free choice as to whether to ratify or not.

The effect of ratification is retrospective, therefore the contract takes place when the agent enters into the transaction not when the principal gives their authority.

Case example
Bolton Partners v *Lambert* (1889)

An agent purportedly accepted an offer from Lambert to buy property belonging to his principal (Bolton), although the agent had no authority to make such a contract. Lambert later tried to withdraw his offer claiming that since Bolton, as principal, had never personally accepted the offer no contract existed. Bolton ratified his agent's actions and demanded that Lambert honour the contract.

   The Court of Appeal held that Bolton's ratification related to the time when the agent accepted the offer and not to the date of ratification. Therefore Lambert's attempted withdrawal was too late.

   Where the third party knows that the agent lacks authority then the presumption is that the purported contract has been made 'subject to ratification' so that ratification will only be effective at the time the contract is actually notified by the principal. Ratification may be either express or implied.

Case example
Waithman v *Wakefield* (1897)

A wife bought non-necessary goods. Her husband kept them, refusing to return them to the seller. It was said that his conduct was an implied ratification of his wife's acts so that he was obligated to pay for them.

The concept of ratification is relatively easy. However, before it can apply four rules need to be satisfied:

1   The agent must inform the third party that they are acting as an agent. Where the agency is undisclosed then the principal cannot ratify. Disclosure of the principal can be by naming them or, alternatively, describing them. It is not enough merely for the agent to say 'I am acting as an agent.'

Case example
***Keighley, Maxstead & Co. v Durant* (1901)**

Roberts, authorized by Keighley Maxstead to buy wheat at a stipulated price, exceeded his authority and bought at a higher price from Durant. Roberts bought in his own name but did intend the purchase to be for Keighley Maxstead. Keighley Maxstead told Roberts that he would take the wheat at the purchase price but later refused to accept delivery.

Keighley Maxstead was not liable to Durant as they could not as an undisclosed principal ratify his action.

---

2   The principal must have been in existence when the act was done. This rule relates to where limited companies are being created and a promoter purports to act on behalf of the uncreated company before registration procedures have been completed. The standard example is *Kelner* v *Baxter* (1866), where a contract to buy wine on behalf of a company yet to be registered could not subsequently be ratified by the company after its actual registration. Now the position is dealt with by statute.

S.36 (c) Companies Act 1985

> Where a contract purports to be made by a company, or by a person as agent for a company, at a time when the company has not been formed, then subject to any agreement to the contrary, the contract has effect as one entered into by the person purporting to act for the company … and he is personally liable on the contract.

3   The principal must have contractual capacity when the act was done as well as at the time of ratification.
    In *Boston Deep Sea Fishing and Ice Co. Ltd* v *Farnham* (1957), the principal, at the date the contract was entered into by the agent, was an enemy alien. Therefore, the ratification was said to be invalid.
    Since the Minors' Contracts Act 1987, a minor, in reaching the age of majority, may ratify the indebtedness incurred while a minor.
4   Ratification must be within the time set or a reasonable time period. Reasonability will be dependent on the circumstances (Re *Portuguese Consolidated Copper Mines Ltd* (1890)).

In addition to the rules given above, a principal must now probably ratify the whole of the contract not part of it (*Suncrop Insurance & Finance* v *Milano Assicurazioni Spa* (1993)), although a much earlier case (*Harrisons & Crossfield Ltd* v *London & North Western Railway Co.* (1917)), said that part ratification was possible. A voidable act can be ratified (*Danish Mercantile Co.* v *Beaumont* (1951)), a void or illegal act cannot be per *Bedford Insurance Co. Ltd* v *Instituto*

Resserguros De Brazil (1984). Once ratification has taken place then the principal must pay the agent for the unauthorized act.

Review question

Laurel, a dealer in diamonds, was authorized by Hardy and Co. to purchase a quantity of gold. A maximum price was given but Laurel was unable to buy at this price. Therefore, Laurel bought at a higher price in his own name and afterwards Hardy and Co. agreed that the cost could be charged to their account.

Subsequently, being able to obtain diamonds elsewhere at a cheaper price, Hardy and Co. refuse to accept delivery and the seller has to sell elsewhere at a lower price. The seller sues both Laurel and Hardy and Co. for damages.

What, in your opinion, will be the likely outcome of the action? Provide reasons and citation for your response.

Duties of an agent

The legal duties imposed on an agent are demanding

A considerable range of duties are owed by the agent to their principal. These are:

An agent must obey the lawful instructions of their principal

Failure to do so will invariably mean the agent will be liable in a breach of contract action. Disobedience includes both acting outside of their actual authority as well as doing nothing at all.

> ### Case example
> ### *Turpin v Bilton* (1843)
> An agent was instructed to insure his principal's vessel but failed to do so. When the uninsured vessel was lost the agent had to compensate the principal.

The remedies available to a principal on his agent disobeying instructions were given by Lord Summer in *Christoforides* v *Terry* (1924). These are:

- a claim for damages for breach of contract;
- recovery of any profit which the agent may have made;
- a refusal to pay the agents remuneration or to give an indemnity.

An agent must work with ordinary skill and diligence

The standard of performance expected is that of the reasonable, average member of the trade or profession in question per *Blundell* v *Stephens* (1920). If the agent does not come from a recognized trade or profession then diligence may equal the agent having taken the same level of care as the principal would have done if acting for themselves (*Davis Ltd* v *Tooth & Co. Ltd* (1937)). If employed to buy and sell the agent must try to their utmost to obtain the best price. Any departure from this will be treated as being a breach of duties.

> **Case example**
> *Keppell* v *Wheeler* **(1927)**
> An estate agent told a potential buyer that a property he had been instructed to sell was already sold. The first buyer in fact had only signed an agreement 'subject to contract' so that the agent was legally still able to accept the higher offer from the second buyer. The agent was held liable to the principal (the vendor) for the difference in price between the first and second buyer.

A gratuitous agent (that is one acting without payment) will be liable for lack of skill or diligence not in contract but in the tort of negligence. The standard imposed is an objective one – that conduct which may reasonably be expected in all the circumstances.

An agent is able by agreement to exclude his own acts of negligence subject to the test of reasonability in the Unfair Contract Terms Act 1977. Some professional agents, e.g. solicitors, have to carry negligence liability insurance by law.

Agents may also be in breach of ss13 and 14 Supply of Goods and Services Act 1982. Section 13 – if a supplier is acting in the course of a business then there is an implied term that it will be provided with reasonable care and skill; s. 14 – the service is to be carried out within a reasonable time.

An agent owes a fiduciary duty to their principal

Because of the initial trust and confidence normally existing between the agent and principal, equity will make the agent subject to a number of fiduciary duties. These 'duties of loyalty' are intended to protect the principal from an agent who abuses their position. As these strict duties derive from equity it is not necessary that the principal and agent be in a contractual relationship; therefore, gratuitous agents are also subject to them. The fiduciary duties are:

In addition to common-law duties equity imposes fiduciary ones

1   *Delegation is not normally allowed*   This is because the relationship between the agent and principal is a personal one. Exceptions to the personal performance obligation where the agent is allowed to employ a sub-agent are.

(a)   Where the principal consented to the delegation when the agency relationship was created (*Quebec and Richmond Railway Co.* v *Quinn* (1858)).
(b)   Where it may be presumed from the circumstances that the agent was intended to be able to delegate (*De Bassche* v *Alt* (1878)).
(c)   Where delegation is the usual practice in the agent's trade or profession, e.g. a county solicitor is allowed to delegate complicated legal work to a specialist city solicitor (*Solley* v *Wood* (1852)).
(d)   Where an emergency occurs making personal performance impossible (*De Bassche* v *Alt* (1878)).
(e)   Where no special skill or confidence is required. The agents duties here will be purely ministerial (that is clerical) (*Allam & Co. Ltd* v *Europa Poster Services Ltd* (1968)).

Normally the principal will not have a contractual relationship with a sub-agent and so be unable to sue them for, say, poor performance. The principal can, however, sue the agent for appointing an incompetent sub-agent (*Balsamo* v *Medici & Another* (1984)).

2 *The agent must not abuse their position for personal benefit*   This is the 'no conflict of interest' rule. The fact that the principal does not lose financially or otherwise will make no difference.

Case example
Armstrong v _Jackson_ (1917)

A instructed his stockbroker (J) to buy shares in a certain company for him. J pretended to buy the shares on the open market but actually sold his own shares in the company to A. Although the price was the same as the open market J did not inform A of the exact source of the shares.

On later discovering the truth, A had the transactions set aside with J being ordered to repay all the sum paid by A for the shares.

In addition the agent must not, without authorization, disclose to anyone confidential information obtained while employed by the principal (*Faccenda Chicken Ltd* v *Fowler* (1986)). To avoid possible conflicts of interest the agent should make full disclosure to the principal.

Some agents, such as banks, may on occasions find it particularly difficult to avoid a charge of conflict of interest where one section of the undertaking will be engaged to give advice, etc., while another section may benefit from having the advice accepted and implemented, hence the corporate practice of having 'Chinese Walls' to deflect conflict of interest accusations.

3 *All profits must be handed over as well as all monies received*   Included in this duty of accounting is the requirement that the agent keep their own money and property separate from that of their principals. Should they not do so then the principal can claim it all. The principal can at any time demand that the agent produces proper accounts.

4 *There must be full and prompt disclosure of all material agency business*   Disclosure has to relate to knowledge that is likely to influence the principal in entering into the contract.

Case example
Heath v _Parkinson_ (1926)

P leased premises and instructed H to sell the outstanding period of the lease. P believed that the owner of the freehold would not allow the premises to be used for a tailoring business. H, knowing that several tailors would buy the lease, contacted the freeholder and got his consent to a tailoring business being carried on. This information was not disclosed to P who sold the lease for a lower sum than he would have done if H had disclosed the information.

H was not entitled to his commission as he had broken his duty of disclosure of agency business.

---

5 *The agent must not accept a secret commission (profit) or take a bribe*   In *Industries and General Mortgage Co. Ltd* v *Lewes* (1949), Slade J said a bribe was:

- the payment of a secret commission made by the third party to the principal's agent;
- knowing that the person receiving it was an agent;
- that the third party failed to disclose to the principal that they had made that payment to the agent.

A more modern case on bribes is *Arrangel Atlas Compania Naviera SA* v *Ishika Wajima-Harima Heavy Industries Co. Ltd (IHI)* (1990), where Leggatt J said a bribe was a commission or other inducement given by a third party to an agent and kept secret from the principal. The key factor is does it lead to a conflict of interest on the part of the agent?

Not all secret commissions will be interpreted as being unlawful.

Case example
Hippisley v *Knee Bros* (1905)

KB were auctioneers engaged by H. They paid for the printing of advertisements and received a trade discount from the printers which they kept for themselves, later saying that a trade custom allowed them to do so. H was charged the full cost of the printing and on discovering the discount refused to pay KB their agency commission.

The Court of Appeal held that KB were entitled to their commission as it related to the sale of the principal's goods and the secret profit did not affect the performance of the sale. However, KB were in breach of their duty not to make a secret profit and had to hand over the discount to H. They were allowed to keep their commission because they had acted in good faith.

The remedies available to the principal on the agent making a secret commission are:

Serious consequences result from an agent accepting an undisclosed payment

- dismiss the agent without notice or compensation;
- recover the secret commission from the agent;
- terminate the contract with the third party (but only if the third party has actual knowledge of what the agent was doing, or had deliberately closed their eyes to it);
- sue the third party for any damages suffered.

Should a bribe be involved then, in addition to the above remedies, the principal may choose between recovery of the bribe or claiming for damages but not both (*Mahesen* v *Malaysia Government Officers' Co-operative Housing Society Ltd* (1979)).

In criminal law the agent and third party may be guilty of committing a crime (see. s.1, Prevention of Corruption Act 1906, and also, if the agent works for a public body, s.1 Prevention of Corruption Act 1916).

Review question

What is the legal status of a third party providing an agent with a day's hospitality on the men's semi-final day at Wimbledon? Assume that no disclosure had been made to the principal.

Rights of the agent against the principal

The agent has the following rights against the principal:

Compared to the principal the agent has modest rights

A right to payment

This will normally be set out in the contract of agency. Should the contract be silent on remuneration then an implied term will mean that the agent is to receive reasonable payment for the work carried out. This is on the basis that the person doing the work could not reasonably be expected to work for nothing, so a reasonable sum should therefore be paid.

The Supply of Goods and Services Act 1982, s.15, says that, subject to an agreement to the contrary, a reasonable sum should be paid to the agent for the service given. If the agreement leaves payment to the discretion of their principal who refuses to use it, then the agent will be unable to enforce the right of payment.

Case example
Re *Richmond Gate Property Co. Ltd* (1965)

A contract between a company and one of its directors said that he was to receive 'such remuneration ... as the board of directors may determine'. As the board never offered him any remuneration he was unable to sue for payment.

To earn remuneration the agent must bring business in for the principal. In *Hodges & Sons* v *Harkbridge Park Residential Hotel* (1940), an agent introduced a government department as the purchaser of the principal's property. No commission was payable as the government department did not contract with the principal but issued a compulsory purchase order to acquire the property.

Also an agent cannot expect payment for a benefit which the principal receives if the act which caused the benefit was outside their appointment.

Case example
Toulmin v *Miller* (1887)

A principal instructed his agent to find a tenant for a property. The agent did this and clearly earned commission. However, the tenant later bought the property but the principal refused the agent commission on the sale. The principal's action was said to be correct in that the agent's instructions had been to find a tenant not a purchaser.

Where the agent is in breach of their duties then unless the principal is prepared to waive the breach the agent cannot enforce the right of payment.

What may be a problem is identifying *when* the agent is to be paid. If the agent is employed to sell then introducing a third party who signs an agreement to purchase but who does not actually complete the contract will mean that the agent is not entitled to payment (*Martin* v *Perry* (1931)); similarly, where the buyer signs the agreement 'subject to contract' then again the agent has no right to payment (*Graham & Scott (Southgate) Ltd* v *Oxlade* (1950)).

Where the seller *refuses to complete* then, in the absence of an express term in the contract of appointment, this will equal a breach of an implied term that the principal (or seller) will not act so as to deprive the agent of their commission (*Alpha Trading Ltd* v *Dunnshaw-Patten Ltd* (1981)). However, if the seller refuses to *sign* the contract then the agent cannot sue for payment; similarly, if the buyer signs an agreement 'subject to contract' but the seller refuses to complete then, again, without an implied term the agent cannot legally demand payment (*Luxor (Eastbourne) Ltd* v *Cooper* (1941)). The justification for this is that the agent must accept the risk that the seller may not go through with the transaction.

A right to a lien

A lien is the right of an agent to retain possession of the principal's goods until an obligation owed to them by the principal has been discharged. Therefore, an unpaid agent may claim the principal's property in their possession as security until they have been paid.

A right to indemnity

Provided that the agent has acted within their appointment then the principal must compensate them for any expense reasonably incurred. Alternatively, the agent may ask for an indemnity when, acting within their scope of authority, they have been found liable in contract or tort to the third party. Should the agent act outside their authority then the right to indemnity is lost.

Case example
Lage v Siemens Bros & Co. Ltd (1932)
Agents who failed to pay custom duty on goods failed in their attempt at claiming an indemnity from the principal. The agents breach of their duty of diligence had been the cause of the fine and it was unreasonable that the principal should pay.

The liability of the agent to the third party

Generally, once the agent has brought about a contract between the principal and the third party then they no longer have any duties or liabilities. Should the transaction they have arranged go 'sour' then it will solely be for the contractual parties themselves to resolve.

Normally the agent has no liability but there are exceptions …

There are, however, a number of exceptions where the agent may remain liable:

1 Where the agent contracts personally, such as signing a contract without any qualification. This may personally bind the agent even though the third party knows the true position.

Words of description 'we, as brokers …' are binding on the agent

Words of representation 'on behalf of …' are not binding on the agent

In order for an agent to escape liability when signing a negotiable instrument on behalf of a principal, they must add sufficient words to their signature to show that they were acting as an agent, or in a representative capacity – S.26(1) Bills of Exchange Act 1882.

2 Where the agent contracts under seal in their own name.

3 Where the agent has acted for a fictitious or non-existent principal. This problem occasionally arises in company law where an 'agent' acted on behalf of a company not yet registered. The normal outcome at common law is that the 'agent' will be personally liable. However, statute law (s. 36(c)(1) Companies Act 1985) will allow the 'agent' to escape liability provided that there was a 'clear exclusion of personal liability' but it must be noted that 'for and on behalf of XYZ Ltd' is insufficient.

4 Where the custom of the particular trade will make the agent personally liable.

5 Where the agent agrees to assume personal liability. This may be where the agent contracts jointly on behalf of the principal and of themselves, or where the agent agrees to be personally liable in order to persuade the third party to contract with an unknown principal.

The doctrine of the undisclosed principal

Here the third party is unaware of the existence of the principal as the agent would have not disclosed either the name or identity of the principal. The third party therefore believes that the agent is the principal party.

For a principal to later take over the contract from the 'agent' would seem to breach the privity rule in contract law as the third party would owe rights and obligations to someone they had not contracted with. Because of this anomaly the law requires that two conditions be satisfied before an undisclosed principal is allowed to take over the contract. These are:

1 That there is an absence of personal consideration. If the third party establishes that they only wanted to deal with the agent or, alternatively, that they never wanted to deal with the principal then the undisclosed principal cannot intervene.

> ## Case example
> ### *Said* v *Butt* (1920)
> B had banned S from attending first night performances. To get around this ban S got a friend to buy a ticket for him. B refused S admittance on the ticket.
>
> S was an undisclosed principal who could not take over the contract made between his friend and B for he well knew that if B had known the truth he would never have sold a ticket to S's friend.

2 That there is a consistency of contract with the agency relationship. If the principal takes over the contract then it must not go against the contract created by the agent. For example, an express term in the contract may prohibit an undisclosed principal from taking the contract over. More commonly such a prohibition term may be implied.

> ## Case example
> ### *Humble* v *Hunter* (1848)
> When making a contract with the defendant the agent described himself as 'the owner of the ship or vessel called the Ann'. It was said that the undisclosed principal could not sue on the contract as the agent, in describing himself as being the owner, had implied that he was the sole contractual principal.

The effect of the undisclosed principal

The following points may be made:

1 The third party can, if they wish, sue either the agent or the principal. This is the common law position e.g. *Clarkson Booker Ltd* v *Andjel* (1964), but now statute may permit a 'second bite at the cherry' (s.3 Civil Liability (Contribution) Act 1978).
2 If the third party decides to sue the principal then they must act quickly or else only the agent will be available for an action.
3 Once the third party has chosen who to sue then it cannot be altered.
4 An individual principal permitted to intervene may sue the third party but subject to any

defence the third party may have against the agent, such as obtaining benefit of a set-off (*Greer* v *Downs Supply Co. Ltd* (1927)).

5 If the principal intended for the agent to disclose, but the agent did not do so, then the principal will have a right of action against the agent.

6 If the principal has taken action against the third party then the agent is unable to take similar action themselves; or if they had commenced an action they must stop it should the principal start their own action.

The agent's implied warranty of authority

An agent who purports to act for a principal, that is who holds themselves out as having the authority to act, implicitly represents that they have the authority of their principal to do so and will be liable to the third party where they have no such authority. The term warranty means a promise or guarantee, so if broken then it is a form of misrepresentation.

The agent has essentially misrepresented themselves

The agent is only guaranteeing that they have the authority to act; they do not guarantee that the contract will be performed. With *del credere,* agent's express contractual terms may say that performance, that is payment by the principal, will be guaranteed.

Liability of the agent is strict so that it makes no difference if the agent honestly believed that they still had the necessary authority. Therefore, fraud or negligence on the part of the agent is not required, only that the third party relied upon the warranty given. However, if the agent acted fraudulently then they may also be liable in the tort of deceit.

Case example
Yonge v *Toynbee* (1910)

Solicitors, acting as agents, were instructed by a client (the principal) to defend him against threatened legal proceedings. Before the proceedings took place the client, unknown to the solicitor, was certified insane. This loss of contractual capacity meant that the solicitors lost their authority to act. However, the solicitors delivered a defence only afterwards learning of the insanity. The plaintiffs (the third party) demanded that the defence be struck out as being invalid and for the solicitors to pay their costs.

The solicitors, in acting for their client, had impliedly warranted that they had the authority to do so when they had not. They were consequently liable for the plaintiffs' legal costs.

Only the third party, not the principal, is able to bring an action for breach of warranty and damages are accessed under ordinary contractual principles per *Hadley* v *Baxendale* (1854). Should the third party know that the agent did not have the authority to act then there will be no misrepresentation and hence no breach of the agent's warranty.

Clearly, as in *Yonge* v *Toynbee* (1910), warranty of the agent's authority can lead to a harsh outcome. To guard against this an agent may ask that their appointment be made under the Powers of Attorney Act 1971 so that the protection of S. 5(1) can be sought.

Statute law may protect an innocent agent from the unfairness of the common law

A donee of a power of attorney who acts in pursuance of the power at a time when it has been revoked shall not, by reason of the revocation, incur any liability (either to the donor or to any other person) if at the time he did not know that the power had been revoked.

The liability of a principal for an agent's frauds, misrepresentation or negligent misstatements

Courts are unwilling to allow principals to hide behind their agents

Vicarious liability will mean that the principal may be liable for the acts of the agent. In respect to an agent's fraudulent acts the principal will be liable where the agent had acted within their actual or apparent authority.

Case example
Lloyd v Grace, Smith & Co. (1912)

The defendants were solicitors who employed a managing clerk to carry out property transfers. The managing clerk fraudulently induced L to transfer two properties which the managing clerk immediately sold and then absconded with the proceeds. The defendants as principals were held liable as that by holding out the managing clerk as being allowed to transfer property they had given him the apparent authority to act as he had. Even though the managing clerk's act was fraudulent for his own benefit he was still acting within the scope of his authority.

The House of Lords' decision in *Lloyds v Grace, Smith & Co.* (1912) was reaffirmed by a later House of Lords' decision in *Armagas Ltd v Mundogas SA, The Ocean Frost* (1986).

Ignorance by the principal that the agent is acting dishonestly will not alter the principal's liability per *Refuge Assurance Co. Ltd v B Ketterwell* (1909).

In respect to all non-fraudulent torts of the agent liability is limited to where the acts are within the scope of their authority (whether within their actual or apparent authority) per *Armages Ltd v Mundofes SA* (1986). Should they act outside the scope of their authority then the agent is termed to be 'on a frolic of their own' and the principal will bear no liability. In *Koorgang Investments Pty v Richardson & Wrench Ltd* (1982), a firm of estate agents (principals) employed a valuer (agent) who gave a negligent valuation. The firm were not liable as the valuer had no authority to make the valuation – he was on a frolic of his own!

Where the third party has a valid action for negligent or fraudulent misrepresentation then both the principal and agent are jointly and separately liable (that is both are liable collectively and individually). Therefore, a third party may try to rescind the contract and/or sue for damages. It is no excuse for the agent to say that they were only following the principal's instructions.

In respect to negligent misstatements, as an agent can owe the third party a duty of care then a third party suffering a financial loss caused by an agent's negligent misstatements can sue the agent for compensation under the Hedley Byrne principal (*Hedley Byrne v Heller & Partners* (1964)). Similarly, provided the agent when making the negligent misstatement, was acting within the scope of their authority then, subject again to a duty of care being owed, the principal may also be liable for the agent's tortuous act.

Termination of agency

The contract of agency can be terminated in the same manner as other contracts:

There is considerable flexibility over methods to end the principal–agent relationship

Completion

If the agent was appointed to carry out certain tasks then once these have been performed the agency will end. Similarly, if the agency was for a stipulated period then on the expiry of that period the agency will end (although a new agency may be created). Should the appointment not be for a fixed period then it is possible that it may end as a result of customary practice within a certain trade or market.

Mutual agreement

Simply the parties agree to end the agency. To make the agreement to discharge legally valid the agent and the principal need to both provide consideration or else have the discharge agreement put into a deed form.

Revocation of the principal's authority

Here the principal will revoke the authority given to the agent. Should the principal not have a valid reason for dismissing the agent, such as the agent being liable for serious breaches of duties, then the principal may well be liable for breach of contract (*Boston Deep Sea Fishing and Ice Co. v Ansell* (1888)). Whether the agent is able to sue for damages will be dependent on the terms of the agreement. It may be that under the contract a period of notice had to be given so that failure to do so will enable the agent to sue for lost future commission (*Martin Baker Aircraft Co. Ltd v Canadian Flight Equipment Ltd* (1955)).

A principal, revoking an agent's authority, needs to inform regular third parties that the agent's authority has been withdrawn. If this is not done then apparent authority may mean that the principal will remain liable for the former agents actions – see *Summers* v *Salomon* (1857).

While most appointments are revocable a limited number are irrevocable. These are:

1 An authority coupled with an interest. This occurs where the agency was created to protect some interest of the agent and without the agents agreement the appointment cannot be revoked.

Termination under completion, mutual agreement, revocation and renunciation are where the parties themselves will deal with the discharge; termination by frustration operates independently of the parties through operation of law.

Case example
Firth v Firth (1906)

The defendant was appointed by a power of attorney to take possession of an estate and to manage it for the principal. The estate was mortgaged to a third party and to support this mortgage the defendant gave a personal guarantee that the mortgage would be paid. The power of attorney made no mention of the guarantee. When the plaintiffs later revoked the defendant's authority and demanded repossession of the estate, the Privy Council held that the authority, as it was coupled with an interest, was irrevocable.

---

2 Where the agent has incurred liabilities for which the principal must indemnify them.

Case example
Read v Anderson (1884)

An agent was employed to place bets for his principal and to pay them if they were lost. After the agent settled a number of bets on the principal's behalf it meant that the agent's authority could not, without agreement, be revoked.

---

3 Where the appointment was made under a power of attorney and expressed to be irrevocable. This is covered by s. 1, Power of Attorney Act 1971 and relates to where the power was given to secure performance of an obligation owed to the agent or, alternatively, given to protect an interest of the agent.

Renunciation by the agent of their appointment

Unless the agreement allows the agent to end the agency or the conduct of the principal justified the agent's action, then the agent may well be liable for breach of contract.

By frustration

Termination by frustration can occur in a number of ways:

- bankruptcy or liquidation of the principal and of the agent if it prevents the agent from performing his or her duties;
- death of either principal or agent;
- illegality, such as the principal being declared, at outbreak of war, an enemy alien;
- impossibility, such as the destruction of the subject matter of the agency or where the agency objective becomes radically different from what the parties intended;
- insanity of either the principal or agent, but under the Enduring Power of Attorney Act 1985, an enduring power of attorney is not terminated by the principals insanity.

The Commercial Agents Regulations 1993 (a shortened overview)

These regulations cover all agreements entered into before or after 1 January 1994. If a contractual term in an existing contract is inconsistent with the regulations then the term will become void.

Agents covered by the regulations

Agents dealing in services, as opposed to goods, are not covered by the regulations

The regulations only apply to a 'commercial agent' who is defined as:

> A self-employed intermediary who has continuing authority to negotiate the sale or purchase of goods on behalf of another person (the principal) or, to negotiate and conclude the sale and purchase of goods on behalf of and in the name of that principal.

Despite the term 'self-employed intermediary' it is believed that a company as well as individuals are covered. A number of agents are excluded, notably distributors who buy and sell goods in their own right and sellers of goods from mail-order catalogues who sell to friends or families. Goods is interpreted to be 'substances, growing crops and things comprised in land by virtue of being attached to it and any ship, aircraft or vehicle'. Services are excluded but clearly problems will surely arise as to what is a service or a good, e.g. computer software.

The form of the agreement

Both the principal and the agent have the right, on request, to a signed document from the other setting out the terms of the agency agreement, including any later variation of it. This right cannot be excluded.

The obligations of an agent

The regulations impose an obligation on the agent to look after the interests of the principal and to act *dutifully and in good faith*. Three particular examples of this duty are provided. The agent must:

- make proper efforts to negotiate and, where appropriate, conclude those transactions they are instructed to take case of;
- communicate to the principal all the necessary information available to them;
- comply with the principal's reasonable instructions.

The obligations of a principal

As with an agent the principal must act *dutifully and in good faith* towards the agent. In particular a principal must:

- provide the agent with necessary documentation relating to the goods concerned, e.g. sales literature, training manuals, etc;
- notify the agent of pertinent matters, e.g. that he or she anticipates that the volume of transactions is likely to be lower than that which the agent could normally have expected;
- inform the agent within a reasonable period of his or her acceptance or refusal of any commercial transaction negotiated or concluded by the agent.

The agent's remuneration or commission

The regulations provide that, in the absence of any agreement as to remuneration between the parties:

> a commercial agent shall be entitled to the remuneration that commercial agents … are customarily allowed, and if there is no such customary practice, a commercial agent shall be entitled to reasonable remuneration taking into account all the aspects of the transaction.

Under the regulations the legal rights of an agent are considerably strengthened

Seemingly, goods under the regulations are to be treated as the same as goods under s. 61(I), Sale of Goods Act 1979 with land itself once again being excluded.

'Commission' means any part of the remuneration which varies with the value of the business transactions. The agent also has the right to demand all information and extracts from the principal's financial records in order to check the amount of the commission due. This right to information is entirely new and cannot be contracted out of.

Payment of commission

Commission becomes due to the agent as soon as either the principal or the third party has performed their obligation under the contract of sale. The agent is entitled to their commission if the principal fails to perform the contract but not if the third party fails to perform. The commissioner shall be paid not later than on the last day of the month following the quarter in which it became due. The provisions concerning payment of commission cannot be contracted out of the detriment of the agent.

After the termination of an agency agreement

Under the regulations an agent will be entitled to commission, notwithstanding the termination of the agency, provided that the transaction was mainly attributable to the agent's efforts and that it was concluded within a reasonable period after the agency agreement was terminated.

Information concerning commission

The regulations impose a duty on the principal to supply their commercial agent with a statement of commission due, showing the method of calculation, not later than the end of the month following the quarter in which the commission was earned.

The termination of the agency contract

Where an agency contract is entered into for an indefinite period and the agreement does not specify notice periods, either party may terminate it on notice. Such notice shall expire at the end of a calendar month and shall be:

- one month during the first year of the contract
- two months during the second, and
- three months during the third and each subsequent year.

Where the agency agreement was entered into for a fixed term then it automatically terminates at the end of that period.

Compensation at termination of the agreement

Compensation is payable on the termination of the agency agreement whether it was for an indefinite period or fixed term. Therefore, if an agency agreement is not renewed compensation is payable even though there is no breach by the principal. To claim compensation the agent must notify the principal that they intend to claim within one year following termination. Compensation is based upon damage suffered by the agent and the agent will have the burden of proof to establish this. While damages are not fully defined in the regulations they are deemed to have been suffered if:

1 Termination has deprived the agent of commission which the proper performance of the agency agreement would have processed for them while providing substantial benefit for the principal.
2 Where termination prejudiced the agent's ability to be reimbursed for expenses incurred in the performance of the contract on the principal's advice.

Non-competition covenants

Any post-termination restraint of trade clause in a commercial agency must:

- be concluded in writing;
- relate to the geographical sea, group of customers and goods entrusted to the commercial agent under the agency agreement;
- last for not more than two years from the date of termination.

Comments on the implications of the regulations

In Britain the principal–agent relationship is one where the principal buys in a service provided by an independent contractor, the agent. Where legal protection is given it is largely the principal who benefits, especially in respect of the wide range of fiduciary duties being owed to the principal, with only modest reciprocal duties being owed to the agent.

The attraction to the principal of having agents in the UK-style relationship is that the relationship was contractual with the contract saying that no commission would be paid until the principal has received payment from the third party and that this could be terminated with a relatively modest period of notice. For the agent the attraction of the relationship was that only in exceptional circumstances would they incur any financial or legal liability in the work undertaken for the principal. Agents then had advantages over direct employees especially as their remuneration could be wholly performance-related, e.g. if they brought in no business then they would be paid nothing. The regulations, following the continental practice, see commercial agents as being akin to quasi-employees. First, they demand that a commercial agent be paid once the principal performs their obligations but not necessarily waiting until the third party has performed theirs, e.g. made full payment to the principal. Second, proper notice has to be given before termination and payment of adequate compensation. Third, as the regulations require a principal to make available his business records for the agent's inspection this has implications in respect of confidentiality. This may mean that principals will begin to keep certain information separate from their financial records so that they may be kept absolutely secret.

It is still too early to say exactly what changes will result from the introduction of the regulations but some commentators have raised the possibility that long term they could see a major diminution in the appointment of commercial agents. Time will tell whether such prophesies come true.

Scotland and Northern Ireland

There are no differences with regard to agency law in England and Wales.

Chapter summary

- The description agent is not derived from what that person does but is based on the relationship between the agent and principal. Therefore, not all who call themselves agents are in fact agents in law.
- It is possible that an agent may legally bind the principal even though the agent may not have express authorization to do so – see implied authority, apparent authority, and authority by operation of law.
- Ratification by a principal of an agent's unauthorized acts is retrospective so that it equals a prior command. The agent is thus treated as having the necessary authority at the time when the act was done. Ratification is subject to a number of conditions.
- The agent will owe the principal a considerable range of duties, the most important of which are termed fiduciary duties which attempt to ensure that the agent will not have a conflict of interest with the principal.
- The agent is not normally personally liable to third parties but in certain circumstances liability can arise, most notably in respect of breach of warranty of authority.
- The methods of terminating an agency contract are the same as discharging contracts generally.
- It is anticipated that the Commercial Agents Regulations 1993 will in the future have a major impact in British agency law.

Case-study exercise

The Hempstead Bank plc has agreed to act for one of their customers – Mr Lucan – while he is absent from England. They act on the following:

1. The bank has been asked by Mr Lucan to find a buyer for a house he owns in Watford but as a result of an oversight they fail to take immediate action. However, on realizing their omission, they agree to sell it to Mr Perry, a newly appointed manager of one of the bank's Watford branches.
2. In acknowledgement of his valued custom, the Bank arranges for an employee to attend an auction in order to bid on his behalf. The employee selected to attend misreads lot no. 132 for lot no. 32 and when he arrives at the auction he discovers that the desired painting has already been sold at a lower price than Mr Lucan was prepared to pay.
3. In an attempt to rectify their failure to obtain the painting, the bank contracts with the art gallery who purchased it to sell it to them at 20 per cent above the auction price but still below the price Mr Lucan would have been prepared to have paid. They promptly inform Mr Lucan of their action but over the next several weeks hear nothing from him.
4. The bank receives a letter from a company registrar saying that a rights issue has been declared on shares owned by Mr Lucan and which the bank is administering for him at an agreed fee. The bank take no action on this matter.

Student task

Apply your knowledge of agency law to the above events and comment on the legal liability, if any, of the Hempstead Bank plc.

Discussion questions

1 An agent exercises powers wider than those expressly given to them. Discuss the validity of this statement.

2 How may an agent be distinguished from:

    (a)   a trustee
    (b)   a bailee
    (c)   a distributor or franchisee
    (d)   an independent contractor?

3 In what circumstances will the agent be personally liable to the third party?

Further reading

An Outline of the Law of Agency (3rd edn), McKensinis and Munday (1992), Butterworth.
This is an excellent and thorough introduction to the subject. Clearly written and easy to follow – recommended.
Bowstead and Reynolds on Agency (16th edn), Reynolds (1995), Sweet & Maxwell.
Fridman's Law of Agency (7th edn), (1996), Butterworth.
These two publications are authoritative books of reference. They are useful for confirmation of accuracy and also for citation.

5 Consumer credit and consumer hire

Introduction

This chapter will examine the regulation of consumer credit and consumer hire agreements by the Consumer Credit Act 1974. Such agreements will, of course, also involve the supply of goods and services, but these aspects are not considered here, and readers should refer instead to Chapter 3.

Dominant role of Consumer Credit Act

It should be noted that a number of proposals for changes in the law are in hand at the time of writing, and some of the proposed changes are referred to below. The reader should always check to determine if any of these changes have been implemented.

Objectives

The Consumer Credit Act 1974 lays down a comprehensive system of controls in relation to most forms of consumer credit and consumer hire agreements. These cover such matters as licensing of businesses, the form and content of agreements, and the regulation of related advertising. It will be shown that the Act is virtually a comprehensive code, and that little form of regulation takes place outside its confines. It will be shown in consequence that agreements falling outside the Act, which will only occur where the contract is a business-to-business contract, are generally unregulated.

Consumer Credit Act as a code

Key concepts

- Credit and hire
- Consumer credit and consumer hire
- Ancillary credit businesses
- Regulated agreements
- Exempt agreements
- Executed and unexecuted agreements
- Licensing
- Running account and fixed sum agreements
- Requirements as to copies
- Linked transactions
- Total charge for credit

- Cancellable agreements
- Credit tokens
- Creditors, debtors, hirers, owners
- Joint and several liability
- Full, intermediate and simple credit advertisements
- Judicial control
- Extortionate credit bargains.

Credit and hire agreements

The Consumer Credit Act defines 'credit' as including the provision of a cash loan and any other form of 'financial accommodation' to an 'individual' (see below). A hire-purchase agreement is a common example. In essence, this is an agreement where one person pays regular instalments for an item, has possession of it for the period of payment, and pays a nominal charge at the end of that period to become full owner. If the amount of credit provided does not exceed £15 000 (it is proposed that this be increased to £25 000), then the agreement is a 'consumer credit agreement'.

Financial limits apply

If goods are hired to an 'individual' (see below), that agreement is a hire agreement (unless it is a hire-purchase agreement, see above), but it will only be a 'consumer hire' agreement if it is capable of lasting more than three months and if the amount of rental does not exceed £15 000 (again there are proposals to lift this to £25 000).

The definition of 'individual'

Under the definition of 'individual' provided in s. 189 of the Act, this will be an individual in the normal sense, but it can also include a partnership or any other unincorporated body of persons which does not itself consist entirely of companies. This means that not only can a partnership be an individual, but so also can an association consisting of a company and a partnership or of a company and an individual. The definition of 'individual' means that a company, or a group of companies, can never count as an individual, and this means in turn that lending to companies falls outside the scope of the Act.

Regulated and exempt agreements

The Act restricts its coverage to those consumer credit and consumer hire agreements which are 'regulated'. This means that the particular consumer credit or consumer hire agreement (i.e. an agreement where the credit or hire payments are within the current limit of £15 000) is one not classified by the Act as 'exempt', since 'exempt' agreements will not be regulated by the Act.

Various agreements exempted from scope of Act

An extensive set of agreements are rendered 'exempt' by s. 16 of the Act. For example, mortgage loans by banks, building societies, insurance companies, friendly societies and local authorities are exempt. The Consumer Credit (Exempt Agreements) Order 1989, made under s. 16 of the Act, also exempts certain agreements where the cost of credit is low or where the number of repayments does not exceed a specified number.

Review questions

1 Explain what is meant by 'credit'.
2 What is meant by a 'consumer' credit or hire agreement?
3 What agreements are 'exempt' and what is the significance of an agreement being 'exempt'?
4 What is meant by an 'individual'?

Credit and hire businesses

If a business consists in whole or in part of the provision of credit or hire under a 'regulated' agreement (see above) then that business is a consumer credit or consumer hire business.

Case example
***Willis* v *Wood* (1984)**

A person who lends money occasionally from his own resources to provide a source of income is not running a consumer credit broker. There is a fundamental difference between lending money and carrying on a consumer credit business.

Licensing

It is a central requirement of the Act that consumer credit and consumer hire businesses, and ancillary credit businesses must be licensed if they are to carry on their activities.

Credit and hire businesses subject to licensing requirements

Though the expression does not appear in the Act, the form of licensing imposed is known as 'positive' licensing. This means that businesses must apply for licences and satisfy certain criteria before they are granted a licence. Applications must be made to the Office of Fair Trading, and s. 25 of the Act requires the Office of Fair Trading (OFT) to grant the application if the applicant can show that they are 'fit' to be awarded a licence; and if they can show that the name under which the licence is sought is not misleading or otherwise undesirable.

The Act requires the OFT, in considering an applicant's fitness, to consider among other things whether the applicant has committed any offence involving fraud, dishonesty or violence; and whether they have engaged in deceitful or oppressive practices, in conduct which, whether unlawful or not, are unfair or improper.

An appeals procedure is set out for disappointed applicants.

Categories of licence

Licences are divided by the Act into standard and group. A standard licence is issued to individual applicants. A group licence is one issued which covers a named group, and can be issued either following an application by that group or on the initiative of the OFT itself. The Law Society has a group licence covering solicitors in practice. Group licences have also been awarded to, among others, the professional bodies covering accountants and to Age Concern. The thinking behind the idea of group licences is that it is much easier to issue one licence embracing an entire group, than to issue standard licences to individual members of the group.

Licences are standard or group

A standard licence lasts for 10 years, and a fresh application is then required. A group licence

System of 'positive' licensing administered by Office of Fair Trading

lasts for such period as the OFT specifies, and this can extend to indefinite duration, which is now normally the case.

Unlicensed trading

Where a business does not have the requisite licence, it commits an offence.

> ### Case example
> ### *R v Priestly* 1983
> The defendant was a motor dealer who pleaded guilty to an offence under the Trade Descriptions Act and to unlicensed trading under the Consumer Credit Act. In the Crown Court, the judge imposed on him a sentence of three months in relation to each offence, to run concurrently. He had an 'appalling' record. The sentence was upheld on appeal since the purpose of the consumer credit legislation was to protect members of the public, some of whom may be unsophisticated in business matters and unsuspicious of clever salesmen, from dealing with those who are not obeying the law.

In addition, any agreements made while unlicensed are unenforceable against the other party unless an order has been obtained from the Office of Fair Trading. Appeals may be made against a refusal to make an order.

Review questions

1 What is meant by a 'consumer credit or consumer hire business'?
2 What is meant by an 'ancillary credit business'?
3 What form of licensing is required of those whose activity is that of a consumer credit or hire business?
4 What matters are looked at when considering an applicant's fitness for a licence?
5 What are the penalties for trading without the requisite licence?

Seeking business

Canvassing off trade premises

'Canvassing off trade premises' occurs when a person solicits the entry of another into a regulated agreement (see above) by making oral representations during a visit to premises, other than business premises, which is carried out for the making of such representations, and which was not carried out in response to a request for a visit made on a previous occasion. This reference to a 'previous occasion' means that a person who knocks unannounced on a door and is asked to come in, even after stating their business, is still canvassing because the invitation was made on the same, not a previous, occasion.

> ### Case example
> ### *R v Chaddha* (1984)
> On 11 occasions, a debtor, or a friend or relative, made the initial approach to the defendant, who was a licensed moneylender. The invitations were not in writing. At each home, the

debtors asked for loans and the defendant laid down certain conditions. It was held that, in putting these conditions, the defendant was seeking entry into a loan and that he was therefore soliciting within the meaning of the Act. Following this ruling, the defendant changed his plea to guilty.

The Act makes it an offence to canvass consumer hire agreements off trade premises only if the licence issued by the OFT (see above) provides for this. The same applies to the canvassing off trade premises of a particular type of consumer credit agreement; that is to say one where the supplier of the relevant goods or services provides the credit themselves, or has any arrangement with a third party for the provision of credit.

It is also an offence to canvass off trade premises an agreement for a cash loan. Any prior request for a visit to discuss such a loan must be in writing, otherwise an offence will still be committed.

Subject to the provision of a determination by the Office of Fair Trading, it is permissible to canvass overdrafts on current accounts. An appropriate determination was made on 1 June 1977.

Circulars to minors

If, with a view to financial gain, a circular is sent to anyone not yet 18, an offence arises if the circular invites that person to borrow money, obtain goods on credit or hire, obtain services on hire, or to apply for information about such matters. Merely sending out general advice on, for example, how to handle finances would not of itself give rise to an offence. The Act only prohibits 'sending', not 'giving'. It is therefore not an offence to stand outside a school and give leaflets away which cover the above matters.

The Act provides for a defence where the sender did not have reasonable cause to know that the recipient was under age. If, however, the material is sent to a school, this defence will not be available.

Unsolicited credit tokens

The Act defines a 'credit token' so as to cover all forms of card or document given by a business which 'undertakes' that its use will allow its user to obtain cash, goods or services on credit.

> **Case example**
> ### *Director General of Fair Trading v Elliot* (1980)
> A firm of shoe retailers sent to former customers a cardboard replica of a credit card. On the reverse it stated: 'valid for immediate use'; the 'sole requirement' is a signature and means of identification; and credit is 'immediately available' if the customer had a bank account. An accompanying leaflet said 'with your card in your hand walk into any … shop, give us your signature, show us simple identification such as a cheque card and walk out of the shop with your purchase and all the credit you need.' The defendants argued that the token was not a credit token because they were not legally obliged to extend credit to someone presenting the card. The divisional court held that it was a credit token because that was the effect of the wording, which 'undertook' the provision of credit. The definition of 'credit token', it was also pointed out, covers a token where credit is provided on the production of the card 'whether or not some other action is also required'.
>
> This was held to be a credit token since it 'undertook' the provision of credit on its face even though credit was granted only to those with bank accounts.

Tight controls on canvassing agreements

It is an offence to deliver or send by post a credit token which the recipient has not asked for in a prior written document. Some credit tokens offering not more than £50 in credit are exempt from this prohibition. It is also lawful to send an unsolicited credit token under a credit token agreement made on a previous occasion, or to send one as a replacement or by way of renewal under an existing agreement.

Review questions

1 What is meant by 'canvassing off trade premises'?
2 Under what circumstances is it (a) lawful and (b) unlawful to canvass an agreement off trade premises?
3 What provisions govern the receipt by minors of information about credit or hire agreements?
4 What is meant by a 'credit token' and under what circumstances may one be lawfully given or sent to an individual?

Advertisements

False or misleading advertisements

The Act makes it an offence for an advertisement to contain information which in a material respect is false or misleading.

Case example
Mersoja v Pitt (1990)
An advertisement for Renault cars stated that the annual percentage rate of charge (see below) was 0 per cent. The evidence showed that any trade-ins accepted were adjusted downwards in order to allow the garage to recover the cost of financing the deal. The deal offered in one particular case was some £250–£300 less than would otherwise have been received if the customer had paid cash or arranged his own finance. The court found that the lower trade-in value was a way of imposing a charge on what was supposed to be free credit. An offence had therefore been committed.

Case example
National Westminster Bank v Devon County Council (1993)
It was held that it was not misleading for an advertisement for a fixed rate mortgage, limited to a set period, not to indicate that the rate might increase once that period had passed. The court pointed out that, in theory, it was possible for the rate to remain unchanged. Compare this with the decision in *Scarborough Building Society* v *Humberside* (1996) where, on the facts, it was not possible to be certain that rates would not change.

The provisions relating to false or misleading advertisements are not restricted to advertisements for regulated agreements (see above). However, advertisements are not covered if they indicate that the credit provided will exceed £15 000 and either that no security, or security other than land, is required. An advertisement is also outside the Act if it indicates that the credit advertised is only available to a company.

Certain other advertisements are outside the Act if they are covered by the terms of the Consumer Credit (Exempt Advertisements) Order 1985/621. For example, certain advertisements relating to credit to be repaid in not more than a stated number of instalments fall outside the Act.

Wide scope given to provisions relating to false or misleading advertisements

Advertisements where goods not sold for cash

It is an offence to advertise specific goods or services as available on credit if they are not also available for cash.

Content of advertisements

Strict rules are laid down for the content of credit and hire advertisements by the Consumer Credit (Advertisements) Regulations 1989/1125. If the advertisement is one which is covered by the provisions of the Act relating to false and misleading advertisements, then it must also conform to these regulations. These provide for just three permitted categories of advertisement: the simple, the intermediate and the full. As these names suggest, the amount of information which must be provided varies with the category chosen. Since a great deal of information is required for full advertisements, and very little for short, advertisers generally choose the intermediate category.

Credit or hire advertisements must choose from three permitted categories

A typical intermediate credit agreement would show: the name and address of the advertiser; a statement that written quotations are available on request; the APR; the amount of credit available; a warning, prominently displayed, that the borrower's home is at risk if repayments on a mortgage are not kept up; and advance payments. It should be noted that not all these features may necessarily appear in an intermediate advertisement, since everything depends on the nature of what is being advertised. A typical full advertisement will contain such information and full repayment details.

A failure to observe the requirements for these categories is an offence.

Case example
Coventry City Council v Lazarus (1996)

Credit advertisements were found to be in breach of the regulations because they did not state:

- that written details were available on request;
- the total amount payable under the credit agreement;
- the total number of repayments required;
- whether the annual percentage rate of interest was variable.

Another advertisement was found to infringe the regulations because it stated that the APR was variable but did not state the annual percentage rate of charge. It also used the words 'incredibly low payments', a comparative term, but failed to state the terms offered by others with whom comparison was made.

The regulations state that any indication that a lesser expense is being imposed than is imposed by others must also indicate who the other persons are and what their terms are.

Quotations

Provisions relating to quotations have now been revoked.

The due diligence defence

A person charged with an offence in relation to advertisements or quotations is entitled to be acquitted if they can show that they committed the offence because of a mistake, reliance on information supplied to them, an act or omission by another person, or an accident or some other cause beyond their control; and if they can also show that they took all reasonable precautions and exercised all due diligence to avoid commission of the offence.

Case example
Coventry City Council v *Lazarus* (1996)

The charges are related above.

   Although the advertisers had pleaded guilty to infringing the regulations, they still claimed to be entitled to rely on the due diligence defence.

   There was evidence before the court that in April 1990 and April 1992 the advertisers had been told by their local trading standards office that certain credit advertisements they had published infringed the regulations. The first of these letters contained a brief summary of the law and also referred to a guidance document published by the Office of Fair Trading. It also advised the advertisers to get in touch with them if they had any queries. The second letter did in fact contain the OFT booklet and again indicated that trading standards would help if asked. This letter was followed within a week by another pointing to further infringements by the advertisers and again offering the help of trading standards.

   Following receipt of the second letter, the advertisers got in touch with the Retail Motor Industry's Federation, since the advertisements related to credit available on the purchase of motor vehicles. They had received back from the Federation advice and information on the drafting of credit advertisements. The advertisers also attempted to follow the OFT booklet which had been sent to them. It was also the case that the advertisers had faxed through to trading standards a copy of one of the advertisements in relation to which they were subsequently prosecuted, but that was on the same day, but after, it had appeared in the press. In these circumstances, the magistrates ruled that the advertisers had satisfied the due diligence defence and so acquitted the advertisers. The prosecution appealed to the divisional court.

   In support of its argument that the advertisers had failed to show due diligence, the prosecution made these points:

1   The advertisers had been able to communicate with the trading standards office by fax and seek their advice, albeit after the offending advertisement had been published.
2   There was no good reason advanced before the magistrates as to why similar enquiries could not have been made before publication.
3   It was open to the advertisers to prepare a draft advertisement in advance of publication and submit it to trading standards for approval and adapt it at the time of each publication to meet the prevailing commercial situation.

   The divisional court had no doubt at all that the magistrates had come to the wrong decision. It said that it 'stands out a mile' that the advertisers should have approached trading standards before publication. It found the prosecution's arguments not just 'compelling', but

---

'over-whelming'. The advertisers failed to take the 'simple precaution' of consulting trading standards before publication.

Seeking advice can be an ingredient in showing due diligence

There was another important issue to be resolved in this case and that was whether the defendants could also show that they had *relied on information supplied*. In the present case, the defendants maintained that they had relied on information supplied, this being the legal advice provided by the Federation.

It was argued by the prosecution that 'information supplied' was not wide enough to include legal advice. The court pointed out that the OFT brochure, and the letters to the defendants from the trading standards office, all advised contact being made with the local enforcement authority. The prosecution's argument that 'information supplied' did not apply to legal advice would mean that anyone taking up this recommendation, but receiving faulty advice, could not make use of the statutory defence. The court found this proposition 'unattractive' and pointed to one dictionary meaning of 'information' as the 'communication of knowledge'. It therefore concluded that the communication of the legal advice was information supplied within the Act and, moreover, that this part of the statutory defence formed an exception to the general principle that ignorance of the law was no defence. However, since the defendants had failed to show due diligence, the case was remitted to the magistrates with a direction to convict.

Legal advice can be 'information supplied'

Review questions

1 To what extent does the Consumer Credit Act control inaccurate advertisements?
2 If specific goods are advertised as being available on credit terms, what further duty is imposed on the advertiser?
3 Explain what categories of advertisement are open to someone advertising credit or hire facilities.
4 What does a person guilty of an offence have to show if they still wish to secure an acquittal?

Making an agreement

The Act does not alter the common law rules regarding offer and acceptance (see Chapter 2). However, it does provide for an extensive range of documentation, with prescribed contents, before a regulated agreement for credit or hire is enforceable.

To begin with, the contract must be in writing and must be set out in the form required by the Consumer Credit (Agreements) Regulations 1983/1553. It must be signed by the customer and by, or on behalf of, the creditor or lender. It must contain all the terms of the agreement other than implied terms (such as those implied by the Sale of Goods Act 1979 as to description, quality and fitness for purpose). Finally, the agreement must also be readily legible when tendered for signature. An agreement which fails to conform to any of these requirements is 'improperly executed' and can be enforced against the customer only on a court order. An application for an order is to be dismissed only if the court considers it just so to do. An enforcement order cannot be made where the customer has not signed the document.

Detailed requirements for enforceable agreements

Meaning and consequences of improper execution of agreement

Copies

Detailed
requirements as
to provision of
copies of
documents

The Act not only requires specific documentation, but it also lays down detailed rules for the provision of copies. The position is as follows. If the agreement is presented personally to the customer, and they are the first one to sign it (that is to say, it has not yet been signed by the creditor or owner), then it must be accompanied by a copy. If the agreement is handed over personally to the customer, and it has already been signed by the other side, then at the same time, a copy of the agreement must be handed over. If the agreement is sent to the customer, it must be accompanied by a copy, whether it has already been signed by the other side or not.

It is also a requirement of the Act that a copy of the agreement, as signed by both parties, must be given to the customer within seven days of the application of the last signature. This will not apply, however, where the customer was the last one to sign, since they will already have received a copy as indicated above. Where this 'seven-day rule' does apply, and the agreement is one that can be cancelled (see below), the copy must be sent by post.

Seven-day rule
for copies not
always
applicable

If the agreement relates to credit-tokens (see above), the seven-day rule is waived so long as the copy is given before or at the time when the credit token is given to the customer.

Where agreement neither sent nor handed over

There will be occasions where the original agreement is neither sent to a customer, nor presented personally. The agreement might, for example, be contained in a brochure available at a display stand or in a newspaper. In such a case, there is no requirement to provide an immediate copy, but the seven-day rule will apply once the agreement has been signed by both parties (see above).

Content of copies

The Act provides that all copies must be accompanied by copies of any document referred to in the copy. However, under the provisions of the Consumer Credit (Cancellation Notices and Copies of Agreements) Regulations 1983, copies of certain documents (such as any Act of Parliament which might be referred to in the agreement) are not required. The regulations also provide that signatures can be omitted from the copies.

If the agreement is cancellable (see below) the copy must contain a cancellation notice. This notice must also be sent by post within the seven days referred to above unless a copy of the agreement is itself required to be sent under the seven-day rule (see above).

Breach of copy requirements

As in the case of an agreement not drawn up in the requisite form, a breach of any of the foregoing copy requirements means that the agreement is 'improperly executed' and so cannot be enforced without a court order. The court is required to dismiss an application for an order if, but only if, it considers it just to do so. However, no enforcement order can be made in the case of a cancellable agreement if the obligation as to a copy of the cancellation notice (see above) was not complied with. Nor can an enforcement order be made in the case of such an agreement if the various requirements as to copies were infringed unless a copy of the agreement as signed by both parties, and of any document referred to in it (subject to the exceptions referred to above) was given to the customer prior to the proceedings in which the enforcement order is sought. No enforcement order can be made, however, if the agreement had not been signed by the customer.

Land mortgages

If the agreement is to be secured on land, special provisions are contained in the Consumer Credit Act designed to ensure that the customer has a special period for reflection on the proposed course of action. First of all, before the agreement is sent to the customer for signature, they must be given a copy of that agreement containing a statement as to their rights to withdraw and (subject to the above exceptions) of a copy of any document referred to in the agreement.

Special rules for agreements secured on land

Second, a copy of the document for signature by the customer must be sent by post not less than seven days from the giving of the above copy.

Third, during what is called the 'consideration period', the other side must refrain from any approach to the customer except in response to a specific request made by the customer once the 'consideration period' had begun. The 'consideration period' begins with the giving of the first copy and ends with whichever of the following is the first to happen: the expiry of seven days after the day on which the agreement was sent to the customer for signature; or their return of the signed document.

If these provisions have been observed, and no notice of withdrawal was received by the other party before a copy of the agreement was sent to the customer for signature, then the land mortgage is 'properly executed' and can be enforced. Breach of these requirements means that the agreement is 'improperly executed' and can be enforced on a court order. An application for such an order must be dismissed if, but only if, the court considers this just. No order can be made if the agreement had not been signed by the customer.

The above provisions do not apply, however, where the land being mortgaged is in fact the land being purchased with the credit. Nor do they apply to agreements for bridging loans provided in connection with the purchase of the land to be mortgaged or any other land. The reason for these exclusions is that if the various formalities detailed above were to apply, in particular the 'consideration period', the normal procedures for the purchase of land by a mortgage would be considerably impeded.

Normal mortgage transactions excluded

Review questions

1   Give an account of the formalities which are required of a regulated consumer credit or consumer hire agreement.
2   What provisions are set out in the Act for ensuring that a customer has a copy of the agreement and what must be contained in that copy?
3   What special provisions are made for cancellable agreements in relation to copies of the agreement?
4   Explain the procedure which must be gone through in the case of land mortgages. Does this apply in all cases of agreements secured on land?
5   Failure to observe the various formalities means that an agreement is 'improperly executed'. What does this mean and how can any problems caused be overcome?

Withdrawal and cancellation

If a person makes an offer, they have a right under normal contractual principles to withdraw that offer at any time prior to acceptance. The Consumer Credit Act does not alter the common-law position, but does expressly state that any form of written or oral notice indicating an intention to withdraw is effective. This is not stated to be exhaustive, so it would still suffice if the other side learns of the intention to withdraw through a third party, whether or not that third party was authorized to pass on the information (see *Dickinson* v *Dodds* (1876)).

Effect of withdrawal

The Act also provides that an indication of withdrawal is validly given if given to anyone who acts for the customer in negotiations for the agreement (such as a solicitor); or if given to a credit broker (see above); or the supplier of the relevant goods or services, if such person was involved in the negotiations leading to the prospective agreement.

The Act provides that withdrawal is to have the same effect as the cancellation of a cancellable agreement.

Cancellable agreements

The Act provides that a regulated agreement is cancellable by the customer if 'the antecedent negotiations included oral representations made when in the presence of the debtor or hirer by a party acting as, or on behalf of, the negotiator.' It is clear from this that if the oral representations were only made by telephone, the agreement is not cancellable. On the other hand, it is enough that the oral representations were made 'in the presence' of the customer. They do not have to be directed at the customer. If, then, representations are made to the wife, but in the presence of the husband who actually signs the agreement, the agreement is cancellable by the husband.

Case example
Moorgate Services Ltd v *Kabir* (1995)

A negotiator in antecedent negotiations (see below) made certain statements as to the suitability of a particular person to be a debtor under an agreement, and that the amount of credit available would be £7000. The Court of Appeal ruled that a statement made during antecedent negotiations will not amount to a 'representation' unless it is a statement of fact or opinion or an undertaking as to the future which is capable of inducing the intended debtor to enter into the agreement. The court ruled that the statements made in this case fell into this category.

Meaning of 'antecedent negotiations' and 'negotiator'

Central to the definition of a cancellable agreement is the concept of 'antecedent negotiations'. This is comprehensively defined by the Act, but may be summarized as referring to negotiations conducted with the customer by the creditor or the owner, by a credit broker (see above) in relation to the particular goods, and by the supplier of the particular goods or services, the acquisition of which is to be financed by the credit. The 'negotiator' is the person by whom such negotiations are conducted.

> ### Case example
> ### *Moorgate Mercantile Leasing Ltd v Gill and Ugolini Dispensers Ltd* (1988)
> A representative from Ugolini paid a visit to Mrs Gill who ran a newsagents shop. She was busy with customers and asked him to leave a pamphlet which he did, writing some information on it. Some of this was incorrect. He returned the following day and she signed an agreement for a dispenser relying on certain misrepresentations made by the representative. It was held that, though misrepresentations had been made, Ugolini were not negotiators and so any statements made by them were not made as agents of the finance company with whom the leasing agreement had been made.

Exemptions from right to cancel

There are agreements which, though falling within the above definition of 'cancellable' are outside the right of cancellation. Agreements cannot generally be cancelled if the credit is secured on land (instead such agreements will generally benefit from the withdrawal provisions available for land mortgages, see above). Agreements will also fall outside the right to cancel if the agreement was signed by the customer on the business premises of some other party.

The period of cancellation

The customer has five days in which to cancel, the period starting from the day after receipt of the 'seven-day' copy or notice of cancellation rights (see above). In certain limited circumstances, the period of cancellation is 14 days following the day on which the customer signed the agreement (see Consumer Credit (Notice of Cancellation Rights) (Exemptions) Regulations 1983/1558).

Notification of cancellation

The agreement, if in the required form, will itself contain a notice of cancellation. However, it is not obligatory to use this, since the Act indicates that any written notice showing an intention to cancel is effective. Apart from serving this notice on the other party, it can also be served on anyone specified in the cancellation notice and on any agent of the other party.

Any form of written notice to cancel suffices

Effects of cancellation

Not only does cancellation cancel the agreement, it also serves to cancel any 'linked transaction'. In broad terms, a 'linked transaction' is one which is ancillary to the credit or hire agreement. A contract of maintenance is a linked transaction if an agreement for the hire purchase of a television set requires such a contract to be taken out. Similarly, a contract for the hire of a freezer might require the customer to take out an agreement for the regular supply of frozen food. This latter would also be a linked agreement. Some linked agreements, however, survive cancellation, and these are listed in the Consumer Credit (Linked Transactions) (Exemptions) Regulations 1983/1560. These specify: insurance contracts; contracts guaranteeing goods; deposit and current accounts.

Subject to exceptions, 'linked transactions' are cancelled as well as main agreement

On cancellation, any sums paid by the customer are repayable, and any sums which would have become payable cease to become payable. If, furthermore, the creditor has paid the supplier for goods before cancellation, as where a finance house buys a car from a car dealer before letting it out on hire purchase to the customer, the creditor is entitled to be repaid by the supplier. Any security given is to be treated on cancellation as never having had effect, and any property lodged for the purposes of security is to be returned.

Cancellation requires restoration of status quo

> ### Case example
> ### *Colesworthy* v *Collman Services Ltd* (1993)
> The owner under a cancellable consumer hire agreement entered into a contract with the defendants for them to become the collection/management agency of the owner. On the instructions of the owner, the customer under the hire agreement paid sums due to the defendants. The customer validly cancelled the agreement and was held entitled to recover monies paid to the defendants. The court said that the defendants were more than collection agents since they were empowered to sue in their own names and to give discharge for payments made.

Cancellation does, however, have only a restricted effect in certain cases where work was done, or goods supplied, to meet an emergency; or where the goods had been incorporated into any land or other thing prior to the notice of cancellation being served. In these special cases, the credit obligations of the customer (such as the paying of interest) are extinguished, but his liability to pay the cash price remains effective.

Effect of cancellation on goods received or given in part exchange

It is possible, if not always likely, that during the cancellation period the customer takes possession of the relevant goods, or gives goods which are taken in part exchange.

Where the customer has taken possession of the goods, their duty is to make them available for collection on receipt of a written request from the other party. While in possession of them they must take reasonable care of the goods, though this obligation lapses after 21 days unless the customer has failed to comply with a written request, in which case the duty of care lasts until the other party recovers the goods.

Provision made for dealing with goods handed over during cooling-off period

In the case of goods taken in part-exchange, the customer has the right to recover the amount of the allowance which was given in relation to such goods. This can, however, be avoided if the goods are returned to the customer within the 10 days following cancellation in substantially as good a condition as when handed over by the customer.

Repayment of credit

The Act contains provisions designed to cater for the situation where, during the cancellation period, a loan is paid over to the customer.

Advancing credit during cooling-off period discouraged

If the customer does cancel, the agreement in fact remains in force so far as it relates to the payment of interest and the repayment of credit. If the customer makes any repayment within the month following cancellation, or before the first instalment was due, then that repayment is interest free. If the customer does not do this, they are still liable to repay only the credit interest following a written request, and on terms as close as possible to that of the original agreement but without extending the period of the agreement. The form in which the written request is to be made is contained in the Consumer Credit (Repayment of Credit on Cancellation) Regulations 1983/1559.

Cancellation outside the Consumer Credit Act

It is also possible to cancel an agreement under the provisions of the Consumer Protection (Cancellation of Contracts Concluded away from Business Premises) Regulations 1987/2117 and the Timeshare Act 1992.

The regulations apply to contracts under which a trader supplies goods or services where those contracts are concluded during an unsolicited visit to the customer's home. Cancellation can take place up to seven days from the making of the contract. The contract cannot in any event be enforced against the customer if they are not provided with a written notice of cancellation. The regulations contain provisions dealing with the recovery of money paid by the customer, the repayment of credit and the return of goods which are broadly comparable with those above. The regulations do not apply to contracts already cancellable under the above provisions.

The Timeshare Act gives certain rights of cancellation in respect of timeshare agreements. These rights do not apply in the case of timeshare agreements which are cancellable under the provisions of the Consumer Credit Act (*Global Marketing Europe* v *Berkshire County Council Department of Trading Standards* (1994)).

Consumer Credit Act not only enactment providing for cancellation

Review questions

1 Under what circumstances can an agreement be cancellable under the provisions of the Consumer Credit Act? To what extent is cancellation permissible under other enactments?
2 What is the immediate effect of cancellation on the relevant contract?
3 Set out the rights of the customer under a cancelled agreement in relation to the recovery of any money they have paid and any goods they may have given in part exchange.
4 To what extent does a customer, who has cancelled an agreement remain liable in respect of any credit received during the cancellation period?

Joint and several liability

One of the most important provisions of the Act is contained in s. 75 which provides for a creditor to be equally liable with the supplier of goods for any breach of contract or misrepresentation committed by the supplier. If, for example, a car dealer provides a car which is not reasonably fit for its purpose contrary to the provisions of the Sale of Goods Act 1979, the customer can sue, at their choice, either the dealer or the finance house which provided them with the credit for the purchase. These provisions only apply if the item obtained with the credit had a cash price of more than £100 but less than £30 000.

Customer has option as to whom to sue

The above provisions have not met with the entire approval of creditors, and there are proposals for change.

Notice before action

The general rule laid down by s. 76 of the Consumer Credit Act is that no action can be taken to enforce a term of an agreement by demanding earlier payment or any sum, recovering possession of goods or land, or treating any rights conferred by the agreement as terminated, restricted or deferred, unless the customer has been given seven days' written notice. The form and content of this notice must conform to the provisions of the Consumer Credit (Enforcement, Default and Termination) Regulations 1983/1561. A copy must also be served on anyone who was a surety for the agreement: if it is not, the security is only enforceable on a court order.

Duty on creditor or owner to give seven days' notice of action

These provisions, however, do not apply where the customer has been in breach of the agreement (for the position where they are in breach, see Default notices). They will apply, for example, where it is provided that the agreement is terminated should the customer become bankrupt, go abroad, or be convicted of a specified criminal offence.

Termination notices

The foregoing provisions do not apply where the creditor or owner wishes to terminate the entire agreement in non-default cases. However, broadly similar provisions covering such cases are contained in s. 98 of the Act. The seven days' notice must also be in the form prescribed by the above regulations and a copy must be served on any surety: if it is not, the security is only enforceable on a court order.

Default notices

In the event of a breach of the agreement by the customer, ss 87 and 88 of the Act regulate the action which the creditor or owner may take. If they wish to: terminate the agreement; demand earlier payment of any sum; recover possession of any goods or land; or treat any right of the customer as terminated, restricted or deferred, they must observe certain formalities.

First, they must send a default notice giving the customer at least seven days' written notice. A copy must be served on any surety: if it is not, the security is only enforceable on a court order.

Second, this notice must be in the form prescribed by the above regulations.

Third, it must indicate: the nature of the alleged breach; the action required to remedy the breach if it is capable of remedy and the date by which the remedial action must be taken; if not capable of remedy, such sum as is required as compensation and the date when it must be paid. Any day referred to must be at least seven days after service of the default notice itself. It is not essential that the default notice actually reaches the customer.

Case example
Lombard North-Central plc v Power-Hines (1994)
The creditor swore an affidavit that he had sent the customer a default notice by post which the customer maintained he had not received. The court pointed to s. 176(2) of the Act which provides for service by post and said that it was designed to apply where, through no fault of the creditor, the default notice was not brought to the customer's attention. It was also held that the court was entitled to assume that, where a letter was not returned, it had been delivered. In addition, the customer had waited some 18 months before making application to the court.

Section 89 provides that if the customer takes the required action by the specified time, the breach of the agreement is deemed never to have taken place.

Duty to provide information

There are a number of sections in the Act imposing a duty on the creditor or owner to supply information to the customer. If the customer makes a written request, and encloses a fee of (currently) 50p, then the creditor or owner must reply within the time allowed by the Consumer Credit (Prescribed Period for Giving Information) Regulations 1983/1569 (usually 12 working days) with full details of the current position under the agreement. The creditor or owner who fails to provide the information within the relevant period is not entitled to enforce the agreement while default continues. If default continues for a month, they commit an offence.

In certain circumstances, such as shop budget accounts, bank overdrafts, certain information is to be sent automatically. No penalty is provided for breach of such a requirement, but it is no doubt the kind of thing which the Office of Fair Trading would take into account as part of its licensing functions (see above).

Customer has statutory right to information

Any information provided is stated by s. 172 to be binding on the creditor or owner, though, if shown to be incorrect, the court may direct such relief as appears to be just.

Termination statements

Section 103 gives a customer the right, on service of a written notice (no fee is payable), to obtain from the creditor or owner a statement to the effect that the agreement between them has been satisfactorily concluded. This must be provided within 12 working days and a failure to comply which lasts for a month gives rise to an offence. The provisions of s. 172 (see above) are applicable.

Customer can seek proof of satisfactory end to agreement

Information from customer

A corresponding duty is also placed on the customer if the agreement requires them to keep the goods in their possession or control. In such a case, s. 80 provides that the customer must, within seven working days of receipt of a written request, provide the creditor or owner with information as to where the goods are. Failure to do so is an offence.

The customer also has duty to provide information

Variation of agreements

It may be that the agreement gives the creditor or owner the power to vary the agreement; the most obvious example being a power to vary the rate of interest. If this is the case, s. 82(1) specifies that the variation is not to take effect unless written notice is given in accordance with the Consumer Credit (Notice of Variation of Agreements) Regulations 1977/328. The basic position is that the particulars of the variation are to be served on the customer, at least seven days being given before the variation takes effect. Where, however, the variation is of the rate of interest, or, in the case of a consumer hire agreement, in the sums payable, it is enough to make an announcement in the national press and also to give notice at the place where the agreement is maintained.

Formalities to observe before agreement can be varied

Review questions

1 In what circumstances can a customer elect to sue either the supplier or the creditor?
2 What formalities are required before the creditor or owner can take action to enforce their rights under the agreement?
3 What rights and duties are imposed on the parties to an agreement in relation to the provision of information?
4 What is it necessary for a creditor or owner to do before they can enforce a variation in the terms of the agreement?

Misuse of credit facilities

The basic provision, set out in s. 83(1) is that the customer under a consumer credit agreement is not liable to the creditor for any loss which might arise from the use of that facility by a third person who is not the customer's agent. This could cover, for example, the pledge by an unauthorized person of the customer's line of credit. It does not, however, extend to a variety of instruments within the Cheques Act 1957, such as cheques, dividend and interest warrants, conditional orders and bankers' demand drafts.

Special provisions apply in relation to misuse of credit-tokens

Furthermore, special provision is made for credit-tokens (see above) by s. 84, the effect of which is as follows. The credit-token agreement must contain the form set out in the Consumer Credit (Credit-Token Agreements) Regulations 1983/1555 – the name, address and telephone number of a person who is to be informed of the loss or theft of the token. If this is done, the customer can be held liable for no more than £50 in the event of such loss or theft, or a smaller amount if the customer gave oral or written notice of loss or theft. Oral notice must be confirmed in writing within seven days. If the agreement does not contain these details, then the customer cannot be held liable for any loss arising from misuse of the token.

Review question

What protection does a person have against the misuse or theft of their credit-token?

Restrictions on remedies in event of default

Protected goods

Section 90 of the Consumer Credit Act deals with 'protected goods'. These are goods obtained under a hire-purchase or conditional sale agreement (see Chapter 3), where the creditor is still owner and the customer has paid at least one-third of the total price. If the customer is in breach of such an agreement, the goods can only be repossessed from them (so they can be repossessed from a third party) on a court order.

A customer who has paid a certain proportion of price protected from 'snatch-back'

An order is not, however, necessary if the creditor seeks repossession for some reason other than breach, as where the agreement provides for recovery of the goods in the event of the customer becoming bankrupt. Nor do these provisions apply where the customer has terminated the agreement (s. 90(6)). Section 173(3) also provides that a court order is not required if the customer gives their consent at the time to repossession. The requirement that consent be given at the time means that consent given in advance, as in the agreement itself, has no validity.

Where the creditor obtains possession in the absence of the required court order, the agreement is terminated forthwith, the customer being released from all future liability and entitled to recover past payments.

Entry on premises

Section 92(1) also requires a court order before the creditor or owner can enter on any premises to recover possession of goods subject to a hire-purchase, conditional sale or consumer hire agreement. Similar restrictions are applied by s. 92(2) when the customer is in breach of a conditional sale agreement relating to land. In both cases, s. 173(3) applies to allow a creditor or owner to dispense with the need for a court order if consent is obtained from the customer at the time.

No entry on premises without court order

Default interest

Section 93 prevents a creditor from obliging the customer who is in breach of the agreement from paying a rate of interest on sums in relation to which they are in default at a rate greater than the rate of interest provided for in the agreement.

Early repayment

The customer under a consumer credit agreement is given by s. 94 of the Act an absolute right at any time, by notice in writing to the creditor, and payment of the balance, to pay off the agreement. They are allowed to deduct from the amount they have to pay any rebate allowable under the provisions of the Consumer Credit (Rebate on Early Settlement) Regulations 1983/1562.

Consumer guaranteed right to pay ahead of time

It has been held when judgement is entered against a defaulting customer, that judgement should be for the full amount and not discounted to reflect any rebate. The debtor only obtains the discount when they pay the judgement or it is enforced against them (*Forward Trust Ltd* v *Whymark* (1990)).

Settlement information

Section 97 of the Act obliges the creditor, within 12 working days of receipt of a written request from the customer, to provide them with full information as to how much is needed to settle the agreement. If they fail to provide the information within that period, they cannot enforce the agreement: if their default persists for a month, they commit an offence. Any statement provided is stated by s. 172 to be binding unless the court decides otherwise.

> ## Case example
> ### *Home Insulation Ltd* v *Wadsley* (1988)
> A credit agreement incorporated a table which set out the rebates to which the customer was entitled in the event of early settlement. When the customer requested settlement information, however, he was quoted the lower figure calculated under the provisions of the Consumer Credit Act. The creditor argued that it was enough that they indicated the sum which they 'in fact' required. The court ruled, however, that the information needed was that 'legally' required, that is to say the sum calculated in accordance with the table incorporated into the agreement. It was also held that it is not open to the parties to such an agreement to waive the requirement that a request for an early settlement statement should be in writing.

Termination of agreements

The Act provides customers with certain guaranteed rights of termination.

Hire purchase and conditional sale

Section 99 gives the customer under a hire-purchase or conditional sale agreement a right at any time to terminate the agreement. This does not apply to a conditional sale agreement relating to land where title has passed to the customer. Nor does it apply to cases where the property in the goods under a conditional sale agreement had already passed to the customer and such property has been transferred to a third party who does not become the customer under the agreement.

Hire-purchase and conditional sale agreements may be terminated

Half the price to
be paid on
termination

If a customer exercises their right to terminate, they are liable to make such payments as are required by the '50 per cent rule'. Section 100 requires them to pay any installation charge to which the agreement committed them, plus one-half of the remainder of the total price. A lesser amount is payable if the agreement provides for a smaller sum or for no sum, or if the court orders a smaller sum when satisfied that such smaller sum represents the amount of the creditor's loss.

Hire agreements

Termination
rights extend to
hire agreements

The customer under a consumer hire agreement is also entitled at any time to terminate it. Section 101 sets out the minimum period of notice, but this can be a shorter period if the agreement so provides. The statutory norm is three months.

There are certain hire agreements which do not fall within these provisions (though the terms of the individual agreements could always allow termination): agreements providing for payments in excess of £900 a year; agreements for the hire of goods in the course of a business where the customer selects the goods and these are bought by the owner (usually known as 'equipment leasing'); and where the goods are leased for the purposes of sub-leasing.

Review questions

1 At what stage do goods become 'protected goods', and what is the nature of the protection offered?
2 In what circumstances can a creditor or owner enter premises to recover possession of goods?
3 Give an account of a customer's rights to pay off an agreement ahead of time.
4 In what circumstances, and subject to what obligations, may a customer terminate an agreement without liability?

Securities

Where a security is given in relation to any consumer credit or consumer hire, or linked agreement, s. 105 requires that security to be in the form prescribed by the Consumer Credit (Guarantees and Indemnities) Regulations 1983/1556. These are confined to guarantees and indemnities given by a third party at the request, express or implied, of the customer. Securities not covered by these regulations do not have to be in any particular form, but they must still be in writing. These provisions do not apply to securities provided by the customer, but that is because the relevant security will be governed by the requirements of the Consumer Credit (Agreements) Regulations 1983/1553 (see above).

Certain
formalities
apply to
securities

In terms broadly similar to those relating to the actual credit or hire agreement (see above), the Act imposes certain requirements before a security can be said to be 'properly executed'. Thus: the security instrument (i.e. the document embodying the security) must conform to the requirements of the above regulations and be signed as required by the regulations by or on behalf of the surety; the document embodies all the terms of the security except for implied terms; the document is legible when presented for signature; and a copy is given to the surety when the instrument is sent for signature. There are also requirements for the provision to the surety of copies of the agreement they are securing.

If these provisions are breached, or if a security is not in writing, the security is enforceable only on a court order. If the application for an order is dismissed on other than 'technical grounds', any security given is deemed to be 'ineffective'. An order is deemed to be dismissed on 'technical grounds' if the court or Director General of Fair Trading so certifies.

Section 106 provides that, where a security is deemed 'ineffective', then it is to be treated as never having been provided; any property lodged with the creditor or owner as security is to be returned 'forthwith'; the creditor or owner must take any necessary action to remove or cancel any entry in a register relating to the security; and any sums realized by the security shall be repaid.

Certain formalities required if security to be enforceable

'Ineffective' securities defined

Duty to provide information

There are provisions as to the supply of information to sureties which parallel those relating to the supply of information to customers (see above). Within 12 working days, and on receipt of a payment of (currently) 50p, the creditor or owner must provide the surety with a copy of the secured agreement, a copy of the security instrument and a signed statement showing the current position under the secured agreement. Failure to comply with these requirements means that the security cannot be enforced while the default continues; and if the default continues for a month, an offence is committed.

Statements provided under the above provisions are binding on the creditor or owner except where the court decides otherwise.

There is also a duty to supply the customer, against following payment of the current 50p fee, with a copy of the security. Failure to do so within the relevant time periods has the effect stated above.

Duty to supply information and copies to surety

Realization of securities

The sale or other realization of securities is potentially subject to control by regulations, but (except for the case of pledges, see below), there are currently no relevant regulations. However, s. 126 of the Act does provide that a land mortgage securing an agreement can only be enforced on a court order. It is possible to avoid the need for such an order if consent to its enforcement is provided at the time and not, for example, in advance.

Anti-avoidance measures

Section 113(i) of the Act provides that no security can be enforced in a way which impose obligations greater than would be if the security were not provided. For example, when a hire-purchase agreement is terminated, the customer is liable for no more than 50 per cent of the total price (see above). The foregoing provision prevents a security being used to obtain more than this.

Section 113(3) provides for rendering certain securities 'ineffective' within the provisions of s. 106 (see above). If, for instance, an agreement is cancelled under the cancellation provisions (see above), is terminated when protected goods are improperly repossessed (see above), the Act provides that any security given in relation to the agreement becomes ineffective. Similar provisions apply when, for example, an enforcement order is not given in the case of an agreement which was not properly executed (see above). However, this will not be the case if the application for enforcement was dismissed on 'technical grounds' (as defined above).

Act not to be evaded by use of security

Review questions

1 What formalities are required in the case of securities and what are the consequences of a failure to observe those formalities?

2 State what rights of information are available both to the surety and the customer in relation to agreements in relation to which there is a security.

3 Indicate the nature of the controls that exit over the realization of securities.

4 What is meant by the expression 'ineffective securities' and to what circumstances does it apply?

Pawns and pledges

The Act creates a separate regime for pawns and pledges. Section 189(1) defines a 'pawn' as any article subject to a 'pledge', and defines 'pledge' as meaning the rights of the person who has taken an article as a pawn. The provisions below do not, however, apply when the article given in pawn is a document of title or a bearer bond.

The person who takes an article in pawn must give a 'pawn receipt'. This must be in the form set out in the Consumer Credit (Pawn-Receipts) Regulations 1983 No 1566. Failure to do so means the commission of a criminal offence. An offence is also committed if the 'pawnee' (that is the person taking the pawn) fails to observe the requirements as to copies and the duty to give notice of cancellation rights (see above).

The provisions of the Act (see above) relating to the form and content of documents, and as to the signing of agreements, will also apply so that any failure in this respect will mean that the agreement is improperly executed (for the consequences of improper execution, see above). This will also be the case, in addition to the commission of an offence, in relation to the provision of copies and notice of cancellation rights.

Redemption period

The Act provides that a pawn can be redeemed at any time within the six months after it was taken. This is the shortest period allowed under the Act, and it can be extended if the period allowed for credit is more than six months, or if a longer period for redemption is separately agreed. If the pawn is not redeemed by the end of the allowed period, it nevertheless remains redeemable until it is realized (see below).

Redemption procedure

The article taken in pawn is to be handed over to the customer when they surrender the pawn receipt and pay the amount owing at any time within the redemption period (see above). If, however, the pawnee knows, or has reasonable cause to suspect, that the person tendering the receipt is neither the owner of the article itself, or authorized by the owner to redeem it, then they are entitled not to hand the article over. A refusal to redeem a pawn without 'reasonable cause' is an offence. It is up to the pawnee to show that they had reasonable cause.

If the pawn receipt has been lost, this can be overcome by the customer making out a declaration in the form prescribed by the Consumer Credit (Loss of Pawn-Receipt) Regulations 1983 No 1567; or, in certain cases, and with the pawnee's agreement, making out a statement in the form prescribed by these regulations.

Consequences of failure to redeem

If the redemption period was six months, and the agreement was for credit not exceeding £25, the pawn becomes the property of the pawnee if it has not been redeemed. In any other case, the pawn becomes realizable at the end of the redemption period.

Realization of pawn

When the pawnee has become entitled to realize the pawn (and note this is different from the case above where the pawn has become their property), they may sell it so long as they have given the period of notice required by the Consumer Credit (Realization of Pawn) Regulations 1983 No 1568 (14 days), though no notice is required if the credit provided was not more than £50. The regulations also provide that, within 20 days of the sale, the customer must be given details of the proceeds of sale.

Customer to receive advance notice of intention to sell pawn

The debt is extinguished if sufficient is realized by the sale to cover the debt, and any surplus is to be paid over to the customer. It has been held that interest is payable on the surplus (*Thomas Mathew* v *Sutton Ltd* (1994)).

If not enough is realized, then the customer is in debt for the amount outstanding. The customer is entitled to challenge the price realized and the expenses incurred, and the burden is then on the pawnee to show that the price or the expenses were reasonable.

Review questions

1 Give an outline of the formalities which must be followed when an item is taken in pawn, and of the consequences which follow a breach.
2 How long has the customer in which to redeem an article given in pawn?
3 State the rights of a pawnee in relation to the article taken in pawn when the period for redemption has passed.
4 What is the position when (a) the amount realized by sale is less than the debt, or (b) is more?

Negotiable instruments

The Act imposes strict controls over the taking of 'negotiable instruments' from debtors, hirers or sureties.

No definition is given in the Act for 'negotiable instrument', so it is best to rely on the definition given in s. 32(1) of the Bills of Exchange Act 1882 defining an instrument as 'negotiable' if it can be 'negotiated', that is to say transferred to another person. A bill, for example, which stated 'Pay X only' could not be transferred and hence is not negotiable. Following enactment of the Cheques Act 1992, this is also the case with cheques marked 'account payee' or 'a/c payee'. A cheque marked 'not negotiable' is, however, still freely transferable (see s. 81 of the 1882 Act). Cheques are generally negotiable instruments, except where marked as above, as are bank notes. See generally Chapter 8 on Negotiable instruments.

Strict controls on use of 'negotiable instruments'

Restrictions imposed

The following provisions of the Act were designed to cover this type of problem. A householder would ask for central heating to be installed and, prior to the work being done, would give the contractor a promissory note or bill of exchange in their favour. This would provide for payment of the price with interest and charges, the whole to become due on default by the householder. The supplier would then negotiate this instrument to a discount house. If a dispute then arose between the householder and the supplier, leading to the householder ceasing payments, they would be liable to pay the discount house the full amount, despite a breach by the supplier. The discount house would be a 'holder in due course' within the Bills of Exchange Act 1882, and would thus take the negotiable instrument free of any defences available to the householder.

The restrictions accounted for

Section 123(1) of the Act states that the only form of negotiable instrument which can be taken to discharge a debt under an agreement or security is a banknote or cheque. Any cheque which is taken must be negotiated only to a bank. Furthermore, s. 123(3) provides that no negotiable instrument, without exception, can be taken as a security for any sums due under an agreement or security agreement. None of the foregoing provisions apply to negotiable instruments within the Consumer Credit (Negotiable Instruments) (Exemption) Order 1984 No 435. This is limited to hire agreements with a connection with a foreign country.

Consequences of breaching these restrictions

If the credit or owner does infringe any of the foregoing provisions, and does so in relation to any sums payable by the customer, the agreement with the customer becomes enforceable only on a court order, though this can be avoided if consent to enforcement is given at the time and not, for example, in advance. The same applies in relation to a security where a negotiable instrument is taken in relation to a sum payable under that security.

The position of the holder in due course

As pointed out above, a holder in due course under the Bills of Exchange Act is entitled to enforce a negotiable instrument without regard to any defences which might be available against the person from whom it was received. To ensure that this does not vitiate the protection created for the consumer by the provisions above, the Act provides that a person wrongly taking a negotiable instrument is not a holder in due course and hence cannot enforce the agreement. This, however, applies only to the creditor or owner under the agreement. If they then negotiate the instrument to a third party taking in good faith, and without notice of the contraventions of the Consumer Credit Act, that third person takes free of any defects in title arising from such contraventions and can enforce the instrument in the usual way. In such an event, however, the Act provides that the customer is entitled to be indemnified by the creditor or owner against any such liability.

Right to indemnity where contraventions occur

Where a cheque is taken, and is not negotiated to a bank (see above), s. 125(2) states that this gives rise to a defect in the title of the party so negotiating. This means that the person to whom it is wrongly negotiated is, if they have notice of the defect, not a holder in due course and hence are unable to enforce the cheque. It will be for the customer to prove that there was such notice. However, if they cannot do so, and becomes liable, then they will, under the provisions referred to above, be able to sue the party who wrongly negotiated the cheque for an indemnity.

Review questions

1 Explain what is meant by a 'negotiable instrument'.
2 What restrictions are placed on the taking of such instruments?
3 Set out the consequences which arise when there is a contravention of the above restrictions.

Judicial control

The Act contains a number of provisions dealing with the exercise of judicial control over consumer credit and consumer hire agreements.

Enforcement orders

There are a number of occasions when an enforcement order is required:

- improperly executed agreements or security agreements;
- where a copy of a notice has not been served on a surety when it should have been;
- when a negotiable instrument has been wrongly taken (for these various points, see the appropriate provisions above).

Various occasions when enforcement order sought

When an enforcement order is applied for, s. 127(1) requires a court to dismiss the application if and only if it considers this just, having regard to prejudice caused to any person and the degree of blame for the contravention and the powers of the court to impose conditions or suspend the operation of an order and to vary agreements and securities. There are also limitations on the making of enforcement orders when agreements were not signed and in the case of cancellable agreements (see above).

Time orders

The court has the power under s. 129 to make a 'time order' if it is just to do so when there is an application for an enforcement order (see above). A time order may also be made on application by a debtor or hirer when a notice before action has been served on them (see above), or when the creditor or owner has brought an action to enforce an agreement or security, or to recover possession or relevant goods or land.

Court may grant extension of time in certain cases

When a time order is made, it must provide for one or both of: the payment of sums owed by such instalments, at such times, as the court, after having regard to means, considers reasonable; the remedying of any breach, other than that of non-payment, within such period as the court specifies.

Section 130 sets out certain matters which are supplemental to the grant of time orders.

Case example
***Southern and District Finance plc v Barnes* (1995)**

In this case, the Court of Appeal stated that the correct approach when considering a time order was as follows:

(i)   whether it is just to make a time order, bearing in mind the position of debtor and creditor;

(ii) that an order is normally to be made for a stipulated time because of temporary financial difficulty;

(iii) that 'sums owed' means every sum due and owing and, where possession proceedings have been brought, this will normally comprise the entire indebtedness;

(iv) that the court may include any amendment of the agreement which is just and which is a consequence of the time order;

(v)   that if, when an order is made, the sum owed is the whole of the outstanding balance, there must be consequences for the term of the loan, the rate of interest, or both; and

(vi) when making a time order, the court should suspend any possession order that it also makes, so long as the terms of the time order are complied with.

Protection orders

Safeguarding the goods

On an application from the creditor or owner, the court may grant an order protecting any property, pending the determination of any proceedings, from damage or depreciation.

Financial relief

Section 132 empowers the court, on an application by the customer under a consumer hire agreement, to grant financial relief if the goods have been repossessed. The application can be not only for relief from payment of sums owed, but also for the repayment of any sums already paid.

Return and transfer orders

In relation to hire-purchase and conditional sale agreements, the court, if it appears just to do so, may make what are called 'return' or 'transfer' orders, but only where an application has been made for an enforcement or time order (see above), or where the creditor or owner has brought an action for repossession.

Court may make order as to ownership of goods

A *return* order is an order for the return of the goods to the creditor. A transfer order is an order for the transfer to the customer of the title to some of the goods, and the return of the others to the creditor.

In making a transfer order, the court has a discretion as to which goods shall become the property of the customer, but such an order can only be made where the paid-up sum exceeds that part of the total price which refers to the transferred goods by an amount equal to one third of the unpaid balance of the total price.

Financial limits to when goods may be transferred

The Act also provides that, where the balance is paid off, title to the goods can pass to the customer, even though a return or transfer order might have been made.

Imposing conditions etc.

Whenever a court exercises its powers to make an order under any of the foregoing provisions, it is empowered by s. 135 to impose conditions on any such order, or to suspend the operation of any term of the order, if this is considered just.

The court is also empowered by s. 136, when making any such order, to include in the order any provision it considers just for amending any agreement or security 'in consequence of a term of the order'. It has been held that this enables the court to change the rate of interest (*Southern and District Finance plc* v *Barnes* (1995) see above).

Extortionate credit bargains

Sections 137–141 of the Act contain provisions relating to the power of the courts to reopen 'credit agreements' where they find the 'credit bargain' extortionate. Hire agreements are not covered, but broadly similar provisions apply in relation to the power of courts to provide financial relief to hirers (see above).

More than regulated agreements covered

It is important to note that the definition of 'credit agreement' is not restricted to 'regulated agreements' (see above). It extends to all credit agreements other than those made with a body corporate or with a partnership of bodies corporate. A loan to an individual of £250 000 would be covered even though that is credit in excess of the amount permitted if an agreement is to be regulated (currently £15 000, see above).

The 'credit bargain' consists of the 'credit agreement', which is the actual agreement for the provision of credit along with any other transactions which are to be taken into account when computing the total charge for credit, such as maintenance and insurance contracts entered into as a term of the agreement.

The credit agreement can only be reopened if the credit bargain is 'extortionate'. This will be the case where the credit bargain requires that the debtor or a relative has to make payments which are 'grossly exorbitant'; or if it 'otherwise grossly contravenes ordinary principles of fair dealing'. A number of factors have to be taken into account, such as prevailing interest rates, the debtor's age, the degree of risk accepted by the creditor, and the degree of financial pressure under which the debtor was at the particular time.

Definition of 'extortionate'

When it decides to reopen an agreement, the court has the general power to 'do justice between the parties'. If it wishes to relieve the debtor or surety from any sum in excess of what is 'fairly due and reasonable', it may: direct accounts to be taken; set aside the whole or part of any obligation; require the repayment of any sum; direct the return of any property; alter the terms of an agreement or security instrument.

Powers of court when reopening an extortionate credit bargain

---

Case example
Castle Phillips Ltd v *Wilkinson* (1992)

The defendants purchased their home in 1980 with a first mortgage which was in arrears by 1983. They also had an unsecured loan and small debts, but their problems could still be resolved. They responded to an advertisement by a sub-broker who suggested a remortgage. They were required to visit a solicitor who said that they would have to pay a fee £1250 to the broker and £840 would have to be returned to the lender as part payment of interest. The agreement was for a bridging loan of £21 000 for between four and six months. The annual rate was 62.9 per cent. The court held that the bargain was extortionate and that the defendants should not be charged with the broker's fee on the advance payment of interest, but at a rate of 20 per cent pa.

Case example
Ketley Ltd v *Scott* (1981)

The defendants were occupiers of a flat owned and occupied by a third party. They were protected tenants. They obtained a valuation of the premises at £24 000 and exchanged contracts with the third party at £22 500. This was in September and notice to complete was given expiring on 6 November. Failure to complete would have meant forfeiture of a £2250 deposit. By 6 November, a mortgage had not been obtained and the defendants visited the plaintiff. A loan of £18 000 was requested by the defendants to purchase premises which they said was worth £30 000. They failed to disclose an overdraft of some £2000 and a guarantee which they had given in respect of certain companies for £5000. The plaintiff, believing the property to be worth about £25 000, agreed to provide £18 000 for three months at an annual rate of 48 per cent. Later that day, the defendants executed a legal charge over the property to secure the overdraft. They then asked the plaintiff to increase the loan to £20 500 to enable completion to take place, and this was agreed to. Later still that day, the defendants, in the presence of their solicitors, signed a legal charge, promissory note and memorandum of agreement. Contracts were exchanged. The defendants defaulted on repayment and the plaintiff took possession proceedings. It was held that, on the facts, this was not an extortionate credit bargain. The defendants had been clearly informed of the true rate of interest and, in view of the nature, speed and value of the transaction, the risk for the plaintiff was high. Further, the defendants were experienced in business matters, and their solicitor was present at the time of signing the documents. Loss of the opportunity to take advantage of a reduced purchase price did not constitute financial pressure on them. The court also held that, even if the bargain were extortionate, it would not be 'just' to reopen it in view of the defendants' own deceit.

Review questions

1 Explain what is meant by a 'time order' and indicate if this can be used to alter the rate of interest payable.
2 What is meant by an 'enforcement order' and what criteria do the courts apply when dealing with applications for such an order?
3 What provisions are available to provide financial relief for someone who hires goods?
4 Explain what is meant by a 'return order' and a 'transfer order'.
5 Indicate the powers available to the court to reopen an 'extortionate' agreement and define what is meant by this expression and how it differs from a 'credit bargain'.

Ancillary credit businesses

Act deals with various professions 'ancillary' to provision of credit or hire

Section 145 of the Consumer Credit Act lists five categories of ancillary credit business. These are credit brokers, debt adjusters, debt counsellors, debt collectors and the operation of a credit reference agency. It should be noted that the Act generally exempts barristers and solicitors from the definition of 'ancillary credit business'.

Credit brokers

In essence, a credit broker is one whose business is that of introducing those seeking a credit or hire agreement to those carrying on a consumer credit or consumer hire businesses. A typical example of a credit broker is the car dealer who refers customers seeking finance to a finance house. Estate agents are commonly credit brokers since they put house buyers in touch with mortgage lenders.

Case example
Hicks v *Walker* (1984)

A motor dealer had lost his consumer credit licence and so could only sell cars for cash. He established a separate credit broking business in part of his premises to which he would direct customers who were seeking credit. The customers did not know that they were dealing with someone other than the dealer. It was held that he was running an unlawful credit brokerage business by referring customers to a finance company.

Case example
Brookes v *Retail Credit Cards Ltd* (1986)

Retail Credit Cards Ltd was a licensed consumer credit business. It made arrangements with a retailer, Visuals Ltd, whereby it would provide credit to Visuals' customers. Visuals printed and displayed in its shop leaflets containing application forms which set out Retail Credit Cards' terms of business. The court held that, while it is clear that a shopkeeper can be a credit broker, it is undesirable to give in advance a definition of 'effecting an introduction'. It did, however, say that the mere provision of display boxes and application forms did not amount to effecting such an introduction.

In determining if a person is carrying on business as a credit broker, no distinction is to be drawn between what a person does as part of selling goods or services, and what they do to assist a customer who specifically seeks help; there is no distinction between transactions initiated by a seller and those initiated by a customer (*R* v *Marshall* (1989)).

Debt adjusting

Debt adjusting arises where a party negotiates on behalf of a customer with a creditor or owner for the discharge of debts; or who takes over, in return for payments by the customer, their obligation to discharge a debt. It can also be any similar activity involving the liquidation of a debt. Accountants and bankers will often be debt adjusters, as will bodies like CABs and Age Concern. The definition does not generally extend to the creditor or owner under the agreement.

Debt counselling

Debt counselling is the giving of advice to customers about the liquidation of debts due under a consumer credit or hire agreement. The definition does not generally extend to the creditor or owner under the agreement. This definition will often also cover those who are debt adjusters.

Debt collectors

Debt collection is the taking of steps to procure payment of debts due under consumer credit or hire agreements. The definition does not generally extend to the creditor or owner under the agreement.

Credit reference agency

Banks not credit reference agencies

A credit reference agency is a business which provides information relevant to the financial standing of individuals, 'being information collected … for that purpose'. This latter part of the definition means that banks will not be such agencies, even though they do provide such information, because the information was not collected 'for that purpose' but was obtained as part of the ordinary part of their business. The same applies to employers who make such information available.

If a credit reference agency is consulted by a business, there are duties as to the disclosure of this fact (see below).

Licensing requirements

Ancillary credit businesses need licences

Unenforceability of agreements when ancillary credit business unlicensed

It is a requirement of the Act that ancillary credit businesses are required to have licences exactly as though they were consumer credit or consumer hire businesses (see above). Section 148 states that an unlicensed ancillary credit business cannot enforce agreements without an order from the Director General of Fair Trading. Section 149 provides that if a consumer credit or consumer agreement is made on the introduction of an unlicensed credit broker, that agreement cannot be enforced without an order from the Director General.

In both the above cases, an appeals procedure lies in respect of adverse decisions of the Director General.

Advertisements

The provisions of the Consumer Credit (Advertisements) Regulations 1989 (see above) apply to advertisements by credit brokers. Although regulations may be made covering debt adjusters and debt counsellors, none have so far.

Canvassing

Canvassing prohibited in relation to certain ancillary businesses

Canvassing in relation to ancillary credit agreements is defined by s. 153 in broadly the same terms as in relation to the canvassing of consumer credit or hire agreements. Section 154 provides that it is an offence to canvass off trade premises the services of a credit broker, debt adjuster or debt counsellor. There is no prohibition in relation to debt collecting or credit reference agencies.

Recovering credit broker fees

If within the six months following the introduction of an individual to a possible source of credit or hire, no agreement is made with that business, then the credit broker is barred by s. 155 from recovering more than £3 in fee or commission for their services. If the credit broker fails altogether to make any introduction, this will count as a total failure of consideration and, under ordinary common-law principles outside the Act, will allow the customer either not to pay or to recover everything they have paid.

Form and content of agreements

The Act provides for regulations setting out the form and content of agreements entered into by an ancillary credit business, but no such regulations have yet been made.

Review questions

1 Give brief definitions of each category of ancillary credit business.
2 Given account of the licensing requirements imposed on ancillary credit businesses, and state the position when a business trades without a licence.
3 To what extent may an ancillary credit business be canvassed off trade premises?
4 What restrictions are imposed on a credit broker as to the recovery of their fee?

Disclosure of credit reference agency consulted

Section 157 of the Act gives customers a right to know if a credit reference agency has been consulted about them when they sought to make a consumer credit or hire agreement. Such a request, however, must be made no later than 28 days after the negotiations for the agreement had terminated, whether successfully or not. Under the provisions of the Consumer Credit (Credit Reference Agency) Regulations 1977, No. 329, the information must be supplied within seven working days. A creditor or owner is obliged by the Consumer Credit (Conduct of Business) (Credit References) Regulations 1977, No. 330 to inform a credit broker as to the name and address of any credit reference agency consulted.

Customers entitled to know who was consulted

Disclosure of information held by credit reference agency

Section 158 of the Act gives an individual the right to submit a written request to a credit reference agency, if accompanied by a fee of £1, to receive a copy of the file held on them reduced into 'plain English'. This means that, if kept in machine-readable form, it must be transcribed into English before being sent to the individual. Under the Consumer Credit (Credit Reference Agency) Regulations, the copy must be sent or delivered within seven working days. This information must be accompanied by a statement in the form set out in the regulations setting out the recipient's right to correct errors.

It should be noted here that, under the provisions of the Data Protection Act 1984, an individual has, subject to certain exceptions, the right to see copies of computer files held on them even if the holders are not credit reference agencies. That Act provides that, if a request for data is made which could be made under the Consumer Credit Act, it will be deemed to be so made.

Section 159 of the Act allows an individual to give written notice that they want their file amended or removed. Within 28 days, the agency must inform them in writing that the entry has been removed or amended (a copy of the amendment also being sent) or that it has taken no action. Within 28 days, and except where the entry has been removed, the individual may send off a notice of correction in not more than 200 words. The agency then has 28 days in which to indicate if it accepts this notice, unless it intends to apply to the Director General of Fair Trading for an order against accepting the notice of correction. Similarly, if the individual does not hear within 28 days that the notice of correction has been accepted, they too may apply to the Director General. If a file is amended or removed, appropriate details must be sent to any business to which, in the six months preceding the individual's request for information, it sent information relating to their financial position. This must be done within 10 working days of notifying the individual of the change or from the time allowed by the Director General for compliance with an order.

Information held on file may be demanded and corrected or removed

Business consumers

The disclosure of information under the foregoing provisions may affect the ability of a credit reference agency to provide a proper service to its subscribers since any copy of the file would be likely to reveal the agency's source of information, and hence those willing to supply such information would probably cease to do so. As a result, an alternative procedure is permitted in the case of business consumers. If the credit reference agency has received the approval of the Director General of Fair Trading, this alternative procedure may be used. The essence of the alternative procedure is that extracts of the file only need be sent, but the individual can approach the Director General if dissatisfied with the extract.

Review questions

1 To what extent has an individual the right to know if a credit reference agency was consulted when they were seeking entry into a credit or hire agreement?
2 Set out the rights open to an individual who wishes to see a copy of a file held on them and what they may do to have entries changed. In what way does the process differ for business consumers?

Chapter summary

The Consumer Credit Act is concerned with agreements made by individuals who enter into credit or hire agreements.

- A licensing procedure is laid down for those in the business of credit or hire. This licensing procedure is administered by the Office of Fair Trading.
- The Act, and regulations made under it, lay down detailed rules as to the form and content of documents, as well as prescribing rules for the sending of copies of documents.
- Certain agreements may be cancelled after they were made.
- A regime of joint and several liability ensures that creditors as well as suppliers are liable for any breach of contract with a customer or for the supply to them of defective goods.
- The Act imposes controls over the way in which business is sought. Canvassing is controlled, as is the sending of unsolicited credit tokens and information to minors.
- Regulations control the content of credit and hire advertisements.
- Elaborate provisions are contained in the Act and associated regulations for ensuring that ample warning is given to customers before any enforcement action can be taken against them or goods are repossessed.
- Customers are given rights of termination in relation to hire-purchase, conditional-sale and hire agreements which are quite distinct from the cancellation provisions.
- Provision is made for the form and content of securities, and for the realization of securities. Separate provision is made where the security is in the form of a pawn or pledge.

- Controls are imposed over the use of negotiable instruments taken under regulated agreements or securities.
- The Act contains provisions for regulating the activities of ancillary credit businesses. These provisions include licensing requirements as imposed on credit or hire businesses.
- The courts are given various powers in relation to agreements. These include the power to issue time orders, return orders, transfer orders and, importantly, the power to reopen extortionate agreements.

United Kingdom application

This chapter applies in its entirety throughout the United Kingdom.

Case study exercise

The Credit Supply Co. is approached by John in his quest for money to buy a new car. He answers an advertisement in the paper and soon receives a telephone call from one of their consultants. They agree to meet at John's home. John advises the consultant that he is unemployed, and has little income beyond the state benefits. He is therefore relieved to be offered £15 000 repayable over 10 years at an annual rate of interest of 75 per cent, at a time when APRs in the marketplace are in the low teens.

The loan agreement is signed and John receives his copy some 14 days later. The loan is credited to his bank one month after the meeting at John's home.

John then goes to a car dealer where he pays cash for the car of his choice. Not long after, the car breaks down and he is advised by one of the motoring associations that it is not of satisfactory quality nor reasonably fit for its purpose, and that he accordingly has a claim against the dealer under the Sale of Goods Act 1979.

John therefore goes back to the dealer's premises only to find that the business has gone into liquidation. Unsure of what to do, he stops his repayments and soon receives a phone call from the Credit Supply Co. advising that action will be taken against him if he does not bring his account up to date within seven days. John fails to do this and the car is repossessed by a security firm acting on the instructions of Credit Supply Co.

Student task

In the light of the above facts, indicate to John what rights he might have against the Credit Supply Co.

Discussion questions

1 It would be administratively easier, and there would be no shortcomings in consumer protection, if the system of positive licensing currently required by the Consumer Credit Act were replaced by a system of negative licensing under which all were allowed to provide credit or hire agreements except where specifically barred by the Office of Fair Trading. To what extent do you agree with this proposition?
2 In what circumstances is an order of the Director General of Fair Trading required before an agreement can be enforced?
3 To what extent does the Consumer Credit Act control ways of seeking business?

Further reading

Consumer Credit Control, Bennion (1976), Longman Professional.
This is a four-volume loose-leaf text and is strongly recommended.
The Consumer Credit Act – A Student's Guide, Goode (1979), Butterworths.
Consumer Credit and Consumer Hire Law – A Practical Guide, Harding (1995), Sweet & Maxwell.
For a background to the passing of the Act, there is the Report of the Committee on Consumer Credit (Cmnd 4596).

6 Advertising and marketing

Introduction

A particularly pervasive aspect of business these days is the extent to which goods or services are not allowed simply to sell themselves. Instead, schemes are constantly being devised which add allure to the product or service in that the prospect of a prize or some other benefit is held out to the purchaser. At the same time, the advertising prepared for products or services, whether or not some such scheme as above is also deployed, not infrequently makes increasingly florid and bold claims for its subject matter. Yet, despite the size and importance of the advertising and sales promotion industry, it is seldom dealt with in texts on business law. This chapter will fill this gap.

Objectives

This chapter will explain both the legal and self-regulatory controls over marketing and advertising. It will concentrate in particular on showing how games and competitions can be lawfully organized by advertising agencies on behalf of retailers and manufacturers generally. There will also be an account of statutory controls over misleading advertising, the controls over broadcast advertising, and an account of the EU background to this legislation.

It will be explained that this legal control is supplemented by a well-developed system of self-regulation operated with the support of, but acting independently of, the advertising industry. Attention will also be given to how the system of self-regulation is enforced.

Key concepts

- Statutory control of promotions with prizes
- Free entry as a way of validating promotions
- Skill as a way of validating promotions
- Trading stamps
- Regulation of advertising claims
- EU legislation
- The radio and television codes
- Self-regulation and the British codes of advertising and sales promotion
- Industry specific codes.

Promotions with prizes: The Lotteries and Amusements Act

Section 1 of the Lotteries and Amusements Act 1976 states that all lotteries are illegal (for the position as regards the National Lottery and other lawful lotteries or distributions of prizes by chance, see Lawful lotteries).

No definition is given in the Act of 'lottery', but this has been made good by the courts which have defined 'lottery' as meaning 'a distribution of prizes by chance': *Taylor* v *Smetten* (1883); *Imperial Tobacco Co. Ltd* v *Attorney-General* (1980).

Case example
DPP v *Bradfute Associates* (1967)

The purchasers of cat food were invited to remove the label and examine the inside. There they would find a bingo card and some numbers placed alongside the card. They were invited to match those numbers with the numbers on the card. If they were lucky enough to match a line, they could then move onto the second stage of the promotion, which was to answer a puzzle which involved some geometric designs. The prizes were therefore won by those who had both a winning card, and who answered the puzzle correctly. The court held that the promotion had two separate stages, and that stage one (having a winning bingo card) was a lottery since winning depended entirely on chance. The prize for succeeding at stage 1 was to proceed to stage 2 (the puzzle). The fact that there might be skill at stage 2 did not prevent stage one from being an illegal lottery.

Free entry

There is nothing in the 1976 Act to state that prizes can be distributed by chance if a promotion is free to enter. This, is, however, the way the courts have interpreted the Act.

Case example
Reader's Digest Association Ltd v *Williams* (1976)

Promotional material was delivered to households in the United Kingdom. Recipients were invited to buy a book. If they did so, they would return certain 'lucky' numbers found in the mail-pack in an envelope marked 'yes'. If they did not wish to buy the book, they could still participate in the draw, but by returning their numbers in the 'no' envelope. The court held that the aim of the 1976 Act was to prevent people from losing money. If it was not obligatory under the terms of a promotion to make a purchase, then the mischief of the Act was not offended, and, in the present circumstances, the promotion was lawful even though it involved a distribution of prizes by chance.

This is why newspaper 'bingo' type promotions, whereby readers win prizes if their 'lucky' numbers match up to the numbers printed in the newspaper are lawful.

Case example
***Express Newspapers Ltd v Liverpool Daily Post Ltd* (1985)**
Cards were distributed via newsagents and the mail to households. By matching the numbers on these cards to those in newspapers, recipients could determine if their cards were winners. The promotion was held to be lawful since there was no compulsion to buy a newspaper. It was always possible to borrow a copy or browse, and hence find out which were the winning numbers without actually buying the paper, even though the aim of the promotion was of course to stimulate sales.

It was said in the *Reader's Digest* case that a promotion will be illegal if a 'substantial number' of those taking part pay to enter. Just what constitutes a 'substantial number' has never been subject to litigation, and must remain a matter of uncertainty. In the *Imperial Tobacco* case, the number of free cards available from shops was very low and disregarded by the court. It was, in effect, a promotion in relation to which a purchase was necessary.

Queries relating to number of those choosing to pay

A question which has arisen in the courts is whether entry is free if a person has to pay to enter a promotion with prizes, but the price charged for the product or service is the normal price; that is to say, there is in effect no charge for taking part in the promotion.

Entry not free even if normal price charged

Case example
***Imperial Tobacco Ltd v Attorney-General* (1980)**
Packets of cigarettes contained scratch cards. Purchasers could determine if they were winners by scratching off various panels. It was argued that since the normal price was charged for the packets, entry into the promotion was free. It was ruled, however, that since a purchase had to be made to participate, that was a purchase for the purposes of the Lotteries and Amusements Act, and entry was therefore not free.

Prior inducement

If there is no advance announcement that a prize draw is to take place from among those who have bought a particular product or service, then, since there was no inducement to spend money to take part in the draw, the mischief at which the 1976 Act is aimed is not offended.

No infringement if no element of inducement

Case example
***Minty v Sylvester* (1915)**
A surprise announcement was made during a theatre production that gold coins were to be distributed that night at random, and also on certain other nights. It was held that there was no unlawful lottery the first time this was done, but that there was on the later occasions since these were announced in advance and payment for the theatre tickets on such occasions was also, because of the element of prior inducement, payment to participate in the random distribution of prizes.

Element of skill

Since a lottery is a distribution of prizes by chance, it follows that, if prizes are won by skill, no offence is committed. Just what constitutes 'skill' in any one case is difficult to determine, since, among other things, it will depend on who is asked to take part. For instance, a promotion directed to the very young will not be as demanding as the skill required of adults. There is little guidance in the case law, but it has been said that any degree of skill, bodily or mental, will suffice providing it is beyond the derisory: *DPP* v *Scott* (1914).

Case example
Andren v Stubbings (1924)
Purchasers of boxes of matches won prizes if they were lucky enough to find a match which burned with a green flame as opposed to the normal blue. It was held that distinguishing colours was not a test of skill.

Case example
John Wagstaffe Ltd v Police (1965)
Prizes were awarded to those who counted up the number of red spots in a window display. This was held not to be a test of skill.

Lawful lotteries

Exemption for National Lottery and others

There are a number of promotions involving the distribution of prizes by chance which might be illegal under the above provisions, but which have in fact been exempted from the ban on lotteries. The most obvious is probably the National Lottery, which was made lawful by the National Lottery Act 1993. Similarly, premium bonds are legalized by the National Loans Act 1967. The 1976 Act itself allows lotteries run by registered societies; and it also contains exemptions for local authority lotteries and those run by those who live or work in the same premises (this allows offices, for example, to run 'Grand National' lotteries). Football pools, bingo and organized betting are also allowed under the terms of the Betting, Gaming and Lotteries Act 1963 and the Gaming Act 1968.

Review questions

1 The 1976 Act makes lotteries unlawful. Define a 'lottery'.
2 What difference does it make if a promotion involves a distribution of prizes by chance, but is free to enter?
3 What is the relevance of skill to the ban on lotteries, and how would you define skill?
4 What is the significance of prior inducement?
5 Why are promotions such as the National Lottery lawful?

Prize competitions

As well as imposing controls over lotteries, the Lotteries and Amusements Act 1976 also controls 'prize competitions'. Section 14 of the Act, which imposes these controls, does not define what is meant by a 'prize competition', but a definition has been provided by the courts.

> ## Case example
> ### *Imperial Tobacco Ltd* v *Attorney-General* (1980)
> See the facts as given above (Free entry). The court held that a prize competition was one which involved the exercise of skill. Since there was no skill in the promotion, it was not a prize competition.

Skill necessary in prize 'competitions'

Rules governing prize competitions

Once it is established that a promotion with prizes is a 'prize competition' (i.e. that an element of skill is involved in winning), s. 14 of the 1976 Act provides as follows:

Rules for prize competitions

1 The promotion must not ask for the results of past events if such result is not ascertained or generally known.
2 The promotion must not ask for the forecasts of the result of future events.
3 All prize competitions must depend to a substantial degree on the exercise of skill.

> ## Case example
> ### *News of the World Ltd* v *Friend* (1973)
> A photograph of a football match was shown in a newspaper with the ball removed. A grid was superimposed on the photograph and contestants were asked to say in which grid the ball was. The prizes were won not by those who had guessed the actual position of the ball but by those who selected the same position as had been selected by an expert panel. The court rejected the argument that contestants were predicting the result of an event (i.e. the decision of the panel following its meeting). It said that to argue that this promotion called for forecasts to be made of an event would be stretching the language further than was warranted.

This ruling opened the way for many promotions to ask for forecasts which do not, on analysis, ask for the forecasts of the result of a future event. One example is to ask what price a share will have at the close of trading on a certain specified day in the future. Another is to ask how much rain will fall on a certain future day. In neither case can it be said, respectively, that the share price or the amount of rain is the result of an event.

Way opened for legal forecasting

It is because of this ruling that there are many promotions on the market which ask for forecasts but which are the right side of the law.

Exercise of skill

Point 3 above stipulated as an additional requirement that winning must depend to a substantial degree on the exercise of skill.

> ## Case example
> ### *Witty* v *World Services Ltd* (1935)
> The readers of a newspaper were asked to state what places in the United Kingdom were represented by nine pictures. More than one place might be suggested by each picture, but each picture was so designed that one name was more fitted than any other. The court held that the winning of the competition depended to a substantial degree on the exercise of skill.

If the particular promotion asks for correct answers to be given to certain questions, but the promoter does not wish to give prizes to all getting the correct answers, a further test of skill must be imposed to reduce those qualifying for the prizes. The most common form of 'tie-breaker', as it is usually called, is to ask contestants to state in not more than a given number of words why they like the particular product or service. The prize(s) then go to the person(s) answering the questions correctly and who have also answered the tie-breaker in the best way as determined by a panel of judges. The wrong approach would be to make a draw from those getting the correct answers.

Case example
R v *Interactive Telephone Services Ltd* (1995)

Contestants were asked to ring a telephone number and to answer a number of questions. Those who answered the questions correctly were placed in a prize draw. The court held that presence of the draw eliminated the effect of the skill shown in obtaining correct answers, with the result that the promotion did not depend to a substantial degree on the exercise of skill.

Payment

It was held in the *Imperial Tobacco* case (1980) that it was not relevant to the legality of a prize competition that a payment was or was not required for participation.

Review questions

1 What is a 'prize competition'?
2 To what extent is it lawful to run a prize competition which asks for the results of events?
3 What has to be done to ensure that winning a prize competition depends to a substantial degree on the exercise of skill?

Trading stamps

Definition of 'trading stamp'

Wide definition of 'trading stamp'

Section 10(1) of the Trading Stamps Act 1964 defines a 'trading stamp' in the widest possible terms. In essence, a trading stamp is any stamp or anything like a stamp, such as a coupon or token, which is obtained following a purchase and which can be exchanged for any kind of benefit, concession, advantage or allowance whatsoever.

This definition goes beyond what is normally thought of as a 'trading stamp', of which the Green Shield stamp is the best known example. A label on a jar of coffee will be a trading stamp if, for example, consumers have to collect three and send off to obtain a free towel. The label is obtained on purchase and can be exchanged for a benefit, i.e. the towel. Similarly, the popular 'Air Miles' promotion involves trading stamps since vouchers for air travel are obtainable following the purchase of a particular product or service.

However, s. 10(1) does exclude stamps which are contained in newspapers or periodicals, such as those coupons which offer 'Xp' off the purchase of a product.

There is also an exemption for stamps which are redeemed by the seller of the particular goods, or the person who sold the goods to the seller; and if, where the retail business concerned is one carried on at six or more establishments, the particular stamps are (a) obtainable at no more than six of those outlets; and (b) the arrangements under which they are redeemed must be entirely separate from arrangements under which other stamps are redeemed.

Where a stamp is within the legislation

Details of promoter

Section 2(2) of the Act requires the name of the company running the trading stamps scheme, or, in the case of an industrial and provident society, the name of that society, to appear on the face of the trading stamp in clear and legible characters.

Certain details to appear on face of trading stamp

Cash value

Section 2(1), in one of the more important aspects to the Act, also states that a trading stamp must bear on its face in clear and legible characters a statement of its value. There is no requirement in the Act as to what this value is to be, and it can therefore be any value chosen by the promoter of the trading stamp scheme. Commonly, trading stamps are given a value of 0.01p.

Trading stamps to have a cash value

It was noted above that the definition of a trading stamp is very wide. Because of this, it is necessary for the cash value to be placed on a wider range of tokens, vouchers and stamps than was probably intended by Parliament. As a consequence, it is not always the case that what might be called these 'unexpected' trading stamps contain the required statement of the cash value, though some do. The fact that no prosecutions ever take place of offending trading stamps probably lies in the fact that no specific authority is obliged to enforce the Act (unlike, for example, the Trade Descriptions Act 1968 which obliges local authorities to enforce its provisions); and because it is probably realized that more falls within the definition of 'trading stamp' than was ever intended.

Display of cash value

Section 7(1) of the Act says that every shop which makes trading stamps available must display a notice indicating the cash value of the trading stamps issued as well as indicating the number of stamps available on any particular transaction. This can be easily done in the case of Green Shield type stamps. However, in the case of what was called above the 'unexpected' trading stamp, this is a practical impossibility. Supermarkets at any one time will have a vast number of different products on their shelves which, for instance, have labels or coupons which are trading stamps under the Act. Assuming that each has a cash value on them, the supermarket would have to have a notice for each product stating the value of that label or coupon, and how much has to be spent to buy that particular product. It is when this aspect to the definition of trading stamp is considered that it becomes plain that that definition was badly drafted.

Redemption for cash

Section 3(1) of the Act gives the person who has collected trading stamps with an aggregate 'cash value' of 25p an absolute right to redeem them for cash. It should be noted that 'cash value' is defined in s. 10(1) as the 'value' stated on the stamp. The problem which can arise here is that the value stated on the stamp might be intended to be the value required under s. 2(1) discussed above. For example, a coupon to be cut off a packet of cereal might state: '50p off next purchase'. This is a trading stamp within the definition given above. If, therefore, the coupon does not also give a specific value to the stamp for the purposes of the Act, that 50p will be such value and the holder can demand 50p in cash.

Section 3(2) of the Act says that the holder of trading stamps who wishes to redeem them for cash can do so in any of the following ways:

- by presenting the stamps at any reasonable time at the promoter's registered office;
- by sending the stamps through the post to that office so long as there are sufficient instructions indicating how the cash is to be paid over;
- in any other way allowed by the promoter.

Redemption for goods

Trading stamps can be redeemed for cash or goods

The holder of trading stamps also has an absolute right to exchange the stamps for goods which is, of course, what happens in the greater number of cases. On redemption for goods, certain obligations are imposed on the promoter. Those in relation to fitness and title are dealt with in the Sale of Goods Act (see above).

Availability of catalogues

The Act does not oblige the promoter of a trading stamp scheme to publish a catalogue but, where the scheme involves, as the traditional trading stamp schemes always do, the exchange of stamps for goods, it will be a practical impossibility to run the scheme without a catalogue.

No compulsion to produce catalogue

Section 5(1) states that, where there is a catalogue, this must indicate the number of stamps needed to obtain the items in the catalogue. The catalogue must also contain a prominent indication of the name of the promoter and its registered office. Section 7(1)(b) requires every shop running a trading stamps scheme to have available a catalogue, if one has been published, where it can be 'conveniently consulted' by customers.

Trading stamp advertisements

Section 6(1) of the Act provides that no advertisement may be published which conveys, or seeks to convey, the cash value of any trading stamps by means of a statement associating their worth with what has to be paid to get them. It would therefore be illegal to say: '£10 worth of trading stamps when you spend £100'. It is only permissible to state: 'Each £1 purchase gives you a trading stamp worth 10p'. It is also made illegal by s. 6(1)(b) to advertise the cash value of a stamp in a way which is misleading or deceptive. Thus, it would be illegal to say: '£5 off your shopping when you collect our trading stamps' if the advertisement did not also indicate the cash value of each stamp and what had to be spent to obtain such a stamp.

Review questions

1 What is a 'trading stamp' as defined by the Trading Stamps Act 1964?
2 To what extent does this definition catch more than stamps such as Green Shield stamps?
3 What is required to be placed on a trading stamp which is within the Act?
4 What are the rights of a holder of trading stamps?
5 Does the promoter of a trading stamp scheme have to publish a catalogue?
6 What rules apply if a catalogue has been published?
7 What rules govern the way in which the cash value of a trading stamp is advertised?

Product claims and descriptions

All forms of product claims and descriptions are covered by the Trade Descriptions Act 1968. It makes it an offence, in the course of a trade or business, to apply a false trade description to goods or to supply goods to which a false trade description is applied. An offence can be committed by written, pictorial or verbal descriptions. There are numerous examples of infringements of the Act, of which the following are a representative selection.

Case example
***Queensway Discount Warehouses Ltd v Burke* (1986)**
Furniture was advertised by the use of photographs showing it in assembled form when in fact it was only available in kit form.

Case example
***British Gas Corporation v Lubbock* (1974)**
A brochure for a cooker stated that it was ignited by a hand held battery torch supplied with the cooker. The torches had, however, been discontinued. This was held to be a false statement as to the composition of the goods and a false statement as to its characteristics.

Case example
***Van den Berghs & Jurgens Ltd v Burleigh* (1987)**
A blend of buttermilk, vegetable oil and butter was sold under the description 'whipping' or 'single'. The packaging suggested the countryside and followed the generally accepted colouring convention for the marketing of cream. A statement described the product as 'the real alternative to cream'. It was held that an offence had been committed. The packaging was likely to deceive the average customer because the general packaging was that associated in the mind of the public with cream. The average member of the pubic was not likely to read what was printed with sufficient care to realize that what was offered for sale was not cream.

What constitutes a 'trade description'

Only those descriptions listed in s. 2 of the Act count as trade descriptions. They are:

1 The quality, size or gauge of goods.
2 The method of manufacture, production, processing or reconditioning.
3 Composition.
4 Fitness for purpose, strength, performance, behaviour or accuracy.
5 Any physical chacteristics not mentioned above.
6 Testing by any person and the results of the test.
7 Approval by any person or conformity with a type approved by any person.
8 Place or date of manufacture, production, processing or reconditioning.
9 Person by whom manufactured, produced, processed or reconditioned.
10 Other history, including previous ownership or use.

The essence of the above list of descriptions is that it can be said they all relate to matters which are either true or false, and not matters of opinion.

The Act applies whether the relevant statements are written or oral.

Case example
Cadbury Ltd v *Halliday* (1975)

Chcolate marked 'extra value' was marketed alongside chocolate bars produced by the same manufacturer which weighed more but which cost the same. The court ruled that 'extra value' was not a trade description because it was not such a description 'in respect of which truth or falsity can be established as a matter of fact'.

Oral statements within the Act

False or misleading

Only listed items are trade descriptions

The Act creates an offence only where the trade description is false. This is defined by s. 3(1) to mean 'false to a material degree'. This would allow the courts to disregard a statement where the falsity was minimal, such as describing a cardigan as 'all wool', when it was in fact 99 per cent wool.

Descriptions must be false to a material degree

Section 3(2) goes on to say that a trade description shall be deemed to be false if 'likely to be taken' for a trade description which is false to a material degree. For instance, if a car's petrol consumption were given as a figure which could only be obtained under conditions not normally available, that statement, while true, would be one likely to be taken as a statement which was false to a material degree (i.e. the likely consumption under normal driving conditions).

Strict liability

Defendant's state of mind irrelevant

It should be noted that the above offence is one of 'strict liability', meaning that it is irrelevant whether or not the person charged knew or should have known that the description was false or misleading. It is, however, necessary that the person charged knows that a false description has been applied (*Cottee* v *Douglas Seaton (Used Cars) Ltd* (1972)).

Review questions

1 What statements are covered by s. 1 of the Trade Descriptions Act 1968?
2 What is meant by 'false' in this context?
3 What are the implications of the offence created by s. 1 being an offence of 'strict liability'?

Statements as to services etc.

Section 14 of the Act provides that an offence arises where a false or misleading statement is made in the course of a trade or business which is known to be false, or which is made recklessly, as to any service, facility or accommodation.

In contrast to the position with product claims and descriptions (see above), this is a 'traditional' offence in that the person charged must have a degree of knowledge before an offence can be committed.

> **Case example**
> **MFI Warehouses Ltd v Nattrass (1971)**
> An advertisement was issued referring to louvre doors which also contained the words 'folding doors gear (carriage free)' and which offered folding door sets on 14 days' free approval. This statement was false, and the question was whether it had been made recklessly. This is defined in the Act as meaning a statement made 'careless whether it be true or false'. It was held that it was enough for the prosecution to show that the person charged did not have regard to the truth or falsity of his advertisement, even though it could not be shown that he had deliberately closed his eyes to the truth, or that he had any kind of dishonest intention.

An offence is committed even though the defendant did not know it was false when published, but knew it was false when communicated to a customer.

> **Case example**
> **Wings Ltd v Ellis (1985)**
> A tour operator advertised that certain hotel accommodation was air-conditioned, but later discovered that this was not the case. On discovering the mistake, the operator took the precautions of giving instructions for amending brochures, informing phone callers and writing to clients who had already booked. Some nine months later, a customer booked a holiday on the strength of an unamended brochure and received no rectification of the false statement. The House of Lords ruled that an offence had arisen when the inaccurate statement was read by the customer because that statement was known at the time to be false.

Promises

If a person promises to do something in the future, and then fails to do so, they may be liable to prosecution under s. 14.

> **Case example**
> **British Airways Board v Taylor (1976)**
> A customer was advised by letter that he had a confirmed reservation on a certain flight. Because the airline deliberately overbooked the flight, this was not so, and in fact there was no seat available for him when he turned up. The House of Lords accepted that promises themselves were not actionable under the provisions of the Act. It would be different, however, where the promise actually contained a representation of existing fact, which was in fact the case here. However, for reasons not related to the Trade Descriptions Act, the defendants were acquitted. See too *Sunair Holidays Ltd v Dodd* (1970) and *Beckett v Cohen* (1973).

Promises generally fall outside the Act

Whether professions are covered

Both s. 1 and s. 14 of the Act refer to descriptions or statements made in the course of a 'trade or business' and questions have arisen as to whether this includes the professions.

The Act covers professions

> ## Case example
> ### *Roberts v Leonard and Bryan* (1995)
> Charges were brought against veterinary surgeons to the effect that they had, by means of a health certificate, applied to calves a false trade description. Noting that the Concise Oxford Disctionary defines 'business' as including a 'profession' the court ruled that the professions were within the Act. See too *R* v *Breeze* (1973).

Review questions

1 What areas are covered by s. 14 of the Trade Descriptions Act which are not covered by s. 1?
2 Consider the extent to which promises are covered by s. 14.
3 Consider the extent to which the expression 'trade or business' covers professional activities.

Disclaimers

Because s. 1 is an offence of strict liability, a number of traders, especially in the motor trade, sought to avoid liability by disclaiming any possible liability should they inadvertently sell goods which were falsely described. This was a particular problem in the motor trade where a dealer might not always know if the milometer was accurate.

> ## Case example
> ### *Norman v Bennett* (1974)
> A contract between two dealers contained a disclaimer of liability for the accuracy of the milometer in the fine print of the contract. The court laid down the rule that, for a disclaimer to be effective, a disclaimer must be as 'bold, precise and compelling as the trade description itself and must be as effectively brought to the notice of any person to whom the goods may be supplied. In other words, the disclaimer must equal the trade description in the extent to which it is likely to get home to anyone interested in receiving the goods.' In the very special circumstances of this case, however, which was a contract beween two dealers who were aware that the accuracy of the milometer was not guaranteed, the disclaimer was upheld.

> ## Case example
> ### *Savory v Dawson* (1976)
> A firm obtained an entry in the Yellow Pages under the heading 'Architects', although no member of the firm was a qualified architect. At the top of each of the pages in the directory, there was, in small print, a reference to another page and on that page there was a statement that the headings were not intended as trade descriptions and did not indicate that a particular professional status or qualification was held. A charge was brought under s. 14. The court said that the words used in *Norman* v *Bennett* (above) were not meant for this type of publication, but there must be still some simultaneous correction which contradicts or disclaims the accuracy of the information wrongly given. In the present case, the link between the disclaimer was insufficient and the prominence of the language of the disclaimer was also insufficient.

> ### Case example
> ### *Newham London Borough* v *Singh* (1987)
> Motor dealers had placed a sticker on the milometer stating: 'Trade Descriptions Act 1968. Dealers are often unable to guarantee the mileage of a used car on sale. Please disregard the recorded mileage on this vehicle and accept this as an incorrect reading.' The court ruled that these steps were more than adequate to bring the disclaimer to the attention of purchasers.

Disclaimers must be fully brought to the attention of the other side

Review question

To what extent is it possible for a party to overcome an inaccurate trade description by the use of a disclaimer, and what are the rules that must be followed?

The 'by-pass' provision

The Act contains in s. 23 provision for charging the person whose act or default caused another person to commit the particular offence. Such person can be charged with committing the offence, whether or not charges are brought against the person who really did commit the offence.

> ### Case example
> ### *Olgeirsson* v *Kitching* (1986)
> A private individual sold a car to a dealer knowing that the milometer reading was false. He was found guilty under this section since he had caused the dealer to commit an offence.

Defences

Section 24(1) provides for a defence where the person charged can prove both the following:

The defence is a 'two-limb' defence

1 That the commission of the offence was due to a mistake, or to reliance on information supplied, or to the act or default of another person, or an accident, or some other cause beyond their control.
2 That they took all reasonable precautions and exercised all due diligence to avoid commission of the offence.

There do not appear to be any cases on what what is meant by 'mistake' or 'accident' in this context. It is, howeer, clear that the 'mistake' must be a mistake by the person charged and that a mistake by an employee is not within the provisions (*Birkenhead Co-Operative Society Ltd* v *Roberts* (1970) and *Butler* v *Keenway Markets* (1974)).

An example of 'reliance on information supplied' was given during the parliamentary debates on the then Trade Descriptions Bill. A tailor might be assured by their supplier that a particular parcel was 'all wool'. A tailor who then made up a suit, and falsely described it as being '100 per cent wool' would be able to say that they relied on information supplied. It would appear that the reading on a milometer can amount to information passed on to a purchaser (*Simmons* v *Potter* (1975)).

When the defendant to a charge is a company, it will have to show that the person said to be 'another' person must not, if an employee of the defendant, be someone who, because of their status, can be effecively treated as the company itself.

> ## Case example
> ### *Becket* v *Kingston Bros (Butchers) Ltd* (1970)
> It was held that the manager of one of a chain of shops who, by failing to read instructions, sold a misdescribed turkey, was 'another person'.

> ## Case example
> ### *Tesco Supermarkets Ltd* v *Nattrass* (1972)
> The defendants owned a large number of supermarkets. They had established a reasonable and efficient system for ensuring that employees complied with the provisions of the Trade Descriptions Act. The shop in question had contravened the pricing provisions of the Act (for the current controls over misleading pricing, see below). This had come about because the shop manager had failed to supervise the work of an assistant. It was held that the manager was 'another person'. He could not be classed as a director or other superior officer of the company. Any such person would not be 'another person' since he would in effect be the company itself. See too *Lewin* v *Rothersthorpe Road Garage Ltd* (1984) where a salesman was also held to be 'another person'.

Due diligence

As a practical matter, it is the second limb of the defence which causes defendants the greatest problem. It is for this reason that more recent enactments such as the Consumer Protection Act 1987 (see below) use only this limb and dispense altogether with the first limb. The cases establish that the courts require a very high standard before a defendant can be said to have taken all reasonable precautions and exercised all due diligence to avoid the commission of an offence.

> ## Case example
> ### *Sherratt* v *Geralds the American Jeweller* (1970)
> The defendants sold a watch incorrectly described as 'waterproof'. Since they had not taken the elementary precaution of dipping it in a bowl of water, they were held not to have exercised due diligence

> ## Case example
> ### *Westminster City Council* v *Pierglow Ltd* (*divisional court*) (1994)
> The defendant was charged with an offence under the Trade Descriptions Act 1968 for falsely describing certain jeans as the manufacture of Levi Strauss. The jeans had been obtained from a business associate in Greece with whom the defendants had been dealing for a couple of years. These were sold to the defendants for £1 or £2 less than the usual UK wholesale price. The goods were examined by the defendants and they appeared to be in order. The Justices held that the defence had been made out. This was even though the description in the

shipping document was 'Blue Jeans type Levi's 501'. In particular, the bench said that it was not 'reasonable or realistic' to expect the defendants to make enquiries of the manufacturer or their suppliers.

The divisional court dismissed the appeal, noting that the supplier had proved reliable over two years and that the price charged by the supplier indicated that the goods were genuine. The court saw nothing in the suggestion that the defendants could have gone back to their supplier for reassurance, since he would merely have repeated what was on the label. Nor was there any merit in the suggestion that contact should have been made with Levi themselves: 'If every time a supplier or retailer comes into possession of a quantity of goods, in order to avoid a possible contravention of the Act he has to go right back to the manufacturer, then the burden which is being placed upon the retailer is far beyond that of establishing that he took all reasonable precautions and exercised all due diligence.'

Case example
The Tesco Case (see above)

The defendants had set up a reasonable and efficient system of instruction and inspection for ensuring that their staff complied with the provisions of the Trade Descriptions Act. Even though the system had broken down on this occasion because of the failure of the store manager to check things properly, this did not mean that they had not shown due diligence.

Personal liability

If the particular offence was committed by a company, the Act provides that any of the following can be charged as well as the company if the offence was due to their neglect or was committed with their consent and connivance: any director, manager, secretary of similar officer, and any person who purported to act in such capacity. The Act makes it clear that this applies also to people holding similar positions in nationalized industries. To prove neglect, the prosecution must show that the relevant person knew the company was applying a false trade description or that they had reasonable cause to suspect it was false (*R* v *McMillan Aviation Ltd and McMillan* (1981)).

Case example
Hirschler v *Birch* (1988)

The director of a company visited Holland where he was shown car parts. A set of lights was sent to England where they were collected by another director. He checked as to their legality and advised the first director that they could be lawfully used in the United Kingdom. In fact, the other director had made only perfunctory enquiries, being more concerned as to whether there was a demand for these lights. The lights were not lawfully marketed in the United Kingdom, but were falsely marked with indications that they were, giving rise to offences under the Trade Descriptions Act. It was held that by failing to satisfy himself that an authoritative source had confirmed the legality of the lights, the offences by the company had been committed because of the neglect of the first director.

Company directors can face personal liability

Innocent publication of advertisement

A defence is provided by s. 25 for the person charged to show that they were a person whose business it is to publish or arrange for the publication of advertisements, and that they received the advertisement for publication in the ordinary course of business and did not know, and had no reason to know, that publication would breach the Act. This will cover newspaper publishers and television and radio broadcasters.

Penalties and prosecution

Section 18 provides for a fine not exceeding the statutory maximum (currently £5000) when a prosecution is brought before magistrates. If taken before the Crown Court, which is what will be done if the prosecution thinks the case to be a serious one, the penalty is a fine (no maximum being fixed) and/or a sentence not exceeding two years.

Case example
_R_ v _Starr_ (1985)

A car dealer had pleaded guilty to turning back the milometers on cars by some 30 000 miles. He appealed against sentence of six months imprisonment, four being suspended. Dismissing the appeal, the Court of Appeal held that any motor trader selling 'clocked' vehicles could expect the courts to give serious consideration to an immediate custodial sentence.

Case example
_R_ v _Gupta_ (1985)

'The appellants' ... [suggested] ... 'that he expected to get a substantial fine. Dishonest secondhand motor-car dealers who "clock" vehicles should expect not to get a substantial fine but a sentence imposing immediate loss of libery _plus_ a substantial fine. It is very important in these cases that not only should dishonest secondhand car dealers be punished, in the sense of losing their liberty, but the very large profits which they make from this kind of behaviour should be taken away from them by way of substantial fine.' See too _R_ v _Hammerton Cars_ (1976).

Clocking demands severe penalties

Prosecutions must be brought no later than three years from the commission of the offence, or one year from its discovery by the prosecutor whichever is the earlier. Proceedings in the magistrates' court must be commenced within 12 months of the commission of the offence.

Case example
Brooks v _Club Continental Ltd_ (1981)

A complaint was made to a trading standards officer about alleged statements made recklessly as to facilities not available on a camping holiday. The initial complaint was made on 19 July. Written statements were given on 26 and 30 September. Informations were laid on 14 November of the following year. The magistrates upheld the defence proposition that the informations were laid out of time. The Appeal was dismissed. There was abundant evidence for the conclusion that the prosecution had 'discovered' the offence more than one year prior to the laying of the informations on 14 November even though the prosecution might have had to make further enquiries as to the identity of the companies involved.

Case example
R v *Shrewsbury Magistrates' Court* (1995)

A fire engine had been built and supplied to the specifications of Shropshire County Council. It was delivered in July 1991. On 21 May 1992, the Deputy Chief Trading Standards Officer of the council heard a radio discussion which indicated that there were problems with the fire engine, and, in the 12 months which followed, he investigated the matter. On 20 May 1993, the Chief Trading Standards Office laid informations under the Act by sending a fax to the Magistrates' Court.

It was accepted that, if the relevant knowledge for the purposes of s. 19 was that of the Trading Standards Department, the informations were laid in time. The Chief and Deputy Trading Standards Officers were the only officers to have delegated authority to institute proceedings under the Act. If, on the other hand, the relevant knowledge was that of other County Council officers, then it was also accepted that the informations were out of time.

The scheme of delegation

The Scheme of Delegation adopted by Shropshire County Council requires the Chief Trading Standards Officer to consult the Chief Executive or County Secretary and Solicitor prior to the institution of proceedings. Normally, this would have meant submission of the file to the County Secretary and Solicitor, whose department normally undertakes prosecution on behalf of the Trading Standards Department. Normal procedure was not, however, followed in this case because civil proceedings were being pursued and it was felt that these should be kept apart from criminal proceedings. As a result, this particular file was not seen by the County Secretary and Solicitor.

There was a meeting on 8 April 1993 of the Policy and Resources Committee at which it was decided that no action was to be taken by the Chief Trading Standards Officer under the Trade Descriptions Act without prior consultation with the Chairman of the Committee.

The divisional court did not find, in either the Scheme of Delegation or those minutes, anything to suggest that it was the County Council rather than the Chief Trading Standards Officer who was the prosecutor. The latter was obliged to consult but, having done so, there was no limit on his freedom to institute and conduct proceedings. Prima facie, the court said, the prosecutor was that party formally initiating the judicial process here by the laying of informations. If this line of argument were correct, the court said, then the informations were laid in time.

The court then went on, however, to consider the position had the prosecutor actually been the County Council. It was the case that the facts material to the present charge were known to the Chief Fire Officer and the Assistant Chief Solicitor in November 1991, more than one year before the informations were laid. Crucially, though, there was no suggestion that either party appreciated that such facts could found a prosecution under the Trade Descriptions Act. The respondents contended that there was no 'discovery' within the Act if there was no understanding of the significance of the known facts.

The divisional court agreed with these latter submissions. Knowledge of the facts without appreciation of their significance, McCowan LJ said, 'would not cause time to run, assuming that the prosecutor was the county council'.

It was acknowledged that the successful arguments put forward by the respondents could have unfair consequences. For example, a chief consumer protection officer and his deputy might be incompetent and have information for more than a year without understanding its significance. An information could still be laid in these circumstances. It would, however, be open to the court in such circumstances to declare the proceedings abusive.

Strict time limits apply for bringing of prosecutions

Review questions

1 Explain the circumstances in which a prosecution can be brought against the person who caused another actually to commit the offence.
2 The defence available to defendants under s. 24(1) is often referred to as a 'two-limbed' defence. Explain what this means.
3 In the first limb of the defence, reference is made to 'mistake' and to 'act or default of another'. In what circumstances do these have effect?
4 Explain what is meant by having to show 'due diligence'.
5 What are the penalties for breach of the Trade Descriptions Act and when is it likely that a prison sentence will be imposed?
6 What time limits apply to the bringing of proceedings?
7 What special defence is available to those who publish advertisements which infringe the Act?

Price claims

Controls on misleading price indications used to be contained in the Trade Descriptions Act but are now contained in Part III of the Consumer Protection Act 1987.

An offence arises if, in the course of any business of theirs, a person gives an indication by whatever means which is misleading as to the price at which any goods, services, accommodation or facilities are available. It is not necessary that anyone in particular was misled (*MFI* v *Hibbert* (1995))

Meaning of 'misleading'

Section 21 of the Act defines 'misleading' in the following ways:

1 A statement that the price is less than in fact it is.
2 A statement failing to indicate that the price depends on certain facts or circumstances. This would cover, for instance, a statement that a voucher can be used to indicate so much off the price, but which does not indicate that it can be redeemed only against items costing not less than a certain sum.
3 A statement failing to indicate that additional charges will be added to the price indicated. This would cover failure to indicate that VAT was payable in addition to the price stated.
4 A statement falsely indicating that a price will be increased or reduced, or will be held as increased or reduced. For instance, an advertisement might indicate a specific saving against the price to be charged after the sale. In fact, the price charged after the sale is the same as that charged during the sale.
5 A statement falsely indicating the facts or circumstances by which the vality of any relevant price comparison is to be judged. This would catch an indication of price which compared the price of one car with that of another without indicating that the price of that other had since been reduced.

Wide definition of 'misleading'

Code of practice

Acting under the provisions of s. 25 of the Act, Parliament approved a Code of Practice for Traders on Price Indications (see the Consumer Protection (Code of Practice for Traders on Price Indications) Approval Order 1988, SI 1988/2078). The Act expressly states that the Code only has evidentiatry status; that is to say, breach of the Code is evidence that the price indication is misleading; compliance with the Code is evidence that it is not.

Code as indicating status of price indication

Case example
Toys 'Я' Us v Gloucestershire County Council (1994)

A retailer was charged with an offence in the following circumstances. A number of toys on the shelves were marked with certain prices. The products also bore a bar code. The problem arose when the products went through the scanner at the checkout because, in a number of cases, the scanner showed a higher price than that indicated on the price ticket stuck on the product. The Act specifically says that it is an offence to indicate a lower price than the price at which the goods are actually available.

The company was convicted before the magistrates and appealed to the High Court. It showed that it had a company policy of always charging the lower price shown on the price tag if the bar code and scanner showed a higher price. This, the High Court ruled, meant that the price at which the goods were 'available' was therefore the price actually marked on the goods. This meant that the company was not guilty of the offence, and so the decision of the magistrates was reversed.

Case example
MFI Ltd v Hibbert (1995)

It is a requirement of the Code that, where a price is claimed as reduced, the higher price must have lasted for at least 28 consecutive days during the preceding six months. Certain advertisements published by MFI did not comply with this requirement, and the prices were held to be misleading.

Case example
Warwickshire County Council v Johnson (1993)

An offer was placed outside a retailers which offered to beat the price charged elsewhere on certain goods. The branch manager refused to honour this promise. It was held that the notice outside the shop was a continuing offer and could only be tested by someone taking up the offer. Since the branch manager had refused to honour the offer, it was therefore misleading. However, an offence can only arise when the person charged is acting 'in the course of any business of his' and this could not cover a branch manager who was neither owner nor having a controlling interest in the shop.

Disclaimers

Although there is no authority, it is presumed that the position as to disclaimers in relation to the Trade Descriptions Act (see above) applies here too.

The 'by-pass provision'

The Consumer Protection Act contains a by-pass provision in terms similar to that of the Trade Descriptions Act (see above). However, the person whose act or default caused the commission of the offence must be acting in the course of a trade or business (*Olgeirsson* v *Kitching* (1986) is thus not good law under the Consumer Protection Act).

Defences

Instead of the two-limbed defence contained in the Trade Descriptions Act (see above), the Consumer Protection Act requires only that a defendant has shown due diligence. The cases cited above may be treated as authorities.

Personal liability

The Consumer Protection Act imposes possible liability on company officers in terms identical to those of the Trade Descriptions Act (see above).

Penalties and prosecution

The time limits for prosecution are the same as for the Trade Descriptions Act (see above). However, while the penalty on summary conviction is the same, the penalty for a conviction before the Crown Court is a fine, without the further possibility of a prison sentence.

Review questions

1 What controls are imposed on 'misleading' price claims by the Consumer Protection Act 1987, and what is the meaning of 'misleading'?
2 What is the function of the Code of Practice for Traders on Price Indications?
3 What responsibility would individuals such as store managers have for breach of the provisions as to misleading pricing?

Advertising control

Advertisements are of course subject to the provisions of the Trade Descriptions Act 1968 (and to such specific legislation as the Medicines Act 1968 and the Food Safety Act 1990). In addition, they are subject to specific statutory control and to a system of self-regulation.

Control of misleading advertisements

The Control of Misleading Advertisements Regulations 1988 (SI 1988/915) implement EC Directive 84/450 on misleading advertisements.

Advertisements not broadcast on radio or television

The regulations give the Director General of Fair Trading certain back-up powers in relation to advertisements which are not broadcast on radio or television (but he can consider cinema advertisements). Regulation 3 also excludes from these back-up powers certain advertisements for financial services.

He is obliged under the provisions of reg. 4(1) to consider complaints that a non-broadcast advertisement is misleading. An advertisement is, according to reg. 2(2) 'misleading' if it 'deceives or is likely to deceive the person to whom it is addressed or whom it reaches and if, by reason of its deceptive nature, it is likely to affect their economic behaviour or, for those reasons, injures or is likely to injure a competitor of the person whose interests the advertisement seeks to promote.' Before he considers any such complaint, however, the Director General may, under the provisions of reg. 4(3), first require the complainant to show that the advertisement has not previously been considered by appropriate 'established means' of dealing with complaints about such advertising. There is no definition of 'established means', but this would include bodies such as the Advertising Standards Authority. The Director General may also need to be satisfied that a reasonable opportunity has been allowed for those established means to resolve the matter, but that they have not done so. He is not, however, required to consider complaints which appear to be frivolous or vexatious. It is also to be noted that there is no compulsion on the Director General to refer an advertisement to 'established means'. The regulations say only that he 'may' so do.

'Established means' may be required first to consider an advertisement

In the exercise of his powers, the Director General is empowered by reg. 7 to obtain and disclose information. Regulation 7(5) also allows him to refer any complaint about an advertisement to any person. This would allow him to refer the matter to such bodies as the Advertising Standards Authority, which he does do from time to time.

Action in court

Regulation 5(2) requires the Director General to give reasons for his decision on whether or not to take court proceedings against an advertisement. No specific right of appeal is provided for in the regulations against a decision, but, as a public official, the actions of the Director General are subject to judicial review, so any decision could be challenged as wholly unreasonable or made in breach of the principles of natural justice.

If he does decide in favour of court proceedings, the Director General is empowered by reg. 5(1) to seek an injunction or an interlocutory injunction (this is an injunction sought before a full trial of the matter in dispute). The court may grant the request if it sees fit, but must first, under the provisions of reg. 6(1), have regard to all the interests involved including the public interest. If an injunction is granted, reg. 6(2) says that it may apply not just to the particular advertisement, but to any other advertisement which is in similar terms or which is likely to convey a similar impression.

Action for an injunction

Case example
Director General of Fair Trading v Tobyward Ltd (1988)

A series of complaints had been made to the Advertising Standards Authority that advertisements for slimming tablets were misleading. These complaints had been upheld, but the advertisements continued to appear. The ASA referred the matter to the Director General who declined to accept undertakings from the advertisers, believing these to be inadequate. An interlocutory injunction was sought. The court granted the injunction saying that, since there was a strong prima facie case that the advertisements were likely to deceive and to affect the

---

> economic behaviour of those to whom they were directed, by encouraging them to buy the product, the injunction would be granted. The court said that it was in the public interest for the court to support self-regulation by granting an injunction where the self-regulatory system had failed. The court also held that, since the Director General had shown a strong prima facie case, he would not be required to give a cross-undertaking in damages.

When hearing an application for an injunction, the court is empowered by reg. 6(3) to require any person seeming to it to be responsible for the publication of the advertisement to provide the court with evidence of the accuracy of any factual claim made in the advertisement. The court must not do so, however, unless it appears to it to be appropriate in the circumstances of the case, having regard to the legitimate interests of the person who would be affected by the requirement as well as of any other person concerned with the advertisement. If the court does make such a requirement, reg. 6(4) goes on to say that if it considers the evidence provided inadequate, or if no evidence is forthcoming, it may treat the factual claim as being inaccurate.

Evidence may be required to prove accuracy of claims

In considering whether or not to grant an injunction, reg. 6(5) says that a court is not entitled to refuse the grant for lack of evidence of damage to any person, or of any intention to mislead or failure to exercise care to ensure that the advertisement was not misleading.

Broadcast advertisements

The regulations apply a different regime in relation to radio and television commercials. These are handled, respectively, by the Radio Authority and the Independent Television Commission. Each body has a duty to consider any complaint that an advertisement is misleading, unless it considers that complaint frivolous or vexatious. Each must give reasons for its decision. If it considers that a complaint is justified, it may ban the broadcast of the advertisement. Each body also has the powers to seek evidence as to the accuracy of factual claims in the same way as the courts.

Differing powers available in relation to broadcast advertisements

It is to be noted that neither body can apply for an injunction. This is because they have the direct power to refuse to broadcast the advertisement, which is equivalent to an injunction.

Review questions

1 When is an advertisement 'misleading' for the purposes of the Control of Misleading Advertisements Regulations 1988?
2 The Director General of Fair Trading has certain powers in relation to misleading advertisements. What are these powers and which category of advertisements fall outside his powers?
3 To what extent do the Regulations seek to preserve the system of self-regulation?
4 What powers are given in relation to the control of broadcast advertisements?

Self-regulation

The British Codes of Advertising and Sales Promotion

The major system of self-regulation in the United Kingdom is that operated by and through the Committee of Advertising Practice and the Advertising Standards Authority. In general, it applies to the print media and not to broadcast advertising.

The Committee of Advertising Practice has as its members the major associations in the advertising industry, such as the Advertising Association, the Newspapers Publishers Association, the Newspaper Society, the Periodical Publishers Association and the Royal Mail. It is CAP which draws up the British Codes of Advertising and Sales Promotion. CAP administers the system of mandatory pre-clearance of cigarette advertising, and gives confidential and free pre-publication advice for all advertisements.

Roles of CAP and ASA

The Advertising Standards Authority, which shares a common secretariat with CAP, was established in 1962. Its chief tasks are to promote and enforce high standards in advertisements, to investigate and adjudicate on complaints, to identify and resolve problems through its own research, to ensure that the system operates in the public interest, and to act as a channel for communications with those having an interest in advertising standards. It has a 12-member council appointed by the chairman. At least half those appointed are unconnected with the advertising industry. All council members sit as individuals.

The ASA publishes, free of charge, monthly case reports which give details of adjudications.

Case example

A complaint was made about a leaflet in a local paper for a one-day sale headed 'LEGAL NOTICE'. The leaflet also included the words 'OUR CUSTOM AND EXCISE NUMBER…' and 'The price comparisons we use on the sets below are taken from The Argos Spring Catalogue and although the furniture on sale today is of the same quality and better, it is not the same make, but you will see what savings you can make by buying today.' The complainant found the use of the headlines and the customs number misleading, and furthermore questioned the validity of the comparison when the goods were not the same.

The advertisers explained that they no longer operated such sales, but offered no comment on the complaint. The publishers of the local paper regretted that they had not fully appreciated the problems with the leaflet, but gave an assurance that they would obtain guidance from the Committee of Advertising Practice before distributing similar material in the future. The ASA considered that the headline and reference to Customs & Excise, together with the use of quasi-legal jargon, gave a misleading impression of what was, in fact, merely a routine privately organized sale. It further considered that the alleged savings were misleading since the products were not the same make. While noting that the leaflet would not appear again, it requested the advertisers not to employ confusing legalese jargon and inappropriate price comparisons in future advertising.

When a complaint is made, the secretariat examines the facts and, if necessary, takes advice from expert external consultants. It then produces a recommendation for the ASA council. Recommendations can, at the request of the secretariat or of those affected, be reviewed by a CAP review panel. The final decision on complaints rests with the council. The secretariat is authorized by the council to take interim action if it is necessary to avoid further harm, for example in the case of a misleading or offensive advertisement or promotion. Appeals against ASA adjudications are made in writing to the chairman and should be accompanied by new evidence, or should demonstrate a substantial flaw in the council's conclusion.

Courts can examine complaint handling

In its dealing with complaints, the ASA is subject to judicial review.

> ## Case example
> ### *R* v *Advertising Standards Authority Ltd, ex parte The Insurance Service plc* (1990)
>
> Insurance Service plc, which provided motor insurance, distributed a circular which, under the heading 'How we can offer lower prices', stated: 'We deal direct with you, the customer. Because we do not have to pay middlemen, we can pass on those savings to you in lower prices.' A complaint was raised about the accuracy of this claim. The secretariat corresponded with the company's managing director who maintained that no payments were made to middlemen. The secretariat's report to the council wrongly stated that he had, in fact, acknowledged that a small proportion of sales were made through intermediaries who received commission. As a result, the council considered and upheld the complaint on the basis of an inaccurate statement as to what the company accepted as the true facts.
>
> The court said that the system established for the consideration of complaints was proper and satisfactory when operated properly and fairly. It had not been so operated in this case because the company had been denied the opportunity to put its case before the council. The court therefore ruled that the decision of the council to uphold the complaint must be quashed.

Sanctions

Sanctions are available to enforce Codes

A number of sanctions exist to ensure that the Codes are complied with. The main media associations belong to CAP, and they agree that their members will not accept offending advertisements. Adverse publicity may result from publication of an adjudication of an adverse report, and the agency which prepared the particular advertisement may lose business. It is in fact quite common for the agreement between the agency and the client to impose the duty on the agency of ensuring that the advertisements which it prepares are in compliance with the Codes. Failure so to ensure will put the agency in breach of contract and hence liable in damages. The Royal Mail may withdraw postage rebates from advertisers whose material offends the Codes. Again, an advertiser or agency may be 'recognized' by a particular association, such as the Newspaper Society, thus entitling it to certain rebates on the advertising it places. Such recognition can be withdrawn if an agency or advertiser produces offending material.

In the last resort, the ASA can refer matters to the Office of Fair Trading for action under the provisions of the Control of Misleading Advertisements Regulations.

Funding

The whole system is funded by surcharges on advertising and direct marketing expenditure. This is collected by the Advertising Standards Board of Finance, a body that operates independently of CAP and the ASA.

European Advertising Standards Alliance

The ASA is a founder member of the European Advertising Standards Alliance. This is based in Brussels and meets on a regular basis to co-ordinate the promotion of self-regulation at a European level. It acts as a focal point for cross-border complaints investigated by individual members. Consumers need only complain to their own self-regulatory authority, no matter where the promotion or advertisement originated.

Review questions

1 What are the functions of the Committee of Advertising Practice and the Advertising Standards Authority?
2 How are the British Codes of Advertising and Sales Promotion enforced?
3 How is this self-regulatory system funded?
4 To what extent does self-regulation operate on a European basis?

Television advertising

The Broadcasting Act 1990 imposes a duty on the Independent Television Commission to draw up a code governing standards and practice in television advertising and the sponsoring of programmes.

The ITC Code of Advertising Standards and Practice produced under this statutory duty applies to all television services regulated by the ITC: that is to say Channels 3 and 4, direct broadcasting satellite services and other satellite services operating out of the UK but not using frequencies allocated to the UK, cable and local delivery services, as well as the Welsh Fourth Channel. Separate provisions apply to teletext.

Code produced under statutory duty

All holders of ITC licences or contracts are required to ensure that any advertising they transmit complies with the Code and to satisfy the ITC that they have adequate procedures to fulfil this requirement. The ITC itself draws up and revises the Code, advises broadcasters on interpretation, monitors compliance and investigates complaints. It has the power to require advertising which does not comply to be withdrawn

Case example

Two versions of an advertisement for Martini appeared to breach the following rule from the ITC Code: 'Advertisements must neither claim nor suggest that any drink can contribute towards sexual success or that drinking can enhance sexual attractiveness.' The advertisement showed a young man in a speedboat entering a port. He notices an attractive young woman sitting at a cafe with an unprepossessing older man. He arrives at the cafe, seizes a bottle of Martini from a passing waiter and two glasses from the bar. He then approaches the table, pours the woman a glass of Martini and one for himself, ignoring the older man. The young man and woman exchange looks and gestures indicating mutual attraction. The young man gets up and walks to the harbourside where he waits. After a brief interval, the woman follows him. As she gets up, her skirt unravels, revealing naked buttocks. The advertisement then cuts to a final scene where another young woman, presumably the young man's girl-friend, is having a tantrum because he has not arrived for a rendezvous.

The TV company said that they did not think that the theme of sexual success was preva-lent in the commercial. Nor did it consider that the drink contributed to sexual success since the couple would have been attracted to each other in any event. The ITC said that it consid-ered this an excessively literal reading of the Code which in any event was to be construed, as it itself said, 'in the spirit as well as the letter'. The TV company also pointed out that the advertisements had been mainly transmitted after midnight. The ITC said that, while this might have been relevant if the Code transgression related to causing offence, it was not relevant to alcohol advertising since the rules apply regardless of the time of transmission. The complaint was upheld and the ITC ordered the advertising to cease.

The 1990 Act expressly reserves the right of the ITC to impose requirements which go beyond the Code. The methods of control open to the ITC include powers to give directions to exclude not only classes and descriptions of advertisements but also individual advertisements, either in general or in particular circumstances.

Television companies are entitled not to accept advertising which they do not wish to carry. This discretion is, however, limited by the Act which states that, in the acceptance of advertisements, there is to be no unreasonable discrimination either against or in favour of any particular advertiser.

It is to be understood that breach of the Code does not of itself give rise to an offence on the part of the advertiser. Private individuals may be able to compel observance of the Code, but only if their private rights are affected or if special damage would be inflicted on them. Otherwise, enforcement lies with the Attorney-General, whose decision as to whether or not to bring an action is not subject to judicial review (see *Attorney-General* v *Independent Broadcasting Authority* (1973) and *Gouriet* v *Union of Post Office Workers* (1977)).

Radio advertising

Statutory code for commercial radio

Under the terms of the Broadcasting Act, the Radio Authority, like the ITC, is obliged to draw up a code which sets standards and practice in advertising and programme sponsorship on independent radio. The remarks made above in relation to the ITC (Television Advertising) may be taken as equally applicable here.

Review question

What duties are imposed on the ITC and the Radio Authority as to advertising standards?

Over the counter medicines

Code for OTC medicines

The Proprietary Association of Great Britain (PAGB) has produced a Code of Standards of Advertising Practice for Over the Counter Medicines, i.e. those available without a prescription.

The PAGB is the national trade association representing the manufacturers of such medicines and food supplements. It is a condition of membership that copy for all medicine advertisements directed at the public, including packaging and point of sale material, is submitted to the Association for assessment against the provisions of the Code. The Association states that it is the duty of all member companies to ensure that their advertisements comply with all statutory and relevant code requirements. The conditions of membership also require members and their advertising agencies to submit all material relevant to the labelling, packaging, advertising and promotion of their products to the public. The association also publishes a separate code covering promotions to health professionals and the retail trade.

And a code for prescription only drugs

The Association of the British Pharmaceutical Industry is the trade association representing manufacturers of prescription medicines. It is a condition of membership that members abide by the Code of Practice. Some 50 companies which are not members of the ABPI have agreed to accept the authority of the Code.

The Code is administered by the Prescription Medicines Code of Practice Authority which is responsible for the provision of advice, guidance, conciliation and training on the Code as well as for the complaints procedure. Complaints are considered by the Code of Practice Panel and, where required, by the Code of Practice Appeal Board.

Review question

In what way do trade associations control the advertising of medicines and drugs?

Chapter summary

- Promotions where prizes are won by chance are lawful if there is no obligation to purchase.
- This does not, however, apply to lotteries such as the National Lottery or premium bonds which are excluded from the general ban.
- Prize competitions, being promotions which involve an element of skill, are lawful if certain specific rules are observed.
- Specific obligations are imposed on those who issue trading stamps.
- An offence arises if a false or misleading description is applied to goods, whether or not there was any intent to mislead.
- An offence arises if a false or misleading statement is made about services, facilities or accommodation, but only if there is an intent to mislead.
- The use of a properly constructed disclaimer may avoid liability.
- Liability may also be avoided by the exercise of due diligence.
- Misleading price claims are controlled by the Consumer Protection Act 1987.
- A Code of Practice acts as a guide to which price claims are misleading.
- The Office of Fair Trading has the power to obtain court injunctions to prevent misleading advertising.
- Advertising in the print media is subject to a system of self-regulation operated by the Committee of Advertising Practice and the Advertising Standards Authority.
- Television and radio advertising is subject to statutory codes of practice.
- The advertising of drugs and medicines is controlled by industry codes.

Case study exercise 1

A coffee manufacturer decides to run the following promotion. All those who buy three jars of coffee, and send the labels to a specific address, will go into a prize draw. The first 100 to be selected will then be contacted by letter and asked a set of general knowledge questions. Those who get all the questions correct will win the advertised prizes.

Although the promotional literature does not say so, all entries have to be in by a specific date; entrants must be aged at least 18; and only one prize can be won per household.

Student task

Consider this promotion in the light of the requirements of the Lotteries and Amusements Act 1976, the Trading Stamps Act 1964 and the British Codes of Advertising and Sales Promotion Practice. You should also consider whether the failure of the promotional material to indicate all the relevant rules could be the subject of a complaint to the Director General of Fair Trading.

Case study exercise 2

A car dealer, who deals in only secondhand cars, decides to advertise a 'sale' in the local papers. The advertisement claims that, for the month of August, the prices will be £1000 below the normal price. The prices are reduced during August, but, for the first three weeks of September, the 'sale' prices are maintained. The advertisement also offered free petrol to any purchaser on their next five visits to the premises.

It is also the case that one of the cars sold during the sale period displayed a false milometer reading. The dealer, who had had previous convictions for 'clocking' had sought to avoid liability by the use of a disclaimer which had appeared in the press advertisements. This had read: 'Trade Descriptions Act 1968. We regret that we are not prepared to vouch for the accuracy of the milometers of any of our cars.' In the case of this particular car, the vehicle had been purchased from a private individual and it appeared that he had clocked the car before trading it in. Before agreeing to accept it as a trade-in, the dealer had looked under the bonnet and had concluded that the state of the engine was about right for the apparent mileage. The purchaser of this car discovered that the mileage was false when he contacted the private individual who had sold the car to the dealer. The purchaser drove the car back to the dealer's premises where he told him what he had learned. The dealer offered to pay compensation of £100, but said that this would take the place of the free petrol offer.

Student task

Consider the possible charges which may be brought under the Trade Descriptions Act against the dealer and the private individual and, in relation to the dealer, whether his price claims put him in breach of the Consumer Protection Act. You should consider in particular whether the facts disclose the presence of a valid disclaimer and whether the dealer can successfully plead the due diligence defence.

Discussion questions

1 The law exercises tight controls over all forms of sales promotions offering prizes. Consider whether this is an accurate summary of the position under the Lotteries and Amusements Act 1976.
2 The control of advertising is as much a matter of legal regulation as of self-regulation. Discuss the validity of this statement.
3 Is it true to say that the way radio and television advertising are controlled stands between legal control and self-regulation?
4 The Trade Descriptions Act 1968, as supplemented by the provisions of the Consumer Protection Act 1987, provides a comprehensive set of controls over all possible forms of misleading claims and descriptions. Is this a fair assessment?

United Kingdom application

The provisions of this chapter apply in their entirety throughout the United Kingdom.

Further reading

Law for Retailers (2nd edn), Brave (1993), Sweet & Maxwell, Chapter 15.
Sales Promotion Law, Lawson (1987), BSP.
Sales Promotion, Advertising of the Law: Legal Guide, Bagehot (1993), Sweet & Maxwell, Chapter 4.
The Law Relating to Trade Descriptions, ed. Harvey, Butterworths.

7   Product liability

Introduction

For many generations products were relatively simple in the methods of their construction, the materials they consisted of and the function they performed. What you saw was what you got. Modern products are immeasurably more sophisticated, incorporating technologies which few consumers really understand. Formerly, a prospective buyer would be able to examine a product to see if it was suitable for their requirements, whereas now it is common for products to be pre-packaged or sold in a 'solid state' form so that a pre-purchase examination is either precluded or else discouraged. Sales literature is generally bland on technical matters but even if this is provided the consumer, as a non-technician, may not comprehend the contents.

Parallel to the growth in product sophistication is the growth in potential harm that modern products may cause. Formerly, for example, household products were mechanical, but now consumer desirables are electrical or electronic; medical products were relatively rudimentary, but now a modern drug is usually a cocktail of pharmaceutical compounds with the potential for serious side-effects. Modern motor cars and aircraft now have many safety features built into them but they also have considerably more parts operating at far higher levels of performance than formerly. Such products are only as safe as the quality control standard of each component part.

Objective

This chapter is intended to cover the common law and statutory approaches to defective products that cause personal injury or damage to property. In respect of the product itself, as opposed to the harm that it causes, damage or loss may be recoverable under contract law or the sale of Goods Act 1979. What is intended to be shown, is that liability for defective products is determined by the standard of care that the law imposes on those responsible for a product being placed into circulation. While product liability covers all products, the chapter attempts to focus on those that are sold to consumers, e.g. non-business buyers.

Key concepts

- Collateral contracts
- The common-law duty of care
- *Res ipsa loquitur* – the thing speaks for itself
- Strict liability under the Consumer Protection Act 1987
- Avoidance of statutory liability.

Liability through contract

While most commercial transactions are done under standard form contracts which contain express terms, a number of *implied terms* are included in all contracts covered by the Sale of Goods Act 1979. Provided that there is a contractual relationship between the parties then the buyer of defective goods will have remedies against the seller for breach of contract.

On investigating a claim for contractual breach it must be established that a term of the contract has in fact been broken. With pre-contractual statements, while they induce someone to enter into a contract, they are not actually part of the contract so that a claim would have to be for misrepresentation not contractual breach. Similarly, if a pre-contractual statement is found to be a trade boast (a seller's over commendation of their wares) then this will be regarded as being a 'mere puff' and again not give rise to an action for breach of contract. However, if neither misrepresentation nor trade boasts are applicable then breach of s. 14 Sale of Goods Act 1979 may apply.

Section 14(2) Sale of Goods Act 1979 imposed an implied condition that goods supplied 'in the course of a business' be of a satisfactory quality. The standard of quality expected was that goods be of *merchantable quality*.

Case example
Shire v *General Guarantee Finance* (1988)

S bought a secondhand motor car and later discovered that eight months earlier it had been written off by insurers for having been submerged in water for over a day. At the time of supply the motor car was said to have been unmerchantable.

Section 14(2) has been amended by s. 14 (2)(a) Sale and Supply of Goods Act 1994 which replaces 'merchantable' with 'satisfactory'. Goods are now of a satisfactory standard if they 'meet the standard that a reasonable person would regard as satisfactory, taking account of any description of the goods, the price (if relevant) and all other circumstances.' The 1994 Act provides guidance as to what factors, in relevant circumstances, will indicate quality of goods. These are:

- fitness for all the purposes for which goods of the kind in question are commonly supplied;
- the appearance and finish of goods;
- whether the goods are free from minor defects;
- the level of safety of the good;
- whether the good is durable.

In contract the liability of the seller is *strict* so it makes no difference whether the defect was known of or not, i.e. there is no need for the fault of a sellor to be proved. The scope of liability covers injury or damage which is the 'reasonable likely consequence' of the breach that was proved to exist, i.e. losses which naturally arise out of a breach but which the buyer could not be expected to predict or guard against. In addition, where special circumstances apply, losses which do not arise naturally may be claimed provided they had been contemplated by both parties at the time they made the contract as the probable result of the breach. These are the two rules in *Hadley* v *Baxendale* (1854) which have been partly put into a statutory form by ss 50(2), 51(2), 53(2), Sale of Goods Act 1979.

> **Case example**
> **Griffiths v Peter Conway Ltd (1939)**
> G bought a Harris tweed coat from PC. G had an abnormally sensitive skin and the coarse tweed material caused dermatitis. G had not disclosed her sensitively to PC.
>
> As the coat would have been safe for virtually everyone else the seller would not be liable.

It is accepted that the greater the potential of harm, the fewer people need to be involved.

Brief overview of other statutes relating to defective goods

Consumer Credit Act 1974

Creditors are liable under s. 56 to consumers for anything said or done by a dealer in the course of negotiations – the dealer is regarded as being the agent of the creditor. Included in s. 56 will be statements made in advertisements (see collateral contracts below).

A creditor may also be liable under s. 75 with 'connected lending' transactions. These are where a creditor lends money to a buyer in order that they may buy goods from a supplier and where the supplier has a pre-existing arrangement with the creditor. Typical creditors caught by s. 75 are the credit token companies such as Visa or Mastercard. The consumer protection given under s. 75 is that where a buyer has rights against a seller for defective goods then these rights also apply against the creditor.

There are advantages in having obtained the defective good on consumer credit terms

Health and Safety at Work Act 1974

A statutory duty under s. 6 is imposed on suppliers of articles and substances *for use at work* to see so far 'as is reasonably practicable' that they will be safe to use. This is a standard of reasonable care similar to that in negligence. Suppliers include designers, manufacturers, distributors, installers and importers. Under s. 6 the burden of proof is reversed in that a supplier has to show that they were not 'negligent'. Also the section will not apply if the product was being misused. Under s. 47(1) the duty is only supported by penal sanctions and does not give rise to civil liability. In practice it is normal that a claim is made by an injured employee against their employer for failing to provide safe equipment or failing to operate a safe equipment or failing to operate a safe system of work.

Supply of Goods (Implied Terms) Act 1973

Under s. 10 (as amended by the Sale and Supply of Goods Act 1994) the implied term as to quality of goods under the Sale and Supply of Goods Act 1994 is to apply to goods on hire purchase.

Supply of Goods and Services Act 1982

In relation to the transfer of goods, such as where they are supplied under an installation or repair agreement, s. 4 (as amended by the Sale and Supply of Goods Act 1994) requires that implied term as to quality of goods under the Sale and Supply of Goods Act 1994 is to apply. In addition s. 9 imposes similar quality obligations on goods being hired.

Products supplied under service agreements are caught by quality provisions

Trading Stamps Act 1964

On the redemption of trading stamps in exchange for goods s. 4 (as amended by the Sale and Supply of Goods Act 1994) there is an implied term that the goods are of satisfactory standard unless defects were specifically drawn to the redeemer's attention or the redeemer examined the goods before redemption and ought to have discovered the defects.

Creation of collateral contracts

Collateral liability may make a producer jointly liable for defective goods

So far in this discussion of liability for breach of contract in relation to defective goods it has been sellers (retailers), suppliers (dealers acting as creditors' agents or installers or repairers), or creditors who have born any liability. With collateral contracts it is producers who may become liable. A collateral contract is where a producer makes a promise to the end user of the product whereby the end user is persuaded to buy the product from someone else. In essence the producer is saying to the end user 'If you buy my goods from a retailer, I promise to provide goods of a certain standard.'

Case example
Andrews v Hopkinson (1956)

The sales manager of a secondhand car dealer assured A, who was relatively ignorant about motor cars, that a 1934 saloon car was 'a good little bus' and also said that 'I would stake my life on it. You will have no trouble with it.' A bought the car on hire purchase terms from a finance company and acknowledged in a delivery note that he was satisfied as to the car's condition. The car was later discovered to have a seriously defective steering mechanism, a defect that a competent mechanic could have discovered.

Clearly there was a contract between A and the finance company but in addition there was also a contract between A and the secondhand car dealer who had, through the sales manager, persuaded A to buy the car by effectively guaranteeing it.

In *Andrews v Hopkinson*, A's consideration for the collateral contract was the purchase of the motor car which was in response to the seller's promise, e.g. 'If you make a contract with the finance company, I promise that the car is in good condition.' The statement 'a good little bus' was a misrepresentation. A collateral contract is enforceable alongside the main one or, alternatively, an independent action on the collateral may be taken.

In exceptional circumstances a producer's advertising or point of sale material may create a collateral contract with the end user.

Case example
Carlill v Carbolic Smoke Ball Co. (1893)

C was persuaded to buy a smoke ball from a retailer because she had relied upon the statements made in the producer's advertisement (CSB Co.) which said that if she bought and used the product as described she would not catch influenza. On catching influenza, and so proving the product defective, C obtained damages from the producer for breach of contract.

Modern advertisements and promotional material will seldom now go as far as making enforceable promises, e.g. Carlsberg is '*probably* the best lager in the world', or Kenco instant coffee is 'as good as a ground coffee' – here value judgements are being made not a definite enforceable promise.

Manufacturers' guarantees

As mentioned, the collateral contract is based upon an assurance or guarantee given by a producer to an end user. More commonly a manufacturer (producer) will provide a purchaser of their goods with an express guarantee. This may be a simple promise such as if a dissatisfied buyer returns a defective bar of chocolate, saying when and where it was purchased, to the manufacturer a replacement will then be given together with a refund of postage. Alternatively, the promise may be more elaborate in saying what the manufacturer undertakes to do and what conditions the dissatisfied buyer must follow. Liability for defects caused by negligence in manufacturer or distribution cannot in, relation to consumer goods, be excluded or restricted by means of a contractual term or notice contained in a guarantee (s. 5(1), Unfair Contract Terms Act 1977).

A reputable manufacturer anxious to protect their business reputation will always want to honour a genuine claim made under a guarantee. But if the manufacturer should refuse to honour a valid guarantee claim then, unless the product was bought directly from the manufacturer, privity of contract will mean that the manufacturer cannot be forced to honour the guarantee promise. If the product was bought direct then the guarantee may have been incorporated into the contract. Even if such incorporation did not take place an action for breach of contract under the Sale of Goods Act 1979 (as amended) would still be possible. Where the product was bought from a retailer then the contract is between that retailer and the buyer with the manufacturer's guarantee being a promise in 'honour' only.

A manufacturer's guarantee may not be enforceable

Review question

The Acme Company uses a marketing campaign to promote sales of its vacuum cleaner. Strap lines proclaim: 'The most powerful vacuum cleaner in the world'; 'Buy Acme, you won't be disappointed'; 'Buy Acme and be swept off your feet'. With each cleaner sold buyers are invited to send off within 14 days of purchase a manufacturer's guarantee card so that they can be registered for a parts-and-labour guarantee. The card asks buyers for details about their age, occupation, marital status, etc. After purchase and registration for the guarantee Andy Handy uses an Acme cleaner only for it to race across the room (sucking up whole tufts of carpet), smash through french windows and explode on the lawn outside.

In relation to what has been covered so far on product liability, discuss any claims Andy Handy may have against the Acme Company.

Liability through negligence

Negligence is a civil wrong (tort) which enables a person suffering harm caused by another's failure to discharge a duty of care to sue for compensation. The following are judicial definitions:

Negligence is based upon a hypothetical 'reasonable man'

> Negligence is the omission to do something which a reasonable man, guided upon those considerations which ordinarily regulate the conduct of human affairs, would do, or do something which a prudent and reasonable man would not do.
>
> Alderson B, *Blyth* v *Birmingham Waterworks Co.* (1856)

Negligence is simply neglect of some care which we are bound to exercise towards somebody.

Bowen LJ, *Thomas* v *Quartermaine* (1887)

If there is a contract between the plaintiff and defendant then the plaintiff may sue concurrently in contract and negligence.

Negligence is then an act or admission of the defendant that causes harm to the plaintiff. The tort is designed to prevent one person causing harm to another but if harm is caused then the defendant, on being found to be at fault, will have to pay damages. As the duty of care imposed by negligence does not arise out of contract, it is possible for a plaintiff who does not have a contractual relationship with the defendant to take action. For a plaintiff to succeed in negligence the burden of proof is on them to establish:

In negligence a contractual relationship between plaintiff and defendent is not required

- that a duty of care was owed to them;
- that the duty of care was broken;
- that the breach of the duty of care caused the plaintiff to suffer foreseeable harm.

Case example
Donoghue v *Stevenson* (1932)

D and a friend visited a cafe where the friend bought her a bottle of ginger beer manufactured by S. D drank most of the ginger beer but eventually noticed the remains of a decomposed snail at the bottom of the opaque bottle. As a consequence of drinking the contaminated ginger beer D suffered severe gastroenteritis. D could not sue the retailer (cafe proprietor) for contractual breach as the contract for the ginger beer had been made between her friend and the cafe proprietor. Instead she sued the manufacturer for negligence. As a defence S alleged that in the absence of a contractual link between himself and D that he could not owe her a duty of care.

The House of Lords held that the correct test in determining if a duty of care is owed is not whether there is a contractual link between the parties but whether a person can reasonably foresee that their acts or omissions may cause harm to another.

In *Donoghue* v *Stevenson* the persons to whom you owe a duty of care to were described as 'neighbours'. Donoghue was a neighbour to Stevenson because it was reasonable for him to foresee that by putting a defective product onto the market, harm may be caused and that harm could be to someone other than the purchaser of the product. The duty, given by Lord Atkin, was said to be:

A duty of reasonable care is owed to end users

A manufacturer of products, which he sells in such a form as to show that he intends them to reach the ultimate consumer in the form in which they left him with no reasonable possibility of intermediate examination, and with the knowledge that the absence of reasonable care in the preparation or putting up of the products will result in an injury to the consumer's life or property, owes a duty to the consumer to take reasonable care.

And in response to whom this duty was owed to, Lord Atkin set out a 'neighbour principle':

You must take reasonable care to avoid acts or omissions which you can reasonably foresee would be likely to injure your neighbour. Who, then, in law, is my neighbour? The answer seems to be – persons who are so closely and directly affected by my act that I ought reasonably to have them in contemplation as being so affected when I am directing my mind to the acts or omissions which are called into question.

Those who are liable

The importance of this decision is that the neighbour principle is not limited to manufacturers but covers everyone involved in the manufacturing process from designers to distributors. In addition it also covers repairers, hirers, suppliers of goods on hire purchase, etc., as well as having more general applications in tort law.

Reasonable forseeability compared to remoteness limits the operation of the duty of reasonable care

---

Case example
Stennet v Hancock and Peters (1939)
A garage negligently replaced a wheel on a lorry and were held liable when the wheel came off and struck a pedestrian.

The significance of Lord Atkin's reference to a manufacturer selling goods, 'in such a form as to show that he intends them to reach the ultimate consumer in the form in which they left him', is that if another person in the product distribution chain, a wholesaler or retailer for example, is responsible for the defect then the manufacturer will not be liable. The form in which the product reaches the end user is not necessarily the exact form in which the product left the manufacturer. It is a finding of fact whether the product would still be in its same form or whether third-party interferences in the product could have taken place.

Novus actus interveniens (a new act intervening) may break a manufacturer's liability

---

Case example
Evans v Triplex Glass Co. Ltd (1936)
E bought a car fitted with a windscreen made by TG. One year after purchase the windscreen shattered and passengers were injured. E alleged that under Lord Atkin's dictum TG had to be liable.

E had still the evidential requirement of showing that it was more probable than not that the injuries were due to faulty manufacture. E was unable to do this because, although he alleged negligence, TG countered by alleging possible faulty fitting of the windscreen, i.e. the possibility that the goods were not in the same state as when they had left the manufacturer.

In relation to Lord Atkin's point about no reasonable possibility of intermediate examination, this is important because, if the manufacturer intended someone to examine the product for defects before having it put into circulation, then, if that examination negligently failed to notice a defect, it ought to result in liability falling not on the manufacturer but on the examiner. Lord Atkin's possibility of intermediate examination is now interpreted as being not the possibility or opportunity of intermediate examination but a 'reasonable probability' of an intermediate examination (*Haseldine* v *Daw* (1941)).

Review question

What do you consider to be the function of the duty of care concept in negligence?

Negligence and contractual liability contrasted

Table 7.1 highlights the differences between claims in negligence and contract.

Table 7.1 *Differences between claims in negligence and contract*

Negligence		Contract
Manufacturer, repairer, supplier	*Who is liable*	The seller (retailer)
A duty of care owed to the plaintiff	*Type of liability breached*	An implied or express contractual term
Whoever suffers foreseeable harm because of the defective product	*Who is able to claim*	Buyer only
Reasonable care, e.g. the defendant must TRY to see that their product is not harmful	*Standard expected*	Strict, e.g. the defendant must SUCCEED in seeing that the product is not harmful
What society expects reasonable people to do, e.g. liability arises independently of the parties	*Source of the expectation*	What terms the parties themselves freely negotiated
Damages that are reasonably foreseeable in that a reasonable man would have foreseen the consequences of his acts or missions. (*The Wagon Mound* (1961)). A claim for the product itself is not possible	*Measure of damage*	Damages that are foreseeable as the probable result of the breach or where the parties contemplated the likelihood of loss (*Hadley v Baxendale* (1854)). A claim for the product itself is possible
Not recoverable (see *Muirhead* v *ITS Ltd* (1985))	*Recovery of pure economic loss* (e.g. loss of future profits by a business harmed by a defective product)	Common – treated as a valid loss
A partial defence under the Act available to the defendant (*Owens v Brimmell* (1977))	*Contributory negligence of the plaintiff* see Law Reform (Contributory Negligence Act 1945)	If the P's negligence is the real reason for the damage then the D will not be liable (*Quinn* v *Burch Bros (Builders) Ltd* (1966)); if the D's negligence only partially contributed to the P's damage then this depends on whether the P's breach of contract can come within 'fault' under the LR (CN) Act 1945

The duty of care

As previously discussed this is based on the judgement of Lord Atkin in *Donoghue* v *Stevenson*. However, even though the defendant has been negligent and the plaintiff in consequence suffers harm, the plaintiff must still show that the duty of care was owed to them.

At all times the plaintiff has the burden of proof in establishing his or her case on a balance of probabilities

> ## Case example
> ### Crow v Barford (Agricultural) Ltd and Holtham (1963)
> C bought a rotary mower made by B from H. The mower had a gap to allow grass cuttings to escape and was started and stopped by the operator placing a foot on the top of the mower directly above the gap. C's foot slipped from the top of the mower and into the gap. He lost two toes.
>
> B was not liable for the danger, being perfectly obvious, meant that the defect did not fall into the Donoghue principle.

Therefore, the duty of care owed in product liability only applies to latent defects, that is defects which are not discernible on a reasonable examination of the product (*Grant* v *Australian Knitting Mills Ltd* (1936)).

Breach of the duty of care

The standard of care expected is that which is reasonable in the circumstances.

> ## Case example
> ### Daniels v R. White Ltd (1938)
> During manufacturer some carbolic acid got into bottles of lemonade. The manufacturer (W) established that they had a 'foolproof' method for cleaning and filling the bottle.
>
> W were not liable. In the circumstances they had acted reasonably and had done enough to ensure that their product was safe.

The standard of care is a variable one expected from a hypothetically average prudent man (or woman). The question asked is how in the circumstances, acting with foresight and caution, would a reasonable man have conducted himself? If such a man was expected to have recognized a potential danger to others and to have dispelled or mitigated it, then if the actual defendant did not take similar action that defendant will be liable for breach of the duty of care.

The likelihood and seriousness of injury will be factors in determining the extent of the duty of care. Where these apply then a defendant is expected to do more to ensure that their products do not cause harm.

The standard of care is a variable one

> ## Case example
> ### Fisher v Harrods (1966)
> A bottle of jewellery cleaner had been bought by a friend and sent to F as a present. When F attempted to use it the bottle exploded and some liquid went into her eyes causing pain and temporary blindness. The explosion had been caused by a build-up of pressure and also by how the bottle had been sealed. No warning had been given on the bottle. Under *Donoghue* v *Stevenson* the manufacturer was probably liable but wasn't worth the powder and shot of

pursuing through the courts. F therefore sued the retailer (H) but as she had no contract with H she sued in negligence.

In court H explained that their practice was to see if goods were fit for their purpose so they admitted to doing no more than testing the product to see if it would work. The court accepted this practice as being reasonable. Thus far F would not be able to show that H had broken their duty of care because they had acted as a reasonably prudent retailer would have been expected to have acted by testing the product to be sold.

F then had to go on to establish that there was something abnormal about the product which meant that H ought to have done more. She succeeded because as the cleaning product had a strong solvent base it was inherently dangerous. This meant that they ought to have questioned the manufacturer more closely and also have looked at the packing instructions.

A cost–benefit approach is controversial in that it introduces financial matter into public safety

When examining whether a defendant has done enough to discharge the duty of care a court may, controversially, apply a cost–benefit analysis to the situation. This approach will mean that where a defendant argues that product safety could only have been improved by a considerable expenditure of money and that it was unreasonable for them to make it, a court will balance notional expenditure against the degree of harm that may have been averted. The greater the anticipated harm the higher the expenditure that the defendant should have incurred on safety protection.

Case example
Walton v British Leyland Ltd (1978)

BL, a motor-car manufacturer, discovered latent defects in wheel bearings on their Austin Allegro model. They estimated that the cost of recalling Allegros for modification at approximately £300 000 and rejected this course of action as being too expensive (they also wanted to avoid bad publicity). What they did do was to tell their approved dealers to remedy the problem when cars came in for routine servicing. W, a passenger, was injured when a wheel came off the car he was travelling in.

Wheel drift was highly dangerous not only to the car driver and passengers but also potentially dangerous to other road users as well. BL ought to have immediately recalled the model. The relatively high expenditure to perhaps modify a small number of rogue cars was no defence.

The causation of loss

The actual cause of the harm may be difficult for the plaintiff to establish

The defendant's failure to take reasonable care of the plaintiff must be the cause of the harm that the plaintiff suffers. In many instances causation will not be a problem. In *Walton* v *British Leyland Ltd* (1978) it was easy to establish, through expert evidence, that as a consequence of the defect in wheel bearings accidents could occur. In other instances the causation requirement may be extremely difficult, such as where injury is in the form of nervous shock, or where so many intervening variables are involved as to make cause and effect almost impossible, on a balance of probabilities, to determine. In yet other instances a product will cause harm but it will be found that no one was negligent. In the Thalidomide tragedy of the 1960s the Distillers Company marketed a new drug. Around 400 women who took the drug during pregnancy gave birth in the UK to children with severe deformities. At the time of the product launch it was not known that this type of drug could cause injury to foetuses so that no warning was given that pregnant women should not take it. While the cause of the deformities was a defective product, in the light of known medical knowledge of the time, the Distillers Company had been following best practices for putting a medical product into the market and therefore could not be said to be negligent.

Problems associated with an action in negligence

As with all litigation, the plaintiff has the burden of proof of establishing, on a balance of probabilities, that the defendant was negligent. Negligence, as we know, requires that a duty of care is owed by the defendant to the plaintiff, that this duty was broken and that the breach caused the plaintiff harm. Courts are increasingly willing to consider, in many novel situations, that a duty of care is owed. However, a plaintiff, especially a private individual, often faces major difficulties over first establishing the breach of the duty of care, and second the caustional requirement.

Proving that the defendant was at fault

Negligence is based on there being somewhere one or more wrong doers (tortfeasors). Unless the plaintiff can show that someone was to blame then the action will be lost. A private individual without benefit of legal aid may find it extremely difficult to satisfy a court that the defendant was sufficiently culpable to be found liable. A sensible plaintiff will only ever take action where the claim is large enough to warrant litigation and against a defendant substantial enough to pay compensation (or having appropriate product liability insurance). This usually means that defendants will be medium- to very large-scale commercial concerns who are easily able to fund a robust defence to a claim with lawyers' and expert witnesses' expenses being written off against profits.

Blame or fault by another is central for a successful action

Indeed a number of commentators have remarked cynically that some corporate defendants, as well as occasionally government departments, use their greater financial resources to intimidate financially weak plaintiffs.

One equitable maximum which may help a plaintiff, by switching the burden of having to prove the defendant negligent, to having the defendant prove that they were not negligent, is the plea of *res ipsa loquitur* or the thing speaks for itself. The necessary conditions plea are:

A successful plea of res ipsa loquitur avoids the plaintiff is having to establish negligence on the defendant's part

1 The 'thing' allegedly causing the harm was under the sole control of the defendant.
2 There is no other direct evidence of what caused the harm (e.g. an alternative, plausible, explanation often is not available).
3 The harm is such that it would not normally have occurred if proper care had been taken by the defendant (e.g. such harm does not normally occur unless someone was at fault).

Res ipsa loquitor applies whenever it is felt by the court that a hypothetical reasonable jury without further evidence would find that such harm was so improbable that it could only have occurred through the negligence of the defendant. The defendant then has the burden of proving the 'notional jury' wrong by establishing that in the circumstances they had, in respect to the plaintiff, taken reasonable care.

> **Case example**
> ***Grant v Australian Knitting Mills Ltd (1936)***
> G, a buyer of a pair of pre-wrapped underpants, contracted dermatitis (a skin disorder) because traces of sulphite had been left in the garment during manufacture.
>
> The circumstances were such that *res ipsa loquitur* applied. The AKM were not able to show that they had taken reasonable care not to allow sulphite to remain in their product when it was put out into the market. Their defence that over four million pairs had been sold without complaint made no difference. The AKM were also found liable for breach of description under ss 13 and 14 Sale of Goods Act 1893 (now the 1979 Act as amended).

Proving that the defect caused the harm

Unfavourable publicity may be a valuable non-legal remedy

This is a finding of fact. With increasingly sophisticated products it is often difficult to show cause and effect. In recent years there have been several instances where pharmaceutical products have been alleged to have harmful side effects or to have made drug addicts of patients. Claimants have found that it is extremely expensive and difficult to establish a causal link between the harm they have allegedly suffered and the pharmaceutical company they hold responsible. Often limited redress is obtained through the plaintiffs gaining favourable media attention with the 'defendant' agreeing to make, without admitting liability, an *ex gratia* payment.

The Consumer Protection Act 1987

Background to the Act

Before the introduction of the Act the major problems with establishing liability for defective products were:

1 A manufacturer of the product could claim that they had taken all reasonable precautions in manufacture and that the defect was therefore too remote for liability to attach. Even if such a claim is spurious it will often tie up a plaintiff in high litigation costs to overcome it.

2 Privity of contract which precludes a customer from suing a manufacturer in contract for a product defect. The customer may sue the retailer in contract for breach of the strict contractual duty owed in respect to the products they sell. However, if the retailer is a small concern not carrying adequate insurance then such an action will be pointless. The customer (and other interested parties) may sue the manufacturer in negligence but the standard owed of reasonable care is lower than that owed in contract.

Strict liability imposes a much higher standard of care

The Act is designed to allow customers (i.e. end-users and others harmed by the defective product) to sue whoever produced the defective product and that person will owe *strict liability* for the harm the product caused. It is intended that manufacturers will be the main target of litigants but attention ought to be taken of the 'development risks' defence and that for property damage there is an 'excess provision' of £275. The title Consumer Protection Act may be misleading, because the Part I provisions of product liability will protect anyone who suffers harm as a result of a defect in a product and not just the consumer as defined in the Unfair Contract Terms Act 1977.

The main motivation for the Act was that it was Britain's response to a 1985 EC Products Liability Directive requiring member states to introduce a regime of strict liability for defective products. Britain was already moving slowly in the direction of strict liability for defective products before the EC Directive arrived. The Act does not slavishly follow the directive but, under s. 1(1), a court is to have discretion in interpreting the Act (and decisions on it of the European Court) so as to follow the intentions of the directives.

1 The Pearson Commission on Civil Liability and Compensation for Personal Injuries recommended in 1978 a system of compensation on the lines of strict liability.
2 The Law Commission recommended in 1977 that the law should be changed to make a producer strictly liable for injuries resulting from defects in products that are put into circulation in the course of a business.

Plaintiff's burden of proof

Liability under the Act is strict so that it will not be necessary for a plaintiff to have to prove that the defendant was negligent. However, the plaintiff will still have to prove:

- that the producer put the product into circulation
- that the product was defective
- that harm was suffered by the plaintiff
- that there is a causal link between the defective nature of the product and the harm suffered by the plaintiff.

If the plaintiff can establish a prima facie defect (a defect at first sight), the onus is then placed on the defendant to disprove liability. With little case law available on the Act it is not clear what exact evidential burden the courts will require claimants to show. The better view is that the onus of proving a defect will not be a demanding one. What may impede some defendants in rebutting the presumption of their liability is if the defective product was so badly damaged that the prima facie defect cannot be determined. However, the causational link between the defect and the harm may be much more demanding.

Parties who are liable

Producers

Endeavouring to make many parties liable, the Act gives a wide definition to 'producer'. A producer is defined by s. 1(2) as:

1 the manufacturer, or
2 the person who wins or abstracts products, or
3 processors, i.e. where a product's essential characteristics are changed by an industrial process who are not only liable for defects caused by their process but also for defects caused by a primary producer who will not be liable. For example a canner of agricultural produce would be liable for harmful chemicals which had been sprayed on a crop by a farmer s. 2(4).

Producer is very widely defined

The Act is very much aimed at manufacturers but it must be noted that where a defective component is installed in a manufactured product, for example defective brake cylinders in a motor car, both the manufacturer of the component part and the manufacturers of the car may be liable.

Supplies and importers

In order to help the plaintiff, the Act allows, in certain circumstances, an action to be brought against own-branders, importers and suppliers.

Own-branders   By s. 2(2)(b), liability is extended to any person who, by putting their name or trademark or other distinguishing mark on the product, holds themselves out as being the producer of the product. Typically, this section will apply to a supermarket's own branded products, but it is possible for an own-brander to avoid liability by making it clear on the product or through point of sale material, that they were not the producer, e.g. Produced for Bloggs Stores plc' or 'Specially selected for Bloggs Stores plc'.

Importers   By s. 2(2)(c), liability is extended to any person who has imported a product into a member state of the EU from a place outside the EU in order, in the ordinary course of any business of theirs, to supply it to another person. Therefore, it is the importer into the EU who is liable, not necessarily the importer into the UK, although if goods are imported directly into the UK from outside the EU, then they are the same.

Suppliers   If it is not possible to identify the producer or importer of a product, s. 2(3) provides for liability on the part of another supplier. This is likely to be the person who supplied the consumer. It is necessary that a person supplied a defective product for there to be liability and this supply must be in the course of business. The supply does not need to be to the ultimate consumer.

The major target of the Act is the manufacturer of the defective product, and so if the supplier is to be liable, four requirements have to be satisfied:

1   The person who suffers the harm must request the supplier to identify the producer, own-brander or importer (s. 2(3)(a)).
2   That request must be made within a reasonable period of the recurrence of the damage (s. 2(3)(b)). 'Reasonable period' runs from the time of the damage, not the time of supply.
3   It must be impracticable for the consumer to identify the actual producer (s. 2 (3)(c)).
4   The supplier fails within a reasonable time after receiving the request to comply with it or to identify the supplier (s. 2(3)(c)).

Thus the supplier may avoid liability by identifying the producer or, alternatively, by identifying their own supplier, who can in turn pass liability along the distribution chain.

Products

Products are defined in s. 1(2) as being any goods or electricity as well as components and raw material incorporated into other finished products.

It is thought unlikely that defective electricity as such can be supplied. However, an action is possible against the producers of defective equipment in the generating process rather than against the producer of the electricity itself. Although not specifically mentioned, water and gas would constitute products as these are tangibles (electricity was specifically referred to as it is an intan-

Margin notes:

Own-branders may avoid liability through an approproate disclaimer of being a producer

A *supplier* is commonly the retailer

gible). Further definition is given by s. 45(1) which is to include 'substances, growing crops and other things comprised in land by virtue of being attached to it and any ship, aircraft or vehicle.'

While products are widely defined, the following are specifically excluded:

1 A building supplied by way of creation or disposal of an interest in land, e.g. a completed house (s. 46(4)). But where materials are incorporated into land under a contract of supply then these products, e.g. building materials, will come under the Act.
2 Nuclear power (s. 6(8)).
3 Agricultural produce which has not undergone an industrial process (s. 2(4)). This would cover such processes as canning, filleting, freezing, and bottling, but as s. 1(2)(c) requires that the process should change the 'essential characteristics' of the product the exclusion should not apply to washing or packaging. Therefore, s. 2(4) protects all persons who supply the produce before it has undergone an industrial process, but after such process has been carried out then the processor is liable for pre-existing defects in the product, as well as those they may introduce themselves. It is anticipated that s. 2(4) will prove difficult to define. The exemption for primary agricultural produce was a consequence of intensive lobbying by the farming industry. It means that consumers suffering harm after buying pick-your-own produce cannot use the Act to gain compensation.

The agricultural produce exemption favours the agricultural industry

Defects

This is explained by s. 3(1) as 'there is a defect in a product… if the safety of the product is not such as persons are generally entitled to expect.' Therefore, the test for determining the level of safety is an objective one; one does not consider the expectations of the particular claimant but the expectations of persons generally. In considering what is meant by 'safety' the court is to have regard to 'all the circumstances' (s. 3(2)) but the Act mentions three specific circumstances which are to be taken into account when deciding if a product is defective. These are:

An objective approach is to be used to determine defects

1 The manner in which, and the purposes for which, the product has been marketed; its get-up (e.g. the dress of the product, such as its container or packaging); the use of any mark in relation to the product and any instructions for, or warnings with respect to, doing or refraining from doing anything in relation to the product.
2 What might reasonably be expected to be done with or in relation to the product.
3 The time when the product was supplied by its producer to another.

The essence of the section is that the product must be safe; if the product is safe but useless then the Act has no application.

Product recall

The Act does not specifically demand that products be recalled for alteration or replacement. However, commercial judgement will often demand that this be done especially as not to do so may result in later negligence claims. Section 3 does encourage appropriate warnings to be given and this will cover not only those made available at the time the product was supplied but also those that ought to have been given later. It may also be pointed out that a product will not always be said to be defective just because a later model contains new developments making it safer. Here s. 3(2)(e) will say that a defect is to be examined at the time when the product was supplied by its producer to another.

Product recall is a matter of both legal and commercial judgement

Market circumstances

Obviously this is a flexible standard and much will depend on how it is interpreted by the courts. The court will have to consider a number of relevant factors. What was the market at which the product was aimed and what sort of advertising or sales promotion was used? If the product is, for example, a child's toy then the target market will clearly be important. The instructions supplied with the product, or an absence of instructions, need to be taken into account to see whether they are adequate.

A more controversial point is the taking into account of the purpose for which the product has been marketed. It is still too early to say whether a court will take into account the comparative social utility of the product and apply a cost–benefit analysis. In the case of a new product launch of a pharmaceutical preparation would the court be willing to say that the risk of product defect was worthwhile given the benefit that the drug was expected to bring in, for example, the treatment of an AIDS patient?

Should a producer want to avoid liability, then it is possible to do so by providing a suitably strongly worded, prominently positioned, notice. The producer's defence would then amount to *volenti non fit injuria* in that the buyer, having been warned of the possible harm, was, on buying and using the product, a willing party to the defect when it occurred. However, poorly worded instructions supplied with a product may make the product defective. This is because warnings and instructions are taken to be part of the product so if they are defective then it rebounds on the product. However, while such a disclaimer notice may avoid liability, it may also cause prospective purchasers to lose confidence in the product, so that sales are curtailed.

Reasonable expectation as to use

Where the defect arises from a production defect, which renders the product unsafe, then there will be liability under the Act. But if the defect is in the design then greater difficulties are created. The court may have to balance the risk of harm against the benefits which were intended to flow from the product in deciding whether the decision to market the product was justified. Perhaps here a court could contrast a carefully calculated decision to market against an out and out gamble.

The conduct of the consumer may also be relevant where he or she has put the product to a use for which it is not intended, e.g. using a blowlamp to dry one's hair! Here the question as to whether an adequate warning was given may be of considerable importance. A failure to warn that a product is not suitable for a particular purpose may give rise to liability, e.g. that fireworks are not suitable for indoor use, or alternatively the failure to warn may relate to how the product is used, e.g. when applying a glue indoors ensure that windows are kept open to dispel the harmful vapour.

The time of supply

Safety is to be judged in terms of the time when the product was supplied. Any improvements in safety after that time will not make the producer liable if the product has not conformed to them. This is subject to the question of whether the producer should have recalled the product if the risk of harm was great, or at least have issued warnings to retailer/service agents to pass on to customers. It ought to be noted that the Act does not specifically demand that defective products be recalled for alteration or replacement. However, commercial reasons will often demand that this be done especially if the producer is wary of further negligence claims (see *Walton* v *British Leyland* (1978)).

Damage

Losses which may be claimed under the Act are death, personal injuries and any loss of or damage to property (s. 5(1)). In respect to property damage certain limitations apply:

1 The amount of any claim must be for £275 or more. For sums up to this amount a claim in negligence may in theory be possible but in practice it may not be worth the risk of litigation, especially since legal aid will not be available.
2 The property must have been of a description ordinarily intended for private use, occupation or consumption.
3 It must have been intended by the person incurring the loss or damage mainly for their private use, occupation and consumption.

The arbitrarily chosen £275 threshold may effectively disentitle some claimants

Therefore, exclusivity of personal use is not actually necessary provided that personal use (as opposed to commercial use) is the predominant use. However, damages for personal injuries are recoverable even if the property was used in a business environment.

In respect to economic loss the following apply:

1 No claim may be made under the Act for pure economic loss.
2 Consequential economic loss relating to personal injury is possible.
3 It remains unclear whether a claim for economic loss resulting from damage to property will be possible. It is believed that the Act will follow *Sparton Steel and Alloys* v *Martin* (1973).

Defences

The available defences are contained in s. 4. They are:

1 The defect was caused by complying with the law – EU or statutory (s. 4(1)(a)). Therefore, a producer will argue that they had no choice but to make the goods that way. Mere compliance with a British Standards Institute specification is not enough, as this will only recommend a minimum standard.
2 That the defect was not in existence when the product was supplied (s. 4(1)(d). To establish this defence the producer must prove that the defect was not present at the time of supply by them. This defence is likely to be the one most commonly used. A producer will endeavour to show that the defect was due to wear and tear, a lack of maintenance, misuse, or interference by a third party after the product was supplied. However, the onus is on the producer to show that there was no defect at time of supply.
3 Where the defendant can show that: 'the state of scientific knowledge at the relevant time was not such that a producer of products of the same description as the product in question might be expected to have discovered the defect if it had existed in his products while they were under his control' (s. 4(1)(e)). This particular defence is commonly known as the 'development risks defence'. For a manufacturer to use this defence they have to show on the balance of probabilities that, given the state of scientific and technical knowledge at the time the product was supplied, no manufacturer of a product of the same description would have discovered the defect. It is technically incorrect to call it a 'state-of-the-art defence'. The defence is so drafted that it will only be available in exceptional circumstances. The EC Product Liability Directive left this defence as an option for

The 'development risks defence' is extremely controversial in that certain hi-tech products may be exempted from operation of the Act

member states. Most member states in fact declined to incorporate it into their respective domestic legislation. The British Government were apparently swayed by lobbying from the pharmaceutical and aviation industries to bring it within the Act. It's inclusion is controversial in that for certain claims it will further defeat the overall objective of the Act in that producers are meant to have strict liability; and, secondly, member states which do not have the defence could become a testing ground for new products.

If the defence is, for example, used by a drug manufacturer where a new drug has caused damage to users, then provided they can show that the correct procedures were followed and no adverse defects with the drug use have been discovered, they would be justified in marketing the drug, provided that it met the knowledge possessed by other such manufacturers.

It appears that the effect of this defence will be to apply a fault-based regime to certain new products. The producer will only be liable where they knew or ought reasonably to have known of the defect, i.e. bring it closer to negligence liability. The burden of proof however will rest on the defendant.

4 The defendant did not supply the product, e.g. it had been stolen or was counterfeit (s. 4(1)(b)).
5 The defendant was not in business (s. 4(1)(c)), e.g. the product was obtained at a jumble sale for a charity (but not a charity shop), or a private sale of secondhand goods. This is the 'Women's Institute Defence'. It is designed to exclude from the Act producers who make products as a hobby, and those products are supplied to another other than in the course of a business.
6 The defect was due to the design of the finished product and that the component manufacturer had been given defective instructions by the producer of the finished product (s. 4(1)(f)). This defence is only available to producers of component parts.

Contributory negligence

The Law Reform (Contributory Negligence Act) 1945 applies (s. 6(4)). Therefore, the count has the power to apportion damages where the plaintiff has been partly to blame for the harm they have suffered.

Limitation

The limitation period runs for three years from the date on which the damage was caused by the defective product, or, alternatively, for three years from the date on which the damage could have reasonably been discovered (Limitation Act 1980, s. 11A(4)).

There is a long-stop provision which prevents any action against the producer more than 10 years from the date on which the product was first put into circulation (s. 11A(3)).

With suppliers of raw materials or component parts and manufacturers of finished products the 10-year period will expire against suppliers of raw materials or component-part manufacturers before it expires against the finished product manufacturer. This may result in manufacturers of the finished product being liable for defective components without recourse to the manufacturer of that defective component. To protect themselves manufacturers of finished products may use a contractual term to say that their supplies are to provide an indemnity for up to 10 years.

Exclusion of liability

The liability of a person to a defendant who has suffered damage caused wholly or partly by a defect in a product cannot be limited or excluded by any contractual term, any notice or in any other manner (s. 7).

Any limitation or exclusion clause is to be ineffective

If, therefore, a plaintiff sued a finished product manufacturer an exclusion would not enable the manufacturer to avoid liability. If, however, the finished product manufacturer then sought to obtain an indemnity from the component manufacturer, an exclusion or limitation clause in the contract between them could block the right to an indemnity sought by the manufacturer.

Review question

In your opinion to what extent has the Consumer Protection Act 1987 given additional protection to consumers who are harmed by defective products?

Product liability – a producer's proactive response

It must be appreciated that the Act provides only a very wide statement of product safety: a product is not safe if it fails to provide the level of safety which persons generally are entitled to expect. The objective expectation of 'persons generally' includes the presentation of the product. With such a general obligation all producers should critically examine their production processes in order to reduce or possibly eliminate the risk of product defects. Internal quality control reviews with external safety audits should periodically be carried out. In more detail the following ought to be considered:

Foresight may enable subsequent liability to be avoided

An establishment-wide policy on claims

Producers should have an internally well-known procedure for handling claims. What ought to be avoided is dealing with them, where the producer makes a range of similar products, on an *ad hoc* basis.

A central collating point for product liability information

A producer ought to have a central database for information on product liability. Claim trends may give advance warnings that a hither unknown problem exists; or a central database may help the development of future policy on product safety. Analysis of statistics should be helpful to make general predictions on future failure frequencies and this may be useful when negotiating product liability insurance cover so as to arrive at a realistic premium for the anticipated risk.

The importance of quality control

Periodic reviews of the efficiency of quality control procedures are essential. Not only will the highest attainable level of quality control reduce claims but insurance underwriters may regard the producer's quality control and testing practices as being of considerable importance when evaluating the risk and premium charged. Quality control may be broken down into:

Design procedures

A full appreciation of any aspect of design which might make a product vulnerable to product failure ought to lead to improvements in design and result in a safer product.

Materials and component supply

Clearly, any raw materials or components bought in should be of the highest standard. In addition the producer should look critically at contractual provisions to satisfy themselves that any liability for defective products is apportioned, between outside suppliers and themselves, to their advantage. In relation to imports from outside the EU, careful considerations need to be given to the question of risk and indemnities.

Production

Obviously, quality control has a major role to play in the manufacturing process. Quality management techniques ought to be of assistance here.

Packaging and distribution

Safe use of the product will mean that fewer claims are made. Therefore, user and installation instructions should be provided with the product. It has to be appreciated that not all end-users are the same, so a producer should anticipate different types and cater for each. Judicial use may be made of warnings, such as that a product must not be used for X purpose or that it must not be used for X unless certain precautions are taken. All literature issued with the product ought to be dated. Records of what literature was issued with what product should be kept, as well as the date when literature was amended or withdrawn. The appropriateness of literature issued with products should not be assumed; it ought to be tested that it does in practice achieve what it is intended to do. Where products are supplied through distributors, producers should consider whether either a contract term or an advisory notice ought to be given to demand that only approved installers fit the product.

Maintain records of inspection and testing

Records relating to each stage in the production process from design to delivery should be kept, together with notes on any remedial action taken when a defect was identified. These records must be kept for the cut-off period of liability under the Act – 10 years from when the product was supplied. However, from the time of making a claim to its adjudication in court may be typically 2–3 years. Therefore, to be safe, records ought to be kept for around 15 years. Many companies date mark their products with the date of manufacture. What is really important is the date of supply.

Product recall and warning system

This is of particular importance in the case of products sold to consumers. The claims policy should have guidelines to say in what circumstances a product recall is to be activated. Once a product recall decision is made then the system must quickly and efficiently swing into action. Similarly, with issuing warnings.

Product liability insurance

Appropriate cover must be taken out, and periodically be reviewed in the light of later knowledge. As claims for product defects grow so underwriters demand more and more knowledge about a product's history – another reason for keeping adequate records.

Criminal law and product defects

In order to improve the safety of consumers, as well as meeting obligations imposed by EU directives, a number of statutory provisions creating criminal offences have been enacted in the last decade.

These are:

- Part II, Consumer Protection Act 1987
- Food Safety Act 1990
- The General Product Safety Regulations 1994.

Whether use of the criminal law in protecting consumers from unsafe products is really effective or merely symbolic is open to dispute. However, in a student text concentrating on civil liabilities, there is insufficient space for a discussion of criminal liability.

Scotland

English law in respect to civil wrongs developed in a piecemeal manner so that it consists of a number of individual torts, whereas Scottish law in the same areas evolved from within a broad general framework of delictual liability, i.e. liability for civil wrongs. However, with negligence English tort and Scottish delict principles are very similar so that case precedents become interchangeable.

Northern Ireland

There are no differences in law between England and Wales and Northern Ireland.

Chapter summary

- To circumvent privity of contract, a collateral contract may be established between the parties, but formation of such a contract is demanding.
- Negligence does not depend on a contractual relationship between the parties, so that anyone suffering harm after using the defective product may claim, irrespective of whether they themselves purchased it.
- Negligence is based on a duty of reasonable care being owed to the plaintiff, with the actual standard of care varying with the circumstances.
- The burden of proof in negligence is on the plaintiff to make out his or her case. Evidential problems may be found in establishing that the duty of care was broken and that the breach caused the plaintiff harm.
- The Consumer Protection Act 1987, introduced as a result of an EC directive, increases the standard of care required from those responsible for putting products into circulation. Liability under the Act is strict, but not absolute in that there are a number of defences available, the most controversial being the 'development risks' defence.
- Producers can take a number of practical measures to avoid or reduce their liability under the Act.

Case study exercise

Machine 'fires' a mystery

Echo report leads to new damage claims

by Hardy Wickes

The great washing machine mystery deepened last week. Following an article in the Echo about two washing machine fires, we received two further telephone calls from owners of Mayyar machines who claim that their appliances had 'caught fire'. But the distributor of these Hungarian made machines, Home Nest, defended their safety record and dispute some of the claims.

Mr Norman Nutt, of Rotherham, said that about three weeks ago flames appeared out of the front of his machine. His wife, Nellie, was just about to go out and leave the washer working when she smelt smoke. He added: 'Luckily I keep an extinguisher in the kitchen and we were able to stop things getting too bad. The kitchen carpet has been completely ruined. I hate to think what would have happened if we had not been there.' Mrs Nutt said the family had just changed from Economy 7 electricity. If they had still been on it, the machine would have been working at night.

Mr Nutt told me that when the Mayyer engineer came, she did not give me a satisfactory explanation about the cause of the fire but said that a new thermostat was needed. Mr Nutt added that he had a new element fitted to the machine by a service engineer two weeks before the fire.

The Echo was also told about the plight of Mrs Hilda McClean of Barnsley. She was out shopping leaving her 19 year-old son, Angus, to load the machine. After it had been going for a while Angus noticed smoke coming from under the washer. Mrs McClean added: 'I came home to find wee Angus panicking at the door saying the washing machine was on fire. I rushed in and went to switch the plug off. As I did so I got an electric shock which threw me towards the burning machine.'

Mrs McClean suffered severe burns to her face and arms. She has been off work for three weeks and does not know when she will return. Mrs McClean, who won the machine in a competition, said she wasn't sure if she wanted it

repaired or not. In a statement issued last week Mr Alec Smart, Marketing Manager, said that Home Nest was 'particularly concerned' by the reports of product failure. He went on to say: 'The safety record of Mayyer products is of prime importance and is a major consideration right from the start of a every project development programme. Every model we buy in is approved by BEAB the British Electrical Approvals Board – or its foreign equivalent. Home Nest also has a stringent quality control system at its distribution centre.'

The Hungarian manufacturer produces over half a million washing machines a year, which are sold throughout Europe. In their statement Home Nest also said that the two machines 'did not catch fire'.

The Nutts' machine was checked and had been subject to some home repairs. The thermostat on it is to be replaced. With respect to Mrs McClean's machine, Home Nest says it does not accept liability, but will as a gesture of goodwill replace it. The Echo will keep you updated in any further developments.

Student task

Apply your knowledge of product liability law to the above events and comment on the legal liability, if any, of Home Nest.

Discussions questions

1 Who is the 'reasonable man' in the eyes of the law? Is he the average man? Does he simply represent the subjective views of the judge? Can the conduct of the reasonable man be sensibly predicted by a legal advisor?
2 At first sight the Consumer Protection Act 1987 represents a major advance for consumers injured by defective products, but on examination that advance is found to be much more limited. Discuss.

Further reading

Product Liability, Clark (1989), Sweet & Maxwell.
Defective and Unsafe Products – Law and Practice, Cotter (1996), Butterworths.

8 Professional negligence

Introduction

The practice of using professional advisors has been firmly established for many centuries. Since ancient times whatever the problem faced by an individual or business there would always be a professional person who for a fee would proffer advice. Because of the increased complexity of modern life, private or business, we are now even more dependent on professional advisors. This growth in complexity has seen professional advisors move from being broad generalists to ever narrower specialists. The solicitor's role as a general practitioner fragments into a number of legal specialisms: conveyancing, trust work, divorce and family matters, etc.; the accountant moves from someone who keeps the books to business manager, taxation consultant or investment counsellor, etc.

What the law has experienced a difficulty with is in making professional advisors liable for negligent advice. If there is a contract in existence between the advisor and client then a legal action for breach of contract is available; where no contract exists then the law for many years was extremely ambivalent. It recognized that defective advice could have serious consequences for those who relied upon it but, whereas with defective products those who suffered a physical injury are able to claim compensation, the law refused to allow those who incurred a financial loss through following defective advice to claim compensation. This refusal worked to the advantage of the professional advisor who avoided liability in tort for the advice he or she gave, but to the detriment of their clients who were left, in the absence of a contract, without a remedy.

The 'mind-block' is that in professional negligence the loss is not a physical one but an economic one. The courts have a similar suspicion of traumatic shock disorders (psychological injuries) which only in recent years has begun to be broken down. Here the law is wary that in relaxing its opposition fraud will flow. Physical injury is more quantifiable; an alleged broken limb can, by means of X-ray examinations, be objectively proved to have been broken, with the severity of the break (simple fracture or added complications) also being shown. Similarly, with non-personal forms of physical damage, such as building damage, once the damage has manifested itself it is possible to see it and assess the amount of compensation needed for repair or to rebuild. Admittedly, not all physical injury or damage can be fitted into this simple cause-and-effect scenario, but the inference is a valid one that in general terms physical injury or damage are, in principle if not always in practice, easier to claim than losses from the pocket.

A second difficulty is that, apart from the possibility of fraudulent claims which would be hard to detect, a willingness to recognize pure economic loss as being on a par with physical injury or damage would lead to a substantial number of claims which would figuratively speaking tend to swamp the court with destitute defendants. This is known as the floodgate argument by which a court will treat an apparently valid claimant with extreme caution lest the ripple effect of its decision lead to serious widespread consequences. A court in exercising a wider view will say that public policy considerations (the floodgate argument) act as a restraint to dispensing justice in one individual instance which will have an adverse effect for the public at large.

However, over the last generation this judicial reluctance to recognize economic loss caused by professional negligence has by increments been broken down. Since the House of Lords seminal decision in *Hedley Byrne* v *Heller & Partners Ltd* (1964), the courts have gradually become more amenable to considering claims for pure economic loss caused by a plaintiff's reliance on negligent advice coming from a professional person.

Objectives

The purpose of this chapter is to draw attention to the particular problems caused by pure economic loss, then to outline how the law has somewhat belatedly granted restricted recognition to claims for loss caused by negligent misstatements and finally to review a number of groups of professionals who have been particularly vulnerable to professional negligence actions.

Key concepts

- Pure economic loss without associated physical injury or other damage
- The *Hedley Byrne* principle
- Derivatives of *Hedley Byrne*, e.g. proximity and special relationship, reliance, expertise, etc.
- Professional negligence in action: groups of professionals before the courts.

Negligence and economic loss

This may be divided into two categories.

Where the economic loss was caused by negligently inflicted physical damage

Financial loss had to be associated with physical damage

Within the law of tort a long-established general principle held that there can be no liability in negligence for pure economic loss unless there was also physical loss or damage.

Case example
Weller v *Foot and Mouth Disease Institute* (1966)

The FMDI negligently allowed foot and mouth viruses to escape from their research centre. As a consequence of their negligence cattle auctions were cancelled. Weller, who were cattle auctioners, sued for lost profit.

As Weller's damage was purely financial with no physical damage, their action had to fail.

The reason why courts are reluctant to allow a plaintiff to recover pure economic loss is largely due to the floodgate argument or ripple effect. If such actions were possible then the courts would, according to the argument, be swamped by plaintiffs pleading economic injury resulting in defendants being forced out of business many times over. In contract there is no ripple effect as the doctrine of privity of contract acts as a brake because only those who have provided consideration, the contractual parties, may claim. In *Weller*, Widgery J provided a graphic scenario of the potential for pure economic loss:

Public policy was used to limit claims

> In an agricultural community the escape of foot and mouth disease virus is a tragedy which can foreseeably effect almost all business in that area. The affected beasts must be slaughtered, as must others to whom the disease may conceivably have spread. Other farmers are prohibited from moving their cattle and may be unable to bring them to market at the most profitable time; transport contractors who make their living by the transport of animals are out of work; dairy men may go short of milk and sellers of cattle feed suffer loss of business.

English courts have long been influenced by the statement of the American judge Cadozo in *Ultramares Corporation* v *Touche* (1931), that with pure economic loss there would be the potential for 'liability in an indeterminate amount for an indeterminate time to an indeterminate class'.

Apart from the floodgate argument another reason for non-recognition of pure economic loss is a suspicion that claims, being difficult to substantiate, could be open to fraud. In *Sparton Steel and Alloys Ltd* v *Martin & Co. (Contractors) Ltd* (1973), a power cable was negligently cut by Martin & Co. which resulted in molden metal solidifying in Sparton Steel and Alloys' factory. Sparton Steel and Alloys lost over a day's production and they sued for all their losses including loss of profits for being unable to process metal until the power cable was repaired. Their claim for physical loss, i.e. the loss of the material actually in the furnace at the time of the power cut, was successful but their claim for loss of profit failed as it was interpreted as being a pure economic loss. Lord Denning in the Court of Appeal justified the general principle of no recovery for pure economic loss:

Fear of fraudulent claims if pure economic loss allowed

> If claims for economic loss were permitted for this particular hazard, there would be no end of claims. Some might be genuine, but many might be inflated, or even false. A machine might not have been in use anyway, but it would be easy to put it down to the cut supply. It would be well-nigh impossible to check the claims. If there was economic loss on one day, did the claimant do his best to mitigate it by working harder the next day? And so forth…

Some commentators have expressed dissatisfaction with Lord Denning's reasoning. They argue that virtually all factories keep production records of daily output; records also relating to dispatch of goods or the delivery of raw materials, etc., may also be inspected to substantiate claims of loss. In addition commentators point out that if the courts are willing to put a monetary amount on losses with no market value, such as a lost eye, or paralysis in a leg, then why be reluctant to become involved with losses that may be investigated in relation to market values, e.g. by inspecting and verifying a company's order book to see whether their level of activity would mean that lost production could not later be made up, etc. Perhaps the courts are not prepared for this level of investigation, or perhaps there is an underlying suspicion that if a fraudulent claim for economic loss is made then fraudulent records to support it can also be produced.

Courts have been unwilling to be too investigative

Lord Denning in Sparton Steel was acutely honest in linking the difficulties of pure economic loss to public policy considerations.

> I think the question of recovering economic loss is one of policy. Whenever the courts show a line to mark out the bounds of duty, they do it as a matter of policy so as to limit the responsibility of the defendant.

The House of Lords in *Junior Books Ltd* v *Veitchi Co. Ltd* (1982) reconsidered the position of pure economic loss and unanimously agreed that there could be liability for economic losses without physical damage to property or persons. In the absence of physical damage the House held that the relationship between the parties was sufficiently close for a duty of care in respect to pure economic loss to be created. The *Junior Books* decision, by breaking with the orthodox position, was felt by many commentators to be 'out on a limb'. In *Muirhead* v *Industrial Tank Specialists Ltd* (1986), the Court of Appeal reverted to the traditional position. They did so by holding that the 'very close relationship' that existed between the parties in *Junior Books*, said by Lord Roskill to be 'as close as it could be short of actual privity of contract', did not exist in *Muirhead*.

The traditional position remains unchanged

In *Greater Nottingham Co-operative Society* v *Cementation Piling and Foundations Ltd* (1988), the Court of Appeal had the opportunity of re-examining *Junior Books* and *Muirhead*. They reaffirmed the orthodox position, per *Muirhead*, that there is still no general liability in negligence for acts or omissions causing pure economic loss. In respect to establishing such liability through the parties having a 'very close relationship' per *Junior Books*, the Court of Appeal held, despite the parties having an actual contractual relationship which required the defendant to take reasonable care, that, notwithstanding the parties being closer than in *Junior Books*, there was no duty of care created in tort whereby the defendants would be liable for the plaintiff's financial losses. *Junior Books* has therefore been sidelined and ought to be treated with caution. If the parties want to protect themselves for pure economic loss then the Court of Appeal in *Greater Nottingham Co-operative* said that they ought to do so be means of contractual terms and not, in the absence of contractual stipulations, to rely on remedies in tort. This stricture follows a plea by Lord Brandon in *Leigh & Sullivan Ltd* v *Aliakman Shipping Co. Ltd (The Aliakman)* (1986):

> where a general rule, which is simple to understand and easy to apply, has been established by a long line of authority over many years, I do not think the law should allow special pleadings in a particular case within the general rule to detract from its application.

In *Leigh & Sullivan* the House of Lords refused to depart from the 'general rule' that pure economic losses are not recoverable in negligence.

Where the pure economic loss was caused by a negligent misstatement

Where a negligent statement causes a loss then it will likely be an economic rather than a physical loss. For many years it was the established position that a pure economic loss caused by a negligent statement was irrecoverable.

> ## Case example
> ### Candler v Crane Christmas & Co. (1951)
> Crane Christmas & Co., accountants, prepared a company's accounts knowing that they would be given to Candler who was considering investing in the company. Candler received the accounts, which due to negligent preparation gave a false impression of the company, and invested in the company. Because of the negligence of Crane Christmas & Co., Candler suffered a financial loss and sued the accounts in negligence.
>
> The Court of Appeal held that Crane Christmas & Co. did not owe Candler a duty of case in tort and hence they were not liable.

With the large increase in professional services the position in *Chandler* v *Crane Christmas & Co.* (1951) was felt by many to be unsupportable. It meant that a professional person, causing someone to suffer an economic loss, could only be liable in contract, or breach of a fiduciary duty, or in deceit. All of these potential liabilities are restrictive. Unless there is a contractual relationship between the provider of the statement and the person suffering the economic loss then liability in contract is excluded, fiduciary relationships are rare and the tort of deceit is difficult to establish. However, the position was changed in a seminal decision in 1964. In *Hedley Byrne Co. Ltd* v *Heller & Partners* (1964), the House of Lords breaking with legal tradition held that a duty of care in negligence could be owed both to client and to third parties. When, for example, giving specialist advice knowing that it would be passed on to a third party who will rely upon it the professional who gave the negligent information or advice will be liable for any pure economic loss the third party may suffer.

The origins of the Hedley Byrne principle

> ## Case example
> ### Hedley Byrne & Co. Ltd v Heller & Partners Ltd (1964)
> Hedley Byrne, advertising agents, were approached by Easipower who asked them to place advertisements on their behalf with media owners. In the advertising industry it is the custom that whoever places an advertisement will be primarily liable to pay for it. To safeguard themselves Hedley Byrne took up a banker's reference on Easipower. The reference provided by Heller & Partners (Easipower's bankers), gave the impression that Easipower were sufficiently financially sound for Hedley Byrne to proceed. Hedley Byrne relied upon the statement from Heller & Partners and placed advertisements for Easipower. The reference from Heller & Partners had in fact been neglectfully prepared because Heller & Partners knew that Easipower were in financial difficulties. Subsequently, Easipower went into liquidation and Hedley Byrne had to pay on their behalf £17 000.
>
> The House of Lords held that previous case law on pure economic loss was no longer correct. Liability for negligence extended to careless statements as well as to careless deeds and in consequence damages could be awarded for pure economic loss as well as for physical injury to persons or property. While liability in law was established, Heller & Partners successfully relied upon an exclusion clause to avoid actually having to pay Hedley Byrne compensation. Also *Hedley Byrne* was a 1964 decision before the Unfair Contract Terms Act 1977 and the Unfair Terms in Consumer Contracts Regulations 1994. Therefore, the validity of exclusion of limitation clauses in professional service contracts, specially in relation to consumers, is unclear.

No common
agreement on
creation of duty
of care

In this important House of Lords decision the judges each gave their own variant of how a duty of care could be created. In his judgement Lord Morris said:

It should now be regarded as settled that if someone possessed of a special skill undertakes, quite irrespective of contract, to apply that skill for the assistance of another person who relies on such skill, a duty of care will arise.

Lord Morris went on to explain how exactly this duty could be created:

If in a sphere in which a person is so placed that others could reasonably rely on his judgement … a person takes it on himself to give information or advice to, or allows his information or advice to be passed on to another person who, as he knows or should know, will place reliance on it, then a duty of care arises.

The burden of
proof is on the
plaintiff to
establish their
allegations

For a plaintiff to succeed in a Hedley Byrne-type action it must be shown that there was a *special relationship* between the parties. This will be achieved by establishing the following:

1 That the defendant claimed to have a special skill and judgement.
2 The defendant knew that the plaintiff would be relying on them, or, alternatively, the information or advice was given in circumstances such that a reasonable person if asked would acknowledge that they knew they were being relied upon.
3 The defendant, not under a contractual or fiduciary obligation to give the information or advice, chose to give it and did so without a disclaimer or clear qualification to show that they did not accept responsibility for the accuracy of it.
4 The plaintiff did in fact rely on the defendant's skill and judgement and in the circumstances it was reasonable for them to do so.
5 The information or advice was negligent and caused the identifiable plaintiff economic loss.

The minority judgement (Lord Reid and Morris) said that a duty of care in such a situation would only arise where the plaintiff had made it clear that they were seeking advice and indicated that they intended to act on it in a certain way, e.g. by investing in the company if the defendant considered the advice was positive.

It is the more restrictive minority view, rather than the broader majority view, that has proved influential in later cases. However, it may be asked whether in the case example below, MLCA did in fact have a certain specialist knowledge of the company they commented on because it was a company within the same group.

Case example
Mutual Life and Citizens Assurance Co. v Evatt (1969)

An influential
Australian Privy
Council appeal
case

Evatt approached Mutual Life and Citizens Assurance asking whether they considered a certain company in the same group as themselves to be a good investment. Mutual Life and Citizens Assurance replied positively on the company and in response to this statement Evatt invested in it. The investment proved bad with Evatt suffering a heavy financial loss.

The Privy Council held that neither Mutual Life and Citizens Assurance or its employees claimed to be professional investment advisors: if agreeing to comment their duty was to answer honestly which they had done. In the circumstances it was unreasonable for Evatt to have relied on Mutual Life and Citizens Assurance as if they were not professional investment advisors.

Case example
Fish v *Kelly* (1864)

Kelly, a solicitor, met a friend on a train and during a conversation casually gave him advice on a point of law.

No duty of care had arisen. In the circumstances it was unreasonable to expect Kelly to know that Fish would be relying on his advice. Fish ought to have asked Kelly to repeat his comments in a more formal situation such as at Kelly's office. Kelly's statements amounted to an impromptu opinion.

See also *Howard Marine and Dredging Co. Ltd* v *Ogden & Sons Ltd* (1978), where Lord Denning said in the Court of Appeal that there would be no liability for 'representations made during a casual conversation in the street; or in a railway carriage; or in an impromptu opinion given offhand; or 'off the cuff on the telephone'.

But in:

Case example
Anderson (WB) & Sons v *Rhodes (Liverpool)* (1967)

Both parties were vegetable wholesalers. A third company was in debt to Rhodes and payment was long overdue. After receiving an assurance from Rhodes that the third company was creditworthy Anderson supplied it on credit with vegetables. On being unable to obtain payment from the third company Anderson sued Rhodes for provision of a negligent misstatement.

As Rhodes were experts in the wholesale vegetable trade they were liable in negligence and had to pay Anderson's losses. It may be queried whether being experts in the wholesale vegetable trade was the pertinant issue. Surely what Rhodes were being asked related not to vegetables but to financial matters, e.g. a wholesale vegetable trader was being treated as if he was a credit reference bureau.

While:

Case example
Chaudhry v *Prabhaker* (1989)

Chaudhry, who had recently passed her driving test, knew nothing about cars and asked her friend Prabhaker to find a suitable second-hand car for her to purchase, but stipulated that she did not want a car previously involved in an accident. Prabhaker, while not a motor mechanic, had some knowledge of cars, and located what he thought was a suitable car in apparently good condition apart from the bonnet which appeared to have been straightened after being crumpled. Chaudhry, on Prabhaker's advice, bought the car for £4500 from the vendor who was a panel beater and sprayer. A few months later Chaudhry discovered that the car had been involved in a very bad accident, had been poorly repaired and was in fact unroadworthy. Chaudhry sued Prabhaker for negligently advising her that the car was in good condition and had not been involved in an accident.

Even friends may be liable under Hedley Byrne

The Court of Appeal held that Prabhaker knew that Chaudhry was going to rely on him and ought to have been warned by the condition of the bonnet, as well as the trade of the vendor, to ask pertinent questions before making his rash statement. Chaudhry was successful in her claim.

Perhaps unwisely Prabhaker's council had conceded that a duty of care was owed, because Stuart-Smith LJ on considering whether a duty of care would arise said that the relationship between the parties is material: if they are friends the true view may be that the advice or representation is made on a purely social occasion and that the circumstances show that there is no voluntary assumption of responsibility.

Review question

Discuss what has to be established in order to successfully sue for professional negligence.

Economic loss and contract

A 'special relationship' is difficult to pin down

The search for a 'special relationship' has been problematic. If the 'neighbour test' in *Donoghue* v *Stevenson* was simply transferred to economic loss then the courts could expect to be flooded by complainants. For instance an expert speaking on a television programme may give advice which many thousands of viewers would act upon; each viewer, if the advice proved negligent, would be a potential litigant. Therefore, mindful of the floodgate argument, the courts have been anxious not to be too generous when formulating and interpreting the special relationship requirement. In *Hedley Byrne* (1964) Lord Devlin asked for a relationship between the parties be 'equivalent to a contract' and this recommendation was later accepted by Lord Templeman who argued, also in the House of Lords, for a relationship 'akin to contract' not a mere 'voluntary assumption of responsibility' (*Smith* v *Eric Bush* (1990)). Also, in *Junior Books* v *Veitchi* (1983), the majority in the House of Lords said that the special relationship between the parties while not creating an actual contract was near to being one, e.g. because there was a contractual chain linking the parties together. And in a later authority, *White* v *Jones* (1993), Lord Mustill argued that special relationship called for a 'mutuality' between the parties in that there is an element in 'reciprocity' present, so that, just as in a contract, both parties must have to do something, e.g. the defendant to perform a task for the plaintiff's benefit, the plaintiff, to rely on the defendant's statement. In *White* v *Jones* the arrangement was, according to Lord Mustill, one-sided and therefore so unlike a contractual relationship that the economic loss complained of could not be claimed. These judicial comments illustrate that with economic loss there is a certain similarity between tort and contract. Indeed some commentators have prophesied that in the future economic loss cases may be reclassified as contract law cases and not as at present tort law cases. If a contractual relationship was found to exist between the parties then a remedy through the Misrepresentation Act 1967 ought to be available.

A full or part contractual relationship is not always needed

However, the courts have not always insisted on a quasi-contractual relationship because, in exceptional situations, a special relationship may be found to exist even though there was a tenuous relationship between the parties and the plaintiff had not relied on any statement made by the defendant. What the courts call for here is not a relationship similar to one in contract but one with a close proximity between the parties. Indeed in the later case of *Spring* v *Guardian Assurance plc* (1994), a House of Lords case concerning economic loss allegedly caused by a negligent reference, Lord Goff stated that in his opinion the basis of the Hedley Byrne principle is an assumption of responsibility by the defendant.

This view would indicate that judgements made in the earlier House of Lords decision in *Smith v Eric S. Bush* (1989) may have been wrong to have cast doubt on the Hedley Byrne assumption of responsibility test. If this proposition is correct then in this context *Smith* v *Eric S. Bush* may be limited to its particular circumstances.

Case example
***Ross* v *Caunters* (1979)**

X, an invalid, was taken care of by Mrs Ross. X asked his solicitor Caunters to prepare a will for him instructing that Mrs Ross was to be a beneficiary. Caunters prepared the will and sent it to X saying that he had to sign it and have it witnessed by two others. X signed it but allowed Mr Ross to be one of the witnesses. The will was returned to Caunters and was placed in the office strongroom. On the death of X Mrs Ross claimed her inheritance but under the Wills Act 1837 the spouse of a beneficiary is an invalid witness. Therefore the will with only one valid witness to it was invalid and Mrs Ross's claim failed. She then sued Caunters in tort for his negligence towards X.

Despite the absence of any contract between Mrs Ross and Caunters and despite Mrs Ross not relying on any statement made to her by Caunters she was allowed to recover damage equivalent to her intended inheritance.

In *Ross* v *Caunters*, the trial judge Sir Robert Megarry V-C chose a middle position between the 'neighbour test' and the 'special relationship' requirement holding that for liability to be founded there had to be a close proximity between the parties with the position of the plaintiff being in the defendant's direct contemplation as someone likely to be closely and directly affected by his acts. Here Mrs Ross had been named in the will and as it bore the signature of Ross as a witness Caunters should have noticed this and asked their client for an explanation. The proximity of the parties was a foreseeable one given that Caunters were contractually bound to meet their client's instruction to see that Mrs Ross inherited after his demise. The fact that Mrs Ross had not relied upon any statement made by Caunters was immaterial. Reliance in economic loss, Sir Robert Megarry V-C said, was merely a form of causation, so provided Mrs Ross established that the cause of her loss was Caunters' negligence then reliance did not matter.

> A 'close proximity' between the parties may be enough

The post-Hedley Byrne position

Unfortunately, the considerable post-Hedley Byrne case law has resulted not in a set of clearly defined principles but in confusion and uncertainty. In a leading House of Lords decision Lord Oliver admitted that it was near impossible to arrive at a general principle that, used to create a relationship between the parties in one situation, could be transferred to another situation (*Caparo Industries plc* v *Dickman* (1990)). As a substitute for general principles what the courts are now seemingly doing is focusing on the degree of fairness inherent in the situation coming before them for adjudication. Where the court is satisfied that there was a major imbalance in the level of fairness between the parties then this will strongly influence their judgement as to whether it is just and equitable to impose a duty of care on the defendant, provided that by imposing a duty of care the floodgates are not opened. This may be a possible underlying explanation for the *Ross* v *Caunters* decision in that most reasonable observers will say that it is unfair that someone who has cared for an invalid does not get, because of the negligence of a legal specialist, a deserved inheritance.

Without transferable principle it appears necessary to adopt a case-law-in-action approach in

> The current position is a confusing one

Judicial caution acts as a brake on the Hedley Byrne principle

order to show how the courts may react to certain situations. What has to be appreciated is that the courts, ever mindful of the floodgate argument, will look at who the information or advice was communicated to. If it was received by an identifiable third party then a loss may be claimed, but if it was received by a class of persons then the courts will say that public policy considerations (a fear of opening the floodgates to litigation) will mean that no one in this class can claim even though causation for their loss is established.

Accountant and auditors

When companies commission financial reports there is clearly a contractual relationship between the compiler of the report and the company so that if the compiler provides misleading information or defective advice they can expect to be sued by the company for breach of contract. But what if a third party examines the compiler's report and relies upon it. If the third party suffers a financial loss because of the compiler's negligence can they sue for compensation?

Case example
Caparo Industries plc v *Dickman* (1990)

Dickman audited the accounts of company X. Caparo Industries had shares in company X and in reliance on Dickman's audit they acquired more shares and made a successful takeover of the company. Subsequently Caparo Industries said that the accounts prepared by Dickman were inaccurate and that Dickman's negligence had caused them a financial loss. The first evidential hurdle was in establishing that Dickman owed them a duty of care.

The House of Lords held that auditor's owe a very limited duty of care. The duty is owed solely to the company that employed them. Therefore, anyone relying on audited accounts cannot claim against the auditor if the accounts are negligently prepared as no duty will be owed to them.

Wider commercial considerations may influence a count in its judgement

In *Caparo* the House of Lords were anxious to limit the class of persons who were owed a duty otherwise, in the event of a negligent audit on a major firm where many investors would be involved, the consequences could easily mean that auditing firms would be forced out of business through having to meet an avalanche of claims (with such potential liability insurers would either refuse to provide professional indemnity cover or only do so at a prohibitive premium). In addition the House was influenced by the statutory purpose of audited accounts on companies. Lord Jauncey said:

> the purpose of annual accounts, so far as members (shareholders) are concerned, is to enable them to question the past management of the company, to exercise their voting rights … and to influence future policy and management. Advice to individual members in relation to present or future investment in the company is not part of the statutory purpose of the preparation and distribution of the accounts.

Caparo is an important case not just in the specific aspect of whom an auditor owes a duty of care to but in that the House of Lords took the opportunity of reviewing the *Hedley Byrne* decision, and providing a more modern restatement of it. Lord Bridge felt that a special relationship would arise:

1 If the defendant knew that their statement would be communicated to the plaintiff who was an individual or a member of an identifiable class.

2 The statement related to a particular transaction or transaction of a particular kind.
3 The defendant knew that the plaintiff would be very likely to rely on it in deciding whether or not to enter into a transaction.

Knowledge, Lord Bridge said, by the defendant had to be established, mere reasonable forseeability of the defendant suffering a loss was not enough. It is seemingly knowledge that creates the proximity between the parties.

The degree of the defendant's knowledge is crucial

In the judgement of Lord Oliver the special relationship was created where:

1 The advice is required for a purpose which is either specified or more generally described and made known, actually or by inference, to the advisor when the advice is made.
2 The advisor is aware, actually or by inference, that their advice will be communicated to others (advisees) in order that it can be used for the purpose specified or generally described.
3 It is known, actually or by inference, that the advice communicated is likely to be acted upon by others for that purpose without further independent inquiry.
4 The advice is so acted upon to the detriment of others.

When examining the conduct of people claiming to have relied upon the advisor's statement an objective standard is to be used. In the circumstances it must have been reasonable for those persons to have relied on the statement and equally it must have been reasonable to expect the advisor to appreciate that their advice was likely to be relied on. From judgement in both *Hedley Byrne* and *Caparo* this appears to be the position, but if the plaintiff's reliance was unreasonable, such as where they follow the advice of a very junior clerk working in a firm of stockbrokers, then it may mean that there is in fact no causation between the alleged reliance and the loss suffered – unreasonable reliance is no reliance.

Reliance is looked at through a reasonable person's eyes

However, if all other requirements are present then it may mean that a defendant can still be held liable under the Hedley Byrne principle even though their reliance was unreasonable but here a court could be expected to reduce the plaintiff's damage claim on the basis that unreasonable reliance equals contributory negligence.

The Caparo decision means that a company making a takeover bid with the price to be paid being largely determined by audited accounts does so at their own risk, because, if the audit was negligently carried out, causing the bidder to pay excessively, then no action will lie against the auditor. Bidders, therefore, are best advised to make their own financial enquiries about target companies and not rely exclusively on audited accounts made for other purposes.

Case example
James McNaughton Paper Group Ltd v *Hicks Anderson & Co.* (1991)

James McNaughton were negotiating over the takeover of a group of companies. The chairman of the target group instructed, at short notice, Hicks Anderson to prepare audited accounts on the group. These accounts were headed 'final drafts' and showed a net loss for the year. Responding to questioning from James McNaughton, Hicks Anderson said that the group were 'breaking even or doing marginally worse'. James McNaughton took over the group but later discovered that the accounts were erroneous in a number of respects and alleged negligence against Hicks Anderson.

The Court of Appeal held that, as the accounts had been prepared for the benefit of the chairman and not for James McNaughton, there was no relationship or proximity between the parties so that Hicks Anderson did not owe James McNaughton a duty of care. In the court's opinion, as the accounts were draft accounts and not final ones, Hicks Anderson could not have been expected to foresee reliance on them by James McNaughton. It would, therefore, not be fair, just and reasonable to impose a duty.

Caparo helpfully summarized

In his judgement in *James McNaughton Paper Group Ltd* v *Hicks Anderson & Co.*, Neil LJ referred to Lord Bridge's *Caparo* statement and then identified a number of factors which may be relevant. These are:

1 The purpose for which the statement is made. In *Caparo* the purpose of an audit report was to enable the shareholders to question the managers of the company, not to assist a third party to make an investment decision; hence the stricture in *Caparo* of the statement having to be made for the specific purpose of being communicated to the recipient.
2 The purpose for which the statement was communicated, for instance who had requested the statement and what they intended to do with it.
3 The relationship between the adviser, the advice, and any relevant third party.
4 The size of any class to which the adviser belonged. So that if there was a single adviser or the adviser came from a small class then it may be easier to infer a duty than if the adviser is one of a large, possibly indeterminate, class.
5 The state of knowledge of the adviser. Did the adviser know of the purpose for which the statement was made? It must be noted that knowledge includes both actual knowledge, and the knowledge that is attributable to the adviser by inference.
6 The degree of reliance by the advisee on the adviser's statement.

The importance of the reliance factor can be seen in the following:

Case example
Morgan Crucible plc v *Hill Samuel Bank Ltd* (1991)

During takeover negotiations the directors and financial advisers of a target company made statements supporting the accuracy of financial statements and profit forecasts intending that a bidder should rely on them. The bidder did so rely and alleged that he suffered loss as a result of the statements being prepared negligently.

The Court of Appeal held that, where the statements were made after an identifiable bidder had emerged, intending that the bidder rely on them, a duty of care might be owed.

Auditors' liability: a response from the profession

Auditors may protect themselves by changing to limited liability status

As a direct consequence of increased vulnerability to claims over negligent misstatements one of Britain's largest accounting firms, KPMG, announced in October 1995 that their major company audit work will be placed into a limited company. The intention of this move is to protect individual partners from the threat of punitive legal action over accusations of professional negligence. In a press release, Colin Sharman, a UK senior partner, explained that the move to incorporated status was a response to the massive rise in litigation against large accountancy firms:

> Firms often pick up the full cost of a company collapse despite being only partially responsible, and when the auditors themselves have not been the subject of fraud or deceit.

The KPMG strategy will mean that partners, who will become audit directors, will no longer be personally liable although the company which is to be created will of course be fully liable for the negligence of its employees. It is anticipated that other accounting practices will follow the lead of KPMG and also place their auditing work within a limited company.

More generally the auditing profession has for some time voiced its concern over the substantial increase in recent years in company auditors' liability claims. The problem is that when a company fails, largely through the fraud or negligence of its directors, all those deemed legally responsible will bear joint and several (that is individual and shared) liability. However, shareholders who have lost their investment will be advised that it is usually pointless to sue those directly responsible, the directors, as they would either have too few assets to pay compensation or, alternatively, they would have placed their assets beyond the reach of any creditor. As a consequence auditors, who by law must carry liability insurance, are an attractive target for a compensation claim.

In a March 1996 discussion paper, 'Finding a Fair Solution', the Institute of Chartered Accountants in England and Wales put forward a proposal that a system of proportionate liability ought to be introduced where blame and liability for company failure are apportioned among those responsible for a company failure. Such systems are already in existence in the USA and Australia. Whether the Department of Trade and Industry will be minded to sponsor enabling legislation for the introduction of proportionate liability is perhaps doubtful. A recently published Law Commission (England & Wales) Report on joint and several liability concluded that no alteration to the current position should be made.

Apportionment of blame: an overseas model?

Solicitors

Barristers and solicitors have immunity from liability for professional negligence while engaged in litigation before a court (*Rondel* v *Worsley* (1969)). For solicitors the area of liability in economic loss in which they seem most vulnerable concerns the negligent preparation and execution of wills. The decision in *Ross* v *Counters* (1980) was referred to earlier; another pertinent decision was: (the use of T in the next sequence of cases represents the person who has made a will: the testator (male) or testative (female)).

Case example
Clarke v *Bruce Lance & Co.* (1988)
T, using his solicitors Bruce Lance, made a will under which Clarke was to receive an interest in T's service station. Later T granted an option to X to purchase on T's death the service station for a fixed price. On T's death the service station was worth more than the fixed price given in X's option. Clarke argued that Bruce Lance owed him a duty to have advised T that the fixed price was an uncommercial proposition and that it would adversely affect Clarke's interest under the will.

It was held that Bruce Lance did not owe a duty of care to Clarke. The courts reasoning was:
(a)   There was an insufficiently close relationship between the parties; Bruce Lance had been subject to T's instructions but could not be expected to have contemplated Clarke as a person likely to be affected by any negligence on their part.
(b)   The grant of the option by T was not intended to benefit Clarke (in fact there had been a conflict of interest between T and Clarke over this).

(c) If a duty of care was owed then it would be owed to an indeterminate class of all potential donors, e.g. a person receiving a gift, or beneficiaries and not just to Clarke (the floodgate argument).

(d) If Bruce Lance had been negligent then it was for T's personal representatives to sue not Clarke.

In contrast to beneficiaries contending that a solicitor's negligence caused them to lose their inheritance there are two cases where claimants contend that a solicitor's negligence caused them to be excluded from becoming a beneficiary under a will. These are:

Case example
Smith v Claremont Haynes & Co. (1991)

T instructed Claremont Haynes his solicitor to prepare a will and to include Smith as a beneficiary. Claremont Haynes knew that T was in poor health but delayed preparing the will and T died before T was able to sign it.

Claremont Haynes had to compensate Smith for the amount he would have received under the will.

Case example
Kesckemti v Rubens Rabin & Co. (1992)

Rubens Rabins, solicitors, failed to provide T with advice concerning a tenancy. In consequence of this omission the property, on T's death, did not pass through his estate.

Rubens Rabins had broken a duty of care owed to Kesckemti (a potential beneficiary) and were liable to pay him compensation.

In both *Smith* and *Kesckemti* the court held that the solicitors were liable in respect to the claimants' expectations. Neither of the claimants had actually lost anything but both had failed to gain a benefit. This is similar to loss of a chance in contractual damages.

The most recent House of Lords decision relating to economic loss caused by a solicitor's negligent omission was:

The latest authority but others will doubtless follow

Case example
White v Jones (1993)

T, having had a reconciliation with members of his family, instructed Jones (a solicitor) to prepare an amended will in order to leave gifts to members of his family who had previously been excluded. Jones negligently delayed carrying out T's instructions and T died without signing the new will. In consequence of Jones's negligent omission White failed to receive a gift of £9000.

The House of Lords held that Jones did owe a duty of care to White and his omission in delaying the preparation of T's will had broken that duty and had caused White an economic loss.

On reflection the decision in *White* v *Jones* (1993) can be accepted as being a fair one in that the tester's wish that on his death White should receive £9000 was honoured; and it was also fair to White as a beneficiary that he would not, because of a solicitor's dilatoriness, lose his expected legacy. However, what is unsatisfactory about the decision is that yet again the judges were unable to find unanimity in arriving at their respective decisions. While not expressly saying that justice and fairness should mean the imposition of a duty of care, these two considerations appear to be woven into Lord Goff's decision. On their own, justice and fairness would be insufficient to establish the necessary proximity between the parties, but Lord Geoff did go on to say that the Hedley Byrne principle should offer a remedy to intended beneficiaries:

> by holding that the assumptions of responsibility by the solicitor towards his client should be held in law to extend to the intended beneficiary who (as the solicitor can reasonably foresee) may, as a result of the solicitor's negligence, be deprived of his intended legacy in circumstances in which neither the testor nor his estate will have a remedy against the solicitor.

In the same case Lord Goff found that Jones could easily have foreseen that his delay might prejudice White's expected legacy. In contrast Lord Brown-Wilkinson, also finding that foreseeability was present and conceding that justice and fairness morally dictated that a duty of care was owed, chose to concentrate on the issue of whether there was sufficient proximity, or in his words a 'special relationship' between the parties. He found, on the ground of the solicitor's having assumed a responsibility to carry out his client's instruction, that there was in fact the required degree of proximity. In a dissenting judgement Lord Mustill came up with a new variant to establish the necessary close relationship between the parties so that a duty of care would be owed. This was that in an assumption of responsibility there had to be between the parties an element of mutuality in that both parties 'played an active part in the transaction from which liability arose'. Mutuality according to Lord Mustill was evidence of a sufficiently proximate relationship to create the duty of care. In the instant case there was, in his judgement, no mutuality and hence no duty of care existed. He also expressed the opinion that it would be wrong in striving to dispense perceived justice to 'create a specialist pocket of tort law, with a special type of proximity, distinct from the main body of doctrine, sufficient to provide a remedy.'

So far in the discussion of a solicitor's liability the clients have all been deceased but in *Hemmens v Wilson Brown* (1993) a transaction involved a living client and a third party. Here, failure by the solicitor to carry out the transaction properly resulted in the intended benefit not being received by a third party – did not give rise to the duty of care, because the client, being still alive, could have rectified the situation had he so wished.

Still little judicial agreement as to what exactly is needed for a Hedley Byrne action

Surveyors and valuers

These are professionals who have been increasingly subject to professional negligence claims.

Case example
Yianni v Edwin Evans & Sons (1982)

Yianni, a first-time buyer, was interested in a certain house. His building society insisted that he should have it valued but also recommended that he had his own structural survey carried out. In their report to the building society (which Yianni did not see) Edwin Evans valued the house at £12 000 and the building society offered Yianni a mortgage, which he took up, at that amount. Yianni later discovered that the house needed £18 000 to put into good condition.

It was known by house surveyors that it was common for first-time buyers not to have their own structural survey but to rely on the valuation prepared for the building society. If the building society gave a mortgage then a first-time buyer was inclined to believe that the property was in good condition. Edwin Evans were deemed to know of this practice and hence they ought to have realized that Yianni would be relying on them to provide an accurate valuation. Edwin Evans were consequently liable.

Case example
Smith v *Eric S. Bush* (1989)

Eric S. Bush gave a valuation on a house to a building society who were considering granting a mortgage on it. A copy of the report was passed on to Smith, the prospective purchaser. The report said that the house was suitable security for the loan. Subsequently, after Smith had bought the house, it was discovered that Eric S. Bush had overvalued the property.

The House of Lords held that, as the report had been prepared by Eric S. Bush knowing that Smith would receive a copy of it, then it was deemed that Eric S. Bush had assumed responsibility to those who would act on the statement made. Proximity had therefore been established and Eric S. Bush owed Smith a duty to take reasonable care over their valuation. Their failure to do so meant that they were liable.

A reminder that for liability to attach there has to be all of these: a duty of care, a breach of that duty, with the loss being caused by the breach.

Case example
Shankie-William and others v *Hearey* (1986)

Mr and Mrs Shankie-William (the first and second plaintiff) engaged Hearey to carry out a survey for dry rot in a flat they intended to buy. Hearey negligently stated that the flat was free of dry rot and Mr and Mrs Shankie-William purchased it. The third plaintiff read Hearey's report and believing that it referred to the whole building bought the flat immediately above the one that had been surveyed. Both flats were subsequently found to have dry rot.

The Court of Appeal held that, in respect to Mr and Mrs Shankie-William a duty of care was owed to them but evidence showed that they would still have bought the flat at the same purchase price even if they had known of the dry rot. Their loss had not, therefore, been caused by his negligence. In respect to the third plaintiff it was found that no duty of care was owed to him.

Review question

Why is there seemingly a difference between how the law treats negligent property surveyors and negligent auditors?

Insurance underwriters

> ## Case example
> ### Henderson and others v Merrett Syndicate Ltd and others (1994)
>
> The plaintiffs were Lloyds' names who were members of syndicates managed by the defendant. Lloyds' names can be either 'direct names' in that the syndicate to which they belong is managed by the members' agents themselves, or 'indirect names' in that the members' agents places names with syndicates managed by other agents and enter into sub-agency agreements with the managing agents of those syndicates. In the action the plaintiffs alleged that the defendants had been negligent in conducting syndicate business and sought to establish that a duty of care was owed to them in tort in addition to any contractual duty that was also owed them.
>
> The House of Lords held that, where a person assumed responsibility to perform professional or quasi-professional services for another who relied on those services then that relationship was itself sufficient to create a duty on the person providing the service to use reasonable skill and care. Therefore, managing agents at Lloyd's owed a duty of care to names who were members of syndicates under their management.
>
> The agents had held themselves out as possessing a special expertise in advising names on underwriting matters. Also the managing agents knew that the names, by giving them authority to enter into contracts, would be relying on their expertise. This duty of care created in tort was unaffected by any contractual relationship that might exist between the parties. Therefore, a plaintiff who had concurrent remedies in tort and contract, could choose, subject to any restrictive contractual term, which remedy to pursue.

Names at Lloyd's have brought many Hedley Byrne-type actions

In *Henderson* v *Merrett* the unanimous decision was given by Lord Goff who said that where a defendant 'assumed responsibility' for the plaintiff's financial position, or where the parties relationship was 'equivalent to contract' then the defendant may be liable for negligence that causes the plaintiff economic loss. The championing of the 'assumption of responsibility' requirement further weakens the House of Lords decision in *Smith* v *Eric S. Bush* (1989) where this requirement was subjected to much criticism.

Disclaimers of professional negligence

It has been common practice for providers of professional services to include in their business terms an exclusion of liability clause. As mentioned earlier the merchant bankers Heller & Partners Ltd were liable in legal principle to Hedley Byrne but as Heller obtained the protection of an exclusion clause no damages in fact were paid. After the decision in *Yianni* v *Edwin Evans & Sons* (1982) it became the norm for surveyors to include a disclaimer of liability over a negligent valuation but their validity was considered by the House of Lords in two later 1989 surveyors cases, *Smith* v *Eric S. Bush* and *Harris* v *Wye Forest District Council No.2*. The legal argument for the surveyors was that on their construction the disclaimer clauses were not there to exclude liability, but were present so as to prevent a duty of care being created. Under the Hedley Byrne principle it is necessary for a plaintiff to show that he or she had reasonably relied upon the statement made by the defendant, however, in absolving themselves of liability the defendants

Disclaimers, while attractive, are fraught with problems

argued that it would be unreasonable for the plaintiffs to rely on a statement made to them and hence a duty of care could not arise. The object of this faintly plausible argument was that if successful it would mean that without an exclusion clause in operation then s. 2(2) Unfair Contract Terms Act 1977 would have no application. S. 2(2) UCTA 1977 covers the restriction, by means of a contractual term or notice, of liability for loss or damage caused by negligence in the cause of a business other than personal injury. Under s. 1(1)(b) negligence includes the breach of any common-law duty to take reasonable care or use reasonable skill. If it can be shown that the term or notice restricting liability was in fact reasonable s. 1(3) then the defendant will escape liability. The House of Lords found that s. 2(2) had to be read in conjunction with s. 13 (which deals with varieties of exemption clauses) so that s. 2(2) did in fact cover the exclusion of relevant obligations or duties and not just the liability once a duty was shown to be owed. The counter-argument was successful. In respect to satisfying the requirement of reasonableness under s. 2(2) the House of Lords asked a number of questions: were the parties of equal bargaining strength? Was it reasonably practicable for the plaintiff to have obtained the advice from another source? How difficult was it for the defendant to provide the advice? Are any public policy considerations involved?

After consideration it was found that in the circumstances the disclaimer was unreasonable. In addition the House of Lords in *Smith* v *Eric S. Bush* also stated that another reason why the disclaimer would be ineffective was that the plaintiff had paid indirectly for the survey to be done. Should the validity of a disclaimer hinge, even in part, on whether the alleged negligent statement had been paid for or not then this is unsatisfactory. In *Spring* v *Guardian Assurance plc* (1994) an employer gave a negligent reference on an employee but as employees do not pay for them then seemingly an employer may attempt to avoid liability for negligent statements contained in a reference by, for example, demanding that an employee sign a waiver of liability before the reference is provided or, more simply, by just telling the employee that no liability for a reference is accepted.

In the context of employee references, if the question of payment proves troublesome then Lord Woolf provided a lifeline in *Spring* by saying that in current employment it is appropriate to regard the employer as obtaining a discernible indirect benefit from giving a reference in that the general practice of provision of references aided recruitment. However, references are commonly provided where no direct or indirect payment applies such as where a friend, doctor, minister of religion or teacher provides it.

Insurance

Appropriate insurance cover is highly recommended

Any professional advisor who offers their services to the public (business or individual clientele) should carry appropriate professional negligence indemnity insurance cover. Indeed, a business buying in a professional service would be advised to contractually require that suitable and adequate insurance is held. More detailed treatment of insurance is given in the chapter on insurance. However, a few observations may be made here.

Professional indemnity insurance

1 Is a contract of indemnity. In return for a premium the insurer will, subject to the terms of the policy, undertake to indemnify the policyholder against loss arising from pre-stipulated causes up to the financial limit given in the policy.
2 Will only reimburse the monies that the policyholder is legally obligated to pay a third

party as a consequence of the negligent performance of their professional activities.

3 May be 'aggregate indemnity', that is any number of claims will be settled by the insurer up to an aggregate sum. Once the aggregate sum is reached then the insured is henceforth on their own. Alternatively, the more modern form is for a policy to be on an 'each and every claim' basis: this means that each claim, during the period of cover, is treated individually and settled on its merits. As there is no upper limit the insurer obviously carries far greater risk so that premiums are correspondly higher.

4 Is subject to normal insurance principles such as utmost good faith whereby the insured must disclose all material facts or circumstances to the insurer. A failure to do so will mean that the insurer may avoid the policy leaving the policyholder uninsured.

5 Will always have an excess whereby the policyholder is required to pay the first part of a claim themselves. The insurers intention in having an excess in the policy is to encourage the policyholder to take care when carrying out their activities. Without an excess the policyholder, who would be fully indemnified, would have no incentive to take care other than the protection of their professional reputation. The excess figure may be based on turnover, e.g. one per cent of a firm's fee income, or a negotiated figure.

6 Will always contain a subrogated rights condition in the policy whereby the insurer will be able on settling a claim to take over the legal rights of the insured. In addition, a policy condition allows the insurer to take over the insured defence. This can result in the insurer electing to contest the claim through the courts, or, alternatively, in settling out of court. The former may damage the insured long-term business relations with a client, as well as causing bad publicity, while the latter may be seen as an admittance of culpability. Where conflicts of interest between the insurer and insured occur then a 'QC clause' in the policy will allow the dispute to be referred to a Queen's Counsel for a legal opinion as to whether a good defence exists. If the QC says that such a defence exists then the insured must either permit the defence to be used by the insurer or else settle the claim themselves without benefit of the policy.

Endangering a valuable business relationship may be avoided by a 'QC clause'

Scotland and Northern Ireland

No additional comments are made.

Chapter summary

- Where economic loss is caused by negligently inflicted physical damage, there can be no recovery of the economic loss unless physical harm or damage was associated with it. The justification for this rule is largely the strength of the floodgate argument.
- To claim *pure economic loss*, that is an economic loss without any physical harm or damage, a plaintiff must come within the Hedley Byrne principle. This requires that the defendant: (a) held themselves out as being a specialist, (b) knew that the plaintiff would rely on them – either actual or implied knowledge, (c) they voluntary assumed, without a disclaimer, responsibility for the accuracy of their statement, and (d) their statement was in fact negligent; also the plaintiff must (e) have relied on the defendant's statement and in consequence suffered loss.
- A number of appellant judges have said that to create a duty of care under the Hedley Byrne principle there has to be a special or proximate relationship between the parties. Unfortunately, there is little unanimity over what the special or proximate relationship consists of, e.g. while some judges call for the relationship to be 'equivalent to contract' others do not go as far.
- A growing body of case law has resulted in the extension of liability for pure economic loss with many professional groups being affected. Accountants when negligently doing auditing work are, however, only liable to the company being audited (unless the audit was specifically commissioned by a party considering taking over the company being audited); solicitors are particularly at risk over any delay in attending promptly to a client's instructions over a will so as to prejudice a legatee; surveyors on providing a negligent property valuation may be liable not only to those who employed them but also be liable in tort to a third party who they knew or ought to have known would be relying on them.
- A disclaimer of liability clause for professional negligence may be used but statute and case law make it difficult for such a disclaimer to be effective.
- Providers of professional services should always hold appropriate professional indemnity insurance. Such cover is subject to normal insurance principles.

Case study exercise

Clare inherited £30 000 on her father's death. In the course of a conversation in the office where she worked with Maurice, a financial journalist, Maurice asked her what she intended to do with her inheritance. Clare replied that she had not made up her mind and was seeking suggestions. Maurice then said, 'Of course it is not really my business to give investment advice to individuals, but if I were you, I should invest in Graphica Ltd, a new computer design company. Although their shares are low at the moment, they are tipped to rise dramatically, as they have developed a revolutionary software package.'

Acting on this advice, Clare invested £30 000 in Graphica Ltd and also passed on Maurice's comments to Donald, a friend, who invested £10 000 in Graphica Ltd. In fact Maurice had confused Graphica Ltd with Graphena Ltd. Graphica Ltd went into liquidation within weeks of Clare and Donald investing in it.

Student task

Advise Clare and Donald who wish to claim in tort damages from Maurice.

Discussion questions

1 The difficult question of liability for pure economic loss has been satisfactorily resolved by recent cases in the law of tort. Evaluate the truth of this statement.
2 In what ways has the Unfair Contract Terms Act 1977 affected potential liability for professional negligence?
3 To what extent is a professional adviser liable in civil law for his or her misstatements?

Further reading

Professional Negligence, Dugdale A. M. and Stanton K. M. (1995), Butterworth.
Comprehensive treatment of the subject.
Textbook on Tort, Howarth D. (1995), Butterworth.
This prize-winning book provides erudite coverage of both professional negligence and product liability.

9 Negotiable instruments

Introduction

This chapter is concerned with negotiable instruments, notably bills of exchange and cheques. It was always possible under the common law for choses in action (such as a debt) to be assigned or negotiated to another. A further development came with the enactment of the Law of Property Act 1925, s. 136 of which created the mechanism for assignment at law of choses in action. An effective assignment under this section enables the assignee to sue the debtor in their own name, but the assignee still obtains no better title than the assignor. The assignee is said to take the chose in action 'subject to equities'.

Certain types of chose in action, however, were long regarded by merchants as being in a special category with distinctive characteristics recognized by the custom of merchants, this being eventually incorporated into the common law. These special types of chose in action, which became known as 'negotiable instruments', were transferable and the transferee was able to sue in their own name. Moreover, such instruments could be transferred easily by delivery, or by delivery and endorsement, without notice to the debtor and, in certain circumstances, it was possible for the transferee to obtain a better title than the transferor. These characteristics, and the possibility of negotiation, are the special features of a 'negotiable instrument'. Among the most prominent of these are bills of exchange and cheques.

Objectives

The relevant law has, for the most part, been codified in the Bills of Exchange Act 1882 and the Cheques Act 1957. This chapter will explain the main provisions of these statutes, dealing especially with the definition of the instruments which come within their scope, the rights and duties of the various parties to the relevant instrument and the various legal incidents attaching to the main negotiable instruments.

Key concepts

- Negotiability
- Bills of exchange
- Promissory notes

- Cheques
- Drawer, drawee
- Endorsement
- Mere holders
- Holder in due course
- Acceptance
- Dishonour
- Discharge
- General and special crossings
- Significance of crossings.

Negotiability

Meaning of 'negotiability'

There is no statutory definition of 'negotiability' or 'negotiable instrument' and whether an instrument is such depends partly on statute and partly on mercantile usage. However, it is commonly accepted that an instrument is negotiable if it can be transferred by endorsement and delivery for value in such circumstances that the transferee takes free from any defects in title of prior parties.

All negotiable instruments will fall into one of two categories: an undertaking to pay a sum of money; and an order to another to pay a sum of money. Examples of such instruments are: promissory notes (see below), banknotes, treasury bills, bearer bonds and bearer debentures, share warrants, bearer scrip certificates and negotiable certificates of deposit, cheques and other bills of exchange (see below), dividend and interest warrants, bankers' drafts and circular notes. The Bills of Exchange Act 1882 governs some, but not all of these instruments.

> **Example**
> A postal order and a £50 note are stolen from X. The thief transfers both to Y. The banknote is a negotiable instrument and Y becomes its legal owner. X cannot recover it and can only sue the thief. The postal order is, however, not a negotiable instrument, though it can be transferred, which means that the thief can give no better title than he has himself. X is therefore entitled to recover it from the thief.

Review question

How would you define a negotiable instrument and its characteristics?

Bills of exchange

'Bill of exchange' defined

The Bills of Exchange Act 1882 codifies the law relating to cheques and other bills of exchange, the most important kinds of negotiable instrument.

Section 3 of the Act defines a 'bill of exchange' as an 'unconditional order in writing, addressed by one person to another, signed by the person giving it, requiring the person to whom it is addressed to pay on demand or at a fixed or determinable future time a certain sum in money to or to the order of a specified person or bearer.'

The parties to a bill

The person issuing the bill is the 'drawer', and the person to whom it is addressed is the 'drawee'. The party in whose favour the bill is drawn is the 'payee'. When the bill is delivered to them, they become a 'holder'. If the 'drawee' later accepts the bill drawn on them, as by signing it, they then become an 'acceptor'.

'Unconditional'

An order will not be unconditional if it directs payment from a particular fund, for this makes the duty to comply with it conditional on that fund having sufficient credit. This differs, however, from an unqualified order to pay, coupled with an indication of the particular fund from which the drawee is to reimburse themselves or a particular account which is to be debited with the particular amount. An order will also not be unconditional if, for instance, it gives a discretion, such as 'Pay X if satisfied with the goods consigned'.

The requirement that a bill must be addressed to a 'specified person or bearer' is not met in the case of an instrument payable to 'cash' (*Orbit Mining & Trading Co. Ltd* v *Westminster Bank Ltd* (1963)).

Date

Where a bill is stated to be payable at the end of a given period, the bill itself must be dated in order to fix the time for payment. If it is not dated, the holder may insert the true date and s. 13 of the Act provides that, if he acts in good faith, the date he inserts will be taken as the true date even if it is not. Dating of a bill is not necessary when it specifies the actual date on which it is to be paid and the Act specifies that no bill is invalid merely because it is undated or post- or ante-dated.

Section 10 defines a bill as payable on demand as a bill which is expected to be payable on demand, or at sight, or on presentation, or as a bill for which no time for payment is specified. The Act also states that where a bill is payable at some fixed or determinable future time, it becomes due and must be paid on the last day of the time allowed for payment or the next following day if the particular day is not a banking day.

An order to pay on the happening of a future event which is not sure to happen is not a bill, neither is an order to pay on or before a specified date (*Williamson* v *Rider* (1963)).

Signature

A duly authorized agent can sign on behalf of a principal; and a signature can be in the form of a mark if this is the habitual form of signature of the signatory (*George* v *Surrey* (1830)).

Section 20 of the Act governs the position where a person signs a blank piece of paper and delivers it to another, intending that it should be completed as a bill. This operates as authority to complete the piece of paper as a complete bill. Such a bill can only be enforced against the signatory if completed within a reasonable time of delivery, and if completed strictly within the limits of the authority provided. A holder in due course (see below), however, could enforce the bill for more than the authorized limit.

Effect of signature in blank

'To or to the order of a specified person or to the bearer'

A bill made payable to 'X or order' is an 'order' bill; whereas a bill made payable to 'X or bearer' is a 'bearer' bill. Section 7(3) of the Act provides that a bill is a bearer bill if payable to a payee who is non-existent or fictitious. If the payee does exist, but was named as a result of fraud, the position is complicated.

> ### Case example
> ### *Bank of England* v *Vagliano Bros* (1891)
> V's clerk forged certain instruments purporting to be bills drawn on V in favour of X, a respectable firm. The clerk forged an endorsement by X in favour of M, under which name he obtained payment. The question at issue was whether the Bank could debit V's account with the amount of these bills. The House of Lords held that a bill was payable to bearer if the payee, while not fictitious, had not been intended to have any rights under the bill; if the insertion of his name, in other words, was a mere pretence. On the other hand, it held that, if there were an intention to benefit the payee, the latter would not be fictitious, and hence the bill would not be payable to bearer, even if the name were inserted because of fraud. In the case itself, the court held that the payee was fictitious and hence the bill was payable to bearer, with the result that the Bank could debit the account.

Review questions

1 Explain what is meant by saying that a bill must be 'unconditional'.
2 Distinguish between 'order' and 'bearer' bills and state which is relevant when the payee is fictitious.
3 To what extent must a bill of exchange be dated and signed? What is the effect of signing in blank?
4 What are the rules as to when a bill is to be payable if it is to be a bill of exchange?

Rights and duties of parties to bill

If a person is to be made liable on a bill, certain requirements must be satisfied.

Criteria for liability

Capacity

This is stated by s. 22 of the Act to be co-extensive with the general capacity to contract (see Chapter 2). The Act further provides that, while a person lacking capacity cannot be liable, other parties thereto can be liable. Companies usually have express or implied authority to draw, endorse or accept bills, and, even if they lack such power, they may be liable on them to a third party under s. 35 of the Companies Act 1985.

Signature

Section 23 provides that a person incurs no liability on a bill unless they signed it as drawer, endorser or acceptor.

Where an agent signs a bill without clearly indicating their status, they will, in accordance with s. 26(1), incur personal liability; and merely adding words such as 'agent' or 'director' will not alter this. To avoid liability, the agent should sign 'J. Bloggs, per pro X Co. Ltd' or 'for and on behalf of X Co. Ltd'. However, the agent will still be liable if there was clear evidence that they intended to assume such liability when signing (*Rolfe Lubell & Co.* v *Keith* (1979)).

Effect of forged signature

Section 24 of the Act provides that a forged or unauthorized signature has no effect.

No claim can be made against someone who signed a bill believing it to be a totally different category of document and this was induced by a misrepresentation, and if the signatory was not negligent.

Effect of mistake

> ### Case example
> ### *Foster* v *Mackinnon* (1869)
> An elderly man signed a bill as endorser mistakenly assuming it to be a guarantee, the mistake arising from the fraud of the acceptor of the document. He had not been negligent and it was held that he was not bound by his signature. See too *Saunders* v *Anglia Building Society* (1970).

Issue and delivery

The Act provides that delivery of a bill is necessary before there can be liability on it and, until delivery, the bill is revocable. This means, for example, that mere endorsement by the payee of an order bill (see above) is not of itself effective: it must be delivered as well. The Act defines 'delivery' to mean the 'transfer of possession, actual or constructive, from one person to another'. Posting a bill does not constitute delivery unless such a method was requested or can be implied (*Thairlwall* v *Great Northern Rly Co*. (1910)).

Section 21, however, provides that a holder in due course (see below) is conclusively presumed to have undertaken a good delivery and can sue all prior parties to the bill, even if they acquired it from a thief.

Review questions

1 What rules as to capacity must be satisfied before a person can be liable on a bill?
2 In what circumstances is (a) an agent liable for their signature to a bill; and (b) a person liable who signed a bill in mistake?
3 Explain the relevance of, and what is meant by, 'delivery' of a bill.

Negotiation of a bill

The payee under a bill of exchange may wish to obtain its value before the date specified in it for payment. They can choose to do this by transferring it to another in return for immediate payment, usually for a sum less than the stated amount. They may of course simply want to make a gift of the amount stated in the bill, or to transfer the sum to another for no particular reason. Whatever the background, the process of transfer is termed 'negotiation', and s. 31(1) of the Act provides that: 'A bill is negotiated when it is transferred from one person to another in such a manner as to constitute the transferee a holder of the bill.' The Act states that the holder of a 'bearer bill' (see above) is the person in possession; in the case of an 'order bill' (also see above), it is the payee or endorsee.

A bearer bill is negotiated by delivery and an order bill by delivery and endorsement.

To achieve negotiation in this latter way, the payee will endorse the bill usually, but not necessarily, on the back under the provisions of s. 32 of the Act. The payee then becomes an endorser and the party to whom it is endorsed, an 'endorsee'. An endorsement which transfers only part of the amount stated in the bill, or which transfers the bill to unconnected endorsees is stated by the Act not to operate as an endorsement.

Method of endorsement

Types of endorsement

The Act provides for various types of endorsement:

1 An endorsement is 'conditional' if, for example, it is endorsed 'Pay X if he supplies agreed goods to Y.' The payer can ignore this condition if they wish, and payment to the endorsee will be valid whether or not the condition is observed.
2 An endorsement 'in blank' does not name or indicate the identity of the endorsee. Following such an endorsement, the bill becomes a bearer bill. It can be converted to an order bill by means of a special endorsement (see below).
3 An endorsement is a 'special endorsement' if it specifies to whom, or to whose order, it is to be paid. An endorsement in blank (see above) can be converted into a special endorsement if the holder inserts a direction to pay themselves or another, or to their order, above the signature of the endorser.
4 An endorsement is 'restrictive' if it prohibits further transfer or expressly states that it is merely an authority to deal with the bill as directed. A restrictive endorsement gives the endorsee the right to receive payment under the bill and to sue anyone whom the endorser could have sued but, unless expressly authorized, cannot transfer this right.
5 A 'subsequent endorsement' arises when there are two or more endorsements and they are taken to have been applied in the order in which they appear unless the contrary is proved.

Review questions

1 What is meant by 'negotiation' and how is this effected in the case of (a) a bearer bill and (b) an order bill?
2 How is a bill endorsed and what types of endorsement are there?

Parties who may
be sued by
holder

Parties liable on a bill

The drawee

The Act provides that a drawee (see above) who does not accept a bill is not liable on it. They may still, however, be liable on the contract or the pre-existing debt in relation to which the cheque was drawn.

The drawer and endorser

The Act provides that a drawer and any endorser accept liability for the bill being honoured and will compensate the holder or any subsequent endorser who is compelled to make payment.

It is open to the drawer or endorser to insert an express stipulation excluding or limiting their own liability to the holder, as by adding *sans recours* or 'without recourse to me'. The use of *sans frais* limits liability to the actual value of the bill, and thus excludes all liability for any expenses arising through dishonour and the subsequent action for enforcement.

The negotiation of a bill without recourse is not uncommon in the export trade and is known as 'forfaiting'.

The acceptor

Once the drawee of a bill has accepted it, they become liable on it.

A stranger

A person may sign a bill, not for the purpose of transferring it, but for the purpose of guaranteeing that it will be honoured. Such a person 'backs' the bill and the Act provides that they are to be regarded as an endorser and can be held liable as such to a holder in due course (see below).

An accommodation party

An accommodation party is a person signing a bill as drawer, acceptor or endorser, but who does so without receiving value for what they do and who signs for the purpose of lending their name to some other person. The Act provides that such a party is liable to a holder for value, even if known to be such a party.

Measure of damages

The Act provides that, on the dishonour of a bill, the damages payable are: the amount of the bill; interest from the time of presentment if the bill is payable on demand and from maturity in other cases; and the expenses of noting and protesting where protest is required (see below). If the bill is expressed as payable in a foreign currency, whether for payment in the United Kingdom or not, the holder is entitled to recover from those liable on the instrument the sum payable either in sterling (applying the rate of exchange prevailing at the time of judgement), or in the foreign currency, with interest until the time of payment (*Miliangos* v *George Frank (Textiles) Ltd* (1976); *Barclays Bank International Ltd* v *Levin Bros (Bradford) Ltd* (1977)).

Review questions

1 What are the respective liabilities under a bill of the drawer, drawee and acceptor?
2 What liabilities attach to a party endorsing a bill and how may he or she restrict these liabilities?
3 To what extent is a stranger and an accommodation party liable in respect of their signature to a bill?
4 What damages are available when a bill is dishonoured?

Parties to whom liability is owed

The holder

The Act defines a 'holder' as the payee or endorsee of a bill who is in possession of it, or the person in possession of a bill which is payable to bearer. If, however, the drawer's signature, or that of any endorser, is forged, the Act provides that the person in possession is not a holder.

Liability is owed to 'holders'

'Mere' holder

The Act provides that a 'mere' holder can sue on the bill in their own name. They may convert an order bill into a bearer bill (see above) by endorsement, and convert a bearer bill into an order bill by special endorsement (see above). However, since a mere holder takes subject to all equities available against any previous parties, their position is less secure than a holder in due course (see

Limited rights of mere holder

below). Though a holder is assumed by the Act to be a holder in due course, their claim on the bill cannot succeed if it is established that they are not a holder for value (see below).

Holder for value

Section 27 provides that any consideration sufficient to support a 'simple contract' suffices to make a holder a holder for value, as does any antecedent debt or liability.

· The basic common law rules as to consideration are modified in two respects by that section. First, each signatory to a bill is deemed to have provided consideration. Second, where value has been given at any time for the bill, the holder is deemed to be a holder for value as regards the acceptor (see above) and as regards all parties to the bill who became parties prior to such time.

Case example
Pollway Ltd v Abdullah (1974)

The purchaser at an auction sale was required to pay 10 per cent of the purchase price of certain property to the auctioneers as agents for the vendor. The purchaser drew a bill in favour of the auctioneers as payees and subsequently stopped payment. The vendor treated this as repudiation and sold the property to a third party. It was held that the auctioneers were entitled to judgement against the drawer of the bill because they had provided consideration. The consideration was their warranty that they had had the vendor's authority to sign a memorandum of authority on his behalf and to receive the purchaser's cheque as reducing his obligation to pay the full price. Alternatively, consideration was provided by the auctioneers agreeing to accept the bill instead of legal tender.

However, unless they are a holder in due course (see below), the holder for value takes the bill subject to equities and to any defect in the title of any of their predecessors.

Holder in due course

A holder in due course is one who satisfies the specific requirements of s. 29 of the Act. These are that:

- the bill is complete and regular on its face;
- the holder became the holder before the bill became overdue and, if it has been dishonoured, before they had notice of this; and
- the holder took the bill in good faith, for value and without notice of any defects in the title of their transferor at the time of negotiation.

Case example
Mackenzie Mills v Buono (1986)

The defendants imported furniture from Italy. Payment was made by bill in exchange for a promise that defective furniture would be replaced. The bill was dishonoured. A further bill was endorsed by the suppliers and handed over to the plaintiff's solicitors who were acting for the suppliers. This too was dishonoured. It was held, in an action by the plaintiffs on the bill, value had been given as between suppliers and defendants since the bill had been given on the understanding that the defective furniture would be made good. This was so even though the defendants could argue in proceedings between them that the consideration for the bill had wholly failed. It followed that the plaintiffs were holders for value and, in the circumstances, also holders in due course.

Consumer Credit Act

It should be noted that breach of certain requirements of the Consumer Credit Act as to the taking of negotiable instruments can deprive a person of the status of holder in due course. For the detail, see Chapter 5.

Rights of holder in due course

Section 38 of the Act provides that a holder in due course holds the bill free from any defect in title of prior parties and free from the personal defences which might be available to those parties among themselves, and they may enforce the bill against all parties liable on it (see above).

Burden of proof

The Act says that a holder is presumed to be a holder in due course. If, however, the bill is shown to be tainted by fraud or illegality, this presumption is displaced, but it can be revived if the holder establishes that, subsequent to that fraud or illegality, value in good faith was given for the bill.

'Complete and regular'

This is a question of fact. A bill will not be complete and regular if any material detail is missing or if it is out of the ordinary. A bill will not be complete if it fails to identify the payee, the sum payable, or a signature necessary to establish the chain of title is missing.

The requirements examined

> ### Case example
> ### *Arab Bank Ltd* v *Ross* (1952)
> It was held that a negotiable instrument had been incorrectly endorsed, in that 'company' had been omitted from the name of the endorsing company. While title passed to the bank, it was not a holder in due course.

'Before the bill became overdue'

A bill payable on demand is deemed overdue when it appears to have been in circulation for more than a reasonable time, this being stated by the Act to be a question of fact. Other bills must be presented on the due day.

If a bill is overdue, it remains valid and transferable, but the transferee obtains no better title than their predecessor.

'Without notice of dishonour'

If a bill has been presented to a drawee and it is dishonoured by non-acceptance or non-payment, a subsequent holder is a holder in due course only if without notice of what has happened. What is meant by 'notice' is discussed below.

'In good faith'

By s. 90 of the Act, something is taken to be done in good faith, where it is done honestly, whether or not done negligently. Careless failure to read a warning communication or advertisement that a bill is stolen does not mean bad faith (*Raphael* v *Bank of England* (1855)), but purchasing a bill for a considerable undervalue may be evidence of bad faith (*Jones* v *Gordon* (1877)).

'For value'

The special meaning attributed to 'holder for value' (see above) does not apply in the case of a holder in due course. This is because the phrase used in the Act is 'he took the bill in good faith and for value', implying that it is the holder themselves who must have provided value.

'Any defects in the title'

The Act provides that the title of a person who negotiates a bill is defective if they obtained the bill, or its acceptance, by fraud, duress, or force or fear, or other unlawful means, or for an illegal consideration, or when they negotiate it in breach of faith, or under such circumstances as amount to fraud.

This list is not exhaustive and is confined to defects which arise from acts of the party negotiating the bill to the person claiming to be a holder in due course. The negotiator, however, may themselves have acted in good faith in taking and transferring the bill, and the defect in title may have arisen through some wrongful act of a prior holder of which they were unaware.

'Notice'

'Notice' means actual notice; that is to say, either knowledge of the facts or a suspicion that something is wrong linked to a wilful disregard of the means of knowledge.

Case example
Sheffield v London Joint Stock Bank (1888)

Money was lent on the security of certain negotiable instruments. These were deposited by the lender with the bank as security for a loan larger than the money he had lent. The bank knew the nature of the lender's business and that he was in the habit of lending money against such securities. He became bankrupt. It was held that the bank was not a holder in due course because it had knowledge of facts which were calculated to put it on enquiry as to the lender's authority to deal in such instruments. In the result, it had no better title to the instruments than the lender and the bank had therefore, on payment of the amounts lent by the lender's clients, to give up the instruments.

'Holder from holder in due course'

The Act provides that a holder who derives title from a holder in due course, and who was not a party to the fraud or illegality which taints the bill, has the rights of the holder in due course as regards the acceptor of the bill and of the parties prior to that holder, even if they have notice of the fraud or illegality.

Case example
Jade International v Robert Nicholas (Steels) Ltd (1978)

The drawer of a bill, which it had transferred to X, and which X had returned to the drawer, was held entitled to rely on this provision and, since X was a holder in due course, the drawer had the rights of such a holder.

Review questions

1 Who is a 'holder' of a negotiable instrument?
2 What are the rights of a 'mere' holder and a holder 'for value', and what constitutes 'value' for this purpose?
3 Explain what is meant by a 'holder in due course'. Give an account of the various ingredients in the statutory definition.
4 What rights are enjoyed by a holder in due course?

Duties of holders

Duty to present for acceptance

There is generally no duty on a holder of a bill to present it for acceptance. It is, though, usually desirable to ascertain if the drawee is willing to accept it because, if they do accept it, they become liable on the bill and the value of the bill is thus strengthened. Furthermore, the Act does require presentation for acceptance when this is required by its terms, or where presentment is necessary to fix the maturity of the bill, that is to say, when it is payable a designated time after sight.

Duty to present for payment

The Act provides that all bills must be presented for payment and that failure so to do discharges the drawer and endorsers, though not the acceptor. Presentation is, however, excused if, after the exercise of reasonable diligence, presentment is not possible. It is also excused if the drawee is fictitious or if presentation is waived.

A bill payable on demand must be presented within a reasonable time. A bill which is not payable on demand must be presented when it falls due or on the next business day if the original day is not a business day. The Act does excuse delay in presentment when the delay is beyond the holder's control and not down to their default, misconduct or negligence. However, once the cause of the delay has gone, the bill must be presented with reasonable promptness if it is not to become overdue. *Duty to present at right time*

> ### Case example
> ### *Yeoman Credit Ltd v Gregory* (1963)
> A bill had been accepted 'payable at NP Bank', but, because the holder was informed by the acceptor's agent that there were no funds at this bank, and that presentation should be made instead at the M Bank, the bill was presented at this bank on the correct day. The M Bank refused payment. On the following day, presentment was made to the NP Bank who also refused payment. The court held that, as the bill had not been presented to the NP Bank on the correct day, the endorser was discharged from liability.

Notice of dishonour

Where a bill is dishonoured through non-acceptance or non-payment, the Act obliges the holder, or someone acting on the holder's behalf, to serve a notice of dishonour on the drawer and any endorser. Failure so to do discharges the particular party from liability on the bill. A holder in due *Action required in event of dishonour* course (see above) who becomes such after the failure is not prejudiced by it. If the requisite notice is given, this acts for the benefit of all subsequent holders and all prior endorsers who have a right to claim payment from the party to whom notice was given.

Form of notice

It is not enough that the drawer or endorser obtains the information as to dishonour indirectly, however impeccable their source. Notice must be in the form prescribed by the Act which states that it must be oral, in writing, or a combination: the return of the dishonoured bill will suffice. A notice of dishonour need not be signed but it must indicate the dishonoured instrument with sufficient clarity.

There are also strict limits for the giving of notice. Such notice must be given within a reasonable time of dishonour. 'Reasonable time' is the day after dishonour where it would be reasonable to deliver the notice by hand; in other cases, it is the day after dishonour or the following day.

The Act does, however, excuse delay in certain circumstances:

1 If caused by circumstances beyond the control of the party wishing to serve notice and the delay cannot be ascribed to their default, misconduct or negligence. For instance, ignorance of the address of the party on whom notice is to be served will excuse delay, so long as the party seeking to give notice did not overlook ordinary and obvious methods for discovering addresses (*Beveridge* v *Burgis* (1812)).
2 If, after reasonable diligence, notice cannot be given or is waived.
3 Notice is dispensed with if drawer and drawee are the same person, or if the drawer lacks capacity (see above) or is fictitious.
4 Notice to the drawer when they are the person to whom the bill was presented for payment, or when they have countermanded payment, or when the drawee or acceptor are not obliged to accept or pay on the instrument.
5 Notice to the endorser is excused if the drawee is fictitious, lacks capacity (and this was known to the endorser at the time of endorsement), or if the endorser was the person to whom the bill was presented for payment.

Duty to note and protest

Only foreign bills covered

Where a 'foreign bill' (see below) has been dishonoured by non-acceptance or non-payment, it must be 'noted and protested'. If this is not done, the drawer and endorsers are discharged from liability. Noting and protesting are not necessary to render the acceptor liable. A 'foreign bill' is one which is either not drawn and payable within the British Isles, or is not drawn within the British Isles on a person residing in the British Isles.

What is meant by noting and protesting

The requirement of noting and protesting involves handing the bill to a notary public who formally presents it for payment or acceptance. Upon dishonour, they make a memorandum on the bill of their initials, their charges, the date and a reference to their register where the details are entered, and they attach a slip to the bill giving the 'answer they receive'. This is 'noting', and it must be done on the day of dishonour or the next business day.

The 'protest' is the formal document recording the fact of dishonour and containing a copy of the bill. The protest may be drawn up at any time after noting. Delay in protesting or noting is excused when the delay comes about because of circumstances beyond the control of the holder and where the delay is not imputable to their default, misconduct or negligence.

Review questions

1 When must a bill (a) be presented for acceptance, and (b) presented for payment?
2 Give an account of the time limits which apply for presenting a bill for payment and indicate when these limits may be waived.
3 What action must be taken, and when, in the event of dishonour by non-acceptance or non-payment?
4 In what circumstances is notice of dishonour excused?
5 What is meant by 'noting' and 'protesting', and when do noting and protesting apply?

Discharge

A bill is discharged when all rights of action on it are extinguished. There are various ways in which this can arise.

Several ways for discharging a bill

Payment in due course

The most common form of discharge is payment in due course, which means payment made on or after maturity to the holder (see above) in good faith and without notice, if such be the case, that the holder has a defective title. Thus, if a holder has obtained a transfer of the bill by fraud, and the acceptor pays the amount of the bill on maturity without knowledge that the title is defective, the bill is discharged.

Acceptor as holder

A bill is discharged when the acceptor becomes the holder of the bill at or after maturity.

Renunciation

When the holder at or after maturity renounces their rights against the acceptor, unconditionally and absolutely, the bill is discharged. The Act requires this to be in writing except where the bill is delivered up to the acceptor. If the bill is then negotiated to a holder in due course (see above) who is unaware of the renunciation, the holder in due course is unaffected by it.

Cancellation

A bill is discharged by intentional cancellation by its holder or their authorized agent. The cancellation must be apparent on the face of the bill. Merely tearing it up, when it can still be put together, is not sufficient (*Ingham* v *Primrose* (1859)). An unintentional or mistaken cancellation has no effect, but where a bill or signature appears to be cancelled, the burden of proof rests on the party alleging that cancellation was unintentional, made by mistake or without authority.

Alteration

The Act provides that, if a bill is materially altered without the assent of all those liable on it, the bill is discharged except against the party who made, authorized or agreed to the alteration. The alteration does not discharge those who endorsed the bill subsequently.

The following matters are expressly stated in the Act to be material alterations: the date; the amount payable; the time of payment; and the place of payment. The list is not exhaustive, and it could well be the case that any alteration which changes the business effect of the bill might be material. Alteration of the name of the payee by the addition of an initial has been held material (*Goldman* v *Cox* (1924)), as has the insertion of the rate of interest in the corner of a bill which provided for the payment of 'lawful interest' (*Warrington* v *Early* (1853)).

If the alteration is not apparent, a holder in due course can enforce the bill as originally drawn. An alteration will be regarded as apparent if the bill would normally be examined by a holder and a reasonably careful scrutiny would have revealed the alteration (*Woollatt* v *Stanley* (1923)).

Review questions

1 List those ways in which a bill of exchange can be discharged.
2 In the case of discharge by payment, what is the effect of the holder having a defective title?
3 State what is necessary for a bill to be discharged by cancellation and renunciation.
4 When is a bill discharged by 'material alteration' and what, in this context, is the significance of an alteration being 'apparent'?

Cheques

Differences between cheques and other bills

The Bills of Exchange Act defines a cheque as a bill of exchange (see above) drawn on a banker and payable on demand. Generally speaking, the provisions of the Act applicable to bills payable on demand apply to cheques.

There are, however, certain aspects to cheques which distinguish them from other bills. Thus, the drawee of a cheque is always a banker. Furthermore, a cheque is never 'accepted' so the rules set out above relating to presentment for acceptance have no application. Again, the rules as to notice of dishonour (see above) are rarely applicable in the case of cheques in order to claim against the drawer because non-payment is almost always due to countermand by the drawer or their lack of funds, and these are both reasons recognized by the Act as dispensing with notice of dishonour. Such notice would, however, normally be required in order to claim against an endorser.

Duties of a bank

Banker and customer in contractual relationship

The relationship of a bank with its customer is contractual. Accordingly, the terms of the contract, express or implied, will govern the relationship of the parties. The most important terms of the relationship are set out below.

Obeying the customer's mandate

A banker is entitled to debit a customer's account with a cheque if that cheque has been signed by an authorized body. Thus, if the bank has authority only to accept a cheque when signed by two parties, but does so when signed by one, it cannot debit the particular account (*Ligget (Liverpool) Ltd* v *Barclays Bank* (1928)).

Honouring cheques

A bank must honour a customer's cheque to the extent that the account is in credit or within the limits of an agreed overdraft. A bank is not in breach of this duty if it dishonours a cheque in excess of the amount in the account, even if the customer has made a deposit sufficient to cover the cheque, if the bank has not had a reasonable time to credit that payment to the account (*Marzetti* v *Williams* (1830)).

Effect of wrongful dishonour

If a bank wrongfully dishonours a cheque, damages can be claimed without proof of actual loss. At one time, it had been the case that parties who were not traders had to show actual loss, but this was regarded as out of date by the Court of Appeal in *Udele* v *Woolwich Building Society* (1995). It may also be the case, though the matter has not been specifically decided, that to indicate that the party presenting the cheque for payment must 'refer to drawer' (i.e. indicating that the account has insufficient funds) when this is not the case gives rise to an action in libel (*Flach* v *London and South Western Bank Ltd* (1915); *Jayson* v *Midland Bank Ltd* (1968)).

Termination of duty to pay

Section 75(1) of the Bills of Exchange Act provides that a bank's duty to pay a cheque drawn on it by a customer ceases when the customer countermands payment. Such a countermand only becomes effective when it reaches the appropriate bank official.

Case example
Curtice v London City & Midland Bank Ltd (1908)

The plaintiff drew a cheque and, the same day, countermanded payment by telegram. This was placed in the bank's letter box but, because of lack of care, it did not reach the appropriate official for two days. The cheque had meanwhile been cashed. It was held that the bank was not liable since the cheque had not been countermanded even though this was due to the carelessness of bank employees. The court also suggested that a countermand by telegram would not be effective, but that it would entitle the bank to postpone payment until the validity of the countermand had been determined. Presumably, this would also apply to fax, e-mail and telephone calls.

Death of customer

Section 75 of the Act also provides that the duty to honour a cheque ceases on notification of the customer's death. It is also accepted that this duty ceases: (a) on a receiving order or the presentation of a petition for winding up; (b) on the service of a garnishee order; or (c) on the banker receiving notice that the customer is not mentally capable of giving a mandate.

Duty of reasonable care

If a company cheque is drawn with the correct signatories to it, but the bank knows or ought to know that it has been drawn for unauthorized purposes, it is liable to the company if it pays out on the cheque (*Selangor United Rubber Estates Ltd* v *Cradock* (1968); *Karak Rubber Co. Ltd* v *Burden (No 2)* (1972)).

Duty of secrecy

The duty of secrecy arises from the nature of the contract between bank and customer. Breach of the duty will entitle the customer to damages which can be substantial if they have suffered actual loss. The duty itself, as laid down in *Tournier* v *National Provincial and Union Bank of England* (1924), is not to reveal any information gained about the customer, subject to certain exceptions:

1 Where disclosure is made under compulsion of law.
2 Where there is a public duty to disclose outweighing the duty to the customer (such as a danger to public order created by the customer's activities).
3 Where the interests of the bank require disclosure so that where the banker is seeking payment of an overdraft, he may state the relevant amount on the writ.
4 Where disclosure is made with the express or implied consent of the customer, as where the latter asks the bank to provide a reference.

None of these exceptions applied in the Tournier case itself where the bank told a customer's employers that his account was overdrawn and that he was probably gambling, the result being that he lost his job. The bank was required to pay damages.

To collect cheques paid in

There should be no delay in presenting cheques

A bank is under a duty to collect for the customer's account cheques paid in by the customer. The bank is then a collecting bank and has the protection of the Cheques Act 1957, if the customer has a defective title to that cheque (see below). The cheque must be presented for payment within a reasonable time. Section 36(3) of the 1882 Act states that this is a question of fact. The Act also says that an overdue cheque can only be negotiated subject to equities, so that the holder is not a holder in due course (see above). The banks generally refuse to honour a cheque which has been in circulation for more than six months.

Duties of the customer

Limited obligation on customer

As noted earlier, the relationship between a bank and its customer is based on contract, and the duties of the customer will be based on the terms, express and implied, of that contract. Little has been imposed on a customer by way of an implied obligation.

> ## Case example
> ### *London Joint Stock Bank Ltd* v *Macmillan and Arthur* (1918)
> A clerk was entrusted with the task of filling in cheques for his employer. He prepared a bearer cheque for £2, the sum payable not being stated in words. The employer signed it, and the clerk added a 1 and a 0 on either side of the 2, and added the words 'one hundred and twenty pounds'. The clerk obtained payment from the bank for £120. It was held that the bank could debit the account since the employer had failed in his implied duty to take reasonable care when drawing cheques.

A customer, however, has no duty to check the accuracy of his statement.

> **Case example**
> ***Tai Hing Cotton Mill Ltd v Liu Chang Hing Bank Ltd* (1985)**
> An employee forged his employer's signature on cheques over a period of six years. Since he did not check his statements thoroughly, the employer failed to notice the loss. The court held that the bank was required to make good the loss, since the employer was not required to check bank statements, nor to operate a system of internal control for detecting fraud.

Estoppel may operate against customer

A customer may, by their conduct, be estopped, or prevented, from alleging that their bank exceeded its authority in paying out on a cheque.

> **Case example**
> ***Greenwood v Martins Bank Ltd* (1933)**
> The plaintiff's wife forged and cashed many of his cheques over a period of time. The plaintiff had discovered this but had not informed the bank. When he later discovered that his wife's explanation of the forgeries was false, he threatened to go to the bank. He then brought an action against the bank to reclaim the money paid on the forged cheques. It was held that he was estopped by his conduct from asserting that the bank had exceeded its authority in paying out on the forged cheques.

Similarly, where a signatory has regularly been allowed by an employee to draw cheques in an unusual manner or for a purpose which would normally be unauthorized, the employer may be estopped from denying the authority of the employee (*London Intercontinental Trust Ltd v Barclays Bank Ltd* (1980)).

Review questions

1 Define a cheque and indicate what differences there are between cheques and bills of exchange generally.
2 What is the nature of the relationship between bank and customer, and what are the main obligations imposed on a bank?
3 Under what circumstances may a bank properly refuse to honour a cheque?
4 Explain the circumstances in which a bank may properly breach its duty of confidence.
5 What are the duties of a customer to the bank?
6 Explain how a customer can be estopped from denying their bank the authority to pay out on a cheque.

Crossed cheques

The nature of crossing

Section 76 of the Bills of Exchange Act provides that a cheque is 'crossed generally' when it bears two transverse parallel lines between which may be added 'and company' (or an abbreviation) or 'not negotiable' or both. The latter is more widely used than 'and company' which nowadays serves no real purpose. The section also permits a cheque to be 'crossed specially' which means that it bears the name of a bank, usually between the parallel lines. Section 77 provides that the crossing may be performed by the drawer or the holder.

Two categories of crossed cheque

The effect of crossing

A crossed cheque must be paid into a bank account and should not be cashed over the counter, even by the payee (unless they also drew the particular cheque). If the cheque is crossed specially payment must be made only to the specified bank.

Effect of disregarding crossing

If a bank makes a payment in defiance of a crossing, and the money is not paid to the 'true owner' of the cheque, the bank is required to pay the money due on the cheque to the true owner. No definition is given of 'true owner', but it will include a holder in due course (see above).

In practice, banks rarely pay crossed cheques over the counter, except where the drawer is also the payee. Should it do so, however, and make a payment to other than the true owner, it may be able to refuse payment to the true owner by relying on one of the statutory defences (see below).

Two types of crossing

It is also the case that, under the Act, a crossing is a material part of the cheque, so that an unauthorized crossing is a material alteration which renders the cheque unenforceable against prior parties who have not consented to the alteration (see above).

Cheques crossed 'not negotiable'

The Bills of Exchange Act provides that, when a cheque is crossed 'not negotiable', it can still be transferred, but a person taking it has no better title than the person from whom they took it.

Cheques crossed 'Account Payee'

This was given statutory protection by the Cheques Act 1992. The crossings 'Account Payee' or 'a/c payee', with or without 'only' operate to render the cheque non-transferable, so that it is valid only as between the parties.

Review questions

1 Explain the difference between a 'general' and a 'special' crossing.
2 What duties are imposed on banks by virtue of a cheque being crossed?
3 What is the significance of a cheque being marked 'not negotiable' or 'account payee'?

Statutory protection for paying banker

There are certain statutory provisions which safeguard a bank from having to make a second payment to the true owner of a cheque when it has already made a payment to a party who is not a true owner.

Section 80 of the 1882 Act provides that if a bank pays a crossed cheque in accordance with its crossing, in good faith and without negligence, it cannot be liable to the true owner if payment was in fact made to another party. The Act also says that the drawer is absolved from liability. If, therefore, a cheque is crossed and sent by post to a company in payment of an account, and the cheque is stolen by an employee of that company and paid into his account, the drawer does not have to make a further payment to that company. It is, however, necessary for the operation of this provision that the bank was not negligent.

Section 60 of the Act applies to crossed and uncrossed cheques. Where an 'order' cheque (see above) is paid in the ordinary course of business and in good faith, the paying bank is deemed to have paid in due course even if the cheque bore a forged endorsement

Bank must be without negligence

Neither ss. 60 nor 80 offer any protection to the paying banker where the customer's signature is forged, or where there has been a material alteration to the cheque (*Slingsby* v *District Bank Ltd* (1931)).

Section 1 of the Cheques Act 1957 gives the paying banker protection where there is no endorsement on the cheque, and the same section affords protection if there is an irregular endorsement, such as a discrepancy between the name of the payee as it appears in the face of the cheque and an endorsement on the back. The protection provided by the Act only applies when the bank is acting in 'the ordinary course of business'. A circular of the Committee of London Clearing Banks lays down what is to be considered as the ordinary course of business.

Protection also provided by Cheques Act

Interpretation of statute aided by circular

Statutory protection of collecting banker

At common law, a bank which collects payment for a cheque on behalf of a person who is not the true owner can be sued by the true owner in conversion or for money had and received (*A L Underwood Ltd* v *Barclays Bank Ltd* (1924); *Bavins Junior and Sims* v *London and South Western Bank Ltd* (1900)). Section 4 of the Cheques Act, however, gives protection to a collecting banker who has acted without negligence.

> ## Case example
> ### *Lloyds Bank Ltd* v *Savory & Co.* (1933)
> Bearer cheques drawn by a firm of stockbrokers in the City were paid to the credit of a housewife's private account. The bank was held negligent since it failed to ask, when she opened the account, the name of her husband's employers. Had it done so, it would have discovered that he was employed by the brokers.

Case example
Marfani & Co. Ltd v *Midland Bank Ltd* (1968)

A cheque for £3000 was signed on behalf of the plaintiff in favour of E. K, who was an employee of the plaintiff, obtained possession of the cheque and, calling himself E, sought to open an account with the defendants. The bank agreed to do this and sought a reference from A who knew K as E and who had been a valued customer of the bank for six years. K withdrew all the money from his account and left the country. The court held that the bank had acted in accordance with current practice and had not been negligent. It did add, though, that the onus lay on the bank of showing that it had taken reasonable care.

Collecting bank as holder in due course

Section 2 of the Cheques Act provides that a collecting bank may become a holder in due course of an order cheque (see above), which is not endorsed, provided that it gives value for the cheque. If it does so become, then it has the usual rights of such a holder (see above) including the right to sue the drawer if the cheque is dishonoured. This statutory provision applies only to unendorsed cheques and not to those which have been irregularly endorsed.

Case example
Westminster Bank Ltd v *Zang* (1966)

An unendorsed cheque drawn by Z was presented for collection by T at his bank for the benefit of T Ltd's account, which was overdrawn. The cheque was dishonoured and returned to T so that he could sue Z, but he discontinued the action and returned the cheque to his bank. The bank claimed to be holders in due course by virtue of s. 2 and thus able to sue Z. It was held that the bank had not given value because interest was charged on the overdraft unreduced by the cheque. It was also said that letting a customer draw against an uncleared cheque would not be 'giving value' unless the bank and customer had first agreed that such drawing was permissible.

Review questions

1 Under what circumstances will a bank be protected if it pays out on a crossed cheque to someone other than the true owner?

2 What protection is available to a bank which pays out on an order cheque which bears a forged endorsement?

3 When is a bank protected if it pays out on a cheque which has not been endorsed or which has been irregularly endorsed? What guidance is there, in this context, as to the meaning of 'ordinary course of business'?

4 What is the position at (a) common law and (b) under statute in relation to a collecting bank which collects payment of a cheque for someone who is not the true owner? Explain, with references, the relevance of negligence in this context.

5 When will a collecting bank become a holder in due course of an order cheque? Explain what is meant by 'giving value' in this context.

Cheques and receipts

Section 3 of the Cheques Act provides that an unendorsed cheque which appears to have been paid by the banker on whom it was drawn is evidence of receipt by the payee of the sum payable by the cheque. Even before the Act, a paid endorsed cheque was treated as evidence of payment (*Egg* v *Barnett* (1800)).

Cheques as receipts

Other negotiable instruments

Promissory notes

A promissory note is defined by s. 83 of the Bills of Exchange Act as an unconditional promise in writing, and signed by the person making the promise, by which they promise to pay on demand or at some fixed or determinable time a specific sum to or to the order of a specified person or to the bearer. Generally, the law relating to bills of exchange also applies to promissory notes, and the maker of the note corresponds to the acceptor of a bill (see above). The maker is primarily liable and the endorsers are in the position of sureties. Since the note is a promise, not an order, to pay, there is no drawee. Generally speaking, the law relating to bills of exchange applies equally to promissory notes.

Bank notes

These are promissory notes which are payable to bearer. When presenting a note for payment, it is not necessary for the bearer to reveal how they came by the note, but if the circumstances aroused the suspicion of the bank, it would be entitled to refuse payment until satisfied of good faith.

Quasi-negotiable instruments

The following documents have some, but not all, of the characteristics of negotiability, but are not themselves negotiable instruments.

Certain documents resemble negotiable instruments

Bills of lading

These are receipts for goods shipped, signed by the carrier or their agent. A bill of lading is a document of title to the particular goods, and possession of the bill entitles the holder to delivery of the goods. It is, however, not a negotiable instrument, so that a transferee obtains no better title than was possessed by the transferor.

Dock warrants

These are documents issued by a dock or warehouse company acknowledging that it holds goods on behalf of the named person or their endorsee. They are documents of title assignable by delivery plus endorsements, but they are not negotiable instruments so the endorsee obtains no better title than the endorser.

American share certificates

These usually have a transfer form printed on the back, and the owner can sign this form leaving the name of the transferee blank. This then operates as a power of attorney to a subsequent transferee to fill in their own name or the name of another, the person named being entitled to apply to the company for registration as a shareholder. Such person obtains no better title than the transferor.

IOUs

These are merely written admissions of the existence of a debt. They are not negotiable but they can be assigned under the provisions of the Law of Property Act 1925. If the IOU contained an express promise to pay, it would be a promissory note (see above).

Miscellaneous banking instruments

Bankers' drafts

These are drafts to order payable on demand, drawn by an office of a bank or on some other office of the same bank. Drafts may be crossed and the crossing has the same effect as the crossing on a cheque (see above). The Cheques Act 1957 extends the protection given to bankers to cover such drafts.

Conditional orders

These are documents ordering payment of money subject to the fulfilment of some stated condition. They may be crossed like cheques and the Cheques Act extends the protection given to bankers to cover such drafts. It should be noted that a document which is apparently a cheque may in fact be a conditional order, as when it carries a statement that it is not to be paid unless an attached receipt is signed.

Dividends and interest warrants

These are drafts issued by a company ordering its bank to pay the stated sum to a named person. They can be crossed like cheques and are covered by the protection given by the Cheques Act.

Deposit receipts

These are acknowledgements by a banker that they hold funds to a certain amount in the name of the depositor. They are not negotiable instruments.

Review questions

1 Explain the nature and effects of a promissory note.
2 What is the status of a banknote and what rights does it give the holder?
3 There are certain documents which have the appearance of negotiable instruments, but which do not have all the incidents of negotiability. Give some examples.
4 What is the status of an IOU?
5 Describe the nature of certain documents classified as 'miscellaneous banking documents'.

Chapter summary

- An instrument is a 'negotiable instrument' if it satisfies the requirements of the Bills of Exchange Act 1882. This Act is a code and it, with the Cheques Act 1957, contains virtually all the relevant law on the subject.
- Cheques and bills of exchange are the most common form of negotiable instrument.
- The key aspect to a negotiable instrument is, of course, that it can be freely negotiated. This can be achieved by endorsement or, in the case of a bearer bill, by simple delivery. There are various categories of endorsement.
- There are a number of parties who can be made liable on a bill of exchange. These include the drawer, the drawee, the acceptor, a stranger and an accommodation party, though an appropriate declaration on a bill can exclude liability.
- Central to the whole concept of negotiability is the position of the party holding the bill. The Bills of Exchange Act distinguishes between a 'mere holder', a 'holder for value' and a 'holder in due course'. The holder in due course is in the strongest position because they, unlike the others, take free of any equities which might attach to the bill.
- Although a holder in due course is not generally obliged to present a bill for acceptance, they are obliged to present it for payment. In addition, they are also obliged to give notice of dishonour when this has occurred. In the case of 'foreign bills', dishonour requires the holder to 'note and protest'.
- A bill is discharged on payment in due course. It can, however, be discharged on acceptance by a holder, by cancellation or by renunciation. A bill is also discharged if it is subject to a material alteration. The Bills of Exchange Act gives a non-exhaustive list of alterations which are deemed to be material.
- Cheques are generally subject to the provisions relating to bills of exchange, but there are differences. For instance, the drawee is always a banker; the rules as to presentment do not apply and those relating to procedure on dishonour are normally inapplicable.
- A number of duties are imposed on a bank towards its clients, such as the duty to observe the customer's mandate, a duty of secrecy and a duty to collect cheques. Little is imposed by law on the customer, though this can be affected by the terms of the contract between the customer and the bank.
- Legislation provides for the effect given to cheques which are crossed and sets out the consequences of certain types of crossing.
- Protection is given, subject to certain conditions, to the banks which collect and which pay out on cheques.
- Cheques can act as receipts.
- Apart from bills of exchange and cheques, there are a number of other instruments which are negotiable instruments, notably promissory notes and banknotes. There are also certain 'quasi-negotiable' instruments such as docks warrants, and bills of lading. There are also a number of miscellaneous banking instruments to which certain incidents attach.

United Kingdom application

The foregoing statements of the law are applicable throughout the United Kingdom.

Case study exercises

Consider the legal implications of the following sets of circumstances.

1   A bill is drawn by A on B in favour of C. It is then endorsed by C in favour of D. It is then stolen from D by a thief who forges D's endorsement and negotiates the bill to E. E in turn endorses it to F who endorses it to G. Does G have title to the instrument? What is the position if B pays G? In what circumstances could B recover the money he had paid to G?
2   A cheque is drawn in favour of C who endorses it to D. It is stolen from D and the thief endorses it to E who endorses it to F who endorses it to G. G has no knowledge of the forgery. What title does G have to the bill and what are his rights, if any, against E and F?
3   A cheque is drawn by A on his bank in favour of C, who is a minor. The minor endorses the cheque to D in return for goods supplied to him by D. A stops payment of the cheque. What are D's rights against C and A?
4   A sells goods to B plc. It is arranged that A will draw a bill of exchange on B plc in favour of A, that B plc will accept the bill and, because A does not consider that the liability of the company offers him sufficient security, that C, a director of B plc, will also sign the bill in his personal capacity. What is the position of C if the bill is drawn and signed by the various parties as arranged?
5   Suppose that A draws a cheque on the X bank in favour of C from whom it is stolen. The thief does not negotiate it but is able to open an account in the name of C at the Y bank. This bank collects the cheque for the thief in the belief that he is C. Under what circumstances would the X bank be entitled to debit A's account if it pays the amount of the cheque to the Y bank? If the cheque were uncrossed and the thief sought payment across the counter at the X bank, what ought the bank to do if it wants protection for paying out on the cheque?
6   A bill is drawn in favour of C who negotiates it to D. He does so because of fraud and misrepresentation on the part of D. D then negotiates the bill for value to E. Under what circumstances can E sue the various parties to the bill? What would be the position of F if E had negotiated the bill to him, whether or not for value?

Discussion questions

1   'The development of electronic funds transfer systems has significantly reduced the importance of negotiable instruments … it is to be expected that over time there will be a further decline in their significance. Yet the advantages of negotiability cannot be denied.' Comment on this observation.
2   When is a cheque deemed to be paid and what improvements would you like to see made to the cheque clearing system?

3　The Review Committee on Banking Services law recommended the enactment of a comprehensive Negotiable Instruments Act which would cover all forms of instrument which possessed stated minimum characteristics (Cm 22, 1989). What do you think such characteristics should be?

Further reading

Byles on Bills of Exchange (26th edn), (1988) Sweet & Maxwell.
This is the leading text on the whole area of negotiable instruments.
Commercial Law (2nd edn), Goode (1995), Penguin.
This deals with commercial law as a whole, but has an excellent section devoted to Money, Payment and Payment Systems which is strongly recommended.
The Law & Practice of Banking (2 volumes) (8th edn), Holden (1993), Pitman.
The leading text on this topic.

10   Banking law

Introduction

This chapter attempts to cover the legal aspects of the banker–customer relationship. Whereas at one time only the relatively wealthy had accounts now it is an exception for a person of working age not to have a banking account. With businesses the incidence of account holding is such that it is unthinkable, apart from a few small, single person businesses, that a modern business could operate for any length of time without the use of banking facilities.

The legal relationship between the parties is largely the outcome of numerous cases (problems) that have gone to the courts for adjudication. The case law that has resulted has been sufficiently flexible to cover over the years most developments in banking, although new technologies may require at some future time statutory intervention to cover the introduction of very recent banking practice.

Objectives

This chapter focuses on the legal relationship between banker and customer. It is intended to show that this seemingly simple relationship may on occasions be more complex than it appears to be. Also to be shown is that the existence of the relationship will result in legal consequences to both parties but especially to a bank which will have major legal obligations imposed on it.

Key concepts

- The definitions of a bank and customer
- The legal basis of the banker–customer relationship
- The bank's duties especially of confidentiality and provision of statements of account
- The customer's duties in relation to cheques
- The bank's responsibilities in respect to provision of references
- The role of the Banking Ombudsman.

The parties to the relationship

The bank

While generally we may recognize a bank it is by no means easy to actually define one. This is especially true when reflecting on the considerable growth in providers of financial services. Are they all banks, whether or not bank appears in their title, or are only some of them banks? If so

A bank is difficult to define legally

which ones? Does it matter whether a commercial body is a bank or, alternatively, a non-bank? The reasons why an answer is important are that:

1 Under the Banking Act 1987 only an approved organization recognized by the Bank of England as an authorized deposit-taker may use the description 'bank' in its title and most have at least £5 million fully paid up capital. Traditionally, many financial businesses were desirous of calling themselves banks, but under the Banking Act 1987 only those meeting the definition of a bank will be permitted to do so. The Act does not, unfortunately, provide a definition of a bank but merely requires that an applicant for the use of bank in its title satisfy certain minimum criteria to be recognized as an 'authorized institution' so as to be able to use the designation bank.

2 The importance of knowing whether an organization is a bank also relates to the statutory protection given to banks under the Bills of Exchange Act 1882 and the Cheques Act 1957.

Definition of a bank

Common-law position

The Court of Appeal decision in *United Dominions Trust* v *Kirkwood* (1966) said that a bank was a body which

- accepts money from and collects cheques for customers
- honours cheques or other withdrawal authorities from its customers, and
- maintains current accounts.

A bank is an undertaking that carries on the business of banking

This decision reaffirmed the traditional view that a bank was identifiable by what it did, e.g. a bank is a body that carries on 'the business of banking'. However, the majority of the Court of Appeal went on to identify a fourth subjective characteristic in that an institution could be a bank because it

- has a reputation as being a bank with other financial institutions.

Reputation is based, according to Lord Denning, on financial stability, soundness and probity, for only the most deserving of financial institutions are to have the appellation bank!

Statutory position

Section 2, Bills of Exchange Act 1882 followed early case law in that a bank is 'a body of persons ... who carry on the business of banking'.

Defining a customer

Defining a customer is important because

- of implications connected with the payment and collection of cheques, e.g. the protection given to banks when they are acting for customers (s. 4, Cheques Act 1957), and
- the various obligations imposed on bank customers by the common law.

As there is no statutory definition, case law has to be considered. From an examination of authoritative case law there must seemingly be some sort of account, current or deposit, held by the potential customer.

To be a customer an account must be held

Case example
Commissioners of Taxation v *English, Scottish and Australian Bank Ltd* (1920)

A rogue opened a current account and one day later paid in a stolen cheque which the bank collected and credited to his account. The rogue then withdrew the proceeds of the stolen cheque and disappeared.

The House of Lords held that a customer is anyone with a bank account; the length of time the account has been opened or the activity of the account does not matter. The bank was collecting a cheque for a customer and hence able to claim statutory protection.

Case example
Great Western Railway Co. v *London & County Banking Co.* (1901)

By arrangement the bank cashed cheques over the counter for a 20-year period. Both the High Court and Court of Appeal said the regular encashment made the payee a customer. However, the House of Lords held that just by cashing a cheque over the counter even for a 20-year period did not mean that the bank had acted for a customer.

The provision of other banking services

The Code of Banking Practice 1994, agreed to by around 300 banks, says that a 'personal customer' is:

> A private individual who maintains an account (including a joint account with another individual …) or who takes other services from a bank.

Exactly what other services will create a banker–customer relationship is open to question. The modern bank is a retailer of a wide range of financial products and it is unreasonable to say that a buyer of any service is automatically categorized as being a customer in the traditional sense. One service that ought to create the relationship is the provision of investment advice.

Case example
Woods v *Martins Bank Ltd* (1958)

W, a young man without business experience, approached MB asking whether their customer Brooks Refrigeration would make a good investment. A branch manager of MB said yes, so W invested through MB £5000 and later opened an account with the bank. Subsequently he made further investments in Brooks Refrigeration. The investments proved to be disastrous with W losing £16 000. Evidence was produced in court which showed that Brooks Refrigeration had been heavily overdrawn through W's investment period and MB's branch manager had been under considerable pressure from his district head office to reduce the debt.

It was held that W had become a customer from the time he gave instructions regarding his first investment and not from when the account was opened.

Review question

1 In *Woods* v *Martins Bank Ltd* (1958) the court accepted that when W approached MB he intended to open an account with them. What if he had no such intention, would he still be said to have been a customer?
2 If the circumstances in *Woods* v *Martins Bank Ltd* (1958) reoccurred could the Hedley Byrne principle be used by W to obtain compensation?

Basis of the banker–customer relationship

Contractual in nature

Express terms

(margin note:) The basic relationship is contractual

As far as operation of the account is concerned it is a *contractual relationship*. If this contract is broken then the innocent party can sue for breach of contract, e.g. if a bank returns a cheque drawn by its customer marked 'refer to drawer – insufficient funds' when there are funds to meet it (wrongful dishonour) then the customer may sue for breach of contract plus a possible action for defamation.

On opening an account a customer may be asked to sign a bank *mandate* and this will provide for the inclusion into the contract of express contractual terms. In addition a customer requesting more than a basic service may be asked to complete other contractual documents such as:

- payment instructions
- consumer credit forms (under the Consumer Credit Act 1974)
- customer agreement forms (under the Financial Services Act 1986).

All contractual terms must pass a test of reasonability as set out in the Unfair Contract Terms Act 1977. Thomas Cook had a clause in their travellers cheques agreement saying that no refund on lost cheques will be made if the loss was caused by the holder's negligence. This clause was upheld as being reasonable.

However, banks using standard form contracts for personal customers, such as the contractual documents listed above, must be aware of the implications of the EC Directive on Unfair Contract Terms in Consumer Contracts now incorporated into regulations. The regulations apply to all unfair contractual terms (not just exclusion or limitation clauses) in consumer contracts where no individual negotiation took place, e.g.

A contract term which has not been individually negotiated shall be regarded as unfair if, contrary to the requirement of good faith, it causes a significant imbalance in the parties' rights and obligations under the contract, to the detriment of the consumer.

s.4, Unfair Terms in Consumer Contracts Regulations 1994

Significantly, in a non-exhaustive list of terms that may be unfair the directive includes any term which allows the seller or supplier to alter the terms of the contract unilaterally without a valid reason specified in the contract or to alter without valid reason any characteristics of the product or service to be provided.

Implied terms

The duties of a banker

These are largely derived from *Joachimson* v *Swiss Banking Corp* (1921). They are:

1 The bank is to receive money and collect cheques, etc., for their customer's account.
2 The bank promises on receipt of proper instructions to repay money held at the branch where the account is kept during normal banking hours.
3 The bank must give reasonable notice before closing a credit account. In *Prosperity Ltd* v *Lloyds Bank Ltd* (1923), a business customer was £7000 in credit when Lloyds gave one month's notice to close the account. This was held to be unreasonable although it may have been sufficient for a private account customer.

A bank's duties are derived from implied terms

Additional duties

4 To inform a customer if their signature has been forged.
5 To maintain a duty of secrecy in relation to the customer affairs.
6 To provide a customer with a pass book or to give regular statements.

Historically, implied terms in the banker–customer contract have been more important then express terms. This importance continues although it is narrowing; banks are being urged to set out for their private customers in simple language exactly what their terms of business are – see the Code of Banking Practice 1992 which requires that customers have clear information about their relationship with their bank.

The duties of a customer

1 To take reasonable care in drawing cheques and writing other orders so as not to mislead the bank or facilitate forgery.
2 To immediately inform the bank of any forged cheque drawn on their account.
3 To pay reasonable bank charges.

A customer's duties are probably less onerous

In the absence of an express agreement, there is an implied right for the bank to make reasonable charges under s. 15 Supply of Goods and Services Act 1982.

4 To issue cheques only if there are sufficient funds in their account to meet them or there is an appropriate agreed lending facility.

Earmarking

This is when a payment has been made into an account to meet a specified cheque which the customer has drawn. The bank must meet this 'earmarked cheque' even though the account as a whole is overdrawn (*Barclays Bank Ltd* v *Quistclose Investments Ltd* (1970)).

Cheque cards

If a cheque is supported by a cheque card then the bank must honour the cheque even if there are insufficient funds in the account to cover it.

> 5 To repay on demand any sums lent by the bank on a current account. In *Williams & Glyn's Bank Ltd* v *Barnes* (1981), it was said that if money is lent on an overdraft and there is no expressed repayment date and no means to imply a repayment date then it is implied to be repayable on demand.

Debtor and creditor

Normally the customer is the creditor and the bank the debtor

It has long been recognized that a banker–customer relationship is one of borrower and lender (*Foley* v *Hill* (1848) or *Joachimson* v *Swiss Banking Co*. (1921)). Where the bank is a debtor, which is the normal position for a credit account, then there is no need for the bank to seek out the creditor (customer). However, with a special account, such as a fixed-term deposit, then probably there is a need to inform the creditor that the fixed term has expired and to then seek instructions.

Agency

A principal–agent relationship can arise in various ways. The main ones are:

An agency relationship is commonly created

1 As a collecting banker by collecting the customer's cheques or other negotiable instruments.
2 As a paying banker by paying on behalf of the customer cheques to third parties.
3 By buying on behalf of the customer stocks and shares, or other investments, or engaging in foreign exchange transactions.

The increased range of financial products offered to customers by retail banks on behalf of third parties or subsidiaries of the bank, make the agency relationship more important than formerly. Where the bank is expressly appointed to act as an agent over a customer's financial affairs the appointment may be under a power of attorney.

Alternatively, a power of attorney may authorize one person (the agent) to operate another's (the principal's) banking account.

Ordinary power of attorney

A bank may receive a power of attorney from an elderly customer

Here the agency will be created by deed under the Power of Attorney Act 1971. The requirements that must be satisfied under s. 1 are:

- it must be in writing;
- it must be fully completed when created so that no details are left for filling in later;
- it must be signed by the principal (the donor) with their signature being witnessed by at least one other;
- it must be sealed – usually achieved with LS (*locus sigilli*) within a circle which replaces an actual seal.

The types of power of attorney

These are:

1 Special or specific powers of attorney. The agent (the donor) is limited to what is given in the deed, e.g. instructions for specific tasks.
2 General powers of attorney. This establishes the agent as being a universal agent.

Enduring powers of attorney

This power is given under the Enduring Power of Attorney Act 1985 and can only apply to individuals. The attraction of an enduring power over an ordinary power of attorney relates to the possibility that the donor may become insane with a resulting loss of contractual capacity, which under agency principles, means that an agent unaware of the insanity would become personally liable for contracts made on the insane donor's behalf (*Yonge* v *Toynbee* (1910)). If the donor of the power is elderly then mental senility may be a real risk.

Under the Act if the deed says that the power conferred is to continue even though the donor becomes insane then provided that the donor has read, or has had it read to them, the deed will then come under the Act. The donee appointed to act for the donor must be an adult or a trust company but not an undischarged bankrupt. It is possible, as with an ordinary power, to have more than one attorney but obviously the fees will be increased.

Should the donor become mentally incapable then the donee's powers are suspended. For their renewal the donee must apply to the Court of Protection for registration of the deed. The donor and any relative(s) specified in the deed must also be notified of the registration.

The following additional points may be made:

1 While registration is being considered the donee will have limited powers to maintain the donor, e.g. to pay domestic bills and medical expenses; and to prevent losses to the donor from occurring, e.g. to maintain property. Any other expenditure will need the approval of the Court.
2 S. 3(4), EPAA 1985 requires that the donee be paid in this interim period.
3 On registration the agent will assume full powers under the deed.
4 Should a donee at any time want to renounce their appointment then they must give notice to the Court.

An enduring power of attorney cannot be suddenly revoked

Bailor–bailee

The provision of safe custody facilities creates a bailor–bailee relationship. Bailment is where goods are delivered by one person (the bailor), to another person (the bailee), on the understanding that the goods will be returned at some future date to the bailor.

A deposit of articles for safe custody creates a bailor–bailee relationship

Trustee

A trust is where one person (the settler) transfers property to a fund which is administered by another person (the trustee) for the benefit of a third party (the beneficiary). It is now common for the larger banks to have their own trustee department or subsidiary companies. With respect to trust business a bank must use reasonable skill and care when carrying out its customer's instructions.

Most banks act as trustees

Fiduciary

A fiduciary relationship is where one person is required to act in good faith towards another. Such relationships occur where one person is in a privileged position and in consequence is not allowed to make a personal profit or to be in a position where their duty and self-interest conflict. A trustee is a fiduciary in relation to the beneficiary.

One writer on banking law (Doyle) says that a fiduciary relationship cannot exist between a bank and its customer. Case law tends to support this contention. However, a special relationship, akin to a fiduciary one, may in exceptional circumstances be created.

A special relationship may equal fiduciary obligations

281

> ## Case example
> ### Lloyds Bank Ltd v Bundy (1975)
>
> B was an elderly farmer whose only asset was his farmhouse. His son's company got into financial difficulties and B guaranteed the company's overdraft using his farmhouse as security. At a later meeting with the bank B increased the security to the full value of the farmhouse. At this meeting the bank manager failed to advise B to obtain independent legal advice but got B to sign various documents to increase the security for the guarantee. B's son defaulted on the loan and the bank made B honour the guarantee.
>
> The Court of Appeal held that the guarantee and security would be set aside. The true relationship between B and LB was one of trust and confidence. This relationship imposed on LB a duty of 'fiduciary care' to work in B's best interest such as by advising him to obtain independent advice. Their failure to do so was a clear breach of that duty.

In this case Bundy regarded the bank manager, whom he had known for many years, as a friend. In relation to a special or fiduciary duty the case may be confined to its facts. The Court of Appeal also found that there was a presumption of undue influence which the bank was unable to rebut.

Selected banking topics in more detail

The bankers' duty of secrecy

The seminal case of a banker's duty of confidentiality was *Tournier v National Provincial & Union Bank of England* (1924)

Tournier's case established the scope of confidentiality

> ## Case example
> ### Tournier v National Provincial & Union Bank of England (1924)
>
> T was £9 8s 6d (£9.43) overdrawn and signed an agreement with the bank to pay this off at £1 per week. T wrote on the agreement the name and address of a firm where he was about to start employment as a commercial traveller on a three-month contract. This repayment agreement was not honoured and the acting bank manager telephoned the firm to find out T's private address; he spoke to two directors. T alleged that during the telephone conversation the bank disclosed that his bank account was overdrawn and his repayment had been dishonoured. The acting bank manager also, it was said, had expressed the opinion that T was betting heavily as he had used cheques to pay a bookmaker. As a result of the conversation the firm did not renew T's contract when it expired.
>
> T brought an action for slander against the bank and for breach of an implied term in the contract that secrecy was to be maintained. Indeed the bank had in their passbooks 'The officers of the Bank are bound to secrecy as regards the transactions of its customers.' In the High Court the bank had the judgement in its favour but T appealed.
>
> In the Court of Appeal Atkins LJ said:
>
> > To what information does the obligation of secrecy extend? It clearly goes beyond the state of the account ... It must extend at least to all the transactions that go through the

> account … It must, I think, extend beyond the period when the account is closed or ceases to be active … I further think that the obligation extends to information obtained from other sources than the customer's actual account.

As to what may be disclosed by a bank Bankes LJ said:

> At the present day I think it may be asserted with confidence that the duty is a legal one arising out of contract and that the duty is not absolute but qualified. It is not possible to frame any exhaustive definition of the duty. The most that can be done is to classify the qualification, and to indicate its limits … On principle I think that the qualifications can be classified under four heads:
>
> 1 Where disclosure is under compulsion by law.
> 2 Where there is a duty to the public to disclose.
> 3 Where the interests of the bank require disclosure.
> 4 Where the disclosure is made with the express or implied consent of the customer.

1 *Disclosure under compulsion by law* (the following is where the bank itself is not a party to any court proceedings). In the Jack Committee Report 1989, 20 statutes were identified under which banks could be compelled to disclose details of customers' financial affairs. Those listed here are merely a small selection of a larger number.

Many statutes can be used to compel a bank to disclose

- S.7 Bankers Book Evidence Act 1879. On the application of any party to legal proceedings a court may order that the applicant party has access to any entries in a banker's books and that copies be taken (*Pollock* v *Garle* [1899]). Such an order will normally only be granted to allow inspection of an account belonging to one of the actual litigants (*Williams* v *Summerfield* (1972)). S.7 also applies to criminal proceedings.
- S.9 (1) Police and Criminal Evidence Act 1984. An order under this Act can compel a bank to produce all its records on a customer, not just the bank books, e.g. interview notes, correspondence, etc. In *Barclays Bank plc* v *Taylor* (1989) (Barclaycard) a bank has a good defence for disclosure when served with a PACE order – also it may plead a public duty to disclose.
  R v *Nottingham Justices ex parte Lynn* (1984) – Fishing trips for useful information is not allowed. *R* v *Andover Justices ex parte Rhodes* (1980) – A spouse may also have their banking affairs investigated. *Barker* v *Wilson* (1980) – Microfilm records come within the Banker's Book Evidence Act 1989 – now part of the Banking Act 1979.
- Ss. 13, 17, Taxes Management Act 1970. S.13: the commissioners of Inland Revenue may ask a bank to prepare and deliver a list of persons beneficially entitled to stock registered in the name of the bank or its nominees per *Att. General* v *National Provincial Bank Ltd* (1928).
  S.17: commissioners may ask a bank to disclose bank interest exceeding £15 p.a. paid or credited to any customer.
- Ss. 431, 432 Companies Act 1985. The Secretary of State for Trade and Industry has powers to appoint inspectors to investigate a company. A company's bankers may be requested to produce all books and documents and to give inspectors all reasonable help.

A bank's legal duty to obey the law overrides any obligation to its customer

Under s. 452 the personal affairs of company officers known to the bank need not be disclosed.

- S. 218 Insolvency Act 1986. On liquidation the Director of Public Prosecutions may have matters referred to him and he has the authority to require a bank to disclose records on their customers.
- Ss. 1, 2 Criminal Justice Act 1987. This allows the Director of the Serious Fraud Office (SFO) to investigate 'on reasonable grounds serious or complex frauds'. (s. 1) Any person, such as a bank, may be questioned and asked to provide documents or other information. (s. 2) A court order is not necessary, merely a notice signed by the investigating officer and countersigned by the Director, SFO. Sealy and Hooley, in *Text and Materials in Commercial Law* 1994, draw attention to a court order that may assist a civil litigant to gain access to a banker's records. This is a *Shapira order* (*Bankers Trust Co.* v *Shapira* (1980)), which as a discovery order helps victims of fraud to trace their money.
- Ss. 7, 8, 24, 27, 31 Drugs Trafficking Offences Act 1986. A restraint order may be obtained to prevent a bank paying out on a customer's account (ss. 7, 8). If a bank is suspicious that a customer is a drug trafficker, or that the account is being used for one, then it must inform the police – a failure to do so will mean that the bank has committed an offence (s. 24).

Holtham v *Commissioner of Police* (1987):

> Suspicion is a state of surmise whose proof is lacking; it is not the provision of proof.

A police officer must, when investigating drug trafficking, obtain a court order so that material must be produced to the police (s. 27). It is a criminal offence when orders are made under the Act for a suspected person to be told by a third party, such as a bank, that he or she is under investigation (s. 31).

The NCIS is growing in importance

- The National Criminal Intelligence Service. The National Criminal Intelligence Service (NCIS) was created to combat drug dealing and football hooligans. In theory any deposit into a banking account, which is not recognized as being a salary, or other regular payment, could lead to a reference to the NCIS. With no minimum sum involved any deposit out of character with that particular account may make a bank notify the NCIS. In 1994 15 000 cases were referred to the NCIS, of which 65 per cent came from the high-street banks. On receipt of a referral the NCIS acts as a central clearing station in that referrals felt to be worth investigating are forwarded to the police force for the area where the account is kept so that they may investigate more fully. Investigations may take months to be completed.
- Ss. 1, 9 Prevention of Terrorism Act 1989. This Act relates to prescribed organizations such as the Irish Republican Army (IRA) and the Irish National Liberation Army (INLA). Relevant authorities may carry out investigation for 'money which is knowingly or having reasonable cause to suspect that it may be used for acts of terrorism'.
- Ss. 105, 117 Financial Services Act 1986. The Securities and Investment Board (SIB) may investigate the affairs of someone who is carrying on an investment business (s. 105).

A public duty to disclose is problematic

2 *A duty to the public to disclose.* A somewhat grey area in law. In Tournier's case it was said that a bank may disclose to protect the bank, interested persons, or the public against fraud or other crime. Therefore, if the bank believed that an account was being used by a

possible criminal or a subversive organization and thought that disclosure would prevent a crime then they would be justified in disclosing.

With the growth of disclosure through compulsion of law, disclosure because of public duty has remained underdeveloped. Interestingly, Sealy and Hooley draw parallels between an accountant's public duty of disclosure and a banker's. The case they cite is *Price Waterhouse* v *BCCI Holdings (Luxembourg) SA* (1992) in which the accountancy firm Price Waterhouse disclosed confidential information on their client to the Bingham Inquiry investigating the Bank of Credit and Commerce International Group.

Should the bank receive a request for assistance from the police then if the customer has already been charged s. 7 Banker's Book Evidence Act 1879 can be used to obtain bank disclosure. If the police only suspect that a crime has occurred then extreme care must be taken because, legally, the police cannot demand that information be given. Normally such requests relate to serious offences. A bank may ask that a letter be sent to them saying that information is 'required for the administration of justice' and giving an undertaking that any information supplied will not be used in court but that the bank will be subpœnaed to give evidence.

Case example
Weld-Blundell v *Stephens* (1920)

Where a customer was trading with the enemy in time of war:

a danger to the State or public duty to disclose may supersede the duty of the agent to his principal

Lord Finlay

---

3 *Where interests of the bank require disclosure*. This is commonly caused by litigation between a bank and its customer. For a case example see *Sunderland* v *Barclays Bank Ltd* (1938) below.
4 *Disclosure with the consent of the customer. Express consent* should seldom cause a problem unless the bank ventures to disclose more than the customer has agreed to. *Implied consent* is dependent on the circumstances.

Case Example
Sunderland v *Barclays Bank* (1938)

Mrs S was a customer of BB. She drew a cheque which was dishonoured for lack of funds. The real reason for the cheque's non-payment was that Mrs S had drawn a number of cheques in favour of bookmakers and BB felt that it was not the type of account on which to allow an overdraft. Mrs S complained to Mr S who advised her to contact the bank. This Mrs S did by telephone with Mr S later interrupting to add his own protests; the bank then told Mr S of the cheques drawn on the bookmakers. Mrs S sued BB for breach of their duty to maintain secrecy. She lost. The circumstances were such that an implied authorization to disclose had been given to the bank.

Would a bank breach its duty of secrecy in answering enquiries about one of its customers from other banks and credit reference agencies? This everyday situation has not really been clarified by the law. The Report of the Younger Committee on Privacy in 1972 said that a bank ought to make it clear to all customers, existing or prospective, how they handle references and to give the opportunity either to grant a standing authority for the provision of references or to ask the bank to obtain their consent whenever a reference was required. The Report of the Jack Committee 1989 recommended statutory codification but this was rejected by the Government as being unnecessary and likely to introduce new difficulties and confusion. The Code of Banking Practice (1994) requires banks to meet a strict duty of confidentiality concerning their customers' (past and present) financial affairs with disclosure only being made for one of the four reasons put forward by Bankes LJ in Tournier's case. The Code also attempts to prevent abuse by banks of their customer database for marketing purposes.

Statements of account

A bank has an implied duty to render statements of account either periodically or on demand. The interval of time between statements is discretional unless an express arrangement is in operation.

Position where the wrong credit balance is given

If a customer honestly believes the credit balance shown on their latest statement to be correct and is not negligent in that belief then he or she may rely on it to draw against that credit balance and if their cheques are dishonoured then the bank can be sued for breach of contract (*Holland* v *Manchester and Liverpool District Banking Co. Ltd* (1909)).

An incorrect credit balance may prejudice the bank

If the bank discovers their error and acts quickly enough then they may ask a court for rectification (correction of error) of the mistake they made. If rectification is not possible then estoppel principles as in Holland above may prevent the bank from recovery of sums incorrectly credited but actually spent by the customer (see also *United Overseas Bank* v *Jiwani* (1976)).

> ## Case Example
> ### *Lloyds Bank Ltd* v *Brooks* (1951)
> The Honourable Cecily Brooks was a beneficiary under a trust entitling her to an income from £2170 6-per-cent preference shares in a company. Due to a mistake in the investment department she was credited with income from 4000 2nd preference shares. Over the years she was credited with an extra £1108. Her defence was that she had relied upon the bank statements as being ones of fact and had in consequence enjoyed a higher standard of living. This alteration of her position was because she honestly believed that her income was greater than what it actually was and in consequence she had spent more in the nine-year period than what she normally would have.
> Her defence was allowed to succeed.

A customer is under no duty to check the accuracy of bank statements given in their pass book (*Kepitagalla Rubber Estates Ltd* v *National Bank of India Ltd* (1909)). The decision in Kepitagalla Rubber Estates has been applied to bank statements (*Tai Hing Cotton Mill Ltd* v *Liu Chang Hing Bank Ltd* (1985).

To succeed in pleading estoppel a customer must establish:

Necessary conditions for estoppel to operate

1 They believed the statement to be correct.
2 They were not negligent in that belief, e.g. if a person of modest means is credited with a large sum then he or she ought to query this.
3 They altered their position through relying on the statement.
4 In consequence of 1–3 it would be inequitable to allow the bank to recover the sum(s) overcredited.

However, if the bank can show that the customer would have entered into transactions whatever their statement showed then point 3 will fail.

Case example
United Overseas Bank v Jiwani (1976)

J had $10 108 in his Geneva bank account. Later UOB received a telex from a Zurich bank transferring $11 000. J was informed of this transfer. At this time J was buying a hotel and sent $20 000 to a Mr Piraric. When UOB received normal written confirmation of the transfer they mistakenly treated it as a new credit of $11 000 and sent J another credit received advice. On receiving this J sent another $11 000 to Mr Piraric for the hotel. J was later sued for the recovery of the second credit.

It was held that the third condition had not been satisfied for J was already committed to buying the hotel.

It will be more demanding for a business person to claim estoppel as they will be expected to know the day-to-day position of their affairs. This will make it difficult for them to show that they acted in good faith when spending money incorrectly credited to the company's account.

Similarly if a customer is unaware of an overcredit then they cannot claim a detriment as a result of the wrongful statement.

Case example
British & North European Bank Ltd v Zalstein (1927)

Z was overdrawn £900 beyond the agreed limit. To conceal this from the bank's auditors a bank manager transferred £2000 to Z's account. Once the manager felt safe from auditor investigation the £2000 was removed from Z's account. Z was completely unaware of what was happening. Later Z was sued for non-payment of his overdraft. Z said that the debt had been extinguished when the £2000 had been entered into his bank statement, e.g. he was attempting to claim the benefit of the credit.

It was held that the debt had not been discharged. There had been no reliance on the incorrect statement.

A customer's failure will mean they will bear the loss

The customer must draw cheques so as to prevent fraud

On a customer's failure to meet this duty a bank, paying out on a forged cheque but doing so in good faith and without negligence, may debit the customer's account.

Case example
London Joint Stock Bank v Macmillan & Arthur (1918)

A clerk made out a cheque for £2 on his employer's behalf. He left an open space between the 2 and the £ sign and omitted to write the amount in words. After obtaining his employers signature he added £120 and wrote this amount in words.

The House of Lords held that the employer had to bear the loss because he had facilitated the fraud.

In this situation a bank is not allowed to take advantage of s. 64 Bills of Exchange Act 1982 by claiming that a material alteration equals no customer's mandate.

Seemingly, any loss caused by the amount being increased will fall on the customer provided:

1 The customers signature was genuine.
2 The alteration is non-apparent and facilitated by the customer's negligence.

Courts are reluctant to extend the customer's duty of care to other parts of a cheque.

Case example
Slingsby v District Bank Ltd (1931)

A cheque having no line between Co. and order read: 'Pay John Priest & Co... or order'. After the drawer signed it a dishonest solicitor inserted in the gap 'per Gumberbirch & Potts'.

It was held that the drawer had not broken his duty of care.

Review question

Caxton & Co, a firm of printers, issued a cheque for £2000 each month for three months to one of their suppliers, David Smith Graphics. Smith altered each cheque to read £12 000 and subsequently obtained payment for that amount from Caxton's bankers, X Bank plc. Despite monthly statements, the forgery did not come to light until the annual audit of Caxton & Co. some four months later, when Caxton & Co. informed the bank of the forgery.

Consider whether Caxton & Co. can successfully claim recovery of the overpayment from X Bank plc.

The customer must advise the bank when they know that their signature has been forged

A failure to provide prompt notice that his or her signature has been forged will mean that the customer will be estopped from denying that the signature is genuine.

Case example
Greenwood v Martins Bank Ltd (1933)

A husband discovered that his wife was forging his signature on his cheques. He did not inform the bank but accepted his wife's explanation that she had been helping her sister who was in financial trouble. Later he found out that his wife had lied. She shot herself and he then sued the bank to recover the value of the forged cheques.

The House of Lords held that the delay in notifying the bank of the forgeries meant he was estopped from denying the genuineness of the signatures.

Courts unwilling to increase the customer's duties

In relation to 'self-regarding duties' the courts have occasionally said that customers ought to do certain things for their own protection. However, a bank has no counterclaim against a customer if they fail to do something to protect themselves. This position, that any 'self-regarding duty' is only advisory, is borne out by the Privy Council's decision in *Tai Hing Cotton Mill Ltd v Liu Chang Hing Bank* (1985). After asking the question whether the somewhat dated cases of *London Joint Stock Bank Ltd v Macmillan* (1918) and *Greenwood v Martin's Bank Ltd* (1933) were still good law Lord Scarman answered by saying that while banks may call for an increase in the standard of care owed by customers the courts would not impose an increased duty. It was, said Lord Scarman, up to the bank either to use their terms of business to gain increased protection or alternatively to persuade Parliament to provide statutory relief. The two cases therefore remain good law.

Tai Hing Cotton Mill Ltd v *Liu Chang Hing Bank Ltd* (1985) is an important and informative case. Particularly good analytical treatment is given on it by Sealy and Hooley, in *Text and Materials in Commercial Law*, 1994.

The provision of safe custody facilities

As already mentioned this creates a bailor–bailee relationship. Formerly there was a difference in the standard owed between paid and unpaid bailees but now there appears to be a single standard. (*Houghland* v *RR Low (Luxury Coaches) Ltd* (1962)). At one time banks used to provide a free safe custody service (the bank being a gratuitous bailee), but now they almost invariable charge for this service. Even if they did not do so they would still be regarded in law as being a paid bailee for provision of safe custody facilities is taken to come within the general banker–customer contract (*Port Swettenham Authority* v *T. W. Wu & Co.* (1978)).

When holding a customer's property the danger is that the bank may later release it to an unauthorized person. This may make the bank liable in the tort of conversion, e.g. the wrongful disposal of another person's property. If they are unable to recover the bailor's (customer's) property then the bank will have to reimburse the value of the property. Liability in conversion is strict so it will not be a defence for a bank to say that they had acted in good faith and were not negligent.

> Conversion is a practical problem for bankers

Case example
Langtry v *Union Bank of London* (1896)

L deposited valuable jewellery for safe custody with UBL. A third party stole and used headed note paper to forge L's purported instructions to hand the jewellery over to the bearer. No judgement was given as the bank settled out of court for £10 000 – an implied admission of liability.

As regards the standard of care expected of banks when acting as bailees a duty of normal care seems the most appropriate. Therefore, if a robber breaks into a bank's strongroom and steals a customer's property the bank will not normally be liable. But if the customer's property was stored in other than a secure place then probably liability would attach.

The procedure that a bank ought to adopt for releasing deposited property may include:

1 On the death of a customer the bank should obtain a receipt for the property from the personal representative when handing over safe custody articles. If the customer's will has been deposited then get a receipt for it signed by all the named executors before handing it over.
2 On deposit by joint account holders, partnerships, or companies, when accepting articles for safe custody the bank ought to obtain specific instructions saying who is entitled to claim repossession and the bank should not depart from these instructions.

In respect to theft of a customer's property by an employee it was formerly argued that a bank would only be liable when property was stolen by the person who was designated to look after it, e.g. a safe custody clerk or key holder. Now, seemingly, liability is extended to any employee (*Port Swettenham Authority* v *T. W. Wu & Co.* (1978)).

Should more than one person claim entitlement to the property deposited then a bank may be advised to make them interplead, that is to take a legal action amongst themselves to determine who is legally entitled to the property, rather than deciding the issue themselves.

In addition to possible liability for conversion, a bank may also face an action for breach of contract. Should a bank attempt to avoid or limit liability by means of a contractual term then the Unfair Contract Terms Act 1977 and, for private account holders the Unfair Terms in Consumer Contracts Regulations 1994, will have to be considered. A bank ought always to ask that articles left with them for safe custody be insured against for loss.

Review question

Mr Harris's sovereigns have been temporarily deposited for the duration of his holiday, a service for which Hallam Bank has made no charge.

1 What is the prime duty of Hallam Bank in this situation?
2 Would the position be different if a charge had been made for the service?
3 What would the position of Hallam Bank be if it released the sovereigns to an unauthorized person?

Trust obligations

As a trust is commonly created by a *trust deed* a bank ought to ask for sight of it (or a certified copy) before opening an account. The deed will say who may sign cheques etc. and the bank should be careful in departing from those designated. Where a trustee is unable to sign cheques etc. the bank may still operate the account but ask other trustees to sign an itemized list of banking transactions every three months saying that they confirm that the account has been operated correctly.

A bank may be deemed to know that a deposit was trust money

With trusts one problematic area for banks concerns the *constructive or implied trustee*. This arises where the bank knew or should have known that money deposited with it was really trust money. In Gross *ex parte* Kingston (1871), an account titled 'police account' meant that funds deposited into it were held for the police. Where there is no notice of a trust then the bank may treat all deposits as belonging to the account holder (*Thomson* v *Clydesdale Bank* (1893)).

In *Barnes* v *Addy* (1874), constructive trusts were divided into two classes. These were *knowing assistance* and *knowing receipt*.

Knowing assistance is where a bank becomes a party to dishonesty and as a consequence it can become liable for all losses suffered by the trust even though some monies may not have passed through the bank account.

In *Baden Delvaux & Lecuit* v *Société Gènerale SA* (1983), it was said that knowing assistance could be derived in several ways. These were:

1 By actual notice of a breach of the trust.
2 By shutting one's eyes to an obvious breach.
3 By intentionally failing to make reasonable enquiries.
4 Through inferred notice such that an honest and reasonable person would know.
5 Through negligence in not making appropriate enquiries.

Seemingly, these may be summarized as actual fraud or dishonesty on the bank's part or a reckless refusal of the bank to make satisfactory enquiries.

Case example
Lipkin Gorman v Karpnale Ltd (1989)

A bank branch manager knew that a partner in a firm of solicitors was a compulsive gambler. Over a period the partner withdrew £323 000 from the client's account and used the money to pay off gambling debts. The firm (LG) sued the bank (K Ltd) as a constructive trustee alleging that the bank ought to have known that the funds were being withdrawn fraudulently.

It was held for the following reasons that the bank was not liable:

1. While the bank manager knew of the gambling there was no direct knowledge of what the withdrawals were being used for.
2. The duty of confidentiality owed to the partner would have been breached if disclosure of the gambling had been made known.
3. If the bank had refused to make payment on the cheques submitted then it would have been in breach of contract.
4. Mere suspicion on the bank's part was not enough to refuse to pay out, e.g. if the bank had wrongfully dishonoured a cheque then it could have been liable in defamation.
5. A bank is not expected to act as a private detective.

Knowing receipt is based on receiving and dealing in trust monies. Liability here is really a lack of integrity but liability is only for those sums which went through the account.

Bank's references – status enquiries (banker's opinion)

It is normal practice for a bank to provide another bank or an approved credit reference agency with a reference on its own customer. When a bank does decide to provide an opinion on a customer's financial position, there is no legal obligation on them to seek out information from elsewhere before giving their reply (*Parsons* v *Barclays Bank Ltd* (1910)). However, their opinion must have been honestly held and based on the facts known to the bank at the time it was given. For the provision of status equiries banks tend to use for this purpose specially printed stationery on which a disclaimer is printed such as 'Confidential – for your private use only and without responsibility'. Despite the wording a person receiving a reference is still able to communicate it to another legitimately interested person. Also such disclaimers are yet to be tested in the courts, to establish whether they pass the test of reasonability given in the Unfair Contract Terms Act 1977 and, but only for private individuals, the Unfair Terms in Consumer Contracts Regulations 1994.

> An opinion honestly held and supported by fact

Set against protecting a customer's rights is a public policy dimension in that the law wants to encourage the practice of providing general references on a person's character and honesty. Provided a bank acted in good faith and the person receiving the information had a justifiable interest in receiving it then the bank will not be liable for defamation as qualified privilege may be pleaded as a defence (*London Association for the Protection of Trade* v *Greenlands Ltd* (1916)).

On providing a reference, even in the form of an opinion, a bank may have to disclose what are normally confidential matters relating to a customer's financial affairs. Permission to disclose is implied from normal banking practice so that there is no need to obtain the customer's express permission. However, the Jack's Committee of 1989 said that there ought to be a legal require-ment for banks to obtain express permission before making disclosure in references. The Jacks

Committee focused on the extent of disclosure that ought to be permitted. It was felt that provision of black information (on a customer in debt) should be treated differently to provision of white information (on a customer in credit). The Code of Banking Practice 1994 did not take up the Committee's suggestion so that debtor and creditor customers are treated on a like for like basis.

The Code of Banking Practice ought to be followed

Previously, a bank would not normally inform a customer that it has received a request for a reference which it intended to provide. However, under s. 7 The Code of Banking Practice 1994 requires banks, on receiving a reference request to advise the customer that a reference request has been received and to explain how the system of banker's references operate.

Provided that the correct procedure is followed a bank is allowed to disclose information (or more accurately to express an opinion) about a customer's financial affairs, however the bank must not disclose specific information about the actual account details but may only disclose in broad terms the financial status of the customer as they know it to be. Specific disclosure would bring the Data Protection Act 1984 into operation. Therefore, the following types of statements ought to be used.

Negative:
'We confirm that X has an account with us.'
'We are unable to speak for your figures.'
'X has only recently opened an account with us; we are therefore unable to speak for your figures.'

Positive:
'X is considered good for your figure.'
'X is considered reliable and trustworthy.'
'X is respectable and good for your figures.'

On providing a reference a bank should be wary of incurring liability under the Hedley Byrne principle.

Case example
Commercial Banking Co. of Sidney Ltd v RH Brown & Co. (1972)

A branch manager gave an over-optimistic reply to a status report request even though the bank headquarters had said that it was worried about the account.

It was held that the reply was reckless and unjustifiable. The bank was consequently liable – the reply equalled fraudulent misrepresentation.

This is an Australian case but it would probably be influential in English law. The bank's attempt at relying on a disclaimer failed.

Finally, it is usual banking practice for a bank not to sign a reference report but merely to initial it. This overcomes the potential pitfall in s. 6 Statute of Frauds Amendment Act 1828 (Lord Tenderden's Act), whereby if it was signed and was found to be wrong then liability for fraudulent misrepresentation would apply.

The banking Ombudsman

A complainant (or group of complainants) who is unable to resolve a dispute with their bank at either branch or higher level may ask the Banking Ombudsman (BO) to intervene and act as an impartial arbitrator between the parties. The objective of the BO is to facilitate the satisfactory, settlement or withdrawal of the complaint. While overwhelmingly most complainants are bank customers this is not strictly necessary as any interested party may complain over the standard of banking service relating to accounts, credit cards, financial products, etc. A complainant must sign a waiver to release the bank from the duty of confidentiality which they owe.

The BO is a voluntary scheme introduced in 1986 by a number of banks covering over 99 per cent of private individual banking customers. The scheme was enlarged in 1993 to include small businesses with an annual turnover of less than £1 million. Originally suggested by the National Consumers Council the scheme is structured with an unlimited company, registered under the Companies Act, being managed by a Board of Directors appointed by member banks in the scheme. Beneath the Board is a seven-member Council of the Banking Ombudsman. The respective duties of the Board and Council are:

The Ombudsman: a complainant's final port of call before litigation

The Board	The Council
(a) to levy contributions from the banking industry to fund the scheme	(a) to appoint the Ombudsman and assess what his terms of reference ought to be (in both instances the Board has final approval)
(b) to agree the budget for the scheme	(b) to prepare a budget for acceptance by the Board
(c) to appoint Council members and confirm the appointment of an Ombudsman	(c) to provide assistance and guidance to the Ombudsman
(d) to approve the Ombudsman's terms of reference and ensure that they are kept	

The BO scheme was introduced because customers in dispute with very large organizations feel dissatisfied with the courts, perceiving technical dangers and uncertainties (Birkinshaw, *Grievances, Remedies and the State*, 1985). Even with a small claims procedure it is still felt by many that 'the courts do not provide an adequate remedy for those with valid complaints against large organizations' (Edell, *The Building Society Ombudsman Scheme: a customers' champion*, 1989).

The banks appear to view the BO scheme as a defensive strategy in that it acts as a useful 'safety valve' for customers who are able to continue with a dispute but to do so through the office of a third party. Of non-trivial complaints less than 5 per cent (less than 1 in 20) are referred to the Ombudsman but referrals are increasing. The increase may be a result of the BO asking for better publicity about the scheme.

The Jacks Committee expressed concern that the banking industry's involvement could seriously undermine the schemes credibility with the public as well as not being convinced that it was really fair. The Committee felt that a statutory scheme should be adopted but this recommendation was rejected by both the BO and the Council of the Banking Ombudsman who argued that it would result in a loss of flexibility as well as the BO having to relinquish the power to make a binding award. The Government agreed with the Council of the Banking Ombudsman (White Paper, 1990) and the scheme remains a voluntary one.

In 1994 the BO awarded damages of just under £1 million to banking customers. The largest award was £70 000. The Ombudsman reported that complaints to his office were down and expressed the view that this may be a result of banks improving other customer services including how they handle complaints.

Finally reference may be made to the Code of Banking Practice 1994. This obligates banks to:

1 Have their own internal procedures for handling customers' complaints fairly and expeditiously.
2 Inform their customers that they have a complaints procedure. Customers wishing to make a complaint are to be told what procedure to follow and what further steps are available if they believe that their complaint has not been dealt with satisfactorily either by the branch or at a more senior level within the bank.

The code also expects that a bank will belong to one of those designated bodies the most appropriate of which for retail banks is the banking ombudsman scheme.

Chapter summary

- The banker–customer relationship in law is derived from case law and is very much based on the objective expectations of the parties.
- In law it is possible for a customer to have a series of legal relationships with a bank, each being dependent on the customer having a different legal status, e.g. as a debtor, bailor, principal, etc.
- Both the bank and its customer will owe various legal obligations to each other but in turn will have a number of rights owed to them.
- The banking ombudsman scheme is intended by the banking industry to offer alternative dispute resolution so as to avoid possible court actions.

Scotland and Northern Ireland

The text of the chapter applies equally to the above.

Case study exercise

Your employer, Dyson Bank plc, has the current account of BacchanBar, a wine bar in which Mr and Ms Vine are the partners. Dyson Bank received a status enquiry on BacchanBar from another bank and, without referring it to the customer, replied as follows:

The BacchanBar,
This is a trading partnership whose assets appear to be fully committed.
The firm does not have a licence to sell alcohol for its wine bar.

It would have been unlawful for BacchanBar to operate without an alcohol licence for its bar. In fact, the firm held the necessary licence.

BacchanBar has failed to obtain a valuable booking as a result of the above reference and the Vines have complained to their branch manager at Dyson Bank about the status reply it gave.

Advise Dyson Bank on the following points:

1 Dyson Bank's right to give status replies on its customers, and any restrictions on that right.
2 The legal points relating to the contents of the above status reply given for BacchanBar.
3 BacchanBar's remedies in the respect of Dyson Bank being in breach of its legal obligations.

Discussion questions

1 (a) Banks act as an agent for their customers in a variety of ways. Explain how agency may arise and what duties the banker will become responsible for.
  (b) Psalter Bank plc have been engaged by a customer, Hardwick, to obtain a second mortgage on his behalf. Psalter Bank arranges mortgage facilities with their subsidiary company Owen Limited, but they do not disclose to Hardwick that it is a subsidiary or that they have received a commission of £300 from them.
  Discuss the legal position in the above.
2 Mrs Forceful is in the habit of collecting her husband's statement from his bank every month. Recently Mr and Mrs Forceful separated, and Mr Forceful now objects that his month's statement was handed to Mrs Forceful without his authority.
  Discuss the legal position in this situation.
3 The bank's common-law duty of confidentiality is really a fiction.
  Discuss.

Further reading

Banking Law, Arora (1993), Pitman.
A very good introduction to the subject. Well presented and student friendly. Recommended.
Law Relating to Banking Services, Palfreman (1993), M & E Handbook.
Good thorough treatment. Easy to follow.
Law Relating to Banking Services, Raby (1992), Pitman.
Law and Practice of Banking Vol: Banker and Customer, (1991), Pitman.
A most impressive authoritative text, Volume 2 covers Securities for Banker's Advances.

11 Insurance (non-marine)

Introduction

As individuals we can readily appreciate the importance of insurance. It is taken out in an attempt to ensure that in the event of a misfortune occurring we at least will obtain financial compensation for the loss or injury suffered. The misfortunes that we commonly guard against by insurance are death, fire, theft (through burglary), accidents that cause property damage and personal injuries.

As with individuals so also with business. A prudent business will always be aware of potential risks and want to protect itself from their occurrence. Not only will property be insured against fire or other forms of damage, but, if appropriate, product liability cover will be taken out to guard against customers or other third parties making compensatory claims for injuries caused by a defective product. Similarly, if the business regularly gives advice or information then a professional indemnity policy would be recommended to cover claims for damages caused by negligent advice. Indeed certain professionals (solicitors and accountants) must by law carry this type of insurance cover. Businesses which are heavily reliant on certain employees may take out a life policy on the life of these key employees. Where employees handle money or other valuable items then fidelity insurance will cover the employer against employee thefts. While it is not really part of this chapter the Employers' Liability (Compulsory Insurance) Act 1969 makes it compulsory for every employer, apart from local authorities and nationalized industries, to insure against liability for injury or disease incurred by their employees and arising in the course of their employment.

Objectives

The purpose of this chapter is to cover the main principles relating to insurance law. These common-law principles, evolved over many years, give judicial protection to the insurer when agreeing to cover the risk that the insured wants protection against.

Key concepts

- The contractual nature of the insurer–insured relationship especially in relation to utmost good faith between the parties
- That a monetary interest, known as an *insurable interest,* is required by the insured, otherwise the policy is treated as being void as a wager

- That only losses *proximate* to the risk covered are recoverable
- That most contracts of insurance are policies of *indemnity*
- That over- or under-insurance can have serious consequences
- That *subrogated* rights may be available to the insurer as well as contribution.

Definition of an insurance contract

Whether a contract is one of insurance is a matter of construction

A policy of insurance is a contract by which one party, known as the insurer, undertakes in return for a premium to pay money to another, known as the insured, on the occurrence of a contingent event, such as death or personal injury, or, alternatively, agrees to indemnify the insured for any loss caused by the risk insured against such as fire or burglary.

The various principles of insurance will be dealt with but a court may well say that a contract is a contract of insurance even though this may be vigorously denied by the parties concerned.

Case example
Department of Trade v St Christopher Motorist's Association (1974)

Members of the association paid an annual fee so that if an event occurred which would prevent them from driving, such as injury or the loss of their licence, then the association would provide a chauffeur (and possibly a car) for up to 40 hours each week for up to 12 months. The Department of Trade said that the association was carrying on an insurance company without the necessary statutory authorization.

It was held that, as there was really no difference between paying for a chauffeur for a member unable to drive and paying the cost of the member themselves arranging for a chauffeur it meant that the aassociation was carrying on an insurance business.

The proposal form

In order to obtain insurance cover inevitably an application form will have to be completed and this is known as a proposal form. The person seeking cover submits the proposal form (offer) to the insurance company and they may either accept or reject it.

The basis clause

The proposal form provides the basis of the contract

Most insurance contracts provide that the completion of the proposal form will become the 'basis of the contract'. This means that the truth of the answers to the proposal form questions is made a condition of the contract. Therefore, the insurer will be able, on the proposal form being completed wrongfully, to avoid liability even if the answer to a question was given innocently or is found to be of no material importance.

Case example
Dawsons Ltd v Bonnin (1922)

A proposal form for a fire insurance policy on a lorry asked where it would be garaged. The proposer innocently gave the wrong address. The proposal was made the 'basis of the contract' and the lorry was later destroyed by fire. The House of Lords held that the insurers were able to repudiate liability since the misstatement, although not material, had been made a 'basis' of the contract.

The 'basis clause' therefore incorporates all the questions and answers of the proposal form into the contract and says that they are all to be treated as being 'warranties' so that however trivial the misstatement the contract may be avoided for breach of 'warranty'.

Warranties and insurance

In contract law a warranty is a secondary contractual term which if broken does not allow the injured party to rescind the contract but only allows a claim in damages for any loss suffered. But when used with a 'basis clause' all statements made by the proposer will become warranties and all warranties in this insurance context are treated as being fundamental terms of the contract, e.g. they are conditions, so that their breach will discharge the insurer from any liability under the policy. However, a slight variation between ordinary contractual conditions and warranties in insurance (which, as mentioned, resembles conditions) is that when a contractual condition is broken the contract is not terminated unless and until the injured party so decides; but with an insurance warranty being broken the contract of insurance automatically ends in respect to the insurer's liability unless they decide to ignore the breach (*Bank of Nova Scotia* v *Hellanic Mutual War Risks Association (Burmuda) Ltd, the Good Luck* (1992)).

Warranties in insurance have a special meaning

The unfairness inherent in the use of insurance warranties has been recognized. The Statement of General Insurance Practice issued by the Association of British Insurers and Lloyd's recommend that for non-commercial insurance:

- no proposal form or policy should convert statements into warranties as to present or past facts
- there will be warnings on proposal forms and renewal notices of the duty of disclosure
- insurers will not repudiate liability for innocent non-disclosure or misrepresentation.

Period of cover

If the period to be covered is expressed to be 'from' or 'after' a named day then the general rule is that it does not include the day so named.

Case example
Isaac v *Royal* (1870)
A policy gave six months' cover from '14 February until 14 August'. The 14 February was excluded but 14 August was included.

Utmost good faith

In most commercial contracts the parties do not need to disclose to each other facts which they know would be of importance to the other party. Contractual negotiations are done on the basis of *caveat emptor* (let the buyer beware) so that the buyer should be cautious as to what he or she is buying and the onus is on them to satisfy themselves that the goods or services are suitable for their needs.

Exceptions to the *caveat emptor* rule can be found in the implied terms of the Sale of Goods Act 1979 (as amended) but also a notable exception relates to insurance contracts. Such contracts are said to be *uberrimae fidei* which means that there has to be the full confidence and frankness between the parties. Therefore, the parties must disclose to each other all information which would influence the other party's decision as to whether or not to enter into the contract. The promisor when seeking insurance cover must disclose to the insurer every fact and circumstance which may

Each party needs to disclose information to the other

influence them in deciding whether to accept the risk and grant cover. Similarly, the insurer should make disclosure of pertinent information to the promisor.

At the bottom of all proposal forms will be a declaration which must be signed by the proposer, e.g.:

> I warrant that the above statements and particulars are true and that no material facts concerning the insurance has been withheld.

As previously mentioned the Statement of General Insurance Practice says that in respect to non-commercial insurances appropriate warnings on proposal forms and renewal notices of the duty of disclosure should be given and that insurers are not to repudiate liability for innocent non-disclosure.

Justification of the utmost good faith requirement

If an insurance company had to investigate whether each question on the proposal form had been answered fully and honestly, together with a general investigation of the applicant's background, then the cost of insurance would become prohibitively high. Knowledge about themselves or the subject matter of the insurance largely lies with the applicant for cover who it is felt would be able unfairly to exploit his or her position to their advantage. To overcome this unequal position the courts have made contracts of insurance ones of the utmost good faith.

Disclosure a result of unequally held knowledge

What has to be disclosed?

All material facts or circumstances must be disclosed whether the insurer has asked specific questions or not. A promisor is not obligated to disclose facts he or she does not know or facts which they cannot reasonably be expected to know. A promisor is only obligated to disclose facts which he or she actually knows or facts which ought reasonably to be known.

Disclosure of all material facts

The Marine Insurance Act 1906, which despite its title applies equally to non-marine insurance, in relation to material facts says in s. 18 (2)(a):

> Every circumstance is material which would influence the judgement of a prudent underwriter in fixing the premium or determining whether he will take the risk.

Whether a failure to disclose is material or not is a finding of fact. Case law gives certain clues.

Convictions

The moral turpitude of the insured has always been of major importance to the insurer.

Case example
Woolcott v Sun Alliance & London Alliance Co. (1978)

W took out a building policy on his house. He was not asked whether he had previous criminal convictions and replied in the negative to the question: 'Are there any other matters you wish to be taken into account?' He omitted to disclose that many years earlier he had been convicted of house burglary. W said that it never occurred to him that his conviction was important and if he had been specifically asked he would have disclosed it. The house was destroyed by fire.

It was held that the conviction was a material fact as it constituted a moral hazard which the insurers would have taken into their assessment whether to accept the risk and if so at what premium.

Woolcott's case can be contrasted with *Reynolds* v *Phoenix Assurance Co.* (1978). R's conviction for receiving stolen property was not material in relation to fire insurance and it was said that criminal convictions would be material depending on their seriousness and the length of time that had elapsed since the insured had been convicted.

Spent convictions

An authoritative writer on insurance law (John Birds) has argued that the Rehabilitation of Offenders Act 1974 ought to mean that when convictions are 'spent' under the Act then they need not be disclosed and any failure to do so will not enable an insurer to avoid liability under a policy. Case law has still to test this matter.

Previous refusal

A refusal by another insurer to accept the risk is a material fact for all insurances apart from marine.

> **Case example**
> ## *Glicksman* v *Lancashire and General Insurance Co.* (1927)
> A firm, consisting of G and H, submitted a proposal form to LGI for burglary insurance. G had been previously refused such cover but the firm itself had never been refused.
> The House of Lords held that G had not disclosed a material fact and the policy was consequentially voidable by LGI.

The latest authority on disclosure in insurance contracts is *Pan Atlantic Insurance Co. Ltd* v *Pine Top Insurance Co. Ltd* (1993). Here the House of Lords held that a circumstance may be material even though a full and accurate disclosure of it would not in itself have had a decisive effect on the prudent underwriter's decision as to whether or not to accept the risk and if so at what premium. The House went on to say that if the non-disclosure of a material fact did not induce the contract then the underwriter is not entitled to rely on it to avoid the contract.

Partial disclosure

Disclosure must be full and complete. A partial disclosure will be insufficient.

Disclosure must be full and complete

> **Case example**
> ## *Hales* v *Reliance Fire and Accident Insurance Co.* (1960)
> A shopkeeper (H) was asked the question in a proposal form 'Are any inflammable oils or other inflammable goods kept on the premises?' H answered that lighter fuel was kept. No disclosure was made that fireworks were kept on the premises in the few weeks leading up to 5 November. Even though the insurance company were aware that shop stock would include in this period fireworks the fire policy was still voidable.

The changing nature of material facts

Material facts or circumstances are important to an insurer for their commercial significance. What is currently commercially significant may well be subject to change.

Material facts change over time

Case example
***Horne* v *Poland* (1922)**

A proposer for burglary insurance failed to disclose that by birth he was a Romanian. Despite being in England since the age of 12 the non-disclosure was said by the court to be material and the insurer was allowed to avoid the policy.

Almost certainly today such non-disclosure would not be held to be material.

A continuing duty to disclose

A material change in circumstances must be disclosed

Once the contract is created then as the insurer cannot, without being in breach of contract, cancel the policy or increase the premiums there is usually no duty to disclose any change in circumstances to the insurer until the insurance is renewed. But if the policy contains a clause saying certain changes in circumstances have to be notified, such as a house being left unoccupied for a long period, then this clause must be followed. However, in the period between submitting the proposal form and creating the contract, which admittedly with the promptness of modern insurers may be relatively short, if any alteration of circumstances occur then the alteration must be made known (*Looker* v *Law Union and Rock Ins Co. Ltd* (1928)). The insurance industry claim that in practice with innocent non-disclosure, where the claim is relatively modest, they seldom take up their right to avoid the policy but only do so where they suspect that the suppression of a material fact was done deliberately. Insurance companies take a long-term business view so that if too many claims were rejected for innocent non-disclosure then the public would lose confidence in insurance and take out far fewer policies.

What need not be disclosed

The proposer may be excused having to disclose

The following need not be disclosed:

1 Facts which reduce the risk to the insurer.
2 Where the insurer says that they do not need to know, such as when asking for details of claims made in, say, the last five years there is an implied statement that they do not want to know about claims made longer than five years ago.
3 Facts which the insurer is taken to know – these are areas of common knowledge.
4 Facts which ought to have been noted by the insurer's medical examiner when the proposer underwent a medical examination.
5 Facts which are excluded by a policy condition, such as where the policy will exclude cover for smoking related illnesses, there will be no need to disclose that you smoke.

Recovery of premiums

Possible if:

A restrictive right to recover premiums

1 The policy is void for some cause apart from fraud or illegality, such as fundamental mistake. However, a term in the policy may say that if the policy is void for whatever reason then the premium will be forfeited (*Sparenborg* v *Edinburgh Life Assurance Co.* (1912)).
2 The policy is avoided for innocent misrepresentation or non-fraudulent disclosure.
3 The policy is cancelled under the statutory cooling-off provisions for life or related cover issued to individuals. An insurer for this type of cover must under s. 65 Insurance

Companies Act 1974 send a notice to the proposer saying that the agreement may be cancelled by the proposer within a 10-day period of receipt of the notice or 10 days from when the premium was paid.

Where the policy is voidable for fraudulent misrepresentation then the insurer does not have to return the premium. Similarly, any illegality, such as there being no insurable interest, will mean that the premiums cannot be recovered unless the insured was not party to the illegality (*Hughes* v *Liverpool Victoria Friendly Society* (1916)).

The Unfair Terms in Consumer Contracts Regulations 1994

The regulations originate from the EC Unfair Contract Terms Directive and apply to contracts which have not been individually negotiated, such as where a contract was drafted in advance and the consumer was not able to influence the substance of a term(s) (s. 3). A consumer is defined as a person acting in a private capacity (s. 2). Therefore, the regulations will apply to virtually all insurance policies taken out by private individuals.

Under the regulations a contract term is unfair where it is contrary to a requirement of good faith in that it causes a significant imbalance in the parties' rights and obligations to the detriment of the consumer (s. 4). In assessing whether a term is unfair a court needs to look at the nature of the service, and at all surrounding circumstances as well as at all the other terms of the contract or another contract if relevant (s. 4). For satisfying the requirement of good faith a court must be guided by Schedule 2 of the regulations:

Additional consumer protection from a European directive

(a) What was the 'respective' bargaining strength of the parties?
(b) Did the consumer receive an inducement to agree the term?
(c) Was the good or service sold or supplied to the special order of the consumer?
(d) To what extent did the seller or supplier deal fairly and equitably with the consumer?

In relation to terms contained in an insurance contract clearly the insurer is in a far stronger position than the consumer seeking cover. Business is done on a predrafted standard form contract with the consumer having to 'take it or leave it'. As for receiving 'an inducement to agree the term' the normal inducement will be a reduction in the premium, or alternatively, more favourable conditions such as a lower excess on the policy. It will be for the insurer to satisfy a court that a genuine inducement was given in return for acceptance of a term which at first sight appears to be exploitative. Fair and equitable dealing will be a finding of fact. With a contract term demanding full disclosure of material facts, any unfairness or lack of good faith may manifest itself not so much in having such a term in the contract but in how an insurer interprets and applies it to claims, e.g. is it used to legitimately protect the insurer against possible fraud, or as a device for the insurer to hide behind in order to legally decline a claim? If a term is found to be unfair then it will not be binding on the consumer but the contract itself will continue if it is capable of continuing without the offending unfair term (s. 5). The Director General of Fair Trading (DGFT) has under section 8 a duty to consider any complaint made to him concerning the unfairness of a contract term and he is able to take appropriate action namely in serving an injunction against the user of the offending contract term. Schedule 3 does contain, for assistance, a fairly long list of examples of terms which may be regarded as being unfair. As the regulations only came into force on 1 July 1995 it may be quite some time before case law starts to flesh out the regulatory requirements.

What ought to be of immediate benefit to consumers seeking insurance is that section 6 requires the insurer to provide an insurance contract in plain, intelligible language. Many insurers, in response to consumer criticisms and the Office of Fair Trading, have in recent years made a conscious effort to make their documentation more consumer friendly but section 6 does impose a more forceful demand. Where terminology is found to be too antiquated, such as the term 'warranty', then replacement terminology may result in meanings well known and favourable to the insurance industry being replaced by new meanings more favourable to consumers. Only time will tell!

Review question

A contract of insurance is one of utmost good faith. To what extent may an insurer avoid liability for non-disclosure or misrepresentation by the insured?

Insurable interest

The insured must have a monetary interest in the insurance subject matter

It is possible to take out insurance to cover the occurrence of most risks. For example, the Wimbledon tennis championships in June are insured against bad weather; female film actresses have previously insured their faces, legs or breasts against accidents; and prospective parents have insured against twins or larger multiple births. However, not all risks can be insured against. Those that are insurable have what is termed an 'insurable interest'. This means that in the event of the subject matter of the insurance being destroyed or damaged the insured will suffer a financial loss. For example a house-owner has an insurable interest in their house for if it catches fire or suffers flood damage then the house-owner will incur a financial loss.

Where a person has no insurable interest then under the Gaming Act 1845 the policy is void as it amounts to no more than a wager. Before the insurable interest requirement it was possible for, say, residents of a street to take out a collective life policy in their favour on the life of the oldest resident. Alternatively, a life policy could be taken out on someone who was to be tried for a capital offence: if the accused was convicted then on the execution of the insured the policyholder made a good profit on their speculation, but if the accused was acquitted then the policyholder merely lost their premium which was effectively their stake money on the wager.

Life assurance and insurable interest

Public policy considerations require an insurable interest

Section 1 of the Life Assurance Act 1774 says that unless there is an insurable interest then an insurance contract will be illegal. A proposer may insure his own life without financial limit or the life of a spouse again without financial limit. In respect to the lives of others then there is a need for the proposer to have when the policy is taken out an insurable interest in the life of the assured but this interest is not necessary at the death of the assured. Despite its title this Act applies to other insurances not just life cover, but it does not apply to merchandise or goods, with money being categorized as goods.

A person taking out an insurance policy is normally termed the insured. With life cover it is the practice to use the term assured. This is because, unlike other insurances dependent on a risk occurring, the death of the person subject to the life cover is assured as we all must eventually die.

> ### Case example
> ### *Harse* v *Pearl Life Assurance Co. Ltd* (1904)
> A son had no insurable interest in the life of his mother who kept house for him. The policy was to cover the mother's funeral expenses but the son had no legal obligation to bury her!

Similarly, a parent has no insurable interest in their child's life (*Halford* v *Kymer* (1830)) as at common law there is no obligation to support a child although s. 17 Supplementary Benefits Act 1976 says there is a legal obligation for a parent to reimburse state benefits given for the maintenance of a child. Insurable interest in respect to other lives are:

- *trial judges* – a life policy for the duration of the trial may be taken out by litigants;
- *theatrical and film directors and film stars* – a life policy may be taken out by the production company;
- a *creditor* can insure the life of a debtor and vice versa;
- an *employer* can take out key person life cover on the lives of essential employees, and
- an *employee* working under a fixed-term contract can take out a policy on the employer's life for the duration of his contract.

Here the policyholder will lose financially on the insured's death

Property and goods cover

In respect to real property (land) the insurable interest must exist when the contract is made but with personal property (goods) it has to exist when a loss is suffered. The principle is the same for life in that the policyholder must have a financial interest in the property insured.

> ### Case example
> ### *Macaura* v *Northern Assurance Co. Ltd* (1925)
> M sold some timber to a limited company in exchange for a majority shareholding. M insured the timber in his own name. The timber was destroyed by fire. NA refused to meet M's claim as M himself had no insurable interest – the timber was owned by the company.

Waiver of an insurable interest

Where the Life Assurance Act 1774 applies then no waiver is possible; where it does not apply then the policy may say that an insurable interest is not required.

The proximity rule

This is a causational requirement in that the real, direct, operative or dominant cause of the loss or damage must fall within the terms of the policy. Should the cause of the loss be excluded under the policy then a claim will fail.

The real cause of the loss or damage must be identified

The burden of proof is on the insured to establish that the alleged event did occur, that it was covered by the policy and that the degree of the loss or damage claimed was suffered. Should the insurer argue that the event causing the loss or damage is excluded then the burden of proof is on them to show this.

> ## Case example
> ### *Winspear* v *Accident Insurance Association* (1880)
> A policy covering death and personal injury excluded accidents caused by natural disease. The insured had a fit while on a bridge over a stream. He fell into shallow water and was drowned.
>
> It was held that the cause of death was accidental drowning. The claim was therefore successful.

Intentional criminal acts

No recovery from an intentional criminal act

If the cause of the loss was derived from an intentional criminal act then the policy will be void to whoever did the act as well as possibly from others who may hope to benefit from the policy.

> ## Case example
> ### *Cleaver* v *Mutual Reserve Life Fund Association* (1892)
> Mr C took out life cover on his own life with Mrs C named as the beneficiary. Mrs C later poisoned him.
>
> Neither Mrs C nor her estate could benefit from the policy.

Only insane suicide is recoverable

The position of suicide is that if it is an insane suicide then the estate of the deceased, subject to any suicide clause in the policy, may recover under the policy but the estate of a sane suicide cannot.

> ## Case example
> ### *Beresford* v *Royal Insurance Co. Ltd* (1938)
> The Honourable Major Beresford, heavily in debt, shot himself dead very shortly before his life policy expired.
>
> It was held that, notwithstanding a clause in the policy saying that a suicide, sane or insane, would not invalid, the policy (provided that it did not occur within two years of the policy being taken out), relatives of the deceased would not be allowed to claim benefit of the policy.

While the public policy considerations in a Beresford-type situation are important it will not slavishly be followed by the court so as to impose injustice on an innocent person suffering loss through a deliberate act of another.

> ## Case example
> ### *Hardy* v *Motor Insurer's Bureau* (1964)
> An uninsured car thief deliberately used a car as a weapon and H was injured. The MIB said that to allow H to receive compensation would be to indemnify an intentional criminal act.
>
> The Court of Appeal held that, if the guilty person himself tried to claim that it would be resisted on public policy grounds, but H was an innocent third party.

A deliberate criminal act does not include an act of negligence or recklessness so that in *Tinline* v *White Cross Insurance Association Ltd* (1921), the insured who pleaded guilty to a man-slaughter charge caused by his negligent driving was still entitled to claim against the policy for accidental injury.

The position of negligence

A loss resulting from the negligence of the insured is still covered by the policy.

> ### Case example
> ### *Harris* v *Polard* (1941)
> A policyholder insured her jewellery against fire damage. On leaving her house unoccupied she wrapped the jewellery in old newspaper and hid them under unlit coal in the fire-grate. On her return she lit the fire temporarily forgetting that the jewellery was hidden beneath the coal. The court said:
>
> > it matters not whether the fire comes to the insured property or the insured property comes to the fire.
>
> The policy covered unintentional loss and this is what had occurred.

Indemnity

All contracts of insurance, apart from life, accident, illness and marine, are ones of indemnity. This means that the insurer undertakes, by payment of money, to make good the loss the insured has suffered. With life, illness and accident insurance the policy will always state the sum assured.

Indemnity insurance is compensation for loss but the insured is only able to recover his or her loss; they are not permitted to make a profit from the occurrence of the insured risk.

> ### Case example
> ### *Darrell* v *Tibbitts* (1880)
> A house was damaged by a gas explosion. The landlord recovered £750 from the insurer. The tenant under the lease was obligated to repair the damage which he did from money received from the local authority who had caused the explosion by their negligence. The insurer was able to recover the £750 as the insured had lost nothing.

Unless a valued policy (see below) is involved then the assessment of indemnity is on the basis of:

1 For a total loss the market value of the property at the time of loss.
2 For a partial loss then the cost of repairs or reinstatement.

Valued policies

This is where the measure of indemnity is agreed when the contract is entered into as opposed to waiting until there is an actual loss. Valuation policies are usually void if there is a gross overvaluation as this would amount to either an illegal wager or a possibility of fraud. Such policies may be taken out to cover loss of profits following fire damage, or to pay an agreed sum if it rains more than a certain amount during, say, the Wimbledon tennis championships (both are forms of business interruption insurance).

If the loss is total then under a valued policy the insured recovers the agreed valued. If a partial loss occurs then the insured will recover a proportion of the agreed value as is represented by the depreciation (damage) in the actual value.

This may be expressed as:

$$\frac{\text{Damage} \times \text{insured value}}{\text{Actual value}} =$$

Case example
Elcock v *Thomson* (1949)

This related to fire insurance. A house with an agreed value of £106 850 was partially damaged by fire. The actual value before the fire was £18 000 and after £12 600. The recovery assessment was:

$$\frac{5400 \times 106\ 850}{18\ 000} = £52\ 055$$

The agreed value here, when compared with the actual value, was suspiciously high.

Position of under insurance and subject to averaging

This is where property is insured for less than its current market value. In periods of high inflation a policyholder may not realize that he or she is underinsured until they make a claim. Here, if the insurers were liable up to the full value of the sum insured, even though a partial loss is involved, it may well mean that a person could pay a similar premium and take the risk that the property would be unlikely to be totally destroyed. In this situation most insurers have a 'subject to averaging' clause in the policy. This means that the insured is taken to be their own insurer for any amount by which they are underinsured.

The insured becomes own part insurer

If, therefore, the insured sum is less than the market value of the property insured, the insurers will only pay the proportion of the loss which the sum insured bears to the value of the property.

An example may make this more clear:

	£	
value of a house	50 000	$^3/_5$ (60 per cent)
house insured for	30 000	
fire damage to house	20 000	$^2/_5$ (40 per cent)
the insured recovers	12 000	

Position of overinsurance and overvaluation

Over insurance gains no additional benefit

Over insurance may arise where premiums are still paid at an original rate even though the original cost of the insured article has been subject to depreciation. For example if a car was bought new for £10 000 and premiums were paid at the appropriate rate but 10 months later the car was written off, the insurer would only pay the market rate at the time of the loss which even if the car was less than one year old would still be considerabley less than the purchase price. It is now popular for insurers to offer new for old policies so then in the event of a claim the insured can expect to receive a new article not the market value at time of loss. Obviously, the advantage of new for old is reflected in the premiums paid.

If deliberate overvaluation of property has occurred then this will equal fraud and the insurer will be able to avoid the policy. Some forms of property, such as antiques or classic cars, do not depreciate but generally appreciate in value. Obviously a policyholder would be wise to allow for a gradual increase in value to be reflected in the policy valuation. However, as future valuation of such articles, even by experts, is somewhat speculative then the insured must choose a reasonable future value and notify the insurer that the value stipulated is not the current one but one for the future (*Hoff Trading Co.* v *Union Ins Co. of Canton* (1928)).

Alternatively, if the policy is renewed annually then each year the policy valuation can be increased although if a professional valuation is required each year then this, on several articles, will be costly on the issued.

Contribution

If there is more than one insurer covering the same risk then the insured can recover the loss from whoever he or she chooses. However, the policy may contain a rateable proportion clause which will say that if property is insured with more than one insurer then each are to pay a proportion of the loss, e.g.:

Each insurer usually has to contribute to the loss

	£
Property worth	15 000
Insured with company A for	12 000
Insured with company B for	9000
Loss suffered	6000

Contribution		
	Company A will pay $^{12}/_{21}$	3429
	Company B will pay $^{9}/_{21}$	2571

Total paid	6000

Subrogation

This principle applies to all insurance contracts which are indemnifiable such as fire and motor insurance but not to life, illness or accident cover. Subrogation is the ability to metaphorically step into the shoes of the policyholder. This means that the insurer is allowed to exploit any contractual or tortious remedy held by the insured against a third party in order to recover all or some of the money which they will have paid out to settle the insured's claim.

Subrogation allows an insurer to take over the insured's rights

---

Case example
Phoenix Assurance v *Spooner* (1905)
S had premises insured with PA. The local authority issued a compulsory purchase notice but the purchase was completed before the premises were destroyed by fire. The local authority then completed the purchase but paid a lower sum because S had by then received some money from PA. PA used subrogated rights in order to sue the local authority for the full compulsory purchase value. Their claim failed as S had agreed with the local authority to take less. PA then successfully sued S for recovery of the sum they had earlier paid her.

At common law subrogated rights only became available when the insurer has fully indemnified the insured.

> **Case example**
> ### Scottish Union and National Insurance Co. v Davis (1970)
> D's car was damaged by the negligence of a third party. D, with SUNI permission, took it to a garage for repair. D was dissatisfied with the repair and after taking it back three times he finally took it to another garage. D then obtained payment directly from the third party and used it to pay the second garage. SUNI later paid the first garage even though D had not signed a satisfaction note. SUNI then sued D for the compensation paid to him by the third party. The right of subrogation would only arise when the insured had been fully indemnified and here the insurer had not done so.

To give insurers more flexibility most policies will contain a clause saying that subjugated rights can operate before indemnification has taken place. Also a policy may say that the insured undertakes on request from the insurer to assign over the right for the insurer to take action against third parties in their own name. Without this facility in the policy the insurer would have to take action indirectly in the name of the insured, who must allow their name to be used, but who of course will not have to personally pay any legal costs.

Review question

Maureen has the following insurance policies:

1 Her house is insured for £100 000 under a valued policy.
2 Her jewellery insured for £20 000 with an average clause in the policy.
3 A painting insured for £40 000 with Insurance Company A and for £60 000 with Insurance Company B.

What could Maureen claim, and against whom if the house burns down destroying both the jewellery and the painting if

- At the time of the fire the house was in fact worth £120 000?
- At the time of the fire the jewellery was worth £40 000 but gems were retrieved from the wreckage to the value of £10 000?
- At the time of the fire the painting was, in fact, worth £60 000?

Requirement of notice

Written notice of loss normally required

All policies require that the insured, to support a claim, provides written notice of the loss and with accident and burglary cover it is common that the policy will require notice to be given 'as soon as possible' or within a stipulated time period. If the insured fails to fulfil this condition precedent then the insurer can deny liability.

> ### Case example
> ### *Verelst's Administrative* v *Motor Union Ins Co.* (1925)
> A motor policy required notice of death by accident in writing 'as soon as possible'. Notice was in fact given one year after the loss was suffered. This was held still to be within the policy condition as the personal representative of the deceased only became aware of the existence of the policy just before notice was given.

> ### Case example
> ### *Adamson* v *Liverpool London and Globe Ins Co.* (1953)
> A policy covering the loss of cash excluded liability for losses not notified within 15 days of the loss. An employee over a two-year period had been stealing money from the employer. It was held that the insured was only able to claim losses within the last 14 days of notice being given, not for the whole period of the thefts.

Must the insured personally notify the insurer of a loss?

> ### Case example
> ### *Lickiss* v *Milestone Motor Policies* (1966)
> A motor policy required that 'the insured' gave notice of any accidents, summons or writs. The insured never himself gave notice of an accident but it was held that the insurers had received valid notice both from the police and from the injured third party.

Miscellaneous matters on accident and fire insurance

Accident insurance

A guaranteed sum becomes payable

Accident cover provides a fixed monetary sum on the occurrence of injury or death (Insurance Companies Act 1982, s.1, Part II). Consequently it is not indemnity insurance. An accident was defined in *Fenton* v *Thorley* (1903) as being:

> an unlooked for mishap or an untoward event which is not expected or designed.

Therefore, injury or death must be due to some unexpected or unintended event which is not natural.

> ### Case example
> ### *Marcel Beller Ltd* v *Hayden* (1978)
> MB, the employer, insured their employees against death caused by 'accidental bodily injury'. An employee, well over the drink-driving limit, crashed his car and was killed. The insurers said that it had not been caused by an accident as it was in fact a reasonably foreseeable result of so much drinking.
>   It was held that, as the deceased had not intended to kill himself it was still an accident. The word was to be given its ordinary meaning (as in *Fenton* v *Thorley*).

Fire insurance

Fire insurance is a contract of indemnity where the insurer undertakes in return for the premium to compensate the insured for loss or injury caused by fire up to a fixed maximum amount. A reminder that as fire insurance is one of indemnity there must be an insurable interest *both* when the policy is taken out and when the loss or damage occurs. Any legal or equitable interest will do, e.g. as an owner, tenant, mortgagee, trustee, etc. If no loss or damage is suffered then there is no entitlement to any money (*Castellain* v *Preston* (1883)). With respect to fire cover the following points may be made:

1 Fire means an actual ignition not just heating.
2 The cause of the ignition does not matter provided that it was not the deliberate act of the policyholder. Therefore, fire caused by lightening or explosion is still covered but fire caused by the arson of the policyholder is not. Whether cover applies to damage caused by the arson of third parties will be dependent on the wording of the policy.
3 Loss through fire includes damage caused by water or foam applied in an attempt to extinguish the fire.
4 At common law there is no legal obligation to use the money received from the insurer to restore the building destroyed or damaged; the insured is able to do what he or she likes with it.

However, statute law s. 83 Fire Prevention (Metropolis) Act 1774 says that anyone with an interest in the building subject to fire loss may require the insured to spend the insurance money on reinstatement of the building. Despite its title the Act applies throughout England and Wales.

Review questions

Laurel and Hardy are shop fitters working on redecorating Burn's antiquarian bookshop. Laurel inadvertently leaves a paint stripper running while he has a tea break. This oversight causes a number of very old bibles to suffer scorch marks. Smelling burning Hardy grabs what he believes is a bucket of water and throws it on a pile of books. The bucket contains not water but paint thinners which Laurel had been using to clean brushes. Suddenly, the whole shop is ablaze with the fire rapidly spreading to the floor above, which is occupied by Madam Rio a clairvoyant. On being summoned the fire brigade eventually control the fire but not until Burn's bookshop is gutted with only the bibles being saved. In addition the basement became flooded with the books stored there being soaked. Madam Rio's premises were extensively damaged and Madam Rio was reported as saying 'If I could have foreseen this I would never have renewed my lease.'

The proprietor of the bookshop, Mr James Burns, makes a claim on the fire policy against BetterSafe Insurance. It is Mr Burn's intention when the claim is settled to buy a farmhouse in the Dordogne.

From an insurance context discuss the above.

Motor insurance and third parties

The Road Traffic Act 1972 makes third-party insurance for death or injury compulsory. A user of a motor vehicle without third-party insurance is guilty of a criminal offence as is the owner of the vehicle (if different from the user). Third-party insurance relates to other road users, pedestrians and to passengers travelling in the insured's vehicle. There is also a requirement of third party property to be covered up to £250 000. If a third party has successfully sued the insured for compensation, but remains unsatisfied then the judgement debt can be enforced against the insurer (Road Traffic Act 1988 ss 151–153).

Alternatively, if a judgement is obtained against the insured who becomes insolvent before the judgement is satisfied then instead of suing as a creditor in the insurer's insolvency (bankruptcy or liquidation), the Third Parties (Rights Against Insurers) Act 1930, s. 1, will allow the injured parties to 'step in to the shoes' of the insured (this is subjugated rights) in order to claim an indemnity from the insurers. This is on the basis that the contract of motor insurance obligated the insurers to indemnify the insured against any claims made under the policy and the Act allows a third party, not withstanding privity of contract, to take over this contractual right.

Another possibility is that if the third party cannot recover damages from the insured for, say, negligence than the third party may take an action for breach of statutory duty.

Case example
Monk v *Warbey* (1935)

W lent his car to a friend. The friend was not covered by insurance when the car crashed injuring M. W's motor policy was restricted to cover only when he was driving. However, M obtained damages through W's breach of the statutory duty to have insurance to cover his friend's driving of the car.

Should any exclusion clause in the policy try to exclude an insurer's liability to indemnify the insured because of age, physical or mental disability, condition of the vehicle, or the number of passengers covered then such an exclusion will be void as far as any third-party claim which may be made. However, restrictions on use of the vehicle, e.g. social and domestic use only, will prevent a third party claiming for injury caused while the car was being used on business.

The Motor Insurers Bureau (MIB) agreed in 1946 that where a driver is not covered by compulsory motor insurance (because insurance was not taken out) that they would meet the claims of unsatisfied third parties. The present MIB agreement, Compensation of Victims of Uninsured Drivers, requires that the third party informs the MIB within seven days of starting legal proceedings against the driver and that subsequently a judgement against the driver (this will include legal costs) is obtained. Subject to certain conditions the MIB will also compensate for third-party property damage.

The MIB undertake to cover an insurance deficiency

Another MIB agreement, Compensation of Victims of Untraced Drivers, will enable hit-and-run victims to claim compensation. Anyone wanting to claim under this agreement must give written notification to the MIB within three years of the event causing the injury or death.

With respect to loss of motor vehicles where a car is stolen and never recovered then the insurers under a comprehensive policy will clearly have to compensate the insured; but where the car is traced but recovery is not possible, perhaps because of a sale by a factor under the Sale of Goods Act 1979, then compensation will still be made. Loss is defined as being theft of the car or its destruction. In *Eisinger* v *General Accident* (1955) a car owner was the victim of a confidence trick. He parted with possession of his car in return for a cheque. The cheque was dishonoured. What he had lost was not the car but the proceeds of its sale.

Insurance intermediaries

These are the various persons who arrange the insurance contract for clients. They fall into the following types:

(a)   a *broker*

(b)   a *Lloyd's approved broker* – only these are able to arrange cover in the Lloyd's insurance market

(c)   an *occasional broker*, such as solicitors

Intermediaries tend to specialize

(d)   a non-Broker Independent Intermediary. Under s. 22 Insurance Brokers (Registration) Act 1977 you cannot call yourself a broker unless you have satisfied a stipulated minimum educational or work experience qualification. However, the Act can be got around by calling yourself a consultant, advisor or specialist but not incorporating the team broker.

(e)   an *agent attached to a particular insurer*. These are often called a *commissioning agent* who are really salespeople. They are independent but enact business for just one company.

(f)   a *new business inspector*. They are employed by an insurance company and are not true intermediaries as they are not agents but they do arrange insurance for the client. The new business inspector has higher status than the commissioning agent.

Whose agent is the intermediary?

In the list given above (e) and (f) are normally the agent of the insurer, whereas (a), (b), (c) and (d) are normally the agents of the insured. This is in spite of their apparent closeness to insurance companies, e.g. receiving information from the company and obtaining from them commission for business introduced. However, a defining factor is that they do not themselves actually accept or reject the proposals for insurance.

Insurance agents and proposal forms

Whose agent is of crucial importance

The 'whose agent' argument is of considerable importance in respect to proposal forms containing incorrect information. If the proposal was completed by the agent, who was the agent of the insured, e.g. by a broker, then the mistake is the insured's responsibility. The insurer will be able to refuse liability on any claim and the insured will be left to possibly claim against the agent for professional negligence. But if the mistake is made by the agent of the insurer, say a canvassing agent (usually a freelance but acting for the insurer) than the insurer will not be able to deny liability on a claim.

Case example
Bawden v *London, Edinburgh & Glasgow Assoc.* (1892)

A personal accident policy was taken out by a one-eyed illiterate man. The proposal form included the question, 'Has the applicant any physical infirmities?' The insurer's agent looked the proposer in the eye, saw the disability, but still wrote down no and then got the proposer to sign the form. The insured later lost his other eye in an accident and made a claim under the policy for compensation.

The agent's knowledge was deemed to be the knowledge of the insurance company. The insured claim succeeded. Bawden's case has been distinguished in later cases.

Case example
Bigger v Rock Life Assurance Co. (1902)

A personal accident policy had been taken out by a publican who later lost an eye when a bottle exploded in his pub. A false answer had been put on the proposal form by the insurer's agent and the insured had then signed the form.

It was held that the insured had a duty to read the answers recorded before signing the form. Therefore the insurers need not honour the claim.

Case example
Newsholme Bros v Road Transport and General Insurance Co. (1929)

In respect to a proposal for motor cover the insured gave the correct oral answer but the insurer's agent wrote down the wrong answer.

The Court of Appeal held that the mistake was the proposer's responsibility and the insurers were allowed to turn down the insured's claim.

In Newsholme's case Scrutton LJ gave as the *ratio decidendi*:

1 If the proposer asks the agent to fill in the proposal form for them, then in doing so they become the agent of the proposer.
2 When the proposer signs the proposal form they are deemed to have read its content.

Halsbury's Laws of England (3rd edn, vol. 22, p. 204) state:

In filling in the answers in a proposal form an insurance agent, except in the case of industrial assurance, is normally regarded as the agent for the proposer, at the request, express or implied, of the latter.

Scrutton LJ also said that where an insurance broker fills up a proposal form on behalf of an insured of full capacity then the insured should not be allowed to hide behind the broker. The courts are only prepared to depart from the general rules where there have been unusual circumstances.

Case example
Store v Reliance Mutual Insurance Society (1972)

A fire and theft policy on a flat lapsed. A new business inspector called on S's wife and persuaded her to have a new policy. A question on the proposal form asked about previous claims – the inspector wrote down none. This was incorrect for there had been a previous fire claim. S's wife signed the completed form. After the insurance had begun a theft occurred. Should the insurer pay the claim or not?

It was held that the insurer had to pay. Firstly, the agent was a high status one who had represented to the insured wife that the form had been completed correctly and, secondly, she was a person of 'low intelligence'.

Insurance agents and claims

If the agent is asked to help negotiate a settlement then can they be the agent of both parties? At one time it was felt that this could be the position but case law no longer supports this view. On claims the agent cannot serve two masters.

Case example:
North and South Trust v *Berkeley* (1971)

The question asked was whether the insured had the right to look at a claims report drawn up by the broker who had arranged insurance cover on carriage of goods by sea. If the broker was the agent of the insurer then confidentiality would mean that the insured could not see it but if the broker was the insured agent's then the insured would have every right to see it.

It was held that the broker was in breach of his duties. As the agent of the insured he had to make the report available to his principal – the insured.

The scope of an insurance agent's authority

Implied authority

This is dependent on circumstances. Where, for example, the insurer gives a cover note to the agent this is an implied authority that the agent has authority to give temporary cover to the insured.

Case example
Murfitt v *Royal Insurance* (1922)

The RI allowed an agent to give oral cover on its behalf for a period of two years. The agent subsequently gave fire insurance cover on an orchard bordering onto a railway line, a spark from an engine led to a fire in the orchard.

It was held that the insurance company were bound by the cover arranged by the agent as he had their implied authority.

This *apparent authority* is based on the principal (the insurer) holding out the agent as having the necessary authority. The doctrine may mean that an insurer is liable for a policy issued by his agent where the insurer fails to notify the insured that the agency has ended (*Willis Faber* v *Joyce* (1911)).

The agent's misrepresentation

Case example
Refuge Assurance v *Kettlewell* (1909)

A life policyholder wanted to give it up but the insurer's agent falsely stated that if the premiums were kept up for a certain period then the holder would get a free policy from the insurer.

It was held that the insurers were responsible for the agent's misrepresentation and had to return the premiums paid after she had requested to end the policy.

But if the insured knows by a contractual clause in the policy that there is some limit to the agent's authority then the principal will not be liable beyond this limit.

Case example
***Horncastle* v *Equitable Life* (1906)**

A life policy on being taken out was worth £5000 but as it was of an endowment type it increased in value annually. A clause in the policy said that terms could be modified by certain people but the agent was not one of those given. The agent said that the policy after 15 years would be worth £7300. In fact after 15 years it was worth only £6100.

It was held that the insurer was not bound by the agent's promise.

Generally, if the insurer's agent informs the insurer over the interpretation of the policy then, should the interpretation be wrong, there will be no misrepresentation as this will be regarded as being a representation of law not fact.

Disclosure of material facts to the insurance agent

Is the knowledge held by the agent also 'held' by the insurer (principal)? This is very important in relation to non-disclosure of a material fact. Just because an agent has material knowledge will not automatically mean that his principal is also deemed to have it as well, for in insurance law this imputed or constructive knowledge principle does not always apply. Therefore, it depends on the circumstances what knowledge will be imputed.

Case example
***Agrey* v *British Legal & Provident* (1926)**

A deep-sea fisherman took out a life policy but he failed to directly inform the insurer that he was a member of the Royal Navy Volunteer Reserve (RNVR) and could in a national emergency be called up for active military service. Instead he told the insurer's agent orally that he was an RNVR.

It was held that the insurer's agent's knowledge was imputed to the insurer; therefore they could not turn down a claim on the grounds of non-disclosure.

Duties of an insurance agent

The duty to obey instructions

An agent must attempt to carry out his client's (principal's) instructions provided they are lawful and do not prejudice professional ethics. Should the agent not be able to carry out his instructions, perhaps the risk cannot be covered for the premium the client is prepared to pay, then the agent should ask the client for further instructions. However, the agent ought to ensure that the client is not left insured (*Rock, Russell* v *Bray Gibb* (1920)).

An agent's duties are demanding

The duty of care

An agent must act with due care in relation to his principal, e.g. show a reasonably competent professional standard. A failure to do so will incur liability in negligence, breach of contract or breach of statute (Sale of Goods and Services Act 1982). In *McNealy* v *Pennine Insurance Co.* (1978) it was said that where the broker acts for the insured, if they are in breach of the duty of care then the measure of damages is the amount of the claim settlement if they had in fact been able to claim successfully from the insurer.

> ### Case example
> ### *Dunbar (Alfred James) v A & B Painters and Economic Insurance Co. Ltd and Whitehouse & Co.* (1986)
>
> A & B P were decorators and had taken out employer's liability insurance for personal injuries to employees. Their usual insurer was X Ltd but when X Ltd considerably increased the premium their broker W placed the cover with E Ltd, stating on the proposal form that A & B P had never been asked for an increase in premiums. The policy E Ltd issued only provided cover for injuries sustained below 40 feet in height. AJD was injured when he fell from a height a little over 40 feet. A & B P agreed damages with AJD and then sought an indemnity from E Ltd, or failing this, an indemnity from W.
>
> The Court of Appeal held that E Ltd could repudiate liability for material non-disclosure of the previous increase in premium. The broker W would be liable as they were the instigator of the non-disclosure. On the evidence E Ltd would most probably have not repudiated the claim if the '40-feet point' had been the only ground available to them.

Should an insurance agent say that even if a policy had been arranged the insurer would not have been liable to honour it and therefore the agent also ought to escape liability as well, then the position seems to be that the courts will look at the likely attitude of the insurer to the claim and not whether the insurer would have been legally liable to pay out on it.

> ### Case example
> ### *Fraser v Furman (Productions) Ltd, Miller Smith & Partners* (1967)
>
> A broker failed to arrange properly an employees' liability policy. The broker argued that no claim would have been paid by the insurer as the insured would have been in breach of a policy condition and therefore could not legally force the insurer to pay out.
>
> In the circumstances it was held that, had the policy been arranged properly, then the insurer would have paid the claim. The broker was therefore liable in damages to the insured.

The duty of care extends beyond disclosure of material facts on proposal forms. For example a broker has a duty to advise the insured about the adverse financial position of the insurer.

> ### Case example
> ### *Osman v Moss* (1970)
>
> A motor insurer was in financial difficulty and this knowledge was generally known in the insurance market. A broker arranging a policy for a client with the financially weak insurer wrote to the client saying that he ought to choose another insurer but did not actually say why. The client insisted on having a policy with the weak insurer who later went into liquidation leaving the client uninsured.
>
> It was held that the client should have been specifically warned of the insurer's financial difficulties.

In *Osman v Moss* (1970) the insured was Turkish with limited English. The case may be confined to its facts and not establish a general principle.

What an insurance agent ought to be careful of is straying outside their area of expertise. Where the broker specializes in life assurance but gives advice on, say, product liability cover then they may be liable unless they inform the client that they are a non-specialist in the matter and await the client's instructions to proceed (*Saginson Bros* v *Keith Moulton & Co.* (1943)).

The duty of good faith

Part of this duty is not to allow any conflict of interest to arise. This is a general rule of agency law but it is possible for an insurance agent, when seeking appropriate cover for a client, to be influenced by the rate of commission paid by an insurer. It is not the practice for brokers to disclose to clients what commissions they receive from insurers.

Lloyd's brokers

These are approved by Lloyd's and insurance cannot be arranged at Lloyd's other than through a Lloyd's broker.

Normally a Lloyd's broker will be the agent of the insured when he or she effects the policy, but becomes the agent of the underwriter as to the premium (*Equitable Life* v *General Accident* (1904)). This liability is due to the Lloyd's Policy Signing Office system of payment to the underwriter even if the broker has not themselves been paid. Should a Lloyd's broker have to personally pay a premium to the underwriter then he or she can recover from the insured.

Chapter summary

- The relationship between the parties (insured and insurer) is contractual with the proposal form being the basic contractual document.
- All terms in the proposal form are to be treated as being warranties but in the insurance context warranties equal conditions.
- Both parties have a contractual obligation to disclose all material facts. For the insurer this means information that will influence his or her judgement as to whether to accept the risk and if so at what premium; should the disclosure obligation be broken then the innocent party can avoid the policy.
- In order to distinguish an insurance contract from a mere wager it is necessary that the person taking out insurance has a monetary interest in the subject matter of the insurance; this interest is termed an insurable interest – in its absence the policy is void.
- A causational requirement known as the proximity rule demands that for a claim to succeed the loss must fall within the cover given and not into an excluded risk.
- Most insurance policies are ones of indemnity meaning that a policyholder can only claim compensation for a loss suffered, but if the policy has a subject to averaging clause, or there is underinsurance, then the insured will only recover a proportion of the loss.
- Should there be more than one insurer for the same risk then if a claim is made against one insurer that insurer can ask other insurers to contribute to the claim settlement.
- Subrogated rights will enable an insurer to take over the legal rights of the insured in order to pursue a claim against a third party.

Scotland and Northern Ireland

The insurance principles discussed in this chapter apply equally to Scotland and Northern Ireland as they do to England and Wales. However, insurers domiciled in Scotland or Northern Ireland will have to be sued in their country of domicility and not the English High Court (*Watkins* v *Scottish Imperial Insurance Co.* (1889)). This requirement can be overridden where the insurer expressly agrees to accept, through an English agent, delivery of legal proceedings documents in England or, alternatively, the insurers conduct will preclude them from denying that valid service of proceedings had taken place (*Moloney* v *Tullock* (1835)). The standard practice is for the insurance policy to contain a clause saying that legal documents will be accepted in England. English insurers will similarly have clauses in their policies saying that legal documents will be accepted in Scotland or Northern Ireland.

Case study exercise

1 Enrico Forzati submits a proposal form for building cover in respect of his house to Northern Insurance. The proposal is accepted and a policy is issued. Several months later the house is damaged when an aircraft, attempting to perform an unauthorized stunt at an air display, crashes onto it. When Enrico makes a claim on the policy the insurer refuses to meet it alleging that Enrico had failed to inform them that he had

(i)   been born in Sicily, Italy where he had spent most of his life, and
(ii) that his house was directly below the flight path a few miles from an airfield.

Discuss whether or not Northern Insurance is legally justified in refusing Enrico's claim.

2 Enrico Forzati's house was valued at £75 000. He had insured it for £50 000 with Northern Insurance and £25 000 with Eastern Insurance for the same cover. The house incurs damage estimated at £10 000. Enrico claims against Northern Insurance for an indemnity.

Explain the rights Northern Insurance will have.

Discussion questions

1 (a) In what way may it be said that the parties to an insurance contract do not negotiate as equals?
   (b) How has the law developed to overcome any unfairness in (a) above?
   (c) What is the legal significance of a proposal form and how would you describe its terms?
2 Discuss the various clauses within an insurance policy that may alter the normal rules of indemnity.
3 Why may the personal representatives of a person who has committed a criminal act not receive payment under the terms of a life assurance policy?

Further reading

Modern Insurance Law (3rd edn), Birds (1993), Sweet & Maxwell.
An excellent introduction to the subject. Recommended.
General Principles of Insurance Law (6th edn), Hardy Ivany (1993), Butterworths.
The Law of Insurance Contracts (2nd edn), Clarke (1994), LLP Ltd.

12 Alternative dispute resolution

Introduction

Alternative dispute resolution (ADR) is methods which attempt to resolve disputes without having to litigate in a court of law. While ADR has been available for many years, compared to other common-law countries (such as the United States, Canada, Australia), Britain has not fully embraced the opportunities that ADR claim to offer. All methods of ADR are based on the mutual consent of the parties in dispute to having it resolved without the assistance of a court of law, together with a willingness to abide by the settlement reached. The belief is that ADR is:

> quicker, cheaper and more user friendly than the courts. It gives people an involvement in the process of resolving their disputes that is not possible in a public formal adversial justice system perceived to be dominated by the abstruse procedures and recondite language of the law. It offers choice: choice of method, of procedure, of cost, of representation, of location.
>
> Lord Mackay. (The Hamlyn Lectures: The Administration of Justice, 1994).

The motivation to seek ADR is largely dissatisfaction with traditional court-based litigation. In May 1995 a survey carried out by the BBC's *Law in Action* programme in conjunction with the National Consumer Council, found that 75 per cent of those questioned thought that the present civil court dispute system was too slow, too complex, too easy to manipulate and too daunting. Indeed only 13 per cent reported that the court system was easy to understand (therefore 77 per cent seemingly found it difficult to comprehend), with 25 per cent saying that they thought courts were well run and that they usually get it right (again seemingly 75 per cent would disagree). Significantly for ADR, in respect of court services, 50 per cent of those questioned expressed the view that they would prefer to 'sit around a table with an independent expert who would assist them to reach an agreement between themselves'. This can be compared to just 8 per cent who stated a preference for a 'full court trial'. This survey evidence confirms an increasing willingness among individuals and probably businesses to submit their disputes to ADR. However, a major problem it must be conceded with ADR is in judging its effectiveness. Studies frequently claim that ADR schemes are highly successful; for example, 80 per cent of mediation cases have been reported to have been successfully settled, but what studies do not reveal is whether or not those disputes would have actually gone on to trial if mediation had not been available.

Objectives

This chapter is designed to provide an overview of the various methods which are being developed to settle commercial disputes in a more amicable way than court-based litigation. The advantages of ADR are that it is claimed to be particularly beneficial to business and these advantages will be outlined.

Key concepts

- Several practical advantages make ADR attractive
- Codes of Practice are encouraged by a quasi-governmental body
- Ombudsmen are industry sponsored
- Mediation and conciliation use the offices of a third party to help broker a settlement
- Mini-trials by shadowing a full trial can give each party their day in 'court' but without the time and expense that a full court hearing would involve.

Litigation

Pertinent questions to ask before commencing litigation

Civil litigation is the most well-known method of resolving disputes but it may be questioned as to whether it is the most effective. It is costly, time-consuming and worrying. Should litigation be considered the following questions ought to be asked:

1. Have I got a good arguable case in law?
2. Am I able to establish my case on a balance of probabilities? (e.g. am I able to assemble the required evidence and witnesses?)
3. Has the other party any defences or counterclaims which may be used?
4. If my action is successful will the other party be able to meet a damage award in my favour as well as being able to pay my legal costs?
5. Do I wish to have future business relations with the other party?

Despite criticisms many argue that the adversarial system adopted by the court is the best way of obtaining the truth. Yet in practice the majority of commercial disputes do not go to court. An out-of-court settlement may be reached by negotiation and compromise. Should this prove impossible then the parties may look to an arbitrator rather than risk the uncertainty of a legal action in the High Court. Therefore, it is highly likely that in the future the role of the legally trained specialist (lawyer) will be lessened by the development of non-adversarial procedures and the involvement of non-lawyers who are able to broker a settlement between parties in dispute.

This impetus is already discernable in private law where, due to ever-increasing costs, legal-aid to litigate is to be displaced by more informal and cheaper ways of settling disputes. Indeed The Lord Chancellor has said that this process must be given priority.

> to move away from lawyers as the first port of call for settling a legal dispute. People would be directed to mediators ... arbitrators and advice workers in law centres and citizens advice bureaux.
>
> Lord Mackay, *The Times*, 4 January 1995

Mirroring the private law industry and commerce, disillusioned with litigation, is moving towards ADR methods which are approved by the CBI and many trade associations. It is noted that the Commercial Court of the High Court has started to encourage parties to consider ADR in cases which come before it.

The Centre for Dispute Resolution

An independent body to promote ADR

In Britain the Centre for Dispute Resolution (CEDR) was established with support from the Confederation of British Industry in 1990. It seeks to promote mediation and other cost-effective approaches to dispute resolution. The CEDR is an independent non-profit making body sponsored by over 250 major companies (e.g. BAA plc, Barclays Bank plc, Eastern Electricity plc), and professional advisors (e.g. Arthur Anderson, the Institute of Directors, the Royal Institution of Chartered Surveyors), which makes it the leading business mediation service in Europe. During its first 18 months the CEDR advised in over £500 million of disputes. In 1995 mediation ranged from a humble boundary dispute between two neighbours, which was resolved within a day, to a US $38 million machinery suppliers contract dispute between a Scandinavian trader and an Asian wood pulp processing company, resolved in three days.

Advantages of ADR

Common between all forms of ADR are a number of claimed practical advantages. These are:

Confidentiality

No adverse publicity results from using ADR. Processes and procedures used ensure privacy with no unwanted parties, such as the media or business competitors, being present. Should one party, on making a settlement, create a precedent, then confidentiality ought to mean that other claimants do not hear of it and so cannot demand similar treatment. With litigation the courts of justice are open to the public; also cases may be reported in the law report or receive media coverage if considered particularly newsworthy.

Bad publicity may be avoided

Choice of the facilitator

The parties are able to select the person (mediator, conciliator) they want. This may be someone they both trust and respect, possibly a person who is also knowledgeable in the matter being disputed. In court-based litigation the parties have to accept whoever is assigned to judge the case.

The parties choose the facilitator

Opportunity to continue the business relationship

The flexibility of ADR enables the parties to come up with the settlement that best fits their situation. The solution to their dispute can be a commercial one as apposed to being legalistic.

The facilitor assisting the parties will be concentrating on finding common ground and ideally there will be a win–win outcome in that both parties can claim to have won something. Should this be the position then each party to the ADR can then sell the settlement more easily to their colleagues.

A win–win outcome is looked for

No one has lost or been humiliated, with litigation there is either a legal victory or defeat. Such a win–loose result is harmful to any future business relationship.

Flexibility

The parties are free to make the procedures that best suit themselves and these can be changed, by mutual agreement, at any time. The ADR process can be fast-tracked or taken more leisurely (most parties do in fact strive for a quick result). Flexibility is also present in relation to remedies. If the parties anticipate having a continuing business relationship then remedies that will assist this may be created. Court-based remedies being more formal lack creativity. Finally with flexibility the parties themselves are always in control of the process whereas with litigation court procedures may control them and result in a feeling that they are too reliant on lawyers to negotiate for them a way through a legal labyrinth.

Cost effectiveness

All ADR schemes should be cheaper than having a dispute resolved through the courts although this may not always apply to arbitration. Not only are high legal costs avoided but the earlier a settlement is reached the greater will be the saving of managerial time. Indeed the parties, within reason, can timetable ADR meetings to suit their own available time knowing that they will not be kept waiting for hours, or days, to state their case or give evidence. Should ADR prove ineffective then all is not wasted as the preparation for ADR will save time in preparing for trial. In litigation key managers may be tied up in assisting with case preparation, or in the trial itself they may have to make themselves available for examination, cross-examination and possible recall over a number of days or weeks.

The types of ADR

Over the years a number of ADR schemes have evolved.

Codes of practice

The Director General of the Office of Fair Trading has a duty to encourage trade associations to promote voluntary codes of practice. These codes include ADR methods of arbitration and/or conciliation in order to resolve disputes with consumers. Examples of trade associations who operate codes of practice include: The Association of British Travel Agents (ABTA) for package holidays; The Motor Agents Association, Scottish Motor Trade Association for motor importers and retailers; Mail Order Traders Association for mail-order trading by agents and the National Association of Funeral Directors for funerals.

Ombudsmen

Like codes of practice this is a business-to-public method of dispute resolution. The aim of ombudsmen is to give quick and inexpensive justice to the weak (individuals) against the strong (large corporations). To achieve this aim legalistic procedures are dispensed with. Ombudsmen exist in a variety of fields e.g. local government, governmental bodies, services, banking, insurance, pensions and building societies.

As an example the insurance ombudsman considered, in 1995, 6438 complaints made by policyholders. In 59 per cent the insurer's decision was upheld while in 35 per cent their decision was revised in favour of policyholders (in the 6 per cent remainder the complaint was withdrawn before the ombudsman made an adjuration). Compensation payments totalled £10 million with the highest award being £177 000 and the lowest £1.41p. In one instance a household insurance policyholder had gone out for the evening and in her absence her house was burgled. The burglars had gained entry through an unlocked ground-floor window. The insurers rejected the claim on the grounds that a policy condition had required her to operate the window locks. However, the police, glazier and insurance loss adjuster all agreed that even if the unlocked window had been locked, it would still not have prevented the burglars gaining entry. The ombudsman accordingly ordered that the claim be paid.

An association of United Kingdom ombudsmen has drawn up operating standards which should be met by all recognized ombudsmen. The association is also anxious that public awareness and acceptance of their role be increased.

Common among ombudsmen is that a finding is normally binding on the organization involved in the adjucation but a complainant does not have to forgo any legal rights so they may, if dissatisfied with the finding, take their dispute through the courts. The weakness of ombudsmen schemes is that they are based on self-regulation and therefore are only seemingly effective where all those in a particular industry belong to and fully support the scheme.

For more detail of a commercial ombudsman scheme see the chapter on banking law where the bank ombudsman scheme is covered.

Mediation

Mediation is the use of a third party to help those in conflict reach an agreement which, unaided, they may never do, or may only do much later in the conflict. This form of ADR originates in industrial relations. Some contracts will have a mediation clause in them saying that in the event of a dispute arising the parties will initially attempt to resolve it through mediation. This will mean that mediation must be tried before a court action can be taken. However, a mediator's suggestions can be rejected so as to open up entry to the courts. Mediators may be nominated by the parties or else a trade association, professional body or local chamber of commerce can be approached for assistance.

The concept of mediation is to assist people to talk to each other in a rational and problem-solving way, to clear up misunderstandings and to clarify issues so as to help negotiations by bringing realism and objectivity to a dispute. Above all the process aims to put back in the hands of the parties responsibility for the outcome of their dispute. The mediator is a facilitator who assists the parties, without prejudice to themselves, to reach their own agreement by informally chairing structured discussions, suggesting possible alternative settlements which, ideally, will bridge the difference between the parties. Lawyers need not be directly involved but can be available to each party for advice. A recent situation which has highlighted mediation is the appointment, under French law, of two mediators in January 1996 to assist negotiations between the £8 billion debt burdened Eurotunnel plc and its creditor bankers. The mediators initially will talk informerly to the company, its shareholders and creditors about finding a mutually satisfactory solution to its financial problems.

A mediator gets the parties to talk constructively to each other

Mediation is attractive in that the parties' preferences and objectives in aiming at a solution are as important as their strict legal rights. What a mediator will avoid is imposing formal outside rules. A judge or arbitrator makes a decision which closes the contest in litigation or arbitration, in a successful mediation the parties themselves agree on the final outcome. Mediation, therefore, leads to a negotiated solution. The fact that the parties have chosen to use it means that they are well on their way to settling their dispute informally. To achieve this the parties, in liaison with the mediator, make their own rules and procedure. Mediation may be divided into two types. First, *evaluative mediation*, where the mediator is allowed to express their personal opinion about the positions taken by the two parties; and second, *facilitative mediation*, where they are prohibited from making personal comment.

With mediation the parties remain in control

Usually the mediator will conduct an open meeting with both parties present. This will establish any common ground and enable differences to be flagged up. The mediator will then have a number of separate meetings with each party in order to find out what each party is willing to accept and thus how far they are prepared to compromise. This may be termed 'shuttle mediation' and it is not necessary that the parties be brought together at the same place or time. When the mediator believes that he or she has sufficiently prepared the way then a series of joint meetings will be arranged.

Should an impasse be reached then the mediator may once more revert to separate meetings until the blockage has been dispelled before continuing with joint meetings. Clearly this process can be slow and one which calls for considerable tact and patience on the mediator's part. Finally, the mediator will announce what he or she understands the outcome to be such as, for example, will allow a contract to be renegotiated on certain new terms, and then ask both parties to confirm their agreement to it by signing it in his or her presence. This agreement will then become binding on the parties so that if it is broken by one of the parties then the other party, if suffering a loss through the breach, can take legal action. Also once the mediation agreement is signed it will mean that litigation over the original dispute is no longer possible. Throughout the process the mediator must scrupulously refrain from giving any indication that they find any fault or apportion any blame to either of the parties. To do so would be unprofessional and destroy any trust that the parties may have in them.

Little to lose
with mediation

As with all ADR methods the advantages of mediation are claimed to be: speed (but not always because shuttle mediation may take some time), cost, privacy and that it may probably preserve commercial relationships. Unless litigation or arbitration are obviously attractive because, for instance, the amount in dispute is extremely large, or a central corporate interest is involved, or one party will materially benefit from delay, then the parties have little to loose in trying mediation. If it does not work then they can walk away and take legal action or go to arbitration. Indeed as mediation is carried out without prejudice to the parties they are free to litigate while mediating. If the mediation is successful then the litigation can be stopped. A success rate of 95 per cent for cases referred to mediation has been claimed.

Studies indicate that most parties would prefer to settle without litigation because of the perceived 'pay back' of there being far less delay, less frustration and aggravation, avoidance of high costs, preservation of business relationships, and far less waste of valuable time for executives.

An interesting overseas mediation development is that adopted by the Supreme and County Courts of Victoria (Australia) which investigated pre-trial conferences making them compulsory for a range of cases. These conferences consist of a court appointed mediator who informally discusses with the parties the likelihood of success and the possible forms of settlement. Should the pre-trial conferences prove unsuccessful then the parties are free to pursue a legal action.

The Australian Institute of Judicial Administration examined the effectiveness of the Victorian pre-trial conference scheme and found that of the cases studied 36 per cent were settled at the pre-trial conference stage, a further 17 per cent settled between the conference and the trial date, with 35 per cent being settled at the court room door, while the remaining 12 per cent went for trial. So far pre-trial conference mediation has not been tried in Britain.

Mini-trials

Somewhat similar in concept to the pre-trial conference is the recent development in Britain of mini-trials derived from the United States. A mini-trial is a method of resolving commercial disputes using techniques of negotiation, mediation and arbitration. The features of a mini-trial are:

1 The parties agree to a mini-trial.
2 The parties exchange documents.
3 A neutral adviser is selected by the parties.
4 At the mini-trial lawyers make shortened presentations of their case aiming to be concise rather than comprehensive.
5 Settlement discussions take place with the neutral adviser's help, if there is still no satisfactory result the parties are free to continue with other forms of dispute resolution usually litigation. However, they may ask the neutral adviser for their opinion on what a judicial outcome would likely be and be guided by that.

New to Britain but established the USA

It may be noted that some commercial judges currently exercise a discretionary role of having a pre-trial review (or a review at some other appropriate stage), informing the parties of possible outcomes if the trial proceeds and that a sensible settlement may be made with consequent savings in time and money. Such a pre-trial review sees the judge acting as a mediator.

Conciliation

Here a third party, the conciliator, assists the parties in dispute to reach an agreement. It is a process of bringing the parties together and encouraging them to talk through their problem. The conciliator adopts the role of an impartial broker who usually, but not always, operates under a framework imposed from the outside. Conciliation is similar to mediation and frequently the two terms are interchanged.

A conciliator is an impartial broker

One variation of conciliation is to combine it with arbitration so that under a contract there will be, on a dispute arising, an obligation to refer the matter to conciliation and if an amicable settlement cannot be reached within an agreed time period to then refer it to arbitration.

Which is the best form of ADR for commercial disputes?

Given the diversity and complexity of commercial activity it is inevitable that disputes will arise but it is often difficult to decide which of the above methods of resolving a commercial dispute would be most appropriate. Each dispute is to a certain extent unique so that no one method is of universal application. One important factor, particularly important in commercial dispute is the relationship of the parties. Should they intend to continue doing business with each other the mediation and/or the mini-trial may enhance the prospect of preserving the relationship.

Scotland and Northern Ireland

No additional comments are made.

Chapter summary

- Many businesses have expressed dissatisfaction with the adverse nature of litigation which results in a win–lose (or even lose–lose) outcome.
- ADR is seen to offer a procedure whereby a dispute is superseded by a new and binding legal agreement (unless the parties do not want it to be binding) which disregards the question of who was right and who was wrong in law. The focus of attention is on which is the best settlement to satisfy the commercial interests of the parties.
- Practitioners of ADR must be impartial, show a high measure of integrity and have a range of people-related skills. They must avoid the temptation to act as a judge by, for example, taking it upon themselves to decide matters of fact or law. Their primary function is to encourage compromise so as to achieve a mutually satisfactory settlement.
- Supporters of ADR claim that it has several advantages over litigation. The advantages are said to be confidentiality, freedom to choose the ADR facilitator, a far greater opportunity to preserve a lasting business relationship, flexibility, effectiveness, and a saving in costs.
- A range of ADR methods are available. These are: Codes of Practice, Ombudsmen Schemes, Mediation, Mini-trials, Conciliation.

Case study exercise

Sheaf & Co. is a partnership which specializes in subcontracting work in the housing construction sector. It is fairly common for a subcontractor in this sector to tender below cost, then on getting the contract to subsequently re-negotiate it. This enables a subcontractor to eventually make a profit.

Sheaf & Co. put in three tenders with Owen plc. Two tenders were accepted, but the third Sheaf & Co. heard is unlikely to be successful. Owen plc is the largest main contractor in the sector and their managing director, Mr Horace Hardman, is the president of the Housing Constructors' Association. Sheaf & Co. have recently started on the two new contracts awarded by Owen plc.

Sheaf & Co. are owed by Owen plc £28 000 on various contracts and are also 'clocking up' £5000 a week on the two contracts recently started. Sheaf & Co. are being pressed by their banks to reduce their overdraft. Within the construction industry it is felt that a house building recession may occur within the next half year. Owen plc are known as a company who leaves it as late as possible to pay subcontractors.

Student task

Offer advice to Sheaf & Co. as to how they may overcome their difficulty.

Discussion questions

1 The alternatives to litigation are much more successful at resolving disputes. Discuss the validity of this statement.
2 Alternative Dispute Resolution excludes both ordinary negotiation where there is no third-party intervention and arbitration, where a third party decides the dispute. Discuss.

Further reading

ADR: A lawyer's guide to mediation and other forms of dispute resolution, A. H. Bevran (1992), Sweet & Maxwell.
This is a helpful guide to mediation.
Resolving Disputes Without Going to Court, A. F. Acland (1995), Random House.
An excellent practical approach to the subject.
ADR: Principals and Practice, H. J. Brown & A. L. Marriott (1993), Sweet & Maxwell.

13 Arbitration

Introduction

When a dispute arises during the progress of a contract it is not necessary that it should automatically go before a court of law for resolution. The parties involved may agree to submit their differences to a third party in whom they have confidence and whose decision they will accept and enforce. To resolve a dispute in this manner, without recourse to the courts, is the essence of arbitration. The impartial third party, to whom both sides of the dispute will put their side of the dispute, is the arbitrator who will consider the evidence and by applying ordinary rules of law make a decision which will be binding and enforceable in the courts. A major feature of arbitration is that a dispute can only be referred to arbitration with the consent of both parties. Indeed commercial contracts often contain clauses where the parties agree in advance to refer any dispute arising from the contract to arbitration.

When examining commercial arbitration particular note should be taken that the principles of law and statutory provisions relating to it do not apply to industrial relations arbitration nor do they apply to consumer arbitration under the small claim procedure of the county court. Similarly not covered is voluntary arbitration of trading associations when dealing with consumers under codes of practice that recommend arbitration to resolve disputes. While certain terms may be used in all these arbitrations, the law and procedures of commercial arbitration are quite different.

The first arbitration statute was the Arbitration Act 1697. The current United Kingdom legislation is the Arbitration Acts of 1950 (the principal act) and 1979. These cover such matters as arbitration agreements, awards, costs and enforcement. The Arbitration Act 1975 was enacted to give effect to the New York Convention which relates to the recognition and enforcement of foreign arbitration awards. As for arbitration procedures the Acts are silent, leaving it to the parties to say how they want their arbitration to proceed to statute.

What issues may be decided by arbitration?

An arbitrator may decide on any disagreement arising during the progress of a contract for which it would be possible to initiate proceedings in a court of law in a claim for breach of contract. This presupposed the existence of an arbitration agreement between the parties either contained in the contract (as it does in many standard form contracts), or arrived at subsequent to the dispute occurring.

Should a contract contain an arbitration clause under which any dispute must be submitted to arbitration then the right of action in court only arises after an award has been made by an arbitrator. Arbitration, long common in the construction and shipping industries, has gradually extended to other commercial fields. In construction an arbitration may be over whether a time extension can be granted, and if so for how long, thereby avoiding a possibility that one side will have to pay liquidated damages for failing to complete a project on time. Often the dispute will be one of fact and this may be termed quality arbitration. An example is where a time extension for interruption of building work caused by bad weather: then a finding of fact is called for. Did it really rain so hard and so prolonged as to cause work stoppage? Couldn't the work programme have been reorganized so as to allow some work to proceed rather than having a complete shutdown? Contrasted with quality arbitration is technical arbitration. This is where the dispute relates to issues of law such as, for example, whether on its construction a time extension clause covered delay caused by bad weather. Where an arbitration relates to issues of both fact and law then they may be termed *mixed* arbitration.

Arbitration versus valuation

An arbitration is where parties to a dispute will agree to have the matter dealt with by a third party who broadly follows a judicial process. A valuation is where a third party is employed to value or assess something but no dispute in fact or law exists between the parties. For instance an accountant may be employed to value shares in a private limited company; or alternatively, an architect may verify for a client that work carried out by a builder is fair and hence payable. Should the valuer not exercise sufficient care then he or she will be liable for professional negligence for any loss caused to their employer, whereas an arbitrator enjoys immunity from a professional negligence action.

Objectives

This chapter attempts to cover the essential aspect of the arbitration process. For an overview of this process please see Figure 13.1. It is intended to highlight potential pitfalls as well as the benefits of this major alternative dispute resolution method.

Key concepts

- The nature of arbitration
- Arbitration agreement
- Merits and demerits of arbitration
- The appointment and removal of an arbitrator
- The arbitral stages.

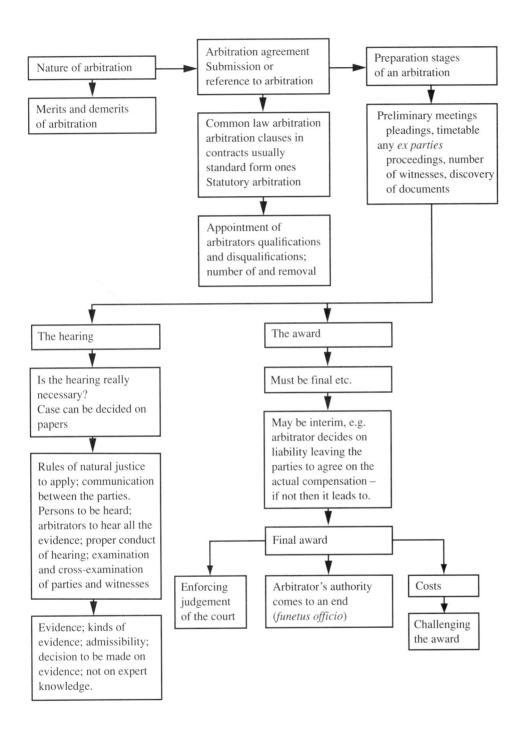

Figure 13.10 Diagrammatic analysis of the arbitral process

The nature of arbitration

Its flexibility

Informality is a major attraction

Arbitration is a convenient way of settling disputes in that, although formal rules of evidence are often applied, it is at the discretion of the arbitrator and the parties. Equally there should be a more relaxed and informal atmosphere than in a court of law. Also the parties may be involved in the decision of when and where any hearing takes place – always assuming that one is necessary.

As a voluntary undertaking

A voluntary approach

It is argued that the voluntary nature of arbitration makes it the most civilized method of resolving commercial disputes. Because of this voluntary approach both parties should feel that a fair decision has been reached and therefore be prepared to carry out the award. But if either party refuses to do so then there are procedures whereby the court can be involved to enforce it.

As a judicial process

Arbitration is a judicial process in that like the courts the arbitrator reaches his/her decision on the evidence presented to him/her and in using their own knowledge and experience. No advice or opinion ought to be taken from anyone else including the arbitrator. In *Fox* v *P. G. Wellfair* (1981) when hearing a building arbitration the arbitrator relied on his own judgement about alleged defects but did not disclose this to the claimants who had no reason to suppose that their evidence was contested. The award was set aside.

In some instances it may be necessary to conduct a full hearing but this will not always be required as the arbitrator can often invoke a decision on the basis of documentary evidence supported by oral evidence from the parties. Also, for smaller claims, *kitchen-table-style* arbitration (derived from the construction industry) may be used. This is where the arbitrator visits the site and inspects the work in dispute. The builder and the client (or their representative) are present, questions are asked and each party has the opportunity to present their case. The arbitrator may there and then say what their decision is and write out a note confirming it. A similar quick informal approach used in quality disputes, particularly in shipping where the matter relates to perishable commodities, is '*sniff and feel*' arbitration. This fact-finding approach is now used in other commercial disputes.

An award is usually final

One crucial point is that with arbitration the award is to all intents and purposes final, because only in special circumstances can an appeal be made to a court of law. As arbitrations are conducted in private there are no 'law reports' on them. The limited cases on arbitration occur when they are appealed to the courts over points of law and are reported in the usual way. However, while this is the general position, in some trade and commodity association standard form contracts an appeal structure may be incorporated in the contractual terms.

Case example
Amalgamated Metal Corp. v *Khoon Seng Co. Ltd* (1977)
The London Metal Exchange standard form contract included the term 'every (arbitration) award shall be conclusive and binding subject to appeal.' The contract, which was held to be valid, then went on to outline an appeal structure.

Arbitration agreements

As mentioned earlier the essence of arbitration is a voluntary agreement. This can arise in the following ways:

- an oral agreement
- a written agreement created before a dispute arises or, alternatively, after a dispute has occurred.

Agreements may be formal or informal

As with contractual terms in other agreements provisions can be expressly provided by, for example, saying that the Arbitration Rules of the Chartered Institute of Arbitrators are to apply, or they may be implied from the circumstances such as by previous dealing between the parties.

Oral arbitration agreements

In line with the general principle of contract law, an oral agreement to use arbitration as a means of settling a dispute is perfectly valid. It is equally binding whether made before or after a dispute has arisen. What must be appreciated is that with this type of agreement the Arbitration Acts 1950 and 1979 do not apply. Therefore, oral arbitration agreements are governed by the common law and in consequence face the following problems:

Common-law regulation is problematic

1 Either party may at any time before the award is made revoke the authority of the arbitrator (*Lord* v *Lee* (1868)). This may be done, perhaps, by a party who believes they are losing the arbitration. In such a situation dismissing the arbitrator has its attractions.
2 Either party may at any time revoke the authority of the arbitrator and then go on to take the dispute to a court of law (*Aughton Ltd* v *M. F. Kent Services Ltd* (1991)). If the arbitration agreement was written, not oral, then such unilateral action would not be possible.
3 The arbitration award can only be enforced by suing for its enforcement in the courts. With written arbitration agreements they came under the Arbitration Act 1950 and s. 26 provides for summary enforcement which is more straightforward.
4 Where statute law requires a written contract (or evidence of it) the lack of a written arbitration agreement may mean that the written arbitration award cannot be enforced – see *Walters* v *Morgan* (1792).
5 As with any oral agreement differences may occur as to what exact terms are meant to apply, with written agreements the 1950 Act may be used to fill in deficiencies but it does not cover oral agreements.
6 Oral agreements can only relate to an existing dispute, not a future one, and to avoid an accusation of incompleteness the arbitrator ought to be named.

Oral agreements are relatively rare but could be created during the course of an arbitration resulting from a written agreement where an arbitrator may be asked to settle differences in addition to those originally identified. However, a sensible arbitrator ought to ask the parties to put their request in writing therefore ensuring that it comes under the Arbitration Acts. This is especially important where later oral alterations could be interpreted as superseding an earlier written agreement.

Written agreement

For the purpose of the Act an 'arbitration agreement means a written agreement to submit present or future differences to arbitration. Whether an arbitrator is named therein or not', s. 32 AA 1950. The application of the Act means that the parties lose total control over the arbitration process which they have with oral arbitration agreements. A written agreement will include a telex – see *Arab African Energy Corp. Ltd* v *Oline produkten Netherland B.V.* (1983) and by analogy also a fax.

Need the agreement be signed?

A signed agreement is probably not required

To come under the Arbitration Acts the agreement must be in writing but the Acts are silent as to whether to be valid the agreement ought to be signed by both parties. The better view is that a signature, even of the one to be made liable, is not essential.

> ## Case example
> ### *Baker* v *Yorkshire Fire and Life Assurance Co.* (1892)
> An insurance policy containing an arbitration clause was said to be a valid arbitration agreement even though the policyholder had not signed it.

When a statutory provision, such as the Statute of Frauds 1677 s. 4, requires a signature then the party who may be found liable needs to have signed it.

Need for certainty

Certainty is essential

As for the agreement itself it must like all contracts be sufficiently certain to be enforceable.

> ## Case example
> ### *Lovelock Ltd* v *Exportles* (1968)
> A contractual clause referred 'any dispute and or claim' to arbitration in England but another clause referred 'any other dispute' to arbitration in Russia.
> The Court of Appeal held that the entire arbitration agreement was void for lack of certainty.

A single document or a set

A need to identify what the parties intended

For convenience a single arbitration agreement is to be preferred. However, it is possible to have an arbitration agreement spread over a number of separate documents provided that, taken as a whole, it can be identified which disputes are to be covered and that arbitration is to apply to them. Also, provided that the terms of an agreement to submit to arbitration are contained in a document or documents, proof that those terms were agreed by the parties to be binding upon them may be derived from outside those documents such as by the conduct of the parties: for oral acceptance or any evidence which satisfies the court that the written terms constituted or formed part of an agreement between the parties see *Zambia Steel & Building Suppliers Ltd* v *James Clark & Eaten Ltd* (1986).

Use of a Scott Avery clause

Scott Avery: litigation only after arbitration

This clause is derived from *Scott* v *Avery* (1856) where in an arbitration agreement the parties agreed not to commence any litigation until after an arbitration award had been made. It was held that such a clause was not illegal as ousting the jurisdiction of the courts but was a condition precedent in that the arbitration award had to be published before either party had access to the courts. *Scott* v *Avery* has set the limits on the freedom of the parties to restrict access to the courts. An arbitration agreement which said that the courts could never be resorted to would be illegal.

Advantages of arbitration

For centuries business people have preferred arbitration to litigation and in the present day the practice appears to be healthy. Some of the advantages claimed for arbitration are given below but a number of the underlying assumptions may be questioned.

Expertise

An arbitrator will usually have expert knowledge in the area in dispute. In many, if not all, cases, the nature of the dispute, in terms of the issues it raises, will determine the academic and professional discipline of the arbitrator. In *Gunter Henck* v *Andre et Cie SA* (1970), Mocatta J was of the opinion that

An arbitrator is usually an expert

> the (arbitration) tribunal … is usually chosen from gentlemen in the trade who may be assumed to know very much more of its technicalities than any judge could hope to know.

It is by normally having lay arbitrators (non-lawyers) that sets British arbitration apart from continental arbitration. However, while expert arbitrators may be preferred for quality (factual) disputes, for technical (legal) disputes they may be less advantageous.

Cost

It may be cheaper to arbitrate than to pursue an action through the courts but it is unlikely to be cheap, yet many authors claim it is an advantage of arbitration that it is cheaper than litigation. Yet to pursue a case through the courts is expensive and often the amount in issue may be relatively modest. For example, in a building dispute the assessment of liability may be based on the respective value of the property. Therefore, a surveyor may inspect a property and value it at £200 000 but fail to notice rising damp. To put the damp penetration right would cost, say, £20 000. In the contract is a term reserving the right to be correct within 5 per cent. The correct value of the property was £180 000 with the surveyors value range between £190 000 – £210 000. If successful the injured party would recover only £10 000 but whether he or she would get their full legal costs is always something of a gamble.

In some instances where formal procedures are adopted, arbitration may be more expensive than litigation. The cost of the hearing will be borne by the parties and this will include the arbitrator's fees (double if there are two arbitrators, triple if three), accommodation costs, secretarial assistance, witness expenses, etc. To set against these costs is the potential speed with which the dispute may be resolved especially as, with limited exceptions, the award cannot be appealed against. Also, it can be noted that with an expert arbitrator there ought to be less need for expensive expert witnesses and arbitrators are able to save time by taking written submissions from the parties as opposed to the often slower oral submissions in a court.

Cost advantage not always easily to determine

From the above discussion it is not possible to be too dogmatic about the relative costs of arbitration or litigation. On balance, probably arbitration, but it must be noted that an arbitrator, usually an expert eminent in his/her profession, commands a not inconsiderable fee, whereas a judge is paid for by the state (it is worth nothing that judges in the commercial court can, on request, act as arbitrators paid for largely by the state!). Arbitration should cost less than court actions but it will depend on the actual circumstances and the complexity of the issues. One author has said that 'Litigation expands to the estimated capacity of the parties to pay' (Parris, *Law and Practice of Arbitration*), therefore, arbitration ought to have the advantage!

Simplicity

A major attraction of arbitration is that the procedure of the hearing can be much more informal and relaxed than that of a court (the rules of procedure in the High Court and county court run to some 3000 and 2000 pages respectively).

The rules of natural justice always operate

An informal approach does not mean no procedure. An arbitrator must follow certain principles. It is a judicial role so he or she must always work within the rules of natural justice. But an arbitrator does have more freedom of manoeuvre than the courts, particularly, where the parties have not agreed in advance any precise procedure. With the permission of the parties the arbitrator can adopt whatever procedure seems most appropriate. The dispute may proceed upon documentary evidence alone; or documents together with written submissions; or a site visit. Alternatively, there may be a formal hearing of the dispute with expert witnesses and lawyers to examine and cross examine.

Speed

Largely as a consequence of relative simplicity arbitration can be quick. In some instances disputes can be resolved within hours, days or a few weeks. In other circumstances they may last for years. Very long arbitrations were criticized in *Peter Cassidy* v *Osuustukkukaupp 1L* (1957) by Derlin J:

> It is of course beyond dispute that if business prefer an expensive and lengthy procedure (arbitration) in this case lasting over three years, to that which the courts provide, they are entitled to have it.

International arbitration may be time-consuming

This remark was made after he dealt with the case in one and three-quarter hours! Where arbitration is more prone to be lengthy is international arbitration. Section 13 (3) AA 1950 has the facility for either of the parties to apply to the High Court to remove an arbitrator who fails to use all reasonable dispatch in commencing and proceeding with the arbitration. If an application under s. 13 (3) is granted then the arbitrator forfeits any right to payment for their services.

Inherent in speed of reaching a final decision is the fact that there is only a limited right of appeal against an arbitrator's award. It, therefore, usually means that the dispute is not 'subjected' to a time-consuming appeal process so that businesses are able to avoid delay in their operation in not having to wait months or years before an appeal is finally dealt with.

Two speedier forms of arbitration, 'kitchen table' and 'sniff and feel' were referred to earlier. A third is called *pendulum*, *flip-flop* or *final arbitration*. Here, each party provides the arbitrator with the figure they believe to be a fair settlement of the dispute. The arbitrator must decided on one of these two sums. Selection of a middle position is not possible. Instead of each side providing an artificially high figure, so as to allow for future compromise, a reasonable sum that the arbitrator is likely to accept must be chosen. This reasonability factor means that the parties settlement figures will be closer than they normally would with unrealistic claims being avoided. A fourth form is *short form* arbitration. This is where the hearing may be restricted to a limited number of days, say one or two, with each party given a specified number of hours to present its claim and defence. The arbitrator also operates under a time restraint in respect of questioning the parties.

Convenience

While the arbitrator is independent of the parties and their powers are considerable regarding the organizing and co-ordinating of the arbital process, nevertheless a careful arbitrator always tries to work with the parties. Therefore, when it is a matter of arranging and timing preliminary meetings or fixing the time and venue of the hearing they will consider the convenience of the parties. For instance meetings out of normal working hours which may take place at a factory, construction site, airport hotel or wherever the parties want.

Where possible the parties' wishes should be met

With litigation it is the convenience of the courts that takes precedence, with that of counsel following and the convenience of the litigants being last. It is not unknown for cases to be listed at around 4 p.m. on the day before the hearing commences with the result that the parties and witnesses may spend days waiting around for their case to be heard.

Privacy

The entire arbitration proceedings takes place in private. Of all the advantages, privacy is the outstanding one. This is commercially significant when it is considered that the whole procedure of a court is in the public domain and as such the public has free access which could lead to undesired publicity and the possible disclosure of trade or commercial confidences.

Privacy is the primary advantage

> ### Case example
> ### *Lonrho Ltd and others v Shell Petroleum Co. Ltd and others (1981)*
> It was alleged by Lonrho that Shell Petroleum had given assurance to the authorities in Northern Rhodesia that they would defy an international oil embargo and continue to supply oil to the constitutionally illegal regime that had declared unilateral independence. Lonrho took their dispute against Shell Petroleum to arbitration but on losing they then appealed to the High Court, the Court of Appeal and the House of Lords thereby ensuring the maximum publicity of Shell Petroleum's dubious business practices.
>
> Also in Shearson Lehman (1989), parties to a private arbitration were ordered to disclose documents to a third party engaged in court proceedings unconnected with the matter being disputed. Similarly, see *Hassneh Insurance Co. of Israel v Steuart J Mew* (1992).

However, in most instances arbitration proceedings remain private as appeals and challenges to arbitration proceedings are rare.

Disadvantages of arbitration

A limited right of appeal

The major disadvantage is the arbitration principle that the award is final. With agreement between the parties an appeal to the High Court on a point of law, that 'substantially effects the right of one or more of the parties' (s. 1 (2), AA 1979), is possible. The grounds for doing so are rather narrow and the main outcome may not be clarification but merely delay in reaching a final conclusion.

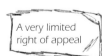
A very limited right of appeal

The joining of third parties

Third-parties cannot be joined

If the dispute involves parties other than those privy to the arbitration agreement, as might occur under construction contracts where an employer, main contractor, and one or more subcontractors may all be in dispute with each other, the award the arbitrator makes is not binding on third parties. Any decision as to the ownership of property or property rights is only binding on the parties to the contract and does not apply to any other party who may be involved. This can be contrasted to a court action where a third party may be joined to the action and be bound by the court's decision.

Complex legal issues

Complex legal issues best left to litigation

When the issue in dispute is one of fact then arbitration is an excellent way in which to resolve it, but if the issue is a substantial one of law it may well be better to litigate. In *Fairclough Dodd & Jones Ltd* v *Vantol Ltd* (1957) a dispute occurred over a term in a standard form contract issued by the London Oil and Tallow Trades Association. Both parties chose to arbitrate but the two arbitrators appointed could not agree. To break the deadlock an umpire was appointed (this is a person charged with deciding any difference between two arbitrators) but said that the matter had to be referred to a court for adjudication. In the House of Lords Viscount Simmonds said:

> Where the substantial issue raises a question of law of general importance which must to the knowledge of the parties, ultimately be determined by a court of law, it is difficult to see what advantage is to be gained by pursuing the tortuous and expensive course of arbitration.

Litigation would most probably be better than arbitration where the dispute is likely to require a reference to the European Court.

Enforcement of the award

A short cut for enforcement

One of the disadvantages of arbitration is that an arbitrator, having reached a decision and made an award, is unable to enforce that award. Should an award not be met, it can only be enforced by taking action in the courts. This is on the basis that a written binding arbitration agreement creates a contract and failure to comply with the arbitrator's award gives rise to an action for a breach of contract. A simple procedure for enforcement is provided by s. 26 AA 1950 (as amended), so that an award may be enforced in the same way as a court order subject to an application for enforcement being approved by the High Court. If the High Court is satisfied that the award is valid then it will enter judgement in favour of the party named and the award may then be enforced in the same way as any other judgement of the court.

Review question

'Where a contractual dispute arises litigation may be subject to difficulties. A more attractive alternative is arbitration'. Critically comment on this statement.

The international dimension

Arbitration may be preferred to litigation where the dispute is between parties in the developed and non-developed world. This is perhaps pertinent where one party is a state or quasi-state body of a former colony for that body may be sensitive about submitting itself to the jurisdiction of a foreign court especially if that court was located in the former colonizing power.

Where the arbitration agreement is contained in an international contract then it must be established what the proper law of the contract is, e.g. which national law will prevail. The starting presumption is that the governing law will be that of the place at which the arbitration is to be held – see *Tzortzis* v *Monark Line A/B* (1968). This presumption may be rebutted by surrounding circumstances. Many international contracts contain a clause saying that any dispute should be subject to the International Chamber of Commerce arbitration. The standard clause being:

What court will have jurdistion?

> All disputes arising in connection with the present contract should be finally settled under the Rules of Conciliation and Arbitration of the International Chamber of Commerce by one or more arbitrators appointed in accordance with the said rules.

The International Court of Arbitration (ICC)

Under the International Chamber of Commerce (ICC) arbitration procedure, the parties are free to submit disputes to arbitrators of their choice and to fix the place and the language of the arbitration, as well as the law applicable to the dispute. In 1994, arbitrators from approximately 50 different countries were appointed and arbitrations were in progress in 30 different countries. The ICC is an international business organization that operates in 140 countries. Within the ICC is an International Court of Arbitration which is the major institution for organizing and administrating international commercial arbitration. The court, created in 1923, received in 1994 348 requests for arbitration. It does not itself resolve disputes (that is left to independent arbitrators nominated by the court) but provides an organizational and supervisory role so as to help overcome obstacles that may arise through arbitral proceedings in international disputes. The court also seeks to ensure that arbitrators' awards are free from defects that jeopardize their enforcement.

The ICC plays an important role in international arbitration

The arbitrator

The person appointed

Anyone may be an arbitrator if the parties agree to their appointment and the individual(s) consent is forthcoming. Clearly the person chosen should have the skill, knowledge and experience to fulfil the obligations imposed. A leading work on arbitration neatly summarizes the position:

Anyone is eligible to be an arbitrator

> Any natural person is capable in law of being the subject of a valid appointment as arbitrator, and of publishing a binding award. If the parties choose to have their disputed resolved by a person who is not equal to the task, they must abide by their choice. Extreme youth or age, mental or physical infirmity, do not deprive an arbitrator of the power to act, or render his award a nullity.

> (Mustill and Boyd, *The Law and Practice of Commercial Arbitration in England*, 1989, p. 247).

However, the arbitral agreement may restrict the appointment.

> ## Case example
> ### *Raheassi Shipping Co.* v *Blue Star Line* (1967)
> The arbitration agreement stated that the arbitrators and umpire shall be commercial men not lawyers. The arbitrators disagreed and on their being unable to agree they appointed a lawyer as the umpire. The court said that the umpires award was invalid due to the irregular appointment.

Appointment of an arbitrator

Appointment is conditional

Unless the arbitration agreement requires one there is no special procedure required to appoint an arbitrator. Also it is not necessary that the appointment be in writing. However, to be valid the appointment must satisfy these conditions:

1 The arbitrator must be notified and requested to accept the appointment. Particular care needs to be taken when 'Atlantic Shipping' type clauses are included. Such a clause requires the arbitration to commence within a stipulated time period or else it will be treated as being abandoned.

> ## Case example
> ### *Atlantic Shipping and Trading Co.* v *Louis Dreyfus & Co.* (1922)
> The arbitration agreement said that if a dispute arose any claim had to be made in writing and the arbitrator appointed within three months ... any departure from this clause will mean that the claim has been waived (that is abandoned) and will be absolutely barred.
>
> It was held that this clause, as it did not actually oust the jurisdiction of the courts, was enforceable.

However, a court may be prepared to use its discretion under s. 27 AA 1950 and grant extra time if it believes that the limit which applies causes 'undue hardship'. In *Liberian Shipping Corp.* v *A. King & Sons Ltd* (1967), Donaldson J interpreted 'undue hardship' as a 'hardship ... greater than that which, in justice, (the claimant) should be called upon to bear'. An extremely short period of time in certain circumstances may well cause 'undue hardship'.

2 The arbitrator must accept the appointment.
3 The appointment of the arbitrator is considered incomplete until it has been notified to the other side. Therefore, neither party may claim that an arbitrator has been appointed until the other party has been notified of the choice. Where each party appoint their own arbitrator notification must be exchanged. If one party appoint and the other does not and a notice of seven clear days of appointment is given and the other party still does not appoint, then the arbitrator who has been appointed becomes the sole arbitrator – s. 7 (b) AA 1950.

The number of arbitrators

Reference may be made to one, two, three or more arbitrators. Should two arbitrators be appointed, they 'may appoint an umpire at any time', and 'shall do so forthwith if they cannot agree' – s. 8 (1) AA 1950, s. 6 (1) AA 1979. To save expenditure on professional fees the parties should ideally agree on a sole arbitrator.

Multiple arbitrators are expensive

Reference to a sole arbitrator

This may occur in one of the following ways:

1 The parties agree in the arbitration agreement.
2 The agreement is silent on the matter so that s. 6 AA 1950 applies; this provision says that unless a contrary intention is expressed then every agreement shall include a clause for the appointment of a sole arbitrator.
3 Where an arbitrator, by the authority of the High Court, has been removed then the court may appoint a new arbitrator.
4 At any time after the appointment of an umpire the court may, on application of either party, appoint the umpire as sole arbitrator.
5 If the agreement is for two arbitrators but only one party appoints an arbitrator then that arbitrator may become the sole arbitrator – s. 7 (b) AA 1950.
6 Where the parties cannot agree on an appointment and the agreement does not provide a procedure to overcome the problem then the court can on the application of either party appoint an arbitrator – s. 10 AA 1950.
7 An arbitration agreement may specify that the arbitrator be a special referee; these are now since the Courts Act 1971 circuit judges. The parties will therefore obtain a highly skilled arbitrator for free!
8 A judge of the commercial court, s. 4 Administration of Justice Act 1970, who can accept appointment as an arbitrator if 'he thinks fit' and the dispute is of a 'commercial character' and the confirmation of the Lord Chancellor is obtained.

Reference to two arbitrators

Each party may appoint their own arbitrator and in the event of any difference or dispute between them they must appoint an umpire – s. 8 (1) AA 1950; s. 6 (1) AA 1979. If there is disagreement over the choice of umpire the two arbitrators may draw lots to resolve it as in Re Hooper (1987), but only if both parties know that the person to be chosen is suitable. If there is a lack of such knowledge on one side then the umpire appointed by such method would most likely be removed as in *European and American SS Co.* v *Crosskey & Co.* (1896).

An umpire may be appointed to reconcile differences

Reference to three arbitrators

Any number of arbitrators may be appointed. The majority will be binding. Should the agreement refer to three arbitrators, one from each side with a third being selected by those appointed, it has the effect of being a reference to two arbitrators with the third acting as an umpire.

The majority will prevail

Appointment of an arbitrator by the court

This may come about as a result of the parties' failure to fulfil their agreement to appoint one; alternative the one appointed may be incapable of acting. Similarly, if an umpire required appointing and is not, or is incapable, then the courts may do so – s. 7 (a) AA 1950. This statutory provision also exists where the contract provides that the appointment of an arbitrator is carried out by a third party.

The removal of an arbitrator, or the revocation of their authority

When the authority of an arbitrator (or umpire) is derived from a written agreement, then unless a contrary intention is expressed the authority and appointment 'is irrevocable except by leave of the High Court' – s. 1 AA 1950.

However, circumstances may arise where the parties, jointly or individually, may wish to challenge the authority of or the appointment of a particular arbitrator. Such a challenge is possible under both common and statute law.

Common law

1 *Breach of contract*

As arbitration arises out of an agreement, therefore, under the basic principles of contract law it can be replaced by a second agreement. Alternatively, one of the parties may commence an action in the commercial court for breach of contract which may be challenged by the other party requesting a stay of action under s. 4 (1) AA 1950. If the court does not grant a stay of action (that is stop the court action and send the case to arbitration) then the arbitration agreement is effectively ended. However, a court will only exercise its discretion to grant a stay in exceptional circumstances, this is because the court would want to uphold written arbitration agreements

> If parties choose to determine for themselves that they will have a domestic forum instead of resorting to the ordinary courts, then … a prima facie (that is at first sight) duty is cast upon the courts to act upon such an agreement.
>
> Lord Selborne, *Willesford* v *Watson* (1873)

If the arbitration agreement is a domestic one, e.g. United Kingdom, then the court has a wide discretion under s. 4 (1) AA 1950, but if the arbitration agreement is non-domestic then the court is limited in its discretion on a stay of court proceedings by s. 1 AA 1950.

2 *Plea of illegality*

This may enable one party to plead that the original contract was illegal and that therefore an arbitration on such a contract would be invalid.

Case example
Taylor v *Barrett Trading* (1953)

In February 1952 Barrett Trading agreed to sell Taylor 1000 cases of Irish stewed steak at 2s 4d a pound. At the time a Meat Products and Canned Meat Order was in force which prohibited the purchase or sale of any such meat at a price of 2s 4d. The seller failed to make delivery and the buyer instigated proceedings under an arbitration clause in the contract. The arbitrators failed to make a decision but the umpire found in the favour of the buyers. The seller appealed on the grounds that the contract was illegal because the price exceeded the maximum permitted by law and therefore that the umpire's decision was unenforceable.

The Court of Appeal held that the seller's argument would succeed.

---

3 *Other remedies*

In addition to breach of contract two other remedies available from the court are a declaration that a party is no longer obligated to arbitrate, and an injunction to prevent the arbitration from continuing.

Statute law

The statutory challenge to the arbitrator's authority may result in the Commercial Court authorizing one of the following:

Impartiality is essential

1 Permission for one of the parties to revoke the authority where the arbitrator is not impartial, or where the dispute involves fraud – s. 24 (1), (2) AA 1950.

Questions of the arbitrator's impartiality will also include showing animosity towards any of the parties or to witnesses. Impartiality may take the form of the arbitrator being connected with one of the parties.

Case example
Veritas Shipping v *Anglo Canadian Cement* (1966)

Veritas challenged the appointment by Anglo Canadian Cement of one Dr Wollersteiner as joint arbitrator. Dr Wollersteiner was the managing director of Anglo Canadian Cement and as an interested party he was not impartial.

The challenge was held to be valid. Dr Wollersteiner was ordered to be removed from office and another arbitrator appointed in his place.

Case example
Catalina v *Norma* (1938)

The 'Catalina' was a steamship of Portuguese ownership and the 'Norma' a motor vessel of Norwegian ownership. The vessels collided with each other off Ushant and the ship owners decided to arbitrate in England before Sir Norman Roeburn. During the hearing the counsel for the Portuguese made reference to a case involving an Italian steamer. The arbitrator, Sir Norman Roeburn, then said:

> The Italians are all liars and will say anything to suit their book. The same thing applies to the Portuguese. But the other side here are Norwegians and in my experience the Norwegians are truthful people. In this case I entirely accept the evidence of the master of the 'Norma'.

This was not the final judgement of the arbitrator, but Sir Norman Roeburn intimated that the vessel 'Norma' was free from blame and that he did not believe the evidence of the Portuguese witnesses.

The Court of Appeal held that the arbitrator had spoken unfairly regarding the Portuguese witnesses and his decision should in consequence be ignored. Another arbitrator was ordered to be appointed by the two parties.

However, some care should be taken because if, in the arbitration agreement, it is openly disclosed that the arbitrator is connected with one party then on signing the agreement the other party cannot later complain of lack of impartiality.

Case example
Jackson v Barry Railway (1893)

A contractor agreed that disputes under the contract should be referred to the arbitration of the buildings owner's engineer.

The Court of Appeal held that the parties must have known at the date of the contract that probably the engineer would not come to his decision on any dispute with an open mind. Therefore, the contractor could not later complain over alleged lack of impartiality.

Less drastic than revoking the arbitrator's appointment is an application to the High Court for an injunction for the arbitration to stop – s. 24 (1) AA 1950.

In practice the naming or designating of a person to serve as an arbitrator is less common that formerly. Now arbitration agreements tend to say that a third party will make the appointment, e.g. that a professional body will nominate the arbitrator. Impartiality may also arise where the arbitrator is also required as a necessary witness – see *Bristol Corporation* v *Aird* (1913).

With respect to fraud, s. 24 (2) AA 1950 allows the party making the allegation to apply to the court to have the arbitration agreement cancelled and for the arbitrator's authority to be revoked. This provision is designed to enable the party accused of fraud to have access to the courts so that they may clear their name. Section 24 (2) is discretional and where the arbitration agreement expressly covers disputes involving allegations of fraud then a court may not give relief – see *Heyman* v *Darwins Ltd* (1942).

2 Removal of the arbitrator and/or setting an award aside for misconduct under s. 23 (1) (2) AA 1950.

This relates to both personal misconduct and to misconduct inarbitral proceedings. These may also be termed *actual* and *technical* misconduct. Actual misconduct is where an improper notice influenced the arbitrator's decision. Technical misconduct is where irregularities in the proceedings occur such as where an arbitrator exceeds their authority, examines witnesses without both parties being present or delegates their authority, etc.

Case example
Pratt v Swanmore Builders and Bakers (1980)

A joint arbitrator was removed for misconduct by reason of his delay caused by a failure to follow a correct procedure. The parties had become confused and delay was due to the arbitrator issuing inappropriate orders.

> ### Case example
> ### *Taylor* v *Barrett Trading* (1953)
> Here the making of an award by an arbitrator on a contract which he knew to be illegal was said to be misconduct on the arbitrator's part.

Misconduct is looked at through the eyes of the court and need not reflect adversely on the good faith, due care, conscientiousness or fair mindedness of the arbitral tribunal in question per Moccata J in *Gunter Henck* v *Andre & Cie SA* (1970). On a misconduct hearing the court again has discretion. What is a major influencing factor is whether one or both parties have lost all confidence in the arbitrator.

Misconduct is a matter for the court

> ### Case example
> ### *Modern Engineering (Bristol) Ltd* v *C. Miskin* (1981)
> Here the arbitrator issued his award in favour of Miskin without bothering to hear Modern Engineering's argument.
>
> In the Court of Appeal, Lord Denning said that both parties should be able to have confidence in the arbitrator and not feel that he was biased towards either. The conduct of the arbitrator was such that he had lost the confidence of at least one of the parties and so should be removed and a new arbitrator brought in. Under s. 25(2) AA 1950 where a court revokes an arbitrator's or umpire's appointment then it may appoint a sole arbitrator, or order that the arbitration agreement shall cease to operate in respect to the matter in dispute.

3 Removal of an arbitrator for being too slow – s. 13(3) AA 1950.

This provision allows an arbitrator or umpire to be removed from office if he or she fail to use all 'reasonable dispatch' in carrying out proceedings and making an award. In *Lewis Emanuel & Sons Ltd* v *Sammut* (1959), an umpire published an award four months late after a summons had been served by the seller. The seller's legal costs would be recovered from the umpire. However, in *Succual Ltd & Pomona Shipping Co. Ltd* v *Harland & Wolff* (1980), Harland & Wolff claimed delay caused by the arbitrators doing nothing. It was found that the arbitrators had done nothing because neither party had asked them to do anything.

Business efficiency is expected

Should s. 13(3) apply then on removal the arbitrator, or umpire, will not be entitled to their remuneration.

Death or bankruptcy of a party

Death of a party to a written arbitration agreement does not discharge the agreement nor does it revoke the arbitration's authority s. 2(1)(2) AA 1950 unless the cause of action dies with the deceased party – s. 2(3) AA 1950. Similarly, written arbitration agreements survive the bankruptcy of a party but clearly it may not be worth arbitrating if the person charged is unlikely to be able to meet an award. If the arbitration agreement was made orally then death of a party will terminate the agreement unless it was expressly agreed to the contrary.

Outcome determined by whether agreement was written or oral

Review question

Discuss the reasons why an arbitrator may be removed from office and also the circumstances for the revocation of an arbitrator's authority.

Preparatory stages of an arbitration

The initial steps

The first step in an arbitration is that a party, or both parties, agree on an arbitrator and appoint one. If the appointing authority is a professional institution then it is from these that the notification of appointment will arise.

The arbitrator must accept the appointment and while, as we have already observed, the law does not insist on it being in writing it is obviously best if it is so.

Once appointed the arbitrator is sent (or if not, calls for) the documents which give authority to the arbitrator to act, namely the arbitration agreement. The arbitrator's authority comes about in one of the following ways:

1 A document which actually sets out who the parties are, recites the dispute and invests the arbitrator with the necessary powers.
2 A clause in a contract states that, in the event of a dispute, it is to be referred to arbitration and that the parties agree on a nomination or that an outside body is called in to nominate.
3 The courts may insist on an arbitration when a case comes before it which includes a clause as in 2 above following a 'stay of action' procedure.

The preliminary meeting(s)

This may take the form of a simple, quick 'kitchen table' meeting or a more substantial meeting. The arbitrator will probably want to know:

1 Is the contract between the parties agreed?
2 Will the contract need interpreting? The object here is to ensure that the dispute is covered by the agreement. This is a matter of construction and case law will be used for guidance.
3 How much, if any, common ground is there between the parties?
4 Are either party going to appoint counsel?
5 Are there any substantial issues of law which may surface during the case?

The arbitrator's instructions or orders

In arbitration, as in court actions, most cases turn on issues of fact and the preliminary meeting(s) is used as a means of putting order into the preparation of the facts prior to a hearing. The following points are likely to be discussed by the arbitrator with any necessary instructions or orders being made:

1 Delivery of points of claim.

2 Particulars of the claim and of any counterclaim.
3 Discovery and inspection of documents.

> **Case example**
> ***Mitchell Construction v East Anglian Hospital Board (1971)***
> Arbitrators asked for Mitchell Construction's personnel files. Mitchell Construction objected on grounds of confidentiality.
>
> The objection was overruled because, as the arbitration hearing would be in private, disclosure was not an important issue.

4 Inspection of property and articles (if required).
5 Arranging any matter which will shorten or facilitate the hearing, e.g. reducing the number of witnesses or simplifying procedures.
6 Adjournment of the proceedings.

Adjournment is at the discretion of the arbitrator who ought to grant it if reasonably possible. However, it may be mentioned that if one of the parties acts deliberately obstructively, such as by refusing to co-operate or even take part, then the arbitrator may act *ex parte* in hearing only one party. Also the Courts and Legal Services Act 1990, by introducing s. 13 (A) into the Arbitration Act 1950 makes it possible for an arbitrator to dismiss a claim if he or she is satisfied that there has been unjustifiable delay by the claimant and that the delay gives rise to a substantial risk that the issues cannot fairly be resolved, or that the delay may cause serious prejudice to the other party.

The hearing

At the hearing the rules of evidence as used in a normal civil court are followed. While the parties are free to represent themselves the practice is for legal counsel to handle the hearing. The claimant (equivalent to the plaintiff), or rather their counsel, will set out their case and call their witnesses. The witnesses will give their evidence and be offered for cross-examination by the respondent (equivalent to the defendant) or their counsel. The claimant is then allowed to put additional questions to their witnesses on matters that arise during their cross-examination. A similar procedure is then adopted by the respondent who will start by setting out their defence and/or any counterclaim they may wish to make. They will then call and examine their witnesses who in turn are offered for cross-examination by the claimant. The next stage is for the claimant to reply to the respondent's defence and, if a counterclaim has been made will provide their defence to it.

A legal procedure is followed

On examining their own witness a counsel must not put leading questions to them which attempt to put answers into their mouths, e.g.

> Q: Do you agree that the machine the respondent delivered was useless to the extent that it was fit only for scrap?

This should be put in a different form:

> Q: Did you examine the machine the respondent supplied?
> A: I did.
> Q: From that examination what condition would you say the machine was in?

If an opposing witness is being examined then leading questions can be put.

Once the above procedure has been completed then the respondent sums up their case in the form of a closing speech. The claimant then has the right of reply. The hearing is now ended. The arbitrator may announce their decision relatively quickly or take time to consider the claims and counterclaims; possibly a site visit may be made. Once the arbitrator has made their decision then, after payment of arbitration charges, the decision is served on the parties and will become enforceable in a similar manner to a judgement debt.

Evidence submitted at the hearing

A decision supported by legal reasoning is required

Unless the parties agree otherwise, an arbitrator is bound under the Civil Evidence Act 1968 by the same rules of evidence as the courts. In 'quality arbitration' (fact finding) the normal rules of evidence are frequently amended either expressly or by implication. In *Mcpherson Train & Co. Ltd* v *S Milham & Sons* (1955), evidence was offered in a letter which was 'not in a form which would strictly be admissible in a court of law' but which the arbitrator accepted. However, the arbitrator must always attempt to decide according to what he or she sees as the legal requirements. They are unable to decide on grounds of personal fairness or by 'striking a reasonable balance' between the parties.

Proof of facts

The complainant has the burden of proof

1 The maker of a statement, e.g. the complainant has the burden of proving what they say is true.
2 All material facts, that is relevant facts in issue, relied upon by the complainant must be proved unless the other party concedes that they are true.

Types of evidence

Evidence can be divided into many different types. The types which an arbitrator is most commonly involved with are:

A mixture of evidence may be used

1 Oral evidence given by witnesses usually under oath at the hearing. If false evidence is given then it amounts to perjury and is punishable by fine or imprisonment.
2 Documentary evidence (originals not copies) under ss. 1–10 Evidence Act 1968. Should a person be unable to attend the hearing then in place of oral evidence documentary evidence may be produced in order to help establish fact.
3 Real evidence in the form of material objects produced for the arbitrator's inspection, or from a site visit, as opposed to oral or documentary evidence.

It is also possible to divide evidence into primary and secondary. Primary evidence is evidence which has, in the circumstances, to be regarded as the best evidence available, whereas secondary evidence is evidence which indicates that better evidence is available. Primary evidence, if available, ought always to be produced while secondary evidence is always rejected in favour of primary evidence on it being admitted.

Expert witnesses

An expert witness is preferred

They offer the arbitrator the best assistance possible in getting at the truth. They are allowed, if need be, to prepare in advance a report from which they can quote when giving evidence. The evidence given is their opinion about the issues and it may be different from ordinary non-expert witnesses who restrict themselves to what they saw, heard or said.

The arbitrator as witness

The arbitrator, as an expert, is entitled to rely on their own knowledge and experience in deciding issues relating to, for example, the quality of goods and may assess for themselves the amount of liability even if no other evidence has been presented – see *Mediterranean & Eastern Export Co.* v *Fortress Fabrics Ltd* (1948). What is important is that the arbitrator, if relying on their own abilities, must inform the parties of their findings and allow them to comment on them. Should the arbitrator wish, then with the agreement of both parties they may call their own witnesses.

If relying on themselves then must disclose this

The Award

A decision without reasons

An award is the decision of the arbitrator upon the submission in an arbitration. When giving it, it is not necessary for the arbitrator to give reasons for the decision and, historically, it was thought best to stay silent on the reasons. It was said in one appeal from an arbitrators award:

> Consider what justice requires and decide accordingly. But never give reasons, for your judgement will probably be right but your reasons will certainly be wrong.

The reason for this reluctance to give reasons when making an award was that if it contained an error on its face then it might be remitted for reconsideration or set aside by the court. In an effort to encourage arbitrators to give reasons for their decisions the Arbitration Act 1979 s. 1 (1) prevents a court from remitting or setting aside an award on grounds of errors of fact or law on its face. However, a party (or both parties) is entitled to ask the arbitrator, in advance of the award being made, to provide reasons for their decision and this will then be known as a reason award. Should the arbitrators fail to provide the required reason than a court can order that he or she do so; a similar order can be made where some special reason meant that a request for a reason award couldn't be made to the arbitrator – s. 1 (5), (6) AA 1950. Alternatively, the parties may agree that no reasons for a decision are to be given and this will mean that no appeal from the award is possible, since the appeals can only be on points of law.

A reason award is always preferred

Opportunity for an appeal

An appeal is a judicial review of an arbitrator's award with respect to questions of law. As previously mentioned the arbitrator's (or umpire's) award is meant to be final unless the agreement expressed a contrary intention such as providing a right of appeal – s. 16 AA 1950. Should the parties wish to exclude an appeal to the courts then they are free to do so provided that it is expressly stated – s. 3 (1) AA 1979.

The right of appeal may be excluded

Where an appeal is made then it has to be either with the consent of all the parties or by the High Court who finds that 'having regard to all the circumstances the determination of the question of law concerned could substantially affect the rights of one or more of the parties' s. 1(4) AA 1979. In order that the court can consider any questions of law it may, if not already provided, require an arbitrator or umpire to give in sufficient detail reasons for the award – s. 1 (5) AA 1979. If the appeal, again solely on a question of law, goes from the High Court to the Court of Appeal then similar restrictions apply, ss. 1 (7), 2 (3) AA 1979, except that the question at issue must be of general public importance. Since the House of Lords decision in *Pioneer Shipping Ltd* v *B. T. P.*

Tioxide Ltd, The Nema (1982), where guidelines (the Nema guidelines) were introduced, the circumstances where courts will interfere with an award on the grounds that the arbitrator made a mistake of law have been considerable limited.

Consent awards

A compromise agreement may foreshorten arbitration

These occur where the parties at some stage in the arbitration enter into negotiations with their advisers but not in the presence of the arbitrator who is not a party to the negotiations. It may be that at an early stage the parties realize from the claims and counterclaims that the arbitration is likely to be long so they may soften their attitude and through a compromise agreement reach an earlier settlement. The outcome of this compromise agreement will be embodied in the award the arbitrator will be asked to make and this may be termed a consent award which will formerly bring the arbitration to a conclusion.

Form of the award

Usually a written award is given

There is nothing in law, either statutory or common, which says the award must be in writing but it is normal practice that it is, with the arbitrator signing it and having it witnessed. If the award is developed orally then it is termed a speaking award with written ones being termed a non-speaking award of which three copies are made, one for either party and one retained by the arbitrator.

On signing, the award is said to be 'published' and to be received by the parties. Following publication the parties have six weeks in which to make application to the court to have the award set aside – see the Rules of the Supreme Court.

The common practice is that the award is divided into two parts:

1 *Recitals*. There is no necessity for recitals, therefore mistakes in it will not be grounds for setting aside the award.

 The recital should be as brief as possible including reference to the arbitration agreement and appointment of the arbitrator. Particular care should be taken to avoid reference to the actual contract or to contractual clauses or to specific contractual documents, as these can then be examined in any legal action which might follow.
2 *The award document*. This is a statement of the decision. It shows which party has been successful and gives the sum to be paid to the claimant or respondent. Under the Arbitration Act 1979 a reason will now probably be given for the decision. Also included will be a statement as to who will pay costs, which may be proportional.

 Interest at $7^1/_2$ per cent under s. 20 Arbitration Act 1950 is due on the sum of the award from the date it is 'published' – unless otherwise stated in the award. This follows the principle of Judgement Debts (Rate of Interest) Order 1971.

The arbitration fees

Payment before publication

The arbitrator will require his or her fees for publishing the award. The arbitrator has a 'lien' that is a right of possession on the award until he or she has been paid. Should no agreement on fees exist, and neither party takes up the award, then the arbitrator may sue on an express or implied promise to pay for services rendered. Should the fee charged be thought too high then an application may be made to the court where a taxing master (an officer appointed to examine costs) will assess the fee – s. 19 (1) AA 1950.

Corrections

The arbitrator has power to correct any clerical mistake or error arising from any accident slip or omission. This is known as the 'slip rule' under s. 17 AA 1950. In case of a serious mistake, as the arbitrator on publishing the award becomes discharged from his or her duty, she or he may make the necessary corrections if it is remitted to him or her by the courts.

Clerical errors may be rectified

The time taken for publishing the award

Unless included in the agreement there is no time limit within which an award should be published. Only if the award is remitted by the court to the arbitrator for further reconsideration is time mentioned where it is stated it should normally be made within three months of the permitted order – s. 22 (2) AA 1950. The main discipline being applied to ensure that arbitrators act as quickly as prudence permits is s. 13 (3) AA 1950 which says that an arbitrator can be removed for failing to use reasonable dispatch.

Promptness is expected

Essentials of a valid award

Before an award can be challenged successfully, there must be some legal defect in it. It is therefore necessary to consider those elements which go to make a valid award, without which the possibility of successful challenge is considerably increased.

Elements for incontestability

1 *It must settle all matters* submitted to the arbitrator and not have become involved with matters outside the arbitrator's jurisdiction.
2 *It must be consistent* and contain nothing ambiguous or contradictory.
3 *It must conform with the submission.* If the agreement contains specific instructions as to how the award is to be made, or when it is to be made, then it must conform to them.

Case example
In Marples Ridgeway & Partners v CEGB (1964)
An arbitrator was asked by the parties at the conclusion of the hearing:

(i)   to issue his award in relation to a specific number of items only in draft form so that the parties might consider how best to proceed; and
(ii) to make no award as to costs until the parties had had time to consider the remainder of his award.

By inadvertence the arbitrator issued his award in final form as to a number of the specified items and purported to make an award as to costs. The High Court held that the arbitrator was guilty of misconduct and that the award should be set aside and remitted back to the arbitrator so that he might comply with the parties request.

---

4 *It must adhere to the agreement* and not decide issues outside of it. An award on issues outside the agreement is void and unless the void part can be severed from the award it will mean that the whole award is also void – see *Buccleuch* v *Metropolitan Board of Works* (1870).
5 *It must be certain* in that the parties must be clear as to what the decision is. If any act, other than payment of money, is needed, then a time limit must be given for its completion.
6 *It must be reasonable, legal and possible* to be carried out. If, for example, the award

requires someone to do an act which is impossible for them to perform then the award would be both unreasonable and incapable of being carried out.

7 *It must be final* in that it resolves unequivocally the dispute. An interim award can be made at any time provided it is expressly stated as being such.

8 *It must be made within the prescribed time limit* set by the parties.

Challenging the award

A limited challenge period

The Arbitration Act 1950, under s. 16, provides that (subject to an agreement making no provision for appeal) the award will be final and binding. However, the Act also makes the provision for the court to remit the award or to set it aside. When applying for setting the award aside the writ is taken out in the Commercial Court (Queen's Bench Division) of the High Court within five weeks of the award being published to the parties.

Costs

Own cost clauses are void

Costs are usually divided into cost of the reference and cost of the award. The costs of the reference are those current from the signing of the agreement to the final award. The costs of the award are the arbitrator's fee and expenses. If there is in the arbitration agreement an own costs clause whereby each party is required to pay their own costs such a clause is void s. 18 (3) AA 1950, as the apportionment of costs is a decision for the arbitrator or, in certain circumstances, the court – s. 18 (1) AA 1950. When the arbitrator decides on the apportionment of costs then they must do so judicially per *Lloyd de Pacifico* v *Board of Trade* (1930). The established practice is for the successful party to be awarded costs.

Enforcing the award

If the unsuccessful party does not pay in accordance with the award, there are two methods by which it can be enforced:

1 The award may be used as a 'course of action' and a writ is taken out to sue for the enforcement of the award. If the arbitration agreement was created orally then this is the only method to enforce the award.

Enforcement may be necessary

2 Enforce the award as a judgement of the court. Section 26, Arbitration Act 1950 says an award by leave of the High Court can be enforced in the same manner as a judgement of the court.

Should the award require that one party does some specific act then, unless a contrary intention is expressed, the arbitrator has the power to order specific performance subject to the normal conditions attached to that remedy – s. 15 AA 1950.

The Arbitration Bill 1995

International arbitration carried out in London is worth annually many millions of pounds and the bill, introduced in December 1995, was a response to a growing fear that London's position as the world's leading arbitration centre was under real threat from continental and far eastern business centres. The bill, sponsored by the Department of Trade and Industry, is largely the work of Lord Justice Saville who, assisted by a committee, identified a number of deficiencies with current arbitration law and procedures and put forward practical solutions to cure them. The deficiencies and solutions are:

1 Current arbitration law is not accessible in that it is derived from a piecemeal development with Arbitration Acts of 1950, 1975 and 1979, being a response to defects in the common law. The bill, if enacted will consolidate arbitration law into a single statute and the use of traditional legalese will be replaced by ordinary English expression.

2 Current arbitrations too often follow court-like procedures and in consequence are more costly than necessary. The solution given in the bill will be to impose a statutory duty on arbitrators to use procedures best suited to the disputes being heard. Oral hearings will no longer be standard and in place of an adversial approach the often quicker and cheaper inquisitorial method may be used.

3 Current arbitration procedures, as given in 2 above, may result in an arbitration becoming a mini-trial with the result that costs escalate alarmingly. The response in the bill is that the arbitrator, unless the parties otherwise agree, may set, irrespective of what is incurred, a limit on the legal costs that can be recovered. As well as keeping legal costs down an underlying objective is to prevent a financially strong party from abusing their dominant position by deliberately running up very high legal costs in the hope of frightening a considerably financially weaker opponent into settling terms.

4 Current arbitration law is perceived as being still too generous with regard to allowing appeals against an arbitrator's award and when an appeal is made the courts are felt to be too willing to overturn the award. The bill proposes that courts will be more restrictive in allowing appeals to be brought, with judicial intervention only being possible in limited circumstances. The intention is to make an arbitrator's award much more final than at present.

Scotland

Two arbitration Acts specifically relate to Scotland. These are:

- Arbitration (Scotland) Act 1984
  This is a short Act of seven sections dealing with arbitration apportionment procedures especially those that a court may adopt on the occurrence of certain eventualities.
- Administration of Justice (Scotland) Act 1972
  Section 3 deals with the power of an arbitrator to state a case to the Court of Session on any question of law arising in the arbitration.

The Arbitration Acts 1950 and 1979 referred to in the chapter only apply to England and Wales.

Northern Ireland

The law is the same as in England and Wales.

Chapter summary

- The nature of arbitration is that it is essentially a voluntary undertaking whereby the parties submit their contractual dispute to an independent third party who, following judicial rules, will reach a decision that will be binding.
- The arbitration agreement can be created orally or in writing. If oral, then the arbitration will be regulated by common-law principles and importantly either party may at any time revoke the arbitrator's authority before an award is made; also an award may only be enforced through a court action. Written arbitration agreements are covered to statute law (Arbitration Act 1950 and 1979) which are more protective to the parties.
- There are both advantages and disadvantages of arbitration. The claimed advantages are: expertise of the arbitrator, cost benefit over litigation, simplicity of procedure, speed of process, convenience for the parties and privacy in that there is no public disclosure (unless an appeal is made). Disadvantages claimed are: modest grounds for an appeal against the award, an inability to join third parties to the action, inappropriateness when dealing with a complex legal dispute and possible problems of enforcing the award.
- The parties are free to appoint who they want as the arbitrator and may appoint more than one. Commonly a sole arbitrator is appointed. In certain circumstances a court may make the appointment.
- An arbitrator may be removed from office on several grounds: breach of contract, illegality (both relate to the arbitration agreement), impartially, misconduct, dilatoriness (all those relate to the arbitrator) and the death or bankruptcy of either party in dispute.
- Arbitration may be broken down into a number of stages: appointment of the arbitrator, preliminary meetings with the parties, delivery of claims and counterclaims together with relevant documents, the hearing (which is subject to the rules of evidence), the award and possible appeal against it.
- The Arbitration Bill, when enacted, will make major changes to existing arbitration law and practice.

Problem question

North and South are two businesses in the recycled paper industry. They regularly do business with each other using the British Recycled Paper Association's (BRPA) terms of business which include the following clauses:

> On the occurrence of any dispute between members which the parties are unable themselves to reconcile, the matter will be referred to arbitration before reference is made to any court of law.

and

> Where the parties are unable to mutually agree on an arbitrator then that appointment will be made by the Association whose choice shall be final.

During a period of falling waste paper prices, North and South fall out over a consignment of waste paper that had been contracted for three months earlier and which North had recently delivered. The claim made by South is that the paper had been contaminated before delivery by oil and is unsuitable for recycling. North counter claims accusing South of deliberately spreading oil over the paper after delivery. The parties are unable themselves to reach an amicable settlement and subsequently the BRPA appoint an arbitrator.

In relation to arbitration discuss the legal implications of the following:

1 The arbitrator appointed was the life president of the BRPA who had recently retired as a director of South.
2 The arbitrator conducted a visit to South's premises and inspected the paper in dispute. While there he refused North's request that a sample of oil from South's fuel tank be taken for matching against the oil on the paper.
3 The arbitrator largely uses his own experience of the industry to reach his decision.
4 At the bottom of the contract between North and South, which only South had signed, the following appeared:

> This contract is invalid until signed by both contractual parties.

North later argues that the arbitration is void as there is no mutually binding arbitration intention.
5 The paper delivered by North was industrial waste that contained high levels of acidtol, a toxic substance the reprocessing of which is banned under an EC Directive.

Discussion questions

1 While arbitration is in theory a method of alternative dispute resolution, in practice it is not. Discuss.
2 An oral arbitration agreement is not worth the breath that creates it. Discuss.
3 How easy is it to appeal against an arbitrator's award?

Further reading

The Law of Arbitration (3rd edn), Gill (1983), Sweet & Maxwell.
While now somewhat dated it still provides good coverage with the attraction of reproducing the arbitration acts in an appendix.
The Law and Practice of Commercial Arbitration in England (2nd edn), Mustill and Boyd (1989), Butterworths.
An authoritative work but somewhat hard to digest.
Handbook of Arbitration Practice, Berstein and Wood (1993), Sweet & Maxwell.
This book is pitched between the other two.

Index